North American
WINE ROUTES

North American
WINE ROUTES

A TRAVEL GUIDE TO WINES & VINES, FROM NAPA TO NOVA SCOTIA

CONSULTING EDITORS
DAN BERGER & TONY ASPLER

PAVILION

This edition first published in 2010 by Pavilion Books

An imprint of Anova Books Company Ltd
10 Southcombe Street
London W14 0RA

www.anovabooks.com

Copyright © 2010 Anova Books Limited

All rights reserved. Unauthorized reproduction,
in any manner, is prohibited.

WRITERS

Tony Aspler, Dan Berger, Christopher Cook, Patrick Fegan,
Doug Frost, Gordon Kendall, Linda Murphy, Laura Ness,
Andy Perdue, Regina Reilly, Renie Steves and Jim Trezise

FOR ANOVA

Project Manager: Fiona Holman
Project Coordinator: Katie Deane
Wine Editor: Maggie Ramsay
Text Editor: David Salmo
Editorial Assistants: Michelle Lo, Sally Worthington
Proofreader: Caroline Curtis
Indexer: Sandra Shotter
Cartography: Barking Dog Art, Bristol, UK
DTP and Layout Design: John Heritage
Colour Reproduction: Rival Colour Ltd., UK

A CIP catalogue for this book is available from the British Library

ISBN 978-1-862-05893-4

1 3 5 7 9 10 8 6 4 2

Printed in China

A Note to Our Readers

The information for this book was gathered and carefully fact-checked by the publisher's researchers and editors. Since site information is always subject to change, you are urged to check the facts presented in this book before visiting a destination to avoid any inconvenience. Anova Books cannot be responsible for any changes or omissions.

Opposite: The winery of Nk'Mip Cellars in southern Okanagan, British Columbia (left); the old round barn at Round Barn Winery, south-west Michigan (center); Nova Scotia vineyards in fall (right)

Contents

About This Book

Over the past decade, wine touring has soared in popularity in both the United States and Canada. More than ever, people are planning getaways centered around wine tasting, and wineries are more than happy to accommodate the demand. But you needn't be a connoisseur to enjoy a wine vacation, nor do you need to travel halfway across the country; a number of wineries cater to all levels of interest, with beautiful scenery and fine cuisine, right in your own backyard.

To help you plan your perfect getaway, we have compiled a guidebook that appeals to wine novices and seasoned connoisseurs alike. From New York to Oregon, Prince Edward Island to British Columbia, *North American Wine Routes* is a comprehensive tome of well-known tours (and hidden gems) across the continent. The tours have been meticulously researched by our regional wine experts; without their help, this book would not be fully realized, and for this reason, we are grateful for their contributions.

Divided into three regions—Western, Central and Eastern—this book features more than 75 tours and 400 wineries. In addition, an easy-to-use detailed map accompanies each tour. Every winery listed is located on the map with a number for easy identification, and the route between the wineries is indicated in the regional color. The inset map gives a geographic pinpoint of the tour within the state.

Each listing includes a full address, phone number, website address and driving directions where appropriate. Icons (see right) are also provided at the end of each listing, whenever relevant. Regional events, wine websites and food and lodging suggestions are listed, too.

Red Wine	
White Wine	
Rose	
Sparkling Wine	
Icewine	
Picnic Area	
Food	
Bed	

Western Region
Central Region
Eastern Region

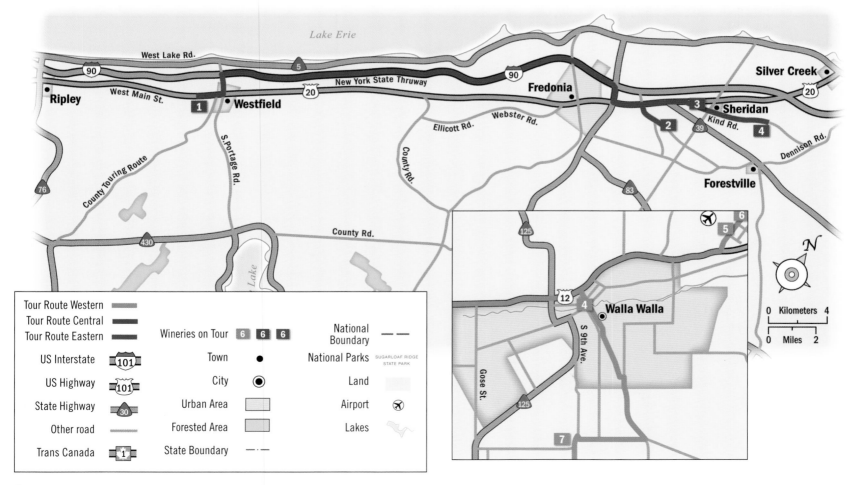

Western Region *Page 16*

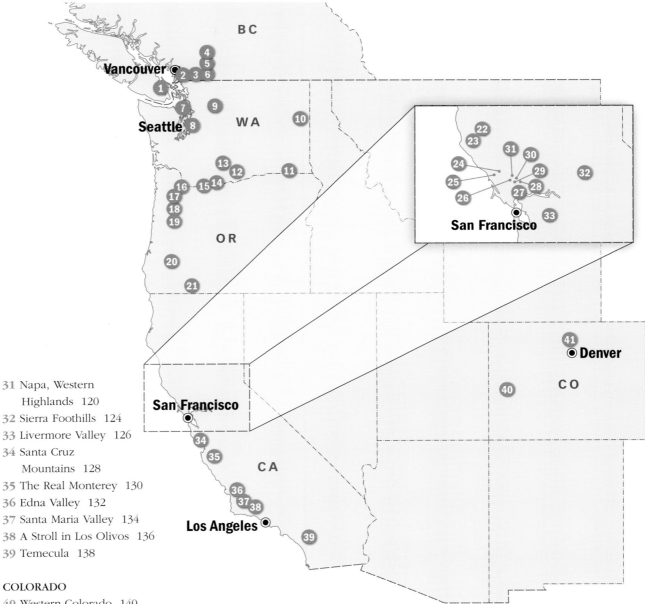

Central Region Page 144

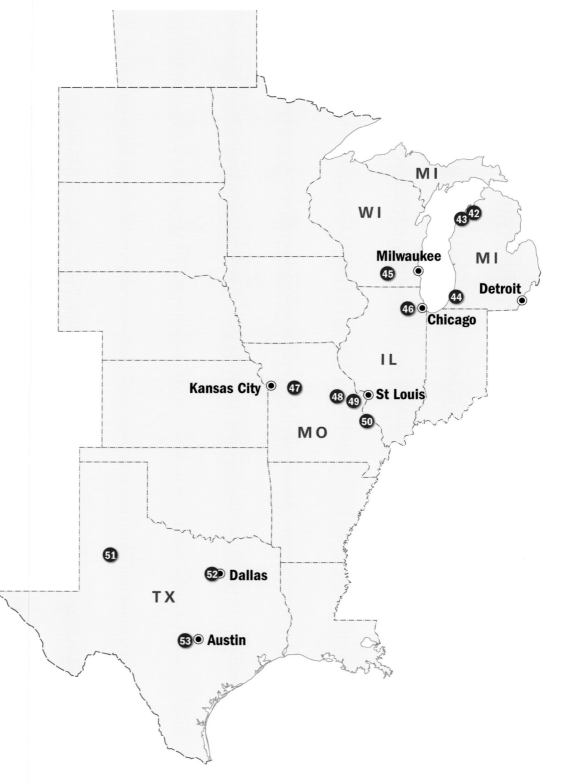

Eastern Region *Page 182*

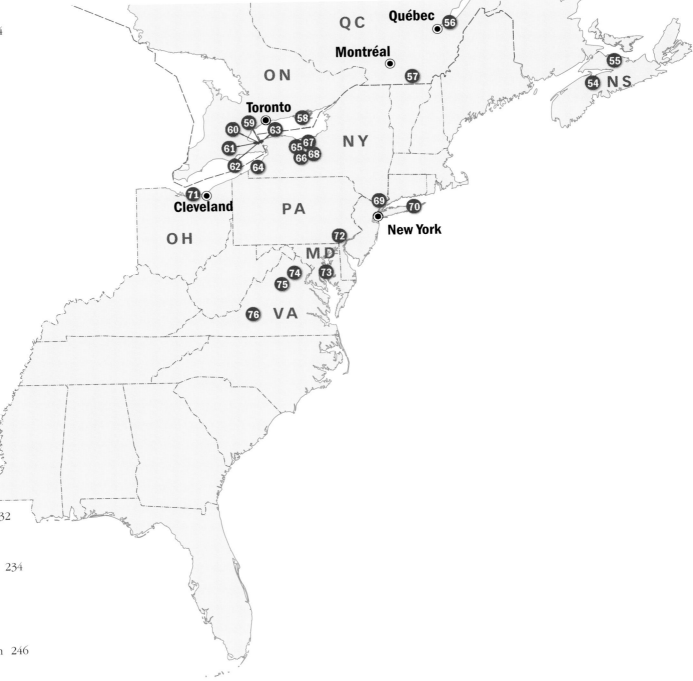

Introduction

One of the best ways to learn about wine is to visit wine regions, see the vineyards and speak to the growers and producers. Immerse yourself in the region, walk through the vineyards, enjoy the local country towns and farmers markets and eat the local food. Wineries can vary from showy and luxurious to downright rustic and laid back.

The best way to do all of this is to plan ahead and even make calls to wineries you are planning to visit. Occasionally, getting the first name of the pourer who will be working on the Tuesday morning you are there will help to get you special "perks" when you arrive.

Advance planning is vital for such issues as meals: Check to see if the wineries you are visiting have cafés nearby or on premise, food to purchase and picnic tables, or nearby bakeries. Follow up on their lodging suggestions, as well as any other travel tips the winery staff can suggest. The more details you get, the easier your trip will be.

What is a wine trail? It is a series of wineries that are all located near one another, which often share a similar trait in their wines. In most cases, there is an affiliation of such wineries that can help coordinate travel (see the "Find Out More" boxes listed within the tours in this book). The wineries along a wine trail usually face similar climate conditions, so although the varietals used may be different among wineries, often the grapes are grown in the same micro-climate, so they will share a common thread.

When to visit Visit wineries early in the day if possible. In high season after noon, tasting rooms can get packed. Staff won't have time to discuss the wines with you. Plan your day so you are at a winery with good picnic/dining facilities at lunchtime. Obviously, it is best to visit during the off-season or midweek. Crush time, late August to mid-October, is busy and buzzing, so don't expect to see the winemaker for more than a few frantic moments! Most wineries are closed on major holidays and many have restricted off-season hours, so always check ahead via the website or give them a call.

How to plan ahead Visit no more than three or four wineries a day. More than that and you won't have time to understand what's happening at each location. Get the true tasting experience by lingering. A leisurely tasting allows you to really savor the wines and make the most of the experience. Don't let the make-an-appointment winery requirement deter you. Some wineries requiring appointments do so because of limitations to their use permits, and/or because they want to make sure they have staff on hand to give guests the attention they deserve. Some simply have limited parking. Appointments can often be made on the morning of your planned visit, though the earlier the notice, the better.

Make the most of your visit Some wineries now offer good food and dining experiences, too, including gourmet picnics and fine restaurant dining. Take advantage of a restaurant or outdoor picnic area to break up the day and, more importantly, to enjoy a spectacular meal or view. If you're more of a do-it-yourself type, bring along your own picnic lunch, buy a bottle of wine at the winery shop and enjoy the view of the vineyards. Some wineries offer cultural experiences, too, such as concerts, art exhibits and spectacular architecture.

Ask questions Get to know the winery and its wines. Even a simple question can proffer valuable information. Start with questions about the founders or the property's founding date. Learning while on a wine tour is the most enjoyable way to get more out of the wine you drink back at home later on. Most staffers are friendly and knowledgeable and are happy to regale you with tales. In smaller wineries, the person behind the tasting-room counter may be the owner and/or winemaker. Only by visiting a winery and/or its tasting rooms can you get a true appreciation for the painstaking work that goes into each bottle, starting in the vineyard.

Please drink responsibly Sample and drink in moderation (the spit bucket is there for a reason and it is not considered impolite to take a small sip and expectorate the remainder; swallowing is not necessary in order to taste the wine properly (see page 13 for more on tasting etiquette). Best bet: Drink a glass of water for every 5 ounces of wine you consume. But best of all is not to taste and drive. Each winery will offer you several samples over the course of a tour, and it's easy to consume too much wine. Plan ahead and choose a designated driver before you begin. There are also other ways of wine touring: via limousine or bike. This book even offers a walking tour (see page 136).

Explore beyond your favorite wines Every winemaker has his or her unique style of winemaking, so a variety of wine (e.g. Merlot, Chardonnay) will taste differently at each winery. Why not try one new grape variety at each visit? Or be even more specific and try just Merlots only—that way, you can explore how a wine changes from vineyard to vineyard, winemaker to winemaker. Remember, too, that some wineries may make very small quantities of a particular wine, sometimes because they are still experimenting and developing their vineyards or because they source the grapes from different places, not always nearby. Also, wine styles may change as a winery develops its strengths or when it changes sources, so on occasion the wines recommended in the book may no longer be in stock.

> Alcohol consumption in the United States is limited to persons over 21 years of age.
> In Canada the provinces listed in this book are as follows:
> British Columbia, Nova Scotia and Ontario: 19 years; Quebec: 18 years

Be creative Always ask if there are wines to buy at the tasting room that are not commercially available in stores. There almost always are, and they can be spectacular! Many wineries now offer older wines (library wines) and special "club" wines that are not available even at the winery for more than a few months. These are wines made in tiny amounts that are often phenomenal.

▲ Wine touring along the Silverado Trail, Napa Valley

Be conscious of tasting fees Some of the tours are in booming tourist destinations, and the more popular wineries in these areas—e.g. in the heart of the Napa—now charge for tasting, partly to discourage visitors preferring quantity over quality. Typical charges range from $2 to $8, but some wineries have a higher fee or may offer a range of tasting options at different price points. Plan well and check in advance, on the winery website or by telephone. Often fees are refundable with purchase. Occasionally, a winery has no fee, per se, but charges a fee for the tasting glass, which you can take home with you.

Relax, have fun, learn and enjoy Allow time to visit other stuff en route. Historic sites are common in wine country areas. Many of the wineries are in spectacular country, where farmers markets abound. So do bakeries, cheese-making operations and local farms. For that reason, avoid chain restaurants and do not ask concierges at fancy hotels where to dine. Best bet is to call a local coffee roasting house a few days before your trip and ask which local restaurants buy their coffee. Local cafés willing to carry locally roasted coffee obviously care a lot about the foods they prepare as well.

When buying wine Many of the wines you'll taste at a winery won't be available anywhere else, so if you like one (or more), buy it then and there. Most wineries will happily give you an empty case to put in the trunk of your car to store your purchases. (Standing up is fine; wines need only be upside down if they will be stored for a long time.) White-foam shipping carriers run about $5 to $10, depending on size.

If you're taking your wines home via airplane, pack so the bottles are impervious to breakage and check them. Better yet, most wineries will be happy to ship your wine directly from the winery to your home. But be forewarned: It's often very hard to get common carriers to ship your wines home for you. Wineries can do this because they have permits, but U.S. consumers are prohibited from buying permits, and most common carriers will not take your purchases. This is a very complicated issue, so check the regulations for your home state before you set off touring in another part of the country.

You may bring Canadian wine across the U.S.–Canadian border, but wine must be declared and duties can apply. If you bring wines into Canada, there is no tax on the first two bottles per person. Additional bottles will be heavily taxed.

When traveling with wine On hot summer days, don't let your wine cook in the back of the car. Your wines will spoil in the heat and the flavors will be spoiled for ever. Buy a cooler bag and some ice packs or even a plug-in device that can cool your wines and keep them protected from spiking temperatures.

Tasting: Wine Do's and Don'ts

Wine-tasting etiquette You and other wine tasters in the tasting room want to be able to evaluate a wine's aroma without competition. Never wear perfumes or after-shave on your tour! Avoid heavy lipstick and use unscented deodorant. Also, smoking immediately before visiting a tasting room spoils the tasting experience for others. Don't worry if fellow visitors at the winery seem to be wine experts and know far more than you do: They probably don't and are just showing off!

To spit or not to spit? A standard glass of wine is about 5 ounces, and tasting-room pours are usually about an ounce, so five pours call for a glass of water to dilute the alcohol. The more you ingest, the less you'll be able to pick up the fine nuances of the more delicate wines. So a good idea is to swirl, sniff, sip, and then use the spit bucket when you have taken sufficient notes so that you'll remember the wine.

Appreciate the flavor "Think while you drink." If you're spending good money on a wine, it really does make sense to take a few moments to appreciate the flavor and personality of what you've paid for. As you sample, think about the sort of foods that will work with it. Heavy reds usually go with char-grilled steaks; Pinot Noir with salmon; Chardonnay with richer seafood dishes.

The ABCs of wine tasting:

Sight Apart from checking if the wine is clear—and with the rise of unfiltered wines, even lack of clarity may not be a bad thing—the colour of the wine (held against a white background) can offer a great deal of insight. Note whether the wine is yellow with green highlights or bronze-ish. The darker the color, the more the wine has been exposed to air and thus will be heavier and richer. Red wines are purple when first made and lose color with age, while white wines are almost water-white when young and go deeper in color over the years.

Smell The smell of a wine may be very similar to the taste or it may be quite different. Some wines have wonderful aroma, but the tastes aren't similar. Some wines smell closed and withdrawn, yet open up wonderfully in the mouth. The best ones emit a heavenly scent that is matched or improved upon by the palate. In any case, swirl the wine gently around in your glass, take a full-blooded sniff of the aroma, and just linger a while, enjoying it and recording the characteristics in your memory. The aroma should give you an idea of the sort of fruit you're getting. Is it more like raspberries or strawberries? Or like plums or raisins? Taking notes can help you recall the wines later.

▲ Follow our guidelines for an enjoyable experience.

Taste It seems silly to have to comment on taste when we all taste so many things every day without apparent difficulty. However, it isn't the tongue that records all the nuances of flavor; it's the nasal cavity. If your nose is blocked or you have a cold, you won't be able to taste well. So take some wine in your mouth and, rather than swallow immediately, just hold it there, breathing in and out through your nose. All the facets of flavor you might have missed will reveal themselves in seconds.

And keep in mind that most wines are best enjoyed with small sips. The larger the quaff, the more alcohol your palate has to deal with, and that can alter the appreciation of wine's great subtleties. Swallowing the wine can give you a sense of whether the amount of alcohol is too great for the wine's structure. The greatest wines in the world are balanced!

Wine classification

American Viticultural Area (AVA)

Before the establishment of the American Viticultural Areas system in 1978, the American appellation system consisted only of vague geographical information as an indication of quality.

There are several levels of appellation:

* State level: the most basic designation. The grapes for a wine so designated can come from anywhere in the borders of the state.

* An individual county: for example, Napa County.

* An American Viticultural Area (AVA): This refers to a distinct grape-growing area marked by specific geographical features and must be approved by the U.S. government, and that approval is based on sound, scientific information which certifies that the wines of a particular AVA conform to similar viticultural characteristics. Normally this sets apart one area of a region from another. AVAs come in all shapes and sizes, from the Ohio River Valley covering 26,000 square miles to ones that cover little more than one winery and a quarter of a square mile (such as Cole Ranch in Mendocino County). It does not guarantee a quality standard, but merely requires that 85 percent of grapes in a wine come from the specified AVA. There are over 190 AVAs, more than 100 of which are in California. Some AVAs are entirely inside other AVAs, such as Green Valley of Sonoma County, which is inside Russian River Valley.

Vineyard designations are not AVAs, but they indicate that a wine came entirely from one vineyard. Some vineyards are very large, and thus the meaning of the designation is blurred. Other vineyard designations are a true indication of quality, since the vineyard is smaller and very carefully tended.

Many other quality statement-based programs for guaranteeing quality have been developed in various areas of the country, but they are not monitored by an agency that can assure that all bottles are technically sound, let alone great wines.

Vintners Quality Alliance (VQA)

In Canada, Ontario and British Columbia wineries are regulated by the appellation VQA (Vintners Quality Alliance), similar to France's AOC, Italy's DOC and Germany's QmP classification systems.

To receive the VQA logo (you'll find it either on the capsule or the label), the wine must be made from 100 percent locally grown, authorized grapes in designated viticultural areas and must be passed by a tasting panel. Wines that do not carry the VQA logo will be a blend of offshore material with Ontario grapes or, in British Columbia, 100 percent offshore material. These wines are labeled as 'Cellared In Canada.'

Words such as "Special Selection," "Private Reserve," "Reserve" or "Barrel Select" do not have any legal definition. Some premium wineries may use these terms to signify their better bottlings, but large companies may also use these terms to help market their lesser ranges, so beware.

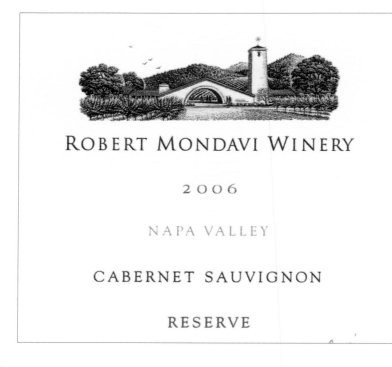

Wine speak: A simple glossary

There is so much myth, mystique, and romance tied up in wine that, consequently, some of the terms you hear may sound scientific, others may sound odd, and some are really little more than the imagination of a wine snob gone rampant! So when a question arises about what you smell in a wine, any answer you give is correct. Do not fear saying the wrong thing. If a wine smells like apple juice, it's perfectly fine to say so—it probably does! Many of the terms in the glossary below will never come up in conversation, and others may be overused. Don't feel out of the loop. This is a business built around chemistry, microbiology, agriculture, and many other disciplines that are foreign to almost all wine lovers. Snobs abound. Ignore them and enjoy your beverage!

Acid/acidity Naturally present in grapes and essential to wine, providing balance and stability and giving the refreshing tang in white wines and the appetizing grip in reds.

Aging An alternative term for maturation. Can take place in the winery (in tanks or barrels) and in the bottle in your home.

Alcoholic content The alcoholic strength of wine, expressed as a percentage of the total volume of the wine. Typically in the range of 7–15 percent.

Alcoholic fermentation The process whereby yeasts, natural or added, convert the grape sugars into alcohol and carbon dioxide.

AVA (American Viticultural Area) System of appellations of origin for U.S. wines. Almost all wines sold in the United States have either a state or an AVA name on the label.

Barrel aging Time spent maturing in wood, usually oak, during which time wine can take on flavours from the wood.

Barrel fermentation Oak barrels may be used for fermentation instead of stainless steel; sometimes this technique gives the wine a rich, oaky flavor.

Barrique The barrique bordelaise is the traditional Bordeaux oak barrel, with a capacity of 50 gallons (225-liters). You may come across the phrase "aged in barrique" in wine lists.

Blanc de Blancs White wine made from one or more white grape varieties. Used especially for sparkling wines made solely from the Chardonnay grape.

Blending The art of mixing together wines of different origin, style or age, often to balance out acidity, weight, etc. Winemakers often use the term "assemblage."

Cellaring The act of laying down wines in a cool, low-light storage location that has constant temperature so the wines (generally red) will take on an added complexity from bottle aging.

Champagne method Traditional method used for all of the world's finest sparkling wines. A second fermentation takes place in the bottle, producing carbon dioxide, which, kept in solution under pressure, gives the wine its fizz. This term may not be used on bottles of U.S. sparkling wine except in certain circumstances. Canada uses the term "traditional method."

Château French for castle: widely used in France to describe any wine estate, large or small, and found in winery names in North America, too.

Corked/corky Wine fault derived from a cork that has become contaminated, usually with Tri-chloroanisole or TCA. The moldy, stale smell is unmistakable. It is nothing to do with pieces of cork in the wine.

Cuvée French for the contents of a s, i.e.ingle vat or tank, but usually indicates a wine blended from either different grape varieties or the best barrels of wine.

Domaine French term for wine estate, and found in winery names in North America, too.

Estate-bottled Bottled at source from a specific location. Usually indicates that the winery grew the grapes, fermented the wine, and bottled it all within the confines of the winery's estate.

Filtering Removal of yeasts, solids and any impurities from a wine before bottling.

Fining Method of clarifying wine by adding a coagulant (e.g. egg whites, isinglass, bentonite) to remove soluble particles such as proteins and excessive tannins.

Fortified wine Wine that has had straight distilled spirits added, usually before the initial fermentation is completed, thereby preserving sweetness. This allows the production of port-style wine, as well as other specialty dessert wines.

Hybrid Grape bred from an interspecific crossing of an American vine species which has natural immunity to the phylloxera louse and the European *Vitis vinifera*.

Icewine A specialty dessert wine of Canada, New York and other cold-infected states. Produced from grapes that have frozen on the vine. Riesling and Vidal are the most common varieties used.

Late harvest A term used for sweeter wines made from grapes left on the vine beyond the normal harvest time, thus concentrating flavors and sugars.

Maturation Term for the beneficial aging of wine.

Meritage American term for red or white wines made from a blend of Bordeaux grape varieties. It rhymes with "heritage" and is used by some 100 or more wineries.

Oak The wood used almost exclusively to make barrels for fermenting and aging fine wines. It adds flavors and tannins; newer oak barrels have a greater impact on the flavor of the final wine.

Oxidation Over-exposure of wine to air, causing loss of fruit and flavor. Slight oxidation, such as that which occurs through the wood of a barrel or during racking, is part of the aging process and, in wines of sufficient structure, enhances flavor and complexity.

Phylloxera The vine louse *Phylloxera vastatrix* attacks vine roots. It devastated vineyards around the world in the 1860s soon after it arrived from the east coast of America. Since then, the vulnerable *Vitis vinifera*, which is used to produce most quality wine, has generally been grafted on to phylloxera-resistant, American rootstocks.

Racking Gradual clarification as well as aeration of wine; the wine is transferred from one barrel or container to another, leaving the lees behind.

Reserve Theoretically a winemaker's finest wine, but the word, having no legal definition in the United States or Canada, has been used indiscriminately and now appears on labels of many ordinary wines.

Second label Usually a lower-priced range of wines, often made by a good producer from surplus grapes, young vines or from the leftovers of rigorous selection for a more prestigious label.

Tannin Harsh, bitter, mouth-puckering astringency in red wine, derived from grape skins, seeds, stems and from oak barrels. Tannins normally soften with age and are essential for long-term development in red wines.

Terroir A French term used to denote the combination of soil, climate and exposure to the sun, i.e. the natural physical environment of the vine. Used by winemakers worldwide.

Varietal Wine made from, and named after, a single or dominant grape variety. A varietal wine in the United States must be made up of at least 75 percent of the varietal listed on the label. In Canada, the wine must be 85 percent of the listed variety.

Vinification The process of turning grapes into wine.

Vintage The year's grape harvest, also used to describe wines of a single year.

Viticulture Vine-growing and vineyard management.

Vitis vinifera Vine species, native to Europe and Central Asia, from which almost all the world's quality wine is made.

VQA (Vintners Quality Alliance) Canadian equivalent of the U.S. AVA system, defining quality standards and designated viticultural areas.

Yield The amount of fruit, and ultimately wine, produced from a vineyard. Measured as tons per acre or tonnes per hectare. Yield may vary from year to year and depends on grape variety, age and density of the vines, viticultural practices, and many other factors including fires, drought, rainfall, pestilence and other factors beyond the winemaker's control.

Western Region

Wine began in the United States with the first settlers making wine from local grapes along the Eastern Seaboard. America's entry into fine wines from *Vitis vinifera* vines didn't begin until the middle of the nineteenth century in California. Thus, it was the Western Region that first made wines that could, at least in theory, be compared with the finest wines of Europe. The key reason was the climate: It was milder in California and far less challenging than it was on the East Coast and in the Midwest.

Fine wines got their start in California in the 1860s after the importation of European vines. Later efforts in Washington and Oregon led to the development of wine industries that soon gained fame locally and eventually worldwide. The West Coast, from the San Diego border to the tip of Washington, had coastal regions that each developed a reputation for fine wines. (Inland regions tend to be too hot for any great wine.) Soon that extended into western Canada with the development of the Okanagan Valley as a fine-wine district.

The classic nature of many of the West Coast wines was so appealing that by the 1970s, 100 years after the first wines were produced in Napa and Sonoma, they were being favorably compared with the best coming out of France. Today's wines are a bit riper and plumper than many wines from the old country.

▲ Vineyards in Sonoma County, California

Vancouver Island

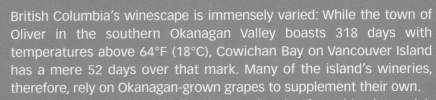

British Columbia's winescape is immensely varied: While the town of Oliver in the southern Okanagan Valley boasts 318 days with temperatures above 64°F (18°C), Cowichan Bay on Vancouver Island has a mere 52 days over that mark. Many of the island's wineries, therefore, rely on Okanagan-grown grapes to supplement their own.

Vancouver Island itself offers an exotic mix of seaside vistas, rich meadowland, lush rain forest and forested mountains. If you are visiting for the day, try to stay long enough for the sunsets; they are amazing, and so, too, are the endless and relaxing views of fir-covered mountains and placid lakes.

Many of the 22 wineries on the island are concentrated along Highway 1, driving north from Victoria toward Duncan—or off side roads from it. For this wine tour, you have to take the ferry from Vancouver to Victoria, a 95-minute crossing, and then drive north along Highway 1.

◄ Vancouver Island offers plenty of wilderness for recreation as well as some excellent wine touring.

1 | Cherry Point Vineyards
840 Cherry Point Rd., Cobble Hill, BC V0R 1L3; (250) 743-1272

Once you turn onto Cherry Point Road, look for the large Cherry Point Vineyards wine barrel at the end of the driveway and turn left. Founded in 1990 on a former mink ranch, Cherry Point was purchased from its founders Wayne and Helena Ulrich in 2004 by the Cowichan Tribes, the largest First Nations community in British Columbia. This made it the second band-owned-and-operated winery in North America (after Nk'Mip Cellars; see page 33) and the third in the world. The Cowichans expanded production, using fruit from other vineyards on their land.

To capitalize on the success of Cherry Point's port-style Blackberry wine (blackberry bushes surround the vineyard), they have built a new solera room to age their fortified wines. The wines on the lowest tier are partially drawn off for bottling and then topped up from barrels of a younger vintage.

The British-born winemaker Simon Spencer makes a range of white and red wines, including two fascinating reds: Bête Noire, from Agria, a Hungarian grape; and Forté, from a hybrid called Castel. The Bistro on the property makes a pleasant place to stop in summer months.

www.cherrypointvineyards.com

2 | Blue Grouse Estate Winery
4365 Blue Grouse Rd., Duncan, BC V9L 6M3; (250) 743-3834

Blue Grouse Estate Winery, named after the bird whose natural habitat it is, lies across Highway 1 from Cherry Point Vineyards. Hans Kiltz's family has owned vineyards in Germany's Rhine region for

▲ The bistro at Cherry Point Vineyards is open in summer months.

more than 300 years. When he and his family immigrated to Canada, they bought a farm in the sheltered Cowichan Valley on Vancouver Island in 1989. On the 31-acre property, carved out of the forest, they found a neglected vineyard, the first to be planted on Vancouver Island. A trained veterinarian specializing in large animals, Kiltz became a farmer; he revived the vineyard and began making wine purely as a hobby. He loved it and, in 1993, established his commercial winery. The wines are made using only fruit from their own estate.

The wood-paneled tasting room under the family home looks out onto the vineyard and the evergreens beyond, making it a relaxing spot to taste the crisp German-style wines, such as the Müller-Thurgau and Bacchus, created by Kiltz and his son Richard. A special treat is Blue Grouse's unique Black Muscat red wine, the only one made in Canada. There is also an oak-aged Pinot Noir.

www.bluegrousevineyards.com

▲ The entrance sign at Blue Grouse Estate Winery

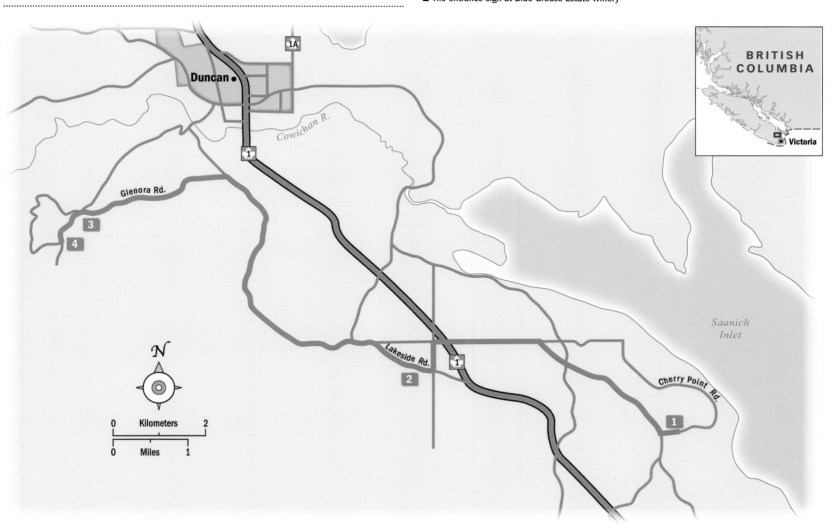

3 | Vigneti Zanatta Winery & Vineyards

5039 Marshall Rd., Duncan, BC V9L 6S3; (250) 748-2338

Once on Glenora Road, you'll see the vineyards belonging to Vigneti Zanatti on your left. The late Dennis Zanatta, true to his Italian heritage, planted vines in 1983 to make his own wine on the dairy farm he purchased in 1958. Those initial plantings on a 5-acre plot, along with more than 100 different varieties, became part of the Duncan Project in the 1980s, a forward-thinking government-sponsored experiment to discover the best wine grapes to grow in this cool region.

Zanatta sent his daughter Loretta to the Veneto region in northern Italy to study winemaking (where she specialized in sparkling wines), and on her return the family opened the first winery on Vancouver Island in 1989. In 1996 the Zanatta family restored their charming 1903 farmhouse, with its wraparound porch, and created a wine bar and restaurant that serves delicious country-style food, which is grown on their farm or by their neighbors (lunches only, Wednesday to Sunday).

Now Loretta and her winemaker husband, Jim Moody, run the winery. As one of the first vineyards established on the island, there's a lot of island wine history here. The winery is one of the few on Vancouver Island to use only grapes grown in its own estate vineyards (Blue Grouse Estate is another; see page 18). Try the sparklers Glenora Fantasia Brut and the Allegria Brut Rosé (there is also a red sparkler), and the table wines Pinot Grigio and Damasco (a white blend).

www.zanatta.ca

▲ Zanatta is still a working farm as well as a winery. This is the old farmhouse.

4 | Godfrey-Brownell Vineyards

4911 Marshall Rd., Duncan, BC V9L 6T3; (250) 715-0504

From Zanatta, continue for about half a mile (1 km) on Marshall Road and then turn left onto the driveway for Godfrey-Brownell, which will take you through a forested area to a deer gate. The vineyards are on your right.

David Godfrey, a former English professor whose family grew grapes on their Cadboro Bay property in the south of Vancouver Island, began looking for a site to plant his own 20-acre vineyard in 1993. It took him five years to find what he was looking for, in the Cowichan Valley, at a price he was willing to pay. Godfrey didn't know then that the property he had chosen had once belonged to a second cousin of his grandmother, whose name was Amos Brownell (hence the name he gave his winery).

Godfrey favors buxom red wines. Try the Pinot Noir and Maltman's Double Red (a blend of Marechal Foch and Gamay Noir), as well as the Chardonnay and Bacchus.

Godfrey-Brownell, in partnership with the Oak Bay Beach Hotel, hosts a gourmet cycling tour through the Cowichan Valley. En route you get to visit a bakery and a fromagerie, before arriving at the winery for a picnic with David Godfrey's wines at the outdoor bar or on the oyster-shell patio with private tables.

www.gbvineyards.com

Springtime at the Butchart Gardens, Brentwood Bay

BUTCHART GARDENS, BRENTWOOD BAY

If you have an extra day to spend on Vancouver Island, you must not miss Butchart Gardens, a 55-acre site in Brentwood Bay, 12.5 miles (20 km) north of Victoria on Tod Inlet at the base of the Saanich Peninsula. Cement magnate Robert Pim Butchart and his wife, Jennie, created a series of gardens on their estate here in the early years of the twentieth century. They turned the mined-out quarry into a sunken garden and over the years created a variety of formal gardens, including a rose garden, an Italian garden and a Japanese garden. In 2004, two 30-foot (9-m) totem poles were installed to mark the 100th anniversary. A commemorative plaque naming Butchart Gardens a National Historic Site of Canada was presented to the Butchart family in 2006. For more information, go to www.butchartgardens.com.

regionalevents

Winter Wine Festival □ January

Held at the Sun Peaks resort, this annual festival showcases revered icewines and the famous wine varietals of the region. Participate in culinary events, wine tastings and educational seminars. **www.sunpeaksresort.com**

Jazz Festival International □ June

Some of the world's best jazz, blues and world beat performers grace the indoor and outdoor stages at Vancouver's most notable music festival.

www.coastaljazz.ca

Abbotsford International Airshow □ August

North America's largest aerial spectacular attracts nearly 300,000 spectators each year. **www.abbotsfordairshow.com**

Penticton Peach Festival □ August

The five-day Peachfest features a range of activities, including live entertainment, fireworks, arts and crafts and parades. **www.peachfest.com**

Victoria Dragon Boat Festival □ August

This premier event takes place in Victoria's Inner Harbour with races, food sampling and plenty of activities. **www.victoriadragonboat.com**

Okanagan Wine Festival □ October

Celebrating the autumn harvest, the Okanagan Wine Festival boasts over 100 events and offers a unique experience for wine lovers. **www.owfs.com**

Fraser Valley

The broad alluvial meadows that cover the Fraser River valley floor make for ideal dairy-farm conditions. The higher ridges, with their sandy loam and red-clay soils, offer better drainage and sun exposure and lend themselves to grape-growing. The sea-level climate virtually eliminates any danger of the vines freezing in winter. While this region does not enjoy the same warm temperatures as the central and southern Okanagan Valley, the growers here compensate by planting cool climate varieties like Bacchus, Siegerrebe, Kerner, Madeleine Angevine, Zweigelt and Maréchal Foch, as well as Chardonnay and Pinot Noir.

A major benefit for the grape and fruit wineries here is their proximity to the greater Vancouver area, which is less than a 45-minute drive away. This valley is the place for those who love the outdoors, whether it's cruising on the river or strolling through Campbell Valley Park. Your winery tour starts at Township 7, south of Langley.

◄ The wide Fraser Valley is one of British Columbia's newer vineyard areas.

1 | Township 7 Vineyards & Winery
21152 16th Ave. (at 212th St.), Langley, BC V2Z 1K3; (604) 532-1766

In 2006 restaurateur Mike Raffan and partners bought this facility and Township 7's winery in Naramata in the Okanagan Valley from the founders, Corey Coleman and his wife, Gwen. The couple had started the Fraser Valley enterprise in a 60-year-old horse barn, which is testimony to the number of riding stables in the neighborhood. Winemaker Brad Cooper, formerly at Stag's Hollow and Hawthorne Mountain in the Okanagan Valley, provides the continuity with the change of ownership.

Unoaked Chardonnay, Chardonnay Reserve, Semillon, Merlot and Seven Stars sparkling wine (made by the traditional method) are all worth trying—and acquiring.

www.township7.com

2 | Domaine de Chaberton Estate Winery
1064 216th St., Langley, BC V2Z 1R3; (604) 530-1736

Domaine de Chaberton was the first winery to be built in the Fraser Valley back in 1991, and today it is the largest, producing some 48,000 cases a year. The original owners, Claude and Inge Violet, planted their vineyard against everyone's advice on a former raspberry farm, naming it after Claude's father's winery in Montpellier, France.

They sold the winery to Hong Kong businessman Anthony Cheng and Vancouver lawyer Eugene Kwan in 2005. The new owners have maintained the character of the original winery—a cluster of dazzling white buildings, including an award-winning French restaurant called Bacchus Bistro (which serves up great bistro cooking with farm-fresh ingredients from the Fraser Valley at both lunch and dinner) and a cedar-paneled Quonset hut that houses the barrel room. Depending on the weather, you can dine indoors or out within sight of the beautifully groomed vineyard.

The emphasis at Domaine de Chaberton is on white German varietals, such as Pinot Gris, Gewurztraminer and Siegerrebe, produced with great care by oenologist Dr. Elias Phiniotis. The reds—Cabernet Sauvignon, a Cabernet Sauvignon-Merlot blend and Shiraz—are sourced from vineyards in the warmer southern Okanagan. Try their Bacchus and the range of wines under the Canoe Cove label.

www.domainedechaberton.com

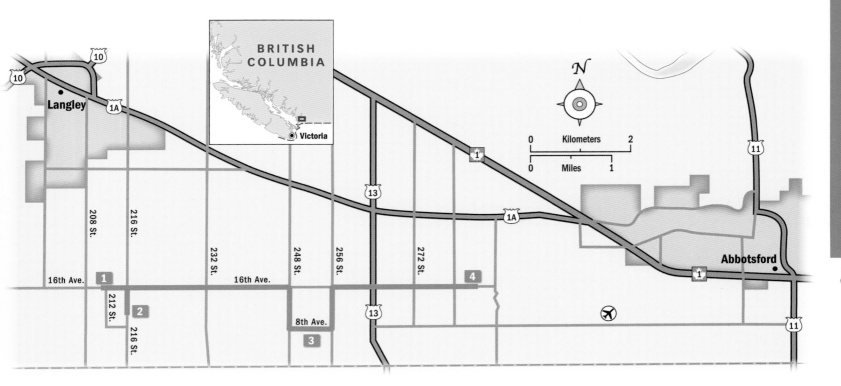

3 | Blackwood Lane Vineyards & Winery
25180 8th Ave., Langley, BC V4W 2G8; (604) 856-5787

Blackwood Lane Vineyards is the newest winery in Fraser Valley. From Domaine de Chaberton, continue along 16th Avenue to 8th Avenue. The winery will be on your right. Blackwood Lane has a Latin motto: *Bonus Vita et Bonus Amici*. Caesar might turn over in his grave at the grammar, but it's meant to translate as "Good Life and Good Friends." Carlos Lee (a restaurateur) and Charles Herrold (rock musician turned winemaker) have combined their talents to produce richly flavored wines with grapes sourced from the southern Okanagan Valley. The ambitious design for the new winery features three perpendicular wine caves excavated into the hillside and an amphitheater for concerts. Their best wines are Bordeaux-style red blends: Try the richly textured Alliance and The Reference.

www.blackwoodlanewinery.com

▲ The Langley region is famed for its lavender farms and events at harvest time.

4 | Lotusland Vineyards
28450 King Rd., Abbotsford, BC V4X 1B1; (604) 857-4188

Continue east on 16th Avenue, which turns into King Road. Proprietors David and Liz Avery used to call their enterprise "A Very Fine Winery," but thankfully changed the name in 2003 to Lotusland, as a tribute to British Columbia and its citizens. The photos of several prominent BC personalities grace the labels of this boutique operation. David Avery maintains an organic vineyard, and as dedicated proponents of green winemaking, the couple power their tractors with biofuels recovered from used restaurant cooking oils. Their wines, from 8.6 acres of vines, include Pinot Grigio, Zweigelt and Cabernet Franc.

www.lotuslandvineyards.com

Similkameen Valley

Similkameen is not as well known in wine circles as the adjacent Okanagan Valley, nor has it been as highly developed as a vineyard area. The Okanagan Valley runs north for 155 miles (250 km); the Similkameen angles northwest for 62 miles (100 km). Currently 11 wineries operate here, though that may well change as the cost of vineyard land rises for favored Okanagan sites.

The wind-blown Similkameen, a former gold-mining area now given over to cattle ranching and horse farms, tends to attract rugged individualists and mavericks who find their own way. The frontier spirit is alive and well in the valley. Keremeos, the town at the end of the tour, hosts an annual three-day Keremeos Elks Rodeo every May, which is well worth attending.

The starting point for this tour is the town of Osoyoos. While you're there, drop into the new wine bar, Bibo, at 8316 Main Street.

◀ The Similkameen River runs through wild and beautiful countryside.

1 | The Seven Stones Winery
1143 Hwy. 3, Cawston, BC V0X 1C3; (250) 499-2144

Driving west out of Osoyoos along Crowsnest Highway (Highway 3) toward Keremeos, you reach Seven Stones in about 30 minutes. In the winery's tasting room is a mural depicting the location of the legendary Seven Stones, individual rock formations throughout the Similkameen Valley.

Winemaker/proprietor George Hanson spent 24 years in the Yukon in the telecommunications industry before moving to the Similkameen Valley to fulfill a lifelong ambition to grow grapes and make wine.

Initially he named his gravity-flow winery Harmony-One, because he saw himself as a conductor orchestrating all the different elements that go into winemaking. In 2005 Hanson and his wife, Vivianne, changed the name to the Seven Stones as homage to the local legend. They felt this would be an interesting theme that could provide valley information to visitors, adding to their experience. The green-painted building that houses the winery and the tasting room is a former workshop situated on sloping benchland overlooking the magnificent Similkameen River Valley and the mountains beyond. The summer heat in the valley has forced

▲ The mountains surrounding the Similkameen Valley

Hanson to install aerial sprinklers in his vineyard to irrigate the vines. They are turned on at night to avoid loss of precious water through evaporation. The emphasis here, as in the rest of the Similkameen because of the heat, is on red wines. Go for the Pinot Noir, Syrah, Meritage and Cabernet Franc (although there is Chardonnay too).

www.sevenstones.ca

2 | Crowsnest Vineyards & Barcello Canyon
2035 Surprise Dr., Cawston, BC V0X 1C0; (250) 499-5129

Driving north to Cawston, turn right at Lowe Drive and left onto Surprise Drive (approximately 10 minutes). Crowsnest is named after Highway 3, the Crowsnest Highway, and it's a true family affair—Olaf and Sabina Heinecke bought the winery in 1998; their daughter Ann makes the wine; their son Sascha manages the sales and oversees the dining aspects.

Set on the windy upper bench of the valley, the winery commands a spectacular mountain view, especially for sunsets. Barcello Canyon is the winery's second label. The bistro serves a German menu, and the newly enlarged covered patio offers a "Picnic on a Platter," as well as such German specialties as rouladen, schnitzel, sauerkraut and bratwurst. Plan to arrive at lunchtime or stay over in the guesthouse for a European breakfast that features cold cuts, cheeses and jams made in-house with the bread baked in a wood-burning oven. Wines to try: Chardonnay Stahltank, Family Reserve Riesling and a white blend called Barcello Canyon Cuvée #3.

www.crowsnestvineyards.com

3 | Orofino Vineyards
2152 Barcello Rd., Cawston, BC V0X 1C0; (250) 499-0068

A left turn on Lowe Drive and another left on Barcello Road will lead you to Orofino, which is 2 minutes away. The winery was named for the mountain that overlooks the property. It's a Spanish term harking back to earlier mining days, meaning "fine gold."

John Weber, a teacher from Swift Current, Saskatchewan—about as far as you can get from wine-growing in Canada—and his wife, Virginia, have hit the ground running with their new winery. The 5.5-acre vineyard was already 12 years old when they acquired it, and those well-seasoned vines provided them with mature fruit. Their pink-stucco building, with its breezeway separating the winery from the tasting room, is the only facility in the country constructed from straw bales. Orofino's earthen walls are 21 inches (54 cm) thick, maintaining a constant temperature inside; they provide sufficient insulation for the barrel cellar and tasting room against the heat of the Similkameen summers. The picnic area is surrounded by the vineyard, trees (almond, oak, quince, maple, and walnut) and

colorful magnolia and bougainvillea. Recommended wines: Pinot Noir, Red Bridge Red (100 percent Merlot), Beleza (a red Bordeaux-style blend) and Riesling.

www.orofinovineyards.com

4 | Herder Winery & Vineyards
2582 Upper Bench Rd., Keremeos, BC V0X 1N4; (250) 499-5595

Continuing along Barcello Road until it becomes Upper Bench Road, you will arrive at Herder (4 minutes), an impressive multi-level winery set against a stark granite cliff face. Californian Lawrence Herder studied winemaking at Fresno State University before embarking on an eight-year winemaking career that took him to B. R. Cohn in Sonoma; his own eponymous winery in Paso Robles; Jackson-Triggs in the Okanagan; and the former Golden Mile Cellars in Oliver. It was great training for the winery that he and his wife, Sharon set up in the Similkameen Valley.

You can picnic here and enjoy a range of well-crafted wines, including Pinot Gris, Chardonnay, Josephine (a red Bordeaux blend) and Cabernet Franc. The art labels are as intriguing as the wines.

www.herder.ca

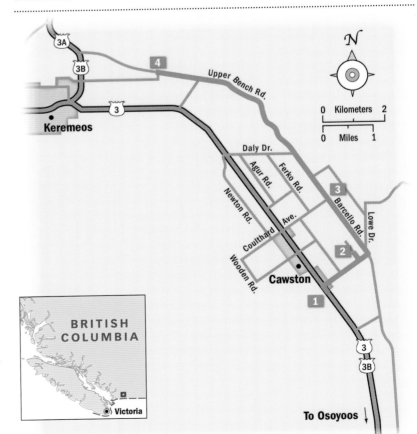

Kelowna, Okanagan

This is the first of three Okanagan tours. Using Kelowna as your starting point, you will drive south along Lake Okanagan, the warmest wine region in Canada, to visit two wineries on the east bank of the lake. Then you will double back to the city and cross the bridge to the west bank for two more visits. Although the distances are not great, you may encounter traffic on the bridge during peak holiday time. All four of the wineries on this tour produce some of the finest wines in Canada and offer food service.

Kelowna, incidentally, is the fastest-growing city in the province, and the area around it produces one-third of all of Canada's apples. Kelowna City Park, which juts out into the lake north of Okanagan Highway 97, is the home of a statue to Ogopogo, a monster that lives in Lake Okanagan and whose legend is said to predate Scotland's Loch Ness monster by 80 years.

◀ Lake Okanagan is one of Canada's top vacation destinations, with miles of lovely parkland.

1 | CedarCreek Estate Winery
5445 Lakeshore Rd., Kelowna, BC V1W 4S5; (250) 764-8866

A 20-minute drive from Kelowna will take you to CedarCreek, one of the most beautiful facilities in the Okanagan. It sits like a gleaming white Mediterranean palace above the eastern shore of the lake, with its garden terrace undulating down to the water. The sloping 48-acre vineyard above the terrace faces Quails' Gate on the other shore (the third stop on this wine tour).

The seminal event in the story of CedarCreek goes back to 1993, when the then winemaker, Ann Sperling, won a platinum medal at the Okanagan Wine Festival for her 1992 Merlot Reserve—the first and only time such an award has been given. This triumph initiated CedarCreek's flagship Platinum Reserve series in 1998. The winery offers three levels of quality—Classic, Estate Select and Platinum Reserve, all stylishly made by Californian winemaker Tom DiBello. Sit on the terrace and sip a cool glass of Chardonnay. Other wines to sample: Ehrenfelser and all the Platinum Reserve wines.

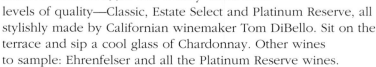

www.cedarcreek.bc.ca

2 | Summerhill Pyramid Winery
4870 Chute Lake Rd., Kelowna, BC V1W 4M3; (250) 764-8000

As you drive north on Lakeshore Road, look for the large pyramid on your right. That will tell you that you've arrived at Stephen Cipes's winery. Cipes is the P. T. Barnum of the British Columbia wine industry. An expatriate New York real estate developer, his showmanship is evident in the huge sparkling wine bottle that appears to float above a giant champagne flute on the winery terrace—an apt metaphor, perhaps, for Cipes's enthusiasm and energy when it comes to his winery. Set behind and slightly above the winery is a model replica of Cheops, the great pyramid at Giza. The structure, at 8 percent of the original's size, is the most recognized icon in the Okanagan and the second such pyramid to be built at Summerhill. Its presence is an ongoing scientific experiment that Cipes has heralded as an overwhelming success when it comes to aging his wines.

On the terrace overlooking the organic vineyards and the lake is the winery's Peace Park, with a half-submerged globe surrounded by flowers and a pole that reads "May Peace Prevail on Earth" in 16 languages. Sip a glass of winemaker Eric von Krosigk's Cipes Brut sparkling wine on the terrace or try some Gewurztraminer. In reds, go for the Platinum Series Merlot or Cabernet Sauvignon.

www.summerhill.bc.ca

3 | Quails' Gate Winery

3303 Boucherie Rd., Kelowna, BC V1Z 2H3; (250) 769-4451

Quails' Gate's 79 acres of vineyard, first established in 1956, run down almost to the edge of Lake Okanagan and slope up to encroaching housing developments on the hills above, which surround the immaculately kept vineyard. Proprietor Ben Stewart has stopped the march of construction by densely planting Pinot Noir, Chardonnay, Merlot and Cabernet Sauvignon.

The contemporary winery stands in sharp contrast to the nineteenth-century settler's cabin that functions as the wine shop. The Old Vines restaurant, known for its great food, is an all-year destination dining facility. It's a relaxing place to dine and to taste the award-winning Stewart Family Reserve wines—especially Pinot Noir, the specialty of winemaker Grant Stanley.

www.quailsgate.com

4 | Mission Hill Family Estate Winery

1730 Mission Hill Rd., Kelowna, BC V4T 2E4; (250) 768-7611

A mere 5-minute drive farther on will take you to British Columbia's most eye-catching winery. If Dionysus, the god of wine, dreamed of a temple to celebrate the fermented grape, he could happily take residence here. Perched on top of a hill above the town of Westbank, in a spectacular setting overlooking Lake Okanagan, this winery is patterned after Robert Mondavi's in Napa Valley. Proprietor Anthony von Mandle totally renovated the property and it is one of the most extraordinary wine facilities you can see on your wine travels, complete with a collection of ancient glassware, a Leger carpet and a Chagall-inspired wall hanging. The most striking feature (in both senses) is the slender 12-story bell tower, whose four bells, commissioned by von Mandl and cast in France, chime every quarter hour.

You access the winery under a large concrete arch that frames the tower and the winery buildings. The feeling evoked is not dissimilar to entering a Greek temple, with its solitude, its sense of calm, the elegant proportions of the buildings, and the open green spaces. Equally dramatic below ground, Mission Hill boasts a magnificent cryptlike barrel-aging cellar that extends in a gigantic L-shape under the winery. Winemaker John Simes, a New Zealander, produces an elegant portfolio of wines, including Select Lot Collection Chardonnay and Merlot, and Reserve Riesling and Pinot Gris.

www.missionhillwinery.com

▲ The Pyramid at Summerhill, used for aging wines

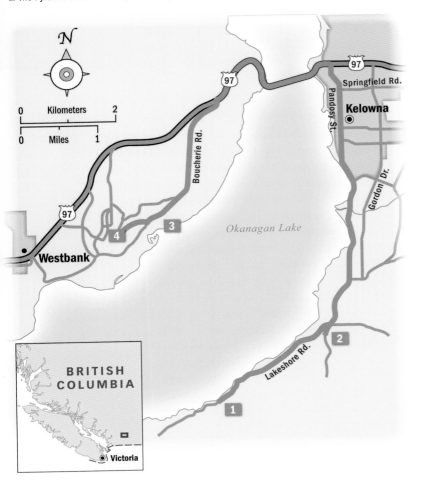

Naramata Bench

As far as wine vistas go, there is no more spectacular a wine vista in Canada than the Naramata Bench, with its vineyards that seem to float above the blue waters of the lake, like a green eiderdown, and which stop just short of a perilous and dramatic cliff drop. Naramata Bench is not appreciably warmer or drier than Kelowna. It's only when you get south of McIntyre Bluff toward Osoyoos that the weather gets warmer and drier.

Here you will find a collection of wines of great quality made from such classic varieties as Cabernet Franc, Merlot, Shiraz, Chardonnay, Pinot Gris and Viognier.

Your starting point is the town of Penticton at the southern end of Okanagan Lake. From downtown Penticton, drive north along the Naramata Road for 5 minutes and you'll come to Red Rooster Winery.

◄ Laughing Stock Vineyards, along the Naramata Bench, has a wonderful view over the lake.

1 | Red Rooster Winery
891 Naramata Rd., Penticton, BC V2A 8T5; (250) 492-2424

In 1990 the Mahrers emigrated from Switzerland and purchased a Naramata apple orchard, which they promptly tore out and planted with vines. Their first vintage was 1997. "Entertain them and they will come," would be a good description of what happened to Red Rooster, the winery that grew. So popular did Red Rooster become, both for its award-winning wines and the hosts' congenial hospitality, that the couple needed more space to welcome visitors and to make wine. They purchased land just outside Penticton and built a new facility of impressive size (30,000 square feet; 2,787 m²), which opened in 2004. The cathedral-like winery building, with its green lawns, a vast "wishing fountain," and shady patio around the wine shop, has made it a great tourist destination. Winemaker Karen Gillis makes top-flight Malbec as well as Pinot Gris, Pinot Blanc, Gewürztraminer and Merlot.

The Mahrers are great supporters of local artists, whose works they display on the second floor of the wine shop. In August the winery holds its annual one-day Bohemian Wine Festival, where artists, sculptors and potters show how they create their works, followed by a silent auction.

www.redroosterwinery.com

2 | Poplar Grove Winery
1060 Poplar Grove Rd., Penticton, BC V2A 8T6; (250) 493-9463

Continue north on Naramata Road and turn left at Poplar Grove Road. Winemaker Ian Sutherland is a fan of Bordeaux red wines. This preference led him initially to plant only Merlot and Cabernet Franc vines, imported in 1993 from Bordeaux, in the 10-acre vineyard that was formerly an apple orchard. Sutherland got off to a flying start when his first red-blend vintage 1995, released in 1997, won a gold medal at the Okanagan Wine Festival that year. Since then he has added Syrah, Pinot Gris and Chardonnay to the portfolio.

In 2007, with his business partner Tony Holler, he built a spanking new winery on a mountainside overlooking Penticton's scenic waterfront. Here you can taste some of the best wines in British Columbia, including the flagship red called The Legacy, a classic Bordeaux blend aged for 24 months in French oak followed by a further 18 months' aging before release, and the benchmark single varietals.

www.poplargrove.ca

3 | Laughing Stock Vineyards

1548 Naramata Rd., Penticton, BC V2A 8T7; (250) 493-8466

Call ahead to make an appointment to taste Laughing Stock wines—
it's worth the effort. From Poplar Grove, return to Naramata Road and
drive north for less than half a mile (1 km). Proprietors David and
Cynthia Enns call it "a serious enterprise with a lighthearted attitude.
And with a name like Laughing Stock, we wake up every day with the
motivation of not living up to our name." The double pun relates to
the couples' financial background. They gave up the investment
business in Vancouver, trading financial stocks on the Vancouver
exchange, for growing vine stocks on a 5-acre site on the Okanagan's
Naramata Bench—a crazy gamble that could, they confess, make
them fit the winery name in the eyes of their former colleagues.

The financial premise is carried over to their labels (which look
like stock quotes) and to the name of their signature Bordeaux-style
red (Portfolio) as well as their red and white blends (Blind Trust).
Their gravity-fed winery, with its barrel cellar, was built into the hillside and opened in 2005. Like all the wineries on the Naramata
Bench, it has a great view of the lake. Try the wines named above as
well as their Chardonnay and Pinot Gris.

www.laughingstock.ca

4 | Lake Breeze Vineyards

930 Sammet Rd., Naramata, BC V0H 1N0; (250) 496-5659

Continue driving north on Naramata Road for about 2.5 miles (4 km),
then turn left on Sammet Road. Winemaker Garron Elmes, a South
African, has been with Lake Breeze since its inception in 1996. The
original owner, Paul Moser, was a South African businessman who
immigrated to British Columbia and re-created a South African–styled
winery complete with a South African winemaker. Moser sold the
winery to Wayne and Joanne Finn, who in turn sold it to Barbara and
Drew McIntyre, Tracey Balland, and Gary Reynolds in 2001.

The small whitewashed winery, which looks as though it has
been transported straight from the Cape, is beautifully sited on the
Naramata Bench overlooking Okanagan Lake, 7.5 miles (12 km) north
of Penticton. True to his South African heritage, Elmes made the first
Pinotage wine in British Columbia, and he does a great job with his
white wines, especially those sold under the Seven Poplars label and
the Semillon.

Set in the vineyard overlooking the lake, the guest cottage with its
wraparound deck is called, for obvious reasons, Artist's View. The
accommodation comes with the caveat that you might get woken
early by a tractor, but, after all, it is a working farm. The Patio
restaurant, open May 1 to mid-October, serves some delicious
Mediterranean-style dishes.

www.lakebreeze.ca

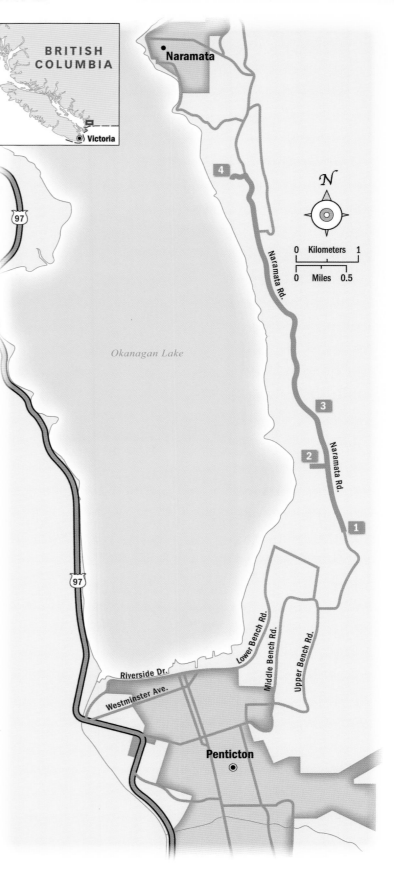

TOUR 6
Southern Okanagan

The Southern Okanagan is the warmest place in Canada, especially as you approach Oliver and Osoyoos. Driving through the region, you will discover the remains of old gold-mining settlements. The terrain here is rock and desert tundra punctuated by verdant stretches of undulating vineyards kept green in this semidesert by the waters of Lakes Vaseaux and Osoyoos.

This tour begins at Okanagan Falls, where you shouldn't miss Tickleberry's, the largest ice-cream seller in the valley, or the Snowy Mountain Chocolate factory. The tour continues south toward the Washington State border on Highway 97 past Oliver, a First Nations settlement and fur-trade and gold-rush stopover, and now the self-styled "Wine Capital of Canada." Osoyoos, at the southern end of the tour, is a popular recreational destination.

◄ Vineyards in the southern Okanagan benefit from endless summer sunshine.

1 | Wild Goose Vineyards
2145 Sun Valley Way, Okanagan Falls, BC V0H 1R0; (250) 497-8919

You reach Wild Goose by taking 10th Avenue in Okanagan Falls and turning south on Maple Street, then right on Sun Valley Way, which is 2.5 miles (4 km) south of the town center. Brothers Roland and Hagen Kruger continue the work their father, Adolf, started in 1990 when he received BC's second farmgate winery license. The family had to clear the slopes of brush and rocks in order to plant their first vines in 1983. "We don't see ourselves as a destination winery," says Hagen Kruger. "We just want to make the best wines we can."

Somewhat off the beaten track and within walking distance to Stag's Hollow Winery, Wild Goose has a folksy, welcoming style: Children (and teetotalers) get fruit-juice samples, while everyone else gets to taste the wines. The Wild Goose white wines are well worth tasting. The family also operates a one-bedroom guest cottage in Oliver at the Mystic River Vineyard site. Winemaker Hagen Kruger's aromatic wines (Riesling and Gewurztraminer) are the highlights, along with Mystic River Pinot Blanc and Autumn Gold, a semi-dry blend. There's a picnic area on the patio, where you can enjoy a bottle of Wild Goose wine. If you want a tour of the winery, make an appointment.

www.wildgoosewinery.com

2 | Jackson-Triggs Okanagan Estate
38691 Hwy. 97 N., Oliver, BC V0H 1T0; (250) 498-4500

Leaving Wild Goose, get back on Highway 97, heading south for 6 miles (10 km). Jackson-Trigg's Tasting Gallery is just off the highway north of Oliver. This is the largest winery in the Okanagan, now under the corporate umbrella of Constellation, and boasts a portfolio of more than 30 wines. Named for its founders, Allan Jackson and Donald Triggs, this winery has carried off more competition medals at home and abroad than any of its competitors. Much of the reason for the success is the quality of the fruit produced in Vincor's extensive vineyard holdings in the southern Okanagan, their meticulous management, and the talent of their young winemakers. The winery—a vast industrial warehouse—is far from glamorous, but the equipment inside is all state of the art. The Tasting Gallery, however, will impress you with its style and comfort as much as its wines. You can sample the wines inside or on the patio. Among the top wines here are Proprietors' Grand Reserve Shiraz, Cabernet-Shiraz, Merlot and all five wines from the Sun Rock Vineyard.

www.jacksontriggswinery.com

3 | Tinhorn Creek

32830 Tinhorn Creek Rd., Oliver, BC V0H 1T0; (250) 498-3743

In Oliver, be sure to stop at the Cock & Bull (34849, 97th Street) or Cantaloupe Annie's (34845 Main Street) for your picnic sandwiches. Another good place to eat is the Crush Pad in the Mesa Hotel (35681, 97th Street, Oliver). A 6-mile (10 km) drive from Oliver will take you to Tinhorn Creek. Winemaker Sandra Oldfield, an American, studied at California's celebrated wine school, UC Davis, where she met her husband, Kenn. The California connection inspired the type of winery the Oldfields created with the Shaunessys in 1993. Sandra Oldfield will tell you that they modeled Tinhorn Creek after Napa Valley's Newton Vineyard on Spring Mountain. Like Newton, this modernistic mustard-yellow building is set majestically on a hillside—in this case, above Oliver's Golden Mile—its entrance embellished by a rock garden and a soothing water fountain. Inside, visitors can watch the winemaking process from interior galleries overlooking the stainless-steel tanks, oak barrels, and the cellar below. The winery takes its name from the creek that runs through the property.

Ever since Tinhorn Creek's 1998 Merlot won Red Wine of the Year at the Canadian Wine Awards, this variety has been Oldfield's signature wine, garnering medals in every competition in which it has been entered. The fruit comes from their 130-acre Black Sage Road vineyard. In 2004 the Oldfields planted more than 600 native shrubs, wildflowers, and bunchgrass in one part of the property. This restored the area to an antelope-brush plant community, creating a natural habitat for BC's endangered wildlife species.

www.tinhorn.com

4 | Hester Creek Estate Winery

13163 326th Ave., Oliver, BC V0H 1T0; (250) 498-4435

The distance between Tinhorn Creek and Hester Creek is about half a mile (1 km). Drive south on Highway 97 and turn right on 326 Avenue. Joe Busnardo planted the original 70-acre vineyard just south of Oliver on what is now the Golden Mile. Between 1968 and 1972 he put in an amazing range of European varietals for his Divino Estate, many from his native Veneto, including Trebbiano—the only winery in the Okanagan to make a wine from this workhorse Italian grape. In 1996 the new owners christened the winery Hester Creek (after the creek that runs in the gully between the neighboring property). Another change of ownership occurred in 2004 when Curtis Garland, owner of a trucking business, bought it and built a new winery with cellars excavated into the hillside. Winemaker Robert Summers, with long experience in Ontario, makes top-flight Bordeaux red varietals

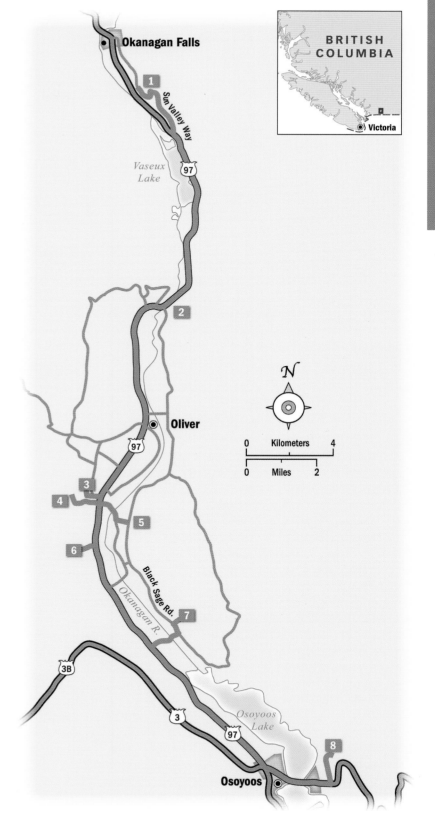

here and a tasty Chardonnay. The vine-covered patio looks out over the vineyard to Black Sage Bench and Mt. Baldy. The winery offers bed-and-breakfast accommodation with vineyard and orchard views.

www.hestercreek.com

5 | Stoneboat Vineyards
7148 Orchard Grove La., Oliver, BC V0H 1T0; (250) 498-2226

Take Highway 97 south from Oliver and turn left on Road 9, past Willow Vineyards, then turn left on 322 Avenue to reach Stoneboat. Lanny Martiniuk and his wife, Julie, bought a 15-acre orchard on the Black Sage in Okanagan back in 1979. They had been growing grapes for about 25 years before they decided to get into the winery business in 2005. Now they've expanded their orchard to 50 acres and they are busier than ever. Outside the tasting room is a replica of a stoneboat, a large, flat sledge used for hauling stones—one was used to clear the stones from the home vineyard in 1984. A drawing of a stoneboat appears on the wine labels. Sample the Pinot Noir and Pinot Blanc as well as the Pinotage, which won the Lieutenant Governor's Award of Excellence for the 2007 vintage.

www.stoneboatvineyards.com

6 | Road 13 Vineyards
13140 316A Ave., Rd. 13, Oliver, BC V0H 1T0; (250) 498-8330

Head back to Highway 97, drive south and turn right on Road 13. Be prepared for a surprise. Peter Serwo, a former builder, constructed a medieval castle for his winery and tasting room, complete with battlements and a conical copper dome; one of its towers is even guarded by a suit of armor. The castle—formerly called Golden Mile Cellars—is positioned in the middle of the 20-acre vineyard Serwo planted in 1982. The view from the castle across the southern Okanagan Valley south of Oliver is spectacular.

Golden Mile Cellars was purchased in 2003 by Mick and Pam Luckhurst. Mick, who had worked in construction, and Pam, a banker, were no doubt impressed by Serwo's chutzpah for building a castle in the desert. Like many before them, they were also wooed into the industry by the romance of wine.

Winemaker Michael Bartier is a Chardonnay specialist who has twice won the White Wine of the Year award at the Canadian Wine Awards. Watch out for his Jackpot single varietal wines, from Pinot Noir to Viognier and the less costly blends called Honest John's Red,

White and Rosé as a tribute to BC premier John Oliver, who introduced irrigation to the valley in the 1920s. You can prebook a barrel tasting here.

www.road13vineyards.com

7 | Burrowing Owl Estate Winery
100 Burrowing Owl Pl., Oliver, BC V0H 1T0; (250) 498-0620

From Road 13, head south again on Highway 97 and turn left at N22 Road, then left on to Black Sage Road. You can't miss Burrowing Hill just along on your right. This southwestern-style gravity-flow winery, constructed in 1998, is set in a sea of vines overlooking Osoyoos Lake at its northern end.

If you climb up to the square tower above the building, there's a walkway with a spectacular 360° vista of the vineyards, granite cliffs, and the lake. The building was originally designed as a 12,000-case facility, but such is the demand for Burrowing Owl wines that they now produce 30,000 cases. Owner Jim Wyse has even built more cellar space under the car park that services visitors to his destination restaurant, The Sonora Room, which offers some of the valley's best cuisine as well as spectacular views from the patio. The winery's 10-bedroom inn on site benefits from a wine lounge and its own cellar, and even has a large outdoor pool and sundeck.

The 180-acre vineyard was planted in 1993 and has been developed with an ecofriendly philosophy. More than 100 bluebird boxes and two bat nurseries have been installed to encourage insect-eating guests to stay and dine in the vineyards. Winemaker Steve Wyse, Jim's son, is particularly strong on his red wines. Try the Cabernet Franc, Syrah, Merlot, Meritage and Chardonnay.

www.bovwine.ca

▲ The restaurant at Burrowing Owl Estate Winery enjoys great views over the vineyards and Osoyoos Lake.

8 | Nk'Mip Cellars

1400 Rancher Creek Rd., Osoyoos, BC V0H 1V0; (250) 495-2985

Take Highway 97 toward Osoyoos and branch onto Highway 3, which will take you through the town to Rancher Creek Road. It's a journey of about 20 minutes to Nk'Mip Cellars. This operation is the first aboriginal-owned winery in North America. The winery's name (pronounced in-ka-meep) comes from the local Salish dialect and means "place where the creek joins the lake." The Osoyoos Indian Band has a history of viticulture dating back to 1968, when members first planted the Inkameep Vineyard. The 32,000-acre reservation that is home to the band contains 25 percent of all vineyard land planted in the Okanagan Valley. Nk'Mip Cellars' attractive labels feature the company logo—a turtle (a symbol of wisdom and vision) painted as a pictograph on an arrowhead (a symbol of the power and heritage of the vineyard). This winery building, reminiscent of the sandstone pueblos of New Mexico, is set dramatically in Canada's only pocket desert, where temperatures can reach 106°F (41°C) and rattlesnakes infest the granite hills behind. Across the lake, you can see Vincor's Osoyoos Larose vineyards. Vincor is a partner in this enterprise. Winemaker Randy Picton makes delicious Riesling, Chardonnay, Merlot and Pinot Noir. Try them over lunch on the patio.

www.nkmipcellars.com

▲ Nk'Mip enjoys spectacular views across Osoyoos Lake to the mountains beyond.

findout more

- **www.winebc.com**
  British Columbia's official wine site with information on tours, wineries and even wine tutorials.

Puget Sound & Islands

The Puget Sound AVA (American Viticultural Area) is a sprawling region. It stretches from the Canadian border north of Bellingham to the state capital of Olympia; an hour south of Seattle and across Puget Sound to the Kitsap and Olympic peninsulas; and all the way to the city of Port Angeles. Within this area fewer than 100 acres of wine grapes are planted. Thus, most wineries rely on grapes from east of the Cascade Mountains, though a few also have estate vineyards planted with such varieties as Pinot Noir, Müller-Thurgau, Madeleine Angevine and Siegerrebe.

Wine lovers looking to explore little-known varieties (always a treat) alongside better-known grapes will enjoy touring the Puget Sound. The region can be divided into three general areas: the northern Puget Sound, around the cities of Bellingham and Mount Vernon; the islands; and the Olympic Peninsula. This tour will take you island hopping.

◀ The garden at Lopez Island Vineyards

1 | Bainbridge Island Vineyards & Winery
8989 Day Rd. E, Bainbridge Island, WA 98110; (206) 842-9463

Gerard and Jo Ann Bentryn planted their vineyards on Bainbridge Island in 1977, and they are fiercely proud of their deep-rooted commitment to local winemaking. The Bentryns were the driving force behind the establishment of the Puget Sound AVA and have been instrumental in promoting sustainable viticulture in the region for the better part of three decades. They produce Pinot Noir, Pinot Gris, Madeleine Angevine, Müller-Thurgau and Siegerrebe from estate grapes, as well as seasonal fruit wines. Their late-harvest botrytis-affected Siegerrebe is one of the most amazing treasures a wine lover will find in the Pacific Northwest.

www.bainbridgevineyards.com

2 | Whidbey Island Winery
5237 S. Langley Rd., Langley, WA 98260; (360) 221-2040

Located near the town of Langley, Whidbey Island Winery produces 3,500 cases a year, using its own cool-climate estate grapes as well as fruit from Eastern Washington. Greg and Elizabeth Osenbach began planting grapes in 1986 and opened their winery in 1992. They craft white wines made from Siegerrebe, Madeleine Angevine and Madeleine Sylvaner grapes grown on Whidbey Island. Other wines include Chardonnay, Viognier, Pinot Grigio, Merlot, Lemberger, Syrah and Sangiovese from the Yakima Valley.

www.whidbeyislandwinery.com

3 | Lopez Island Vineyards
724 Fisherman Bay Rd., Lopez Island, WA 98261; (360) 468-3644

Owner/winemaker Brent Charnley planted his 6-acre vineyard in 1987 and farms it organically. From estate grapes, he crafts Siegerrebe and Madeleine Angevine, and he supplements them with Cabernet Sauvignon, Merlot, Malbec, Chardonnay and blends from Yakima Valley and Red Mountain grapes. He also makes three fruit wines, using locally grown apples, pears, raspberries and blackberries.

Lopez Island Vineyards is in a rustic setting, and the sense of passion that goes into the viticulture and winemaking resonates throughout. Often the vineyards are harvested by members of the surrounding community.

www.lopezislandvineyards.com

4 | San Juan Vineyards

3136 Roche Harbor Rd., Friday Harbor, WA 98250; (360) 378-9463

Located in a century-old schoolhouse on San Juan Island, San Juan Vineyards was established in 1996 by Yvonne Swanberg.

Six acres of estate grapes account for about a third of the winery's 4,500-case production, with the rest supplemented by grapes from the Yakima Valley in Eastern Washington. The estate vineyards include Pinot Noir, Siegerrebe and Madeleine Angevine. The Siegerrebe in particular has gained national acclaim in recent years. From Yakima Valley grapes, San Juan makes Merlot, Syrah, Chardonnay, Riesling, and red and white blends.

www.sanjuanvineyards.com

The Seattle skyline from Puget Sound

GETTING TO THE WINERIES

Your best choice for getting from winery to winery on this tour is a Washington State Ferry. Bainbridge Island is a short 30-minute ride from downtown Seattle, and Whidbey Island is a 20-minute ride from Mukilteo, near Everett. You can also drive to Whidbey Island by driving north to Mount Vernon, then through Anacortes and down through Whidbey Island.

Getting to the San Juan Islands (particularly San Juan and Lopez islands) will mean driving to Anacortes and taking a ferry through the islands. It stops at four islands on the way to Sidney, British Columbia. In the summer months this ferry ride is extremely popular, so advance reservations are highly recommended.

findout more

- www.visitsanjuans.com
  A great guide to San Juan, Lopez and Orcas islands.

- www.wsdot.wa.gov/ferries
  Washington State Ferries schedule.

- www.pugetsoundwine.org
  Puget Sound Wine Growers Association. Great information on wineries, vineyards and viticulture.

Seattle to Woodinville

With a population of more than 3.3 million people, the greater Seattle area is easily the largest region in the Pacific Northwest. With the growth of the state wine industry, many wineries have gravitated to this area to take advantage of the region's population and tourism. However, the vast majority of the grapes used in the wines made here are from east of the Cascade Mountains.

Seattle has a long history of urban wineries, going back to the repeal of national Prohibition in 1933. By far the largest concentration of wineries in the Seattle area is in Woodinville, a suburb northeast of the city. Chateau Ste. Michelle has called Woodinville home for more than 30 years and has been a draw for hundreds of thousands of visitors annually; this has acted as a magnet for wineries wanting to take advantage of those crowds. Wineries from eastern Washington are also opening second tasting rooms in Woodinville.

◀ The tasting room at Chateau Ste. Michelle, Washington's flagship winery

▲ The historic Chateau Ste. Michelle in Woodinville is one of Seattle's top attractions.

1 | Chateau Ste. Michelle
14111 N.E. 145th St., Woodinville, WA 98072; (425) 488-1133

Chateau Ste. Michelle is Washington's flagship winery. It is the state's oldest winery, its most recognized and its most visited. It started in 1934 as two competing wineries—National Wine Co. and Pommerelle—and the grand winery in Woodinville was built in 1976.

Today more than 400,000 visit Ste. Michelle annually. In addition to being open daily for wine tasting, the chateau puts on a summer concert series that draws top artists and plays host to the annual Auction of Washington Wines, which raises millions of dollars for the Children's Hospital in Seattle. The spacious grounds are a perfect setting for a picnic.

Ste. Michelle is the state's second largest (after its sister winery Columbia Crest) and is the world's largest producer of Riesling, crafting 1 million cases annually in more than a half-dozen styles. The winery bottles dozens of different wines and some are available only through the tasting room. Head winemaker Bob Bertheau is especially proud of his Muscat Canelli, an off-dry white wine. Ask if any rare icewines are being poured, or see if any Ethos wines are available, especially Cabernet Sauvignon, Syrah or Chardonnay.

The chateau also serves as the corporate headquarters for Ste. Michelle Wine Estates, the company that runs top wineries in Washington, Oregon and California's Napa Valley. It uses about two-thirds of all the wine grapes grown in Washington.

www.ste-michelle.com

2 | Columbia Winery
14030 N.E. 145th St., Woodinville, WA 98072; (425) 488-2776

Directly across the street from Chateau Ste. Michelle is Columbia Winery. It was set up in 1962 by a group of wine-loving University of Washington professors, who started it as Associated Vintners. By the late 1970s, the name changed to Columbia Winery and the group brought in David Lake, a Master of Wine who served as winemaker for the next quarter century. He introduced Syrah and Pinot Gris to the state, as well as many other innovations. Lake retired in 2005 and passed away in 2009.

The spacious tasting room was remodeled in 2009. From the extensive range of wines, look out for the Red Willow Syrah, Small Lot Series Barbera and Milestone Red.

www.columbiawinery.com

EST. 1962

COLUMBIA WINERY

SYRAH
COLUMBIA VALLEY

3 | Brian Carter Cellars
14419 Woodinville-Redmond Rd. NE, Woodinville, WA 98072; (425) 806-9463

Brian Carter is one of Washington's most recognized and celebrated winemakers. He started in 1980 at the Paul Thomas Winery and later moved to Washington Hills Winery in the Yakima Valley, where he helped build that operation into one of the state's best.

He began to make wines under his own label in 1997 and opened Brian Carter Cellars in 2006 to much fanfare and success. Carter's focus is on blends, and he crafts many styles, from Bordeaux to Super-Tuscan, to Rhône to Spanish. The tasting room is in a quaint building in Woodinville, and Carter is in the process of building a new winery nearby (see photos on page 38).

www.briancartercellars.com

37

▲ Brian Carter (inset) and his current tasting room

4 | JM Cellars
14404 137th Pl. NE, Woodinville, WA 98072; (206) 321-0052

Located just around the corner from Chateau Ste. Michelle and Columbia, JM Cellars is a small winery but a big favorite for wine tourists. Owners Peggy and John Bigelow launched the winery in 1999 with 350 cases of wine made in their basement, then moved to their current location a year later. They craft wines using grapes from such top vineyards as Seven Hills, Klipsun, Ciel du Cheval and Boushey.

JM's focus is on red wines, with the flagship Bordeaux-style blend Tre Fanciulli leading the way. They also craft a Chardonnay and a dessert wine made from Semillon.

www.jmcellars.com

5 | Novelty Hill Winery
14710 Woodinville-Redmond Rd. NE, Woodinville, WA 98072; (425) 481-5502

The Alberg family launched Novelty Hill in 2000, and it has been in the capable hands of winemaker Mike Januik from the beginning. Januik, a Washington winemaker since 1984 and former head winemaker for Chateau Ste. Michelle, helped the family decide to plant its estate Stillwater Creek Vineyard in the Frenchman Hills of Washington's Columbia Valley. The vineyard is one of the best in the state—especially as it is so young, planted in the late 1990s—and is the backbone of Novelty Hill's wines. Try the Stillwater Creek Vineyard Cabernet Sauvignon, Sauvignon Blanc, Syrah or Merlot.

Novelty Hill started out in a warehouse in Woodinville, but it opened its beautiful new facility in 2007. Januik's own eponymous winery is also housed here and shares the tasting room.

www.noveltyhillwines.com

▲ Novelty Hill's stunning new tasting room

6 | DiStefano Winery

12280 Woodinville Dr. NE, Woodinville, WA 98072; (425) 487-1648

Here is the classic story of a nuclear engineer turned winemaker. Mark Newton's love for wine started in the early 1980s after a visit to a California sparkling-wine producer. He launched his winery in 1984 with the intent of producing bubbly, then refocused his efforts on reds and whites in the early 1990s. The cozy tasting room opened in 2000.

Today DiStefano is recognized as one of the state's top red wine producers. Under Newton's direction, DiStefano crafts elegant Bordeaux-style wines—both blends and varietal Cabernet Sauvignon and Franc—and has recently added such Rhône varieties as Viognier, Syrah and Grenache.

www.distefanowinery.com

7 | Cadence Winery

9320 15th Ave. S, Unit CF, Seattle, WA 98108; (206) 381-9507

Ben Smith and Gaye McNutt launched Cadence Winery in the late 1990s and quickly gained acclaim for Smith's suave winemaking style, which focuses on reds. In 2006, they enjoyed their inaugural harvest from Cara Mia, their estate vineyard on Red Mountain. From the beginning, Smith has focused on vineyard-designated red blends, all from Red Mountain.

The winery is in a warehouse district in south Seattle and is open by appointment (and well worth the effort to make a call or drop an e-mail in advance).

www.cadencewinery.com

8 | The Tasting Room

1924 Post Alley, Seattle, WA 98101; (206) 770-9463

How would you like to taste the wines from seven wineries all in one stop, while enjoying yourself in the world-famous Pike Place Market? You can at The Tasting Room in downtown Seattle.

You can taste wines from Camaraderie Cellars (Port Angeles), Wilridge Winery (Seattle), Naches Heights Vineyards (Naches), Harlequin Cellars (Touchet), Mountain Dome (Spokane), Wineglass Cellars (Zillah) and Latitude 46 (Touchet).

The Tasting Room has opened a second operation, in Yakima, which features three wineries and presents itself as a destination for hiking and picnicking amid 80 acres of vineyards and sagelands.

www.winesofwashington.com

The Herbfarm restaurant has a legendary wine cellar.

WOODINVILLE—A MAGNET FOR WINE LOVERS

Woodinville is home to at least 50 wineries and tasting rooms. It is a simple drive from downtown Seattle and should take you less than 30 minutes, depending on traffic. A trend in recent years has been wineries from eastern Washington opening second tasting rooms in Woodinville. There are plenty of amenities in the area, known as the "east side" because it's on the east side of Lake Washington (not to be confused with eastern Washington, which is on the east side of the Cascade Mountains).

Because of wine tourism, many great places to eat and stay have popped up in Woodinville in the past decade. Across the street from Chateau Ste. Michelle is The Willows Lodge, one of the finest hotels in the Puget Sound region. It shares a parking lot with the Barking Frog and Herbfarm restaurants—both superb. The Herbfarm's nine-course meals and 20,000-bottle cellar are legendary. Dining there is the quintessential Northwest culinary experience.

find out more

- **www.woodinvillewinecountry.com**
  Woodinville Wine Country is the umbrella organization for Woodinville-area wineries.

- **www.ssaw.info**
  The South Seattle Artisan Wineries is a group of eight small producers clustered together in the SODO (south of downtown) district of Seattle.

Lake Chelan

For decades, Lake Chelan has been the playground for Washington State residents. Situated in the Cascade Mountains about three hours' drive from Seattle, Lake Chelan is a tranquil and popular destination—especially in the summer for families wanting a brief vacation, as well as in the winter when snowmobiling and other winter sports are in vogue. Chelan has also been an agricultural haven for the better part of a century, though primarily in apples and cherries rather than grapes. However, as the fortunes of the famed Washington apple industry have waned, entrepreneurial orchardists have begun to convert trees to vineyards. Since 1998, more than 250 acres of wine grapes have been planted, and wineries have followed.

Lake Chelan is easy to divide into two areas: the south shore and the north shore. Starting from the town of Lake Chelan, all of the wineries are clustered on either side and are easy to reach.

◄ Vineyards planted along the southern shores of Lake Chelan

1 | Tsillan Cellars
3875 Hwy. 97A, Chelan, WA 98816; (509) 682-9463

Tsillan Cellars (pronounced the same as the lake) is the grandest winery in Lake Chelan. Retired dentist Bob Jankelson was inspired by multiple visits to Italy and has carved a Tuscan-style villa out of a former Red Delicious apple orchard that now grows some of the finest grapes in Washington.

Tsillan is one of the largest producers in the region, with about 7,000 cases annually. And it also makes some of Lake Chelan's best wines. Since opening in 2004, Tsillan has rolled out one award-winning wine after another, starting with Gewürztraminer, Riesling, Pinot Grigio and Chardonnay, followed by such reds as Syrah and Italian-inspired blends.

The tasting room, in the style of an Italian villa complete with stone columns and a bell tower, is Napa-like in its amenities and style. The beautifully landscaped grounds are also well worth a leisurely stroll, thanks to a tranquil waterfall and stunning views of the vineyards and lake.

Tsillan's on-site restaurant is Sorrento's, operated by the family that runs the restaurant with the same name in San Francisco.

A visit to the Lake Chelan area is not complete without a stop at Tsillan Cellars.

www.tsillancellars.com

2 | Vin du Lac
105 Hwy. 150, Chelan, WA 98816; (509) 682-2882

Larry Lehmbecker, owner of Vin du Lac, is crafting some of the finest red wines in Washington, all from a perch overlooking the southern end of Lake Chelan—and all while still practicing law in Seattle.

▲ Tsillan Cellars' Tuscan-style villa was inspired by the owner's many visits to Italy.

This winery started life as Chelan Wine Co., but Lehmbecker realized many wineries would want to capitalize on the regional name and early on decided to change the name to Vin du Lac, which means "Wine of the Lake." He and partner Michaela Markusson have created a comfortable winery in a wonderful location that includes a tasting bar and restaurant in the renovated 1920s' orchard farmhouse. Half the property is still a working orchard. Expect live music on Saturday evenings during the summer.

Vin du Lac's best wines are Cabernet Franc, Cabernet Sauvignon, Syrah, Viognier, Riesling and Sauvignon Blanc, but it really is hard to go wrong with any of Lehmbecker's offerings.

www.vindulac.com

3 | Benson Vineyards Estate Winery
754 Winesap Ave., Manson, WA 98831; (509) 687-0313

Not far behind Tsillan Cellars in grandeur is Benson Vineyards on the lake's north shore. The Benson family completed construction of its new Mediterranean-inspired tasting room and grounds in 2009, which provides one of the area's most sweeping views of the valley and lake. Benson was the first winery to produce wines completely from estate grapes, and winemaker Scott Benson is crafting some stunning wines. The best is a Sangiovese, but don't overlook the Viognier, Pinot Noir, Cabernet Franc, and red and white blends.

Though there is no on-site restaurant yet at Benson Vineyards, expect some kind of food service in the near future. Meanwhile, picnickers are more than welcome to enjoy their food while sipping on wine and taking in the stunning vistas.

www.bensonvineyards.com

4 | Hard Row to Hoe Vineyards
300 Ivan Morse Rd., Manson, WA 98831; (509) 687-3000

Judy and Don Phelps launched their operation in 2006 with the name Balsamroot Winery. While they like the name (and the indigenous plant it was named after), nobody could remember it—even their best customers.

So in 2008 they renamed the winery Hard Row to Hoe. A local legend was the inspiration and goes something like this: More than a half century ago, a brothel opened for business. One entrepreneur set up a rowboat taxi service to take local miners across the lake to the house of ill repute. Thus the name Hard Row to Hoe.

The winery is having a lot of fun with the name by designing the tasting room to look like an old-time bordello, complete with a red light over the restroom. And one of the wines, a red blend, is called Miss de Miner.

Not to be lost amid the fun name and history are the wines, which are superbly made—mostly from Columbia Valley grapes—and well worth seeking.

www.hardrow.com

findout more

- **www.lakechelanwinevalley.com**
  The website of the Lake Chelan Wine Valley Association includes the latest information about new wineries, visiting hours and more.

- **www.lakechelan.com**
  The Lake Chelan Chamber of Commerce site is a great resource for planning a trip to the region.

- **www.cometothelake.com**
  Includes 101 things to do in Lake Chelan and other amenities.

- **www.washingtonwine.org**
  Website for the Washington Wine Commission and a great planning tool.

Spokane

Washington State's second-largest city is in the northeastern corner of the state, about two hours from the heart of Washington wine country. Though not a traditional wine-touring region, Spokane has developed into a destination in the past decade, in part because of its population and in part because of its proximity to northern Idaho—a playground for Pacific Northwesterners. Even though the city still has a bit of the Wild West–frontier feel to it, it is home to dozens of great restaurant choices. If you're looking to treat yourself, The Davenport is one of the finest establishments there.

About a dozen wineries are in the Spokane area, and all rely on grapes from the Columbia Valley—the vast grape-growing area southwest of the city. Touring Spokane wineries can take anywhere from a long day to a leisurely three-day weekend.

◀ The Spokane area is wheat country so the local wineries have to source their grapes farther afield.

1 | Barrister Winery
1213 West Railroad Ave., Spokane, WA 99201; (509) 465-3591

Attorneys Greg Lipsker and Michael White turned their winemaking hobby into a full-time profession in 2001, when they opened Barrister. Success has come quickly and often, as the pair produce some of the finest red wines on the West Coast. Evidence of this includes top honors in every important wine competition from Seattle to Los Angeles.

The wine that has scored a bull's eye among serious wine lovers is Barrister's Cabernet Franc, which is eerily consistent in its quality at the highest level. Lipsker and White also craft highly regarded Syrah, Cabernet Sauvignon, Merlot and a blend called Rough Justice. In recent vintages, the two have begun to craft some white wines, too. The winery is open Fridays and Saturdays or by appointment. This is a must-stop if you're interested in tasting some seriously great wine.

www.barristerwinery.com

2 | Lone Canary Winery
109 S. Scott St., Suite B2, Spokane, WA 99202; (509) 534-9062

Mike Scott was the winemaker at nearby Caterina Winery for the better part of a decade before launching Lone Canary with two partners. The first releases were wines from the 2002 vintage. The winery gets its name from the American Goldfinch, or wild canary, which is Washington's official state bird.

The wines are nothing short of remarkable and are vastly underpriced for their quality. Conway crafts a wide variety of styles, including Italian (Sangiovese, Barbera and Pinot Grigio) to Bordeaux style (Sauvignon Blanc, Merlot, Cabernet Sauvignon and blends) to Rhône (Syrah). Lone Canary is producing stellar wines, and its tasting room is well worth a visit.

www.lonecanary.com

3 | Latah Creek Wine Cellars
13030 E. Indiana Ave., Spokane, WA 99216; (509) 926-0164

Mike Conway launched Latah Creek in 1982, at around the same time he was involved in helping to start Hogue Cellars in Washington's Yakima Valley. He started out at E&J Gallo in the early 1970s and worked his way up as a lab tech before becoming a winemaker.

The focus at Latah Creek is good quality at modest prices. Balance

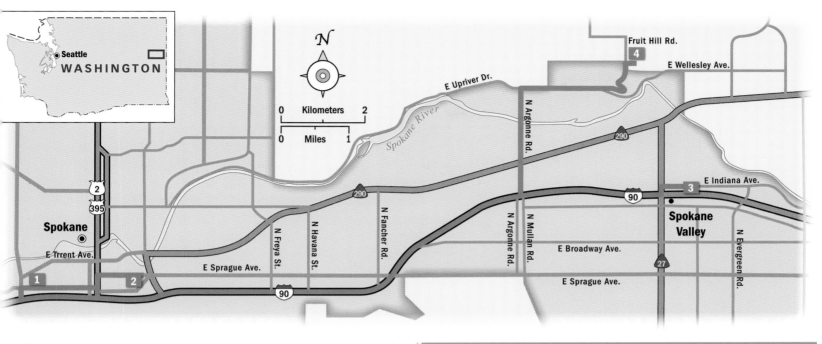

...nd flavor are premium, and Conway's wines cater to palates up and ...own the sophistication scale. One of his best-sellers is an off-dry ...lend of Riesling and huckleberry juice called Huckleberry d'Latah. ...ine lovers should be sure to try Italian-style Sangiovese, limited-...roduction Winemaker's Reserve Red and bright, off-dry Moscato ...'Latah. Mike's wife, Ellena, runs the tasting room and gift shop, ...hich is among the most friendly you will find anywhere.

...ww.latahcreek.com

4 | Arbor Crest Wine Cellars
4705 N. Fruit Hill Rd., Spokane, WA 99217; (509) 927-9463

...he grande dame of Spokane wineries is ...rbor Crest, a beautiful facility perched on a ...ill some 400 feet (122 m) above the ...pokane River. Second-generation ...inemaker Kristina Mielke-van Loben Sels ...nd her husband, Jim, oversee the operation ...tarted by her parents and uncle in 1982. ...he main feature on the expansive grounds ...s the aptly named Cliff House, built in 1924. ...rbor Crest puts on more than a dozen ...oncerts each year.

Arbor Crest made its name early on with ...auvignon Blanc, and while it remains a ...taple, beautifully balanced reds now take center stage, including ...abernet Sauvignon, Syrah, Merlot and Bordeaux-style blends.

...ww.arborcrest.com

regional events

Taste Washington! ▢ April
This is the destination to go for wine connoisseurs and foodies alike. Attendees have the opportunity to sample wines from over 140 wineries and gourmet food from 85 regional restaurants.   www.tastewashington.org

Bite of Seattle ▢ July
More than 60 restaurants and 30 food product companies participate in Seattle's premier culinary event.   www.biteofseattle.com

find out more

• www.visitspokane.com
Spokane Convention and Visitors Bureau.

• www.spokanewineries.net
Spokane Wineries Association.

• www.washingtonwine.org
Washington Wine Commission—a great planning tool.

Walla Walla Valley

For the past decade the hottest wine region in the Pacific Northwest has been the Walla Walla Valley. And what makes Walla Walla so special? Red wine, particularly Syrah and Cabernet Sauvignon. While a large percentage of the wines made here use grapes from the broader Columbia Valley, some of the best come from local vines.

The growth of the Walla Walla Valley is nothing short of stunning. The first winery to open in the modern era remains its most famous: Leonetti Cellar (1978), followed by such producers as Woodward Canyon in 1981. By the early 1990s just a half-dozen wineries called the valley home. Then waves of wineries opened, starting in 1995 and still continuing. These days more than 130 wineries are in the Walla Walla Valley. For touring purposes, the valley can be divided into roughly four regions: west of town on Highway 12; downtown; at the airport; and south of town, toward Oregon.

◀ Woodward Canyon vineyards make a rare splash of green in the barren Walla Walla Valley.

1 | Woodward Canyon Winery
11920 W. Hwy. 12, Lowden, WA 99360; (509) 525-4129

Located in a restored 1870s farmhouse, Woodward Canyon is the second-oldest winery in the valley. Owner/winemaker Rick Small has built his reputation over the past three decades with Cabernet Sauvignon, crafting some of the finest and most distinctive in the New World. His "Dedication Series" Cabernet honors a Walla Walla Valley pioneer on the label each year, and the wine is among Washington's most collectible. Small's "Artist Series" Cab is often equal to the task, showing off fruit from different vineyards. Merlot and Chardonnay are other specialties of this top-quality producer.

www.woodwardcanyon.com

2 | L'Ecole Nº 41
41 Lowden School Rd., Walla Walla, WA 99362; (509) 525-0940

One of the valley's oldest wineries (open in 1983), L'Ecole is still one of its best. Marty Clubb is the owner and winemaker for this winery, set in an old schoolhouse, and he crafts some of the valley's most remarkable Cabs, Merlots, Syrahs, red blends and Semillons. The winery's iconic label—

▲ L'Ecole Nº 41, set in an old schoolhouse, is one of Walla Walla's most famous wineries.

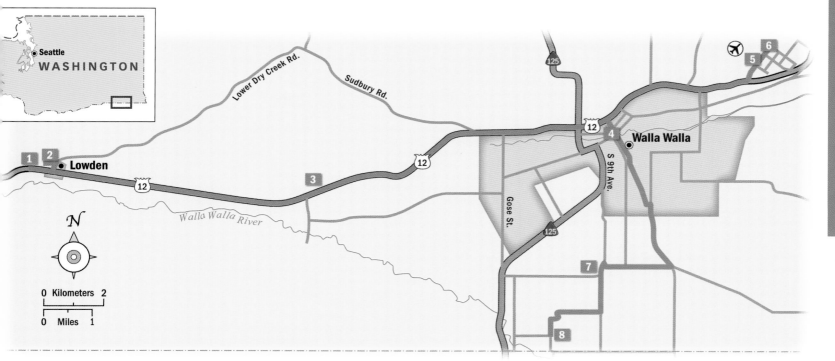

drawing of the winery building—was created by one of the children in the family. The school theme is played up throughout L'Ecole, right down to the tasting bar, which is a chalkboard. The town of Lowden, which is west of Walla Walla, was once known as Frenchtown, thus the French name for "school."

www.lecole.com

3 | Reininger Winery
5858 W. Hwy. 12, Walla Walla, WA 99362; (509) 522-1994

Six miles (10 km) west of town, in a couple of converted potato sheds, is one of the stars of Walla Walla. Chuck Reininger, a former mountain-climbing guide, caught the wine bug in the early 1990s while in college in Seattle. He and his wife, Tracy (a Walla Walla native), opened their eponymous winery in 1997, and the resulting wines quickly gained fame. Reininger is best known for its Cabernet Sauvignon, Merlot and Syrah—all from Walla Walla Valley grapes.

www.reiningerwinery.com

4 | Seven Hills Winery
212 North 3rd Ave., Walla Walla, WA 99362; (509) 529-7198

Casey McClellan opened this winery in 1988 in Milton-Freewater, Oregon, a town about 15 miles (24 km) south of Walla Walla. More than a decade later, he and his wife, Vicky, relocated the winery to

Sunset in the famous Seven Hills Vineyard

THE OREGON CONNECTION

While a few wineries have started to pop up on the Oregon side of the Walla Walla Valley, the vast majority are in Washington. That said, many of the valley's finest grapes come from south of the border. In fact, one of Washington's most famous vineyards is actually about 3 miles (5 km) into Oregon territory. Seven Hills Vineyard is co-owned by the trio of Gary Figgins (Leonetti Cellar), Marty Clubb (L'Ecole Nº 41) and Norm McKibben (Pepper Bridge Winery). The three use about half of the fruit from the more than 200 acres of vines, with the rest sold to more than 25 other producers.

downtown Walla Walla, sharing a historical building with one of the region's finest restaurants, Whitehouse-Crawford.

McClellan's winery is named after Seven Hills, a vineyard he and his father planted in the early 1980s that is now one of the Northwest's most famous. While he makes a wide array of wines, his most cherished efforts are Cabernet Sauvignons, Merlots and red blends from the state's top vineyards.

www.sevenhillswinery.com

5 | Tamarack Cellars
700 C St., Walla Walla, WA 99362; (509) 526-3533

One of the earliest wineries to open in an old World War II–era building at the Walla Walla Regional Airport was Tamarack Cellars. Owner Ron Coleman launched his winery in 1998 with the intention of making a few hundred cases of Merlot. Now it's a several-thousand-case winery that is considered one of Walla Walla's finest.

Merlot remains Coleman's trademark wine, though his Cabernet Sauvignon, Syrah and red blends are nothing short of remarkable. Perhaps his most famous wine is a nicely priced blend called Firehouse Red, named after the building Coleman's winery occupies (once the airport's firehouse).

www.tamarackcellars.com

▲ Cabernet Sauvignon is one of the success stories of Washington vineyards.

6 | Dunham Cellars
150 E. Boeing Ave., Walla Walla, WA 99362; (509) 529-4685

Winemaker Eric Dunham got his start as an assistant winemaker for L'Ecole N° 41 (see page 44). He launched this winery, which he owns with his parents, with the 1995 vintage. He quickly gained a cult following for his Cabernet Sauvignon, though his finest efforts might have been saved for his Syrah wines, which continually and remarkably come out at or near the top of one peer-group judging after another.

Dunham was one of the first wineries to embrace the Walla Walla Regional Airport as its home. Its large building provides ample space for wine production and also a cozy and comfortable tasting-room

▲ New vineyard plantings in the Walla Walla Valley show little signs of slowing down.

▲ Eastern Washington provides the bulk of the grapes for all Washington wine.

experience. Eric Dunham's artistry doesn't stop with his wines. He also puts paint to canvas to create many of the works of art that grace Dunham Cellars' labels.

www.dunhamcellars.com

7 | Dusted Valley Vintners
1248 Old Milton Hwy., Walla Walla, WA 99362; (509) 525-1337

Wisconsin natives Chad Johnson and Corey Braunel set up their winery south of downtown Walla Walla in 2003 and, from their 100 acres of vineyards, have been crafting utterly stunning Cabernet Sauvignon and Syrah wines since their first release. The wines are remarkable in their consistency at the highest level of the Northwest wine industry, regularly earning top marks in judgings and blind tastings.

findout more

- **www.wallawallawine.com**
  The best source of information on wine touring is the website for the Walla Walla Valley Wine Alliance.

- **www.wallawallawinenews.com**
  This combination of blog, news and calendar site offers a lot of great insights on what is happening in and around the valley.

The pair have a great sense of humor to go along with the talented winemaking, as evidenced in just about every aspect of the winery. This makes Dusted Valley Vintners a great stop on the Walla Walla wine trail.

Not satisfied with success from their main label, Johnson and Braunel have launched a second label, called "Boomtown," that puts the spotlight on high quality and value—a combination every wine lover seeks.

www.dustedvalley.com

8 | Northstar Winery
1736 J.B. George Rd., Walla Walla, WA 99362; (866) 486-7828

Northstar, part of the Ste. Michelle Wine Estates stable, is a winery created with the sole purpose of crafting the world's finest Merlot. For many years the winery existed in a virtual state, using space at other Ste. Michelle facilities in Eastern Washington. However, in 2002, Northstar got a permanent home south of Walla Walla in a bucolic location facing the Blue Mountains.

Northstar's Merlots regularly rank among the best in the New World—and often fare well against the great standard bearers from Bordeaux's Right Bank. In recent years Northstar has strayed ever so slightly from its Merlot roots, producing small amounts of a Bordeaux-style blend called Stella Maris and crafting tiny amounts of such varieties as Cabernet Franc, Petit Verdot, Syrah and Semillon. For the most part, these wines are available only at the winery.

www.northstarmerlot.com

WALLA WALLA AMENITIES

Before the rush to become a wine town, Walla Walla was a bit short on food and lodging. But with its fame in the past decade has come superb eating establishments and places to stay.

Whether you are looking for white-tablecloth treatment or leisurely Northwest style, you will find it, primarily in the downtown area. The Marcus Whitman Hotel is *the* place to stay.

Getting to Walla Walla is not difficult. Flights from Seattle, Portland, Spokane and Boise arrive regularly—and they land conveniently close to a number of wineries, in case you're looking to jump off the plane and into a tasting room literally across the street from the terminal building.

Red Mountain

To be honest, Red Mountain, on the dry eastern edge of the Yakima Valley, is neither red nor a mountain, but "Brown Ridge" wouldn't be much of a name. It is, however, an amazing place to grow wine grapes, perhaps the best in Washington. It is one of the warmest regions in the state, so red-wine grapes are king here, especially Cabernet Sauvignon, Merlot and Syrah, though many other varieties are grown, including Sangiovese, Nebbiolo and Cabernet Franc.

Vineyards began to replace sagebrush in the mid-1970s, and the region grew slowly through the mid-1990s. In the past decade a veritable land rush has occurred, pushing up land prices and creating a tremendous amount of growth—in both vineyards and wineries. Today Red Mountain is home to about a dozen wineries, and that is expected to double in the next decade.

◀ Red Mountain is one of the best places in the state for growing quality wine grapes.

1 | Chandler Reach Vineyards

9506 W. Chandler Rd., Benton City, WA 99320; (509) 588-8800

This winery, one exit west of Red Mountain on Interstate 82, is slightly in no-man's land—it isn't part of Red Mountain but is far closer to it than it is to Prosser, the heart of the Yakima Valley (see Tour 13). Passing it up would be a shame because owner Len Parris has created a Tuscan-inspired oasis amid the sagebrush landscape of Eastern Washington.

Parris, inspired to enter the wine industry after a visit to Tuscany in 1997, purchased 42 acres of north-facing land opposite Red Mountain and built a stunning winery complete with a handsome colonnade that would not look out of place in the swankier parts of Chianti Classico or Montalcino.

His vineyards surrounding the winery focus entirely on classy red varieties, including Cabernet Sauvignon, Merlot, Cabernet Franc, Syrah and, of course, Sangiovese, Tuscany's classic red grape. Parris produces about 5,000 cases per year. He makes a Viognier to complement the reds, using fruit purchased from another vineyard.

www.chandlerreach.com

▲ The stylish tasting room at Fidelitas Wines

2 | Terra Blanca Winery & Estate Vineyard

34715 N. DeMoss Rd., Benton City, WA 99320; (509) 588-6082

Keith Pilgrim has built an amazing winery on his 300-acre estate on the lower reaches of Red Mountain. Pilgrim arrived from California in the early 1990s with the dream of owning a winery. By 1997 he had opened the first winery in Washington with caves, where he stores his red wines in the barrel. A decade later Pilgrim had constructed a stunning Italian-themed building that architecturally rivals anything in the Pacific Northwest. Adjacent to the spacious tasting room is a demonstration kitchen, where cooking classes are held.

His flagship wine is a Bordeaux-style blend called Onyx, though he also crafts Syrah, Cabernet Sauvignon, Merlot, Malbec and an array of other reds, whites and dessert wines, primarily from his estate grapes.

www.terrablanca.com

3 | Fidelitas Wines

51810 N. Sunset Rd., Benton City, WA 99320; (509) 588-3469

Owner Charlie Hoppes is one of Washington's most respected and recognized winemakers. After working for Chateau Ste. Michelle as its red winemaker for several years, Hoppes helped launch Three Rivers Winery in Walla Walla, then started Fidelitas with the 2000 vintage. He built his modest yet stylish tasting room on a 5-acre plot on Red Mountain in 2007 and planted 3.5 acres of Cabernet Sauvignon in 2009.

Thanks to his experience of than 20 vintages in Washington, Hoppes understands where the best grapes are grown and the importance of working closely with top growers. Thus, he has access to incredible fruit from vineyards such as Champoux, Boushey, Ciel du Cheval, Stillwater Creek and Conner-Lee.

Increasingly, Hoppes has focused on Bordeaux varieties, particularly Cabernet Sauvignon, though he also favors Merlot, Malbec and Semillon. The wines tend to show elegance and power and can be aged for years or minutes, depending on the needs of the customer.

www.fidelitaswines.com

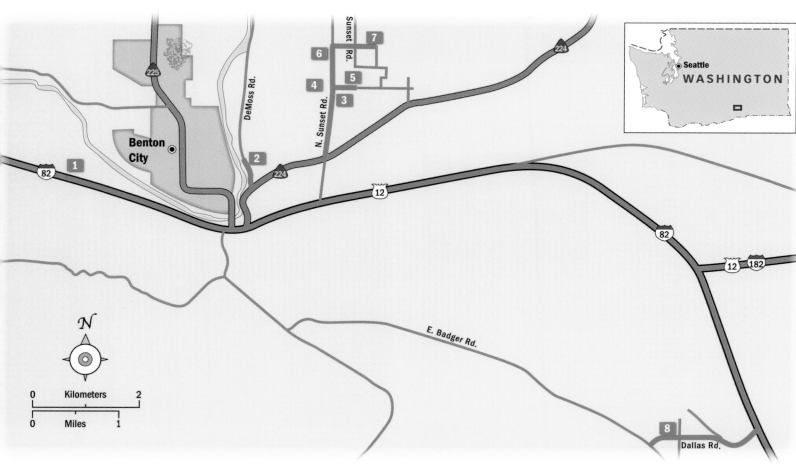

▲ Kiona, once a basement operation, is now a beautiful facility overlooking the Yakima Valley.

4 | Kiona Vineyards & Winery
44612 N. Sunset Rd., Benton City, WA 99320; (509) 588-6716

In 1975 John Williams and Jim Holmes (who now owns Ciel du Cheval Vineyard across the road) planted the first grapes on the Red Mountain ridge, and they harvested the fruits of their labor in 1978. For nearly three decades, Kiona's tasting room was in the basement of the family home.

However, in 2007 the winery moved to a new, $3-million facility right next door, and it now includes a spacious tasting room. Second-generation winemaker Scott Williams crafts a wide variety of wines, from Zinfandel, Merlot, Cabernet Sauvignon, Sangiovese and red blends to Riesling, Chenin Blanc, Chardonnay and even icewine. If there is a signature wine, it's probably Lemberger, a red wine that has been championed by Kiona for its entire history and which is more at home in Germany's Württemberg region.

www.kionawine.com

▲ The grand winery at Hedges Family Estate

5 | Hedges Family Estate
53511 N. Sunset Rd., Benton City, WA 99320; (509) 588-3155

Tom Hedges grew up in nearby Richland, Washington, and caught the wine bug when he began selling it in the Far East. In 1987 he launched his namesake winery and is one of the people responsible for bringing classic Bordeaux-style red blends to Washington.

At a time when most Washington wineries' tasting rooms were little more than afterthoughts, Hedges had a vision of how grand the industry could be. The Hedges winery, opened in the mid-1990s, remains one of the state's grandest, inspired by French-style chateaux. Long before Red Mountain gained official appellation status in 2001, Hedges championed the sense of place that the grapes, vines and soil of this ridge evoke in the resulting wines.

Hedges is best known for its red blends, and it offers three: Red Mountain Reserve, Three Vineyards and CMS (Cabernet-Merlot-Syrah). The latter, an inexpensive wine, has a white counterpart (Chardonnay-Marsanne-Sauvignon). Winemaker Pete Hedges also crafts a port-style dessert wine.

www.hedgesfamilyestate.com

6 | Hightower Cellars
19418 E. 583 PR NE, Red Mountain, WA 99320; (509) 588-2867

Tim and Kelly Hightower started their eponymous winery in 1997 in Woodinville, where Tim worked for one of the state's largest producers. In 2002 they purchased 15 acres of land high on Red Mountain, built their winery and planted 10 acres of Bordeaux varieties: Cabernet Sauvignon, Merlot, Cabernet Franc, Malbec and Petit Verdot. They also purchase grapes from top vineyards on Red Mountain as well as in the Horse Heaven Hills and Walla Walla Valley. The resulting wines show elegance and firmness, typical of Red Mountain wines.

www.hightowercellars.com

7 | Col Solare
50207 Antinori Rd., Benton City, WA 99320; (509) 588-6806

High above other wineries on Red Mountain is Col Solare, a joint venture between the Antinori family of Tuscany (which began making wine in the 1380s) and Ste. Michelle Wine Estates. The operation produces two wines: a high-end Bordeaux-style red blend called Col Solare and a more modestly priced blend called Shining Hill (which is the translation of Col Solare from Italian). The state-of-the-art $6.5-million facility opened in 2007. The winery is open for private tastings by appointment only, and it is well worth the effort.

www.colsolare.com

▲ Col Solare's new winery stands high on Red Mountain.

8 | Goose Ridge Estate Winery
16304 N. Dallas Rd., Richland, WA 99352; (509) 628-3880

Goose Ridge faces Red Mountain across Interstate 82 and, in fact, shares the same aquifer. The Monson family began planting the vineyard in the late 1990s and now has about 1,400 acres planted, making it the state's largest contiguous wine grape vineyard.

Charlie Hoppes of Fidelitas oversees winemaking for Goose Ridge and knows all the best vines in the vineyard. Cabernet Sauvignon, Merlot, Syrah and red blends are all great choices.

The tasting room is just a few minutes' drive from Red Mountain. It was remodeled in 2009, when the Monson family invested in a massive winemaking facility nearby, leaving more room for entertaining visitors.

www.gooseridge.com

RED MOUNTAIN AMENITIES
Because of its size and agricultural focus, Red Mountain offers no food or lodging. However, the communities of West Richland, Richland, Kennewick and Pasco are nearby and are home to nearly 200,000 people. Thus, you'll find plenty of hotels and motels in all price ranges just a few minutes away from Red Mountain. And with them come several choices for restaurants—everything from national chains to local and regional choices. There's also plenty of shopping and several golf courses nearby, as the Tri-Cities area is the economic and population hub of Washington wine country.

Yakima Valley

Washington's Yakima Valley is the Pacific Northwest's original wine country. It was here that William Bridgman first planted wine grapes in 1917, then opened a winery soon after the Repeal of Prohibition. It was here that Walter Clore took a job with Washington State University in the 1930s and began to promote planting grape vines like some sort of Johnny Appleseed. And it was here that the federal government granted the Northwest its first official American Viticultural Area in 1983.

The Yakima Valley is Washington's second-largest appellation, and within it are three smaller AVAs (Red Mountain, Snipes Mountain and Rattlesnake Hills). From a wine-touring perspective, the Yakima Valley can be split into three main areas: Zillah in the west, Prosser in the middle, and Red Mountain in the east. This tour focuses on the first two areas (for Red Mountain, see Tour 12).

◀ In the dry Yakima Valley, the irrigated valley floor contrasts sharply with the bleached uplands.

1 | Sagelands Vineyard
71 Gangl Rd., Wapato, WA 98951; (800) 967-8115

This winery is one of the first you will encounter when entering the Yakima Valley from the city of Yakima. It opened in 1984 as Staton Hills Winery and was uneven in its quality for its first 15 years. However, it was purchased by the Californian Chalone Wine Co. in 1999, and its fortunes turned quickly. Today it is owned by the large Diageo wine group.

Sagelands uses grapes from what it terms the "Four Corners" of Washington wine country: the Wahluke Slope to the north, the Horse Heaven Hills to the south, the Walla Walla Valley to the east and the Rattlesnake Hills to the west (which is the appellation it is in).

Sagelands is best known for its economically priced and oft-awarded reds, particularly its Cabernet Sauvignon and Merlot.

www.sagelandsvineyard.com

2 | Piety Flats Winery
2560 Donald-Wapato Rd., Wapato, WA 98951; (509) 877-3115

This conveniently located tasting room adjacent to Interstate 82 is one of the fun little stops in the Yakima Valley. Piety Flats is a historical name for the community of Donald (neither of which can be found on maps today).

The building dates back to 1911 and in recent years has been home to the Donald Mercantile. Those in the know make it a must-stop on summer trips through the Yakima Valley, particularly for the amazing peach sundaes. Another draw are the wines made by David Minick (of Willow Crest Winery, Prosser). Fairly priced, the highlights are Riesling, Black Muscat and a red blend, Mercantile Red.

www.pietyflatswinery.com

3 | Claar Cellars
1001 Vintage Valley Pkwy., Zillah, WA 98953; (509) 829-6810

Situated right next to Interstate 82 in Zillah, Claar Cellars is one of the most conveniently located tasting rooms in the Yakima Valley.

Claar Cellars' vineyards and winemaking facility are actually about 50 miles (80 km) to the east, in an area north of Pasco, overlooking the Columbia River. The Whitelatch family planted the vineyard in 1980 and launched the winery in 1997, with a focus on Riesling, Merlot, Sangiovese and red blends. The winery is known for its solid quality and reasonable prices.

www.claarcellars.com

4 | Hyatt Vineyards

2020 Gilbert Rd., Zillah, WA 98953; (509) 829-6333

Hyatt Vineyards is one of the older wineries in the Yakima Valley, having been established in 1983. It was one of the first wineries to embrace Merlot as Washington's primary red grape and continues to craft some of the state's best in that category.

Hyatt's 180 acres of estate vineyards surround the property, making a stop here in the bucolic Rattlesnake Hills an enjoyable one.

Hyatt crafts everything from bold Zinfandels and Cabernet Sauvignons to suave icewines. Of particular delight are two versions of wine made from the rare Black Muscat grape. Also of note is Roza Ridge, the winery's premium label, which highlights the reserve-level wines from Hyatt Vineyards.

www.hyattvineyards.com

▲ The view from Sagelands Vineyard toward Mount Rainier, Washington's highest mountain

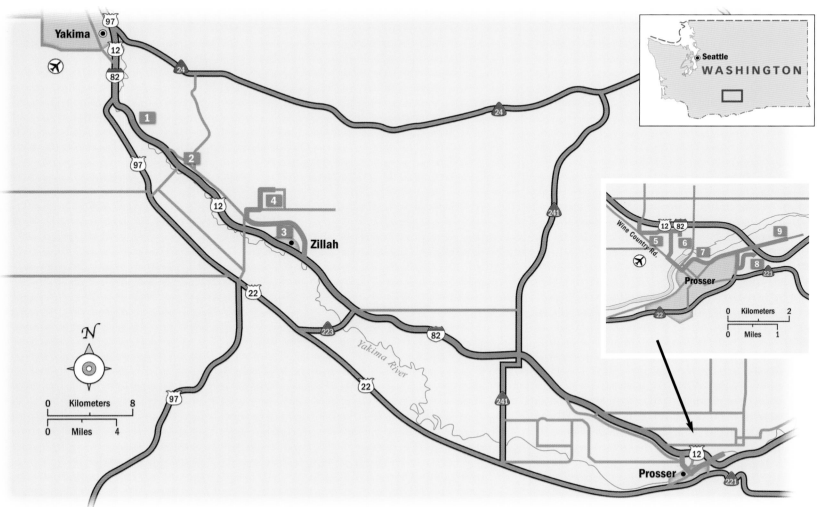

5 | Thurston Wolfe Winery
588 Cabernet Ct., Prosser, WA 99352; (509) 786-3313

Wade Wolfe and Becky Yeaman launched Thurston Wolfe in 1987, but at the time, Wade was heavily involved in the wine industry—first at Chateau Ste. Michelle and later at Hogue Cellars—so the winery never evolved beyond boutique status, until he retired to focus on Thurston Wolfe full-time.

Today he is crafting some of the state's most interesting and delicious wines. Wolfe has never feared straying into lesser-known varieties hardly found elsewhere in Washington, as one can tell by such offerings as Petite Sirah, Zinfandel, Primitivo and Lemberger. He also crafts several port-style wines and an extremely popular white blend of Pinot Gris and Viognier.

The tasting room is in the Vintner's Village, just off Interstate 82 and within walking distance of a dozen other wineries.

www.thurstonwolfe.com

6 | Winemaker's Loft
357 Port Ave., Prosser, WA 99350; (509) 786-2705

The Winemaker's Loft is not a winery but rather an incubator with room for up to seven wineries under one roof. It is in the aptly named Vintner's Village just off Interstate 82 in Prosser, giving the area one of the highest concentrations of wineries in the state, with more than a dozen within strolling distance of each other.

As is the nature of incubator-style wineries, the list of tenants tends to revolve. That said, the current wineries will likely stay for at least two to four years. They include Apex Cellars, Maison Bleue, Coyote Canyon and Tasawik.

The Winemaker's Loft is a beautiful Tuscan-style building complete with a fountain and courtyard at the entrance, with each tasting room just a few steps from its neighbor.

7 | Desert Wind Winery
2258 Wine Country Rd., Prosser, WA 99350; (509) 786-7277

The Fries family owns 540 acres of prime vineyards on Washington's Wahluke Slope as well as Duck Pond Cellars in Oregon's Dundee Hills. But Desert Wind Winery in Prosser is its masterpiece.

The winery overlooks the Yakima River near Interstate 82 and is a true destination. The stunning tasting room and gift shop serve up estate wines, including red blends, Merlots, Syrahs, Cabernets, Viogniers, Sauvignon Blancs and more. Adjacent to the tasting room is a restaurant open for lunch and dinner. A conference facility can handle a couple hundred people, and a large patio provides beautiful views of the Yakima Valley. To top it off—literally—are

▲ Desert Wind Winery is a perfect spot to relax after a long day of wine touring.

guest rooms on the second floor that rival any smart Seattle hotel for luxury and attention to detail. If you want to wind down after a long day of wine touring, you can even order a massage.

www.desertwindwinery.com

---

8 | Snoqualmie Vineyards

660 Frontier Rd., Prosser, WA 99350; (509) 786-5558

Snoqualmie is a winery that finally has a home. It started in western Washington in 1984. When it was purchased by Ste. Michelle in 1991, it moved around the Columbia Valley to the wine giant's various production facilities. In 2003 it moved to its current location, which is likely to be more permanent. The winery is in a retrofitted warehouse with a comfortable tasting room and gift shop, with a lovely seating area outside next to a bubbling fountain.

In recent years longtime Snoqualmie winemaker Joy Andersen has begun to produce wines under the "Naked" moniker, meaning they use certified organic grapes (though the wines themselves are not necessarily organically produced). In addition, she crafts a number of bottlings that are of stunning quality at modest prices. Look especially for Snoqualmie Riesling, Merlot, Cabernet Sauvignon, Syrah, Gewürztraminer and Chardonnay.

www.snoqualmie.com

---

9 | Kestrel Vintners

2890 Lee Rd., Prosser, WA 99350; (509) 786-2675

How many wineries are prominently featured in a murder mystery? In Washington State, not many, but Kestrel qualifies because it was a focal point of the 2009 novel *For the Sake of the Vine*. Kestrel has also been making some killer wines in its fairly short history (it opened in 1999). Using primarily estate grapes from 30-year-old vines, Kestrel crafts luscious Merlots, Cabernet Sauvignons and red blends, as well as elegant Viogniers and Chardonnays.

Kestrel's most famous and successful wine was a bit of an accident. The winemaker was looking to produce a value-priced red blend and came up with Lady in Red, a nonvintage bottling whose label depicts a woman in a red dress. The wine is now Kestrel's most popular. Looking for something to nibble on while wine touring? Kestrel's tasting room offers a fine selection of regional and international cheeses.

www.kestrelwines.com

▲ The Cabernet Sauvignon grapes of Kestrel Vintners are crafted to produce a dark, rich red wine.

YAKIMA VALLEY AMENITIES

The Yakima Valley has long had a well-earned reputation for a dearth of good places to eat and stay. However, for the most part, the former problem has been eradicated. Prosser, in particular, has blossomed with high-quality, locally owned restaurants. Picazo 7 Seventeen leads the way, while CG Bistro also is a strong contender. In nearby Sunnyside, Snipes Mountain Brewery also is a strong choice. And in Zillah, it's hard to beat El Ranchito.

In terms of lodging, choices remain limited, with few B&Bs and most other choices being chain motels.

find out more

- **www.wineyakimavalley.org**
  Wine Yakima Valley is the umbrella organization for wineries and vineyards within the appellation.

- **www.rattlesnakehills.com**
  All about touring wineries within the Rattlesnake Hills AVA.

Columbia River Gorge

The lower Columbia River Gorge is among the most beautiful drives in America. Drop in a couple dozen wineries and you have a great destination on your hands.

The Washington side of the Gorge is more rural and rugged than the Oregon side (see Tour 15), south of the river. Even the small towns are few and far between. And the two-lane highway tends to be at higher elevations than the Oregon side, so the views are even that much more spectacular.

Plenty of grapes are grown in the Gorge. In the eastern area big reds are the norm, especially Zinfandel, Cabernet Sauvignon and Merlot. Moving east, temperatures drop and precipitation rises, giving way to cooler-climate grapes such as Gewürztraminer, Riesling and Pinot Noir. This dramatic change helps make this a fascinating region.

◀ The Columbia River Gorge is one of the Pacific Northwest's most scenic destinations.

1 | Wind River Cellars
196 Spring Creek Rd., Husum, WA 98623; (509) 493-2324

Located high in the hills above the Columbia River just below Mount Adams is this picturesque winery. It started in the mid-1980s as Charles Hooper Family Winery, then changed names when Kris and Joel Goodwillie purchased the operation in 1997.

The Goodwillies craft a wide variety of wines, including Riesling, Pinot Noir, Syrah, Cabernet Franc, Chenin Blanc, Pinot Gris and Chardonnay. One of their finest efforts is called Port of Celilo, a fortified dessert wine using Lemberger, a red grape of Austrian origins. If the views and wines aren't enough to bring you to Wind River Cellars, how about a whitewater rafting trip on the White Salmon River that concludes with a wine tasting at the winery?

www.windrivercellars.com

2 | Syncline Wine Cellars
111 Balch Rd., Lyle, WA 98635; (509) 365-4361

James and Poppie Mantone were drawn west through their love for wine. They met while working at an Oregon winery, fell in love and followed their dream of owning a winery across the Columbia River to Washington. Since launching Syncline in 2001, the Mantones have gained a near-cult following for their elegant and balanced wines, which use grapes from throughout the Columbia Valley and Columbia Gorge AVAs. Their estate vineyard, Steep Creek Vineyard, is next to a series of high cliffs rising straight out of the Columbia River. Syncline's early focus was on Rhône varieties, particularly Syrah, Mourvedre, Grenache, Counoise, Viognier and Roussanne, though they also craft Pinot Noir and a few other wines.

www.synclinewine.com

3 | Cascade Cliffs Vineyard & Winery
8866 Hwy. 14, Wishram, WA 98673; (509) 767-1100

This humble-looking winery, which sits atop basalt cliffs 400 feet (120 m) above the Columbia River, is producing some blockbuster wines. Owner Bob Lorkowski became fascinated with wine, thanks to his grandfather, who was a moonshiner. Lorkowski worked at different wineries before purchasing Cascade Cliffs in 1997 and expanding the vineyards to 23 acres. He grows mainstream grapes such as Merlot and Cabernet Sauvignon, as well as pioneering plantings of Petite Sirah, Zinfandel, Nebbiolo and Barbera.

www.cascadecliffs.com

Maryhill Museum of Art is set on extensive grounds.

WHAT IN THE SAM HILL..?

The region near Goldendale is known as Maryhill and was named by railroad executive Sam Hill after his wife, Mary. He built a mansion overlooking the Columbia River and later converted it to a museum, now the Maryhill Museum of Art. The museum is near Maryhill Winery and includes several fine works, including original Rodins. He also built a replica of Stonehenge, a memorial to the 13 men from Klickitat County who died in World War I.

4 | Maryhill Winery

9774 Hwy. 14, Goldendale, WA 98620; (877) 627-9445

A destination winery by any definition, Maryhill Winery is perched atop a cliff overlooking the Columbia River with majestic Mount Hood to the southwest. It is a dramatic setting, which is part of what inspired the owners Craig and Vicki Leuthold to launch their dream here in 2001.

Starting with 4,300 cases of wine a year, they've expanded to produce more than 70,000 award-winning cases and have opened a 4,000-seat amphitheater that attracts top musical acts each summer. Maryhill's claim to fame is Zinfandel, California's versatile red grape. Zinfandel was hardly planted in Washington until Maryhill's 2002 vintage won Best in Class at a 2004 competition in the heart of California's Zin country.

www.maryhillwinery.com

findout more

- **www.columbiagorgewine.com**
  Columbia Gorge Winemakers.

- **www.crgva.org**
  Columbia River Gorge Visitors Association.

- **www.maryhillmuseum.org**
  One of Pacific Northwest's top cultural destinations.

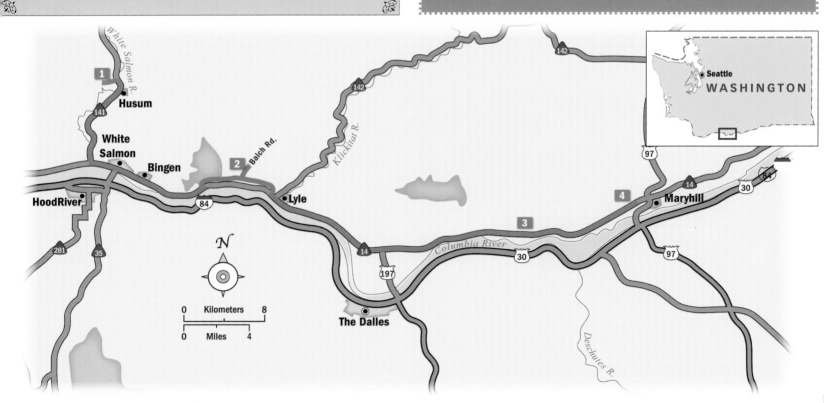

Columbia River Gorge

Though only the broad Columbia River separates the Oregon and Washington sides of the Lower Columbia River Gorge, the two regions could not be more different. The fact that a four-lane interstate runs along the Oregon side of the Gorge has probably helped it develop more and receive more visitors; it's an easy drive from Portland, 80 miles (129 km) to the west. As a result, the cities of Hood River and The Dalles are vastly larger, comparatively, than any of the small communities on the north side of the river. Thus, there is so much more to choose from when it comes to dining, lodging and other amenities.

More than a dozen wineries dot the Oregon side of the Gorge between Hood River and The Dalles. Most are smaller producers, primarily relying upon grapes from the region, though some fruit comes from the Willamette Valley to the west and the Columbia Valley to the northeast.

◄ Mount Hood, seen here from Phelps Creek Vineyards, towers over the vineyards in this part of Oregon.

1 | Phelps Creek Vineyards

1850 Country Club Rd., Hood River, OR 97031; (541) 386-2607

Bob Morus began planting his vineyard near Hood River in 1989 and now has 30 acres of vines, primarily planted to Pinot Noir and Chardonnay. When he launched the winery with the 2004 vintage, he hired Rich Cushman, a Hood River native and one of Oregon's finest winemakers who had spent 25 years working in the Willamette Valley. That move quickly set Phelps Creek's reputation as a serious winery on the rise. Cushman also makes his own wines at the winery, sold under the Viento label.

www.phelpscreekvineyards.com

2 | Cathedral Ridge Winery

4200 Post Canyon Dr., Hood River, OR 97031; (541) 386-2882

In 1985 Don Flerchinger started a little winery in Hood River, focusing on German grape varieties. The results were brilliantly crafted Riesling and Pinot Gris wines sold under the name of Flerchinger Vineyards.

Nearly two decades later, Flerchinger retired and sold the winery to Robb Bell, who renamed it after a ridge on nearby Mount Hood. Bell hired Michael Sebastiani of the famed California winemaking family, changing the focus from white to red wines. The results have been superb—Sebastiani's wines have transformed Cathedral Ridge into one of Oregon's top producers. Try the Viognier, Zinfandel and Cabernet Sauvignon Reserve.

www.cathedralridgewinery.com

▲ The owner, Bob Morus, pouring wine for visitors at Phelps Creek Vineyards

Columbia R.

84 **30**

84 **30**

Post Canyon Dr.

Post Canyon Dr.

2

Rand Rd.

30

84

4

3
● Hood River

Hood R.

35

May Dr.

Balmont Dr.

12th St.

Fairview Dr.

Belmont Dr.

281

Country Club Rd.

N

0 Kilometers 1

0 Miles 0.5

Barrett Dr.

281

Portland

OREGON

3 | The Pines 1852
202 State St., Hood River, OR 97031; (541) 993-8301

In the late 1800s Louis Comini settled in the Columbia River Gorge near The Dalles and planted grapevines from his native Genoa, Italy. For decades these Zinfandel vines went untended until Lonnie Wright came along in 1982 and revived them. For the better part of two decades, Wright sold his grapes to others, particularly Peter Rossback of Sineann winery in Newberg, Oregon. Beginning in 2001, Wright held back some of his grapes and launched his winery—with Rossback as his winemaker.

The tasting room in downtown Hood River also operates as an art gallery that showcases regional artists.

www.thepinesvineyard.com

4 | Quenett Winery
111 Oak St., Hood River, OR 97031; (541) 386-2229

This winery took its name from the journals of Lewis and Clark, who refer to Quenett Creek—now Mill Creek—as the area where they set up camp near The Dalles on their journey to the Pacific Ocean in 1805.

The focus here is on Italian varieties—Sangiovese, Zinfandel and Barbera—along with traditional French varieties such as Cabernet Sauvignon, Merlot and Syrah.

The tasting room doubles as a wine bar and is open till 8 p.m. on Fridays and Saturdays, when live music is often part of the ambience.

www.quenett.com

findout more
- **www.columbiagorgewine.com**
  Columbia Gorge Wine Growers.
- **www.crgva.org**
  Columbia River Gorge Visitors Association.
- **www.hoodriver.org**
  Hood River County Chamber of Commerce.

GREAT WINE AND WIND
The Columbia River Gorge, particularly around Hood River, is a haven for wind surfing. In the summertime it would be unusual not to see the river dotted with wind surfers. In fact, more than a few winemakers and restaurateurs have been drawn to this region because of their love for the sport. So even if you don't plan to try it out, you'll still benefit from it in the form of great food and wine.

Around Portland

At more than 2 million residents in and around the city, Portland is Oregon's largest city and, as such, is the center of culture and entertainment. Few wineries call Portland home, however, because Yamhill County—the heart of the Oregon wine industry—is just a 45-minute drive away. That said, there is no shortage of wine tasting in the city of roses, thanks to numerous wine shops, wine bars and restaurants.

Portland probably doesn't have the same reputation for food as its fellow West Coast big cities (San Francisco, Seattle and Vancouver, in particular), but one of the real joys of staying in the city is the top chefs' fierce dedication to using regional ingredients from the area's many high-quality farmers.

For this tour, two of the destinations are Forest Grove, a bedroom community about a half-hour drive to the west, on Highway 26.

◀ Montinore Estate is one of Oregon's largest wineries and an easy drive from Portland.

1 | Oregon Wines on Broadway
3515 S.W. Bdwy., Portland, OR 97205; (503) 228-0126

The best place in the entire state to try a broad range of Oregon wines is this wine shop and wine bar in downtown Portland.

At any given time, Oregon Wines on Broadway serves up sips or glasses of 30 Oregon wines, primarily the state's famous Pinot Noirs. A few whites and a handful of Washington reds also are on tap.

If you're hungry, bread, cheeses, olives and other munchies are available. A great place to relax or take in some serious wine tasting.

www.oregonwinesonbroadway.com

2 | Hip CHICKS do WINE
4510 S.E. 23rd Ave., Portland, OR 97202; (503) 234-3790

When this winery opened in a warehouse district of Portland in 2001, it was a little difficult to take it seriously. The name, the goofy labels and the less-than-serious attitude of the owners/winemakers had aroused a great deal of curiosity as to the seriousness of the venture, yet the wines were pretty good from the start, and they continued to mature over the years, even if Laurie Lewis and Renée Neely blissfully did not.

These days the winery's name and whimsical labels hardly raise an eyebrow, as it seems everybody is trying to capture a level of,

well, hipness that has been here since the beginning. The prices have stayed startlingly reasonable and quality remains good. Try the Drop Dead Red, Sangiovese and Pinot Gris.

The Hip Chicks have opened a second tasting room, in the Yamhill County town of Newberg.

www.hipchicksdowine.com

3 | SakéOne
820 Elm St., Forest Grove, OR 97116; (503) 357-7056

If you are interested in checking out the only American-owned saké producer in the United States, you are in the right place. SakéOne started in the mid-1990s as Momokawa, changing to its current name in 1998.

Saké, of course, is wine made from rice and is most famous in Japan, where the process has been refined for centuries. SakéOne makes a number of different styles of saké, from G, short for Genshu (a Japanese term for premium-grade saké), to several flavored sakés under the Moonstone label. The fruit-infused sakés—including such flavors as pear, raspberry and plum—were a category created by SakéOne in 1997 and remain the company's top medal winners.

www.sakeone.com

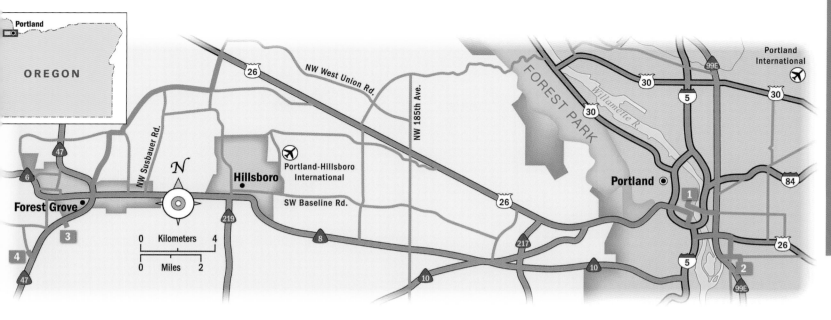

4 | Montinore Estate

3663 S.W. Dilley Rd., Forest Grove, OR 97116; (503) 359-5012

The sleepy community of Forest Grove is home to one of Oregon's largest wineries.

Established in 1987, Montinore got its name from the original owner's love for his home state of Montana, thus "Montana in Oregon" became "Montinore."

The vineyards now top 250 acres, which are the sources for all of Montinore's wines. The offerings include a number of single-block Pinot Noirs that stand tall alongside many of the state's best, as well as Riesling, Pinot Gris, Gewürztraminer and Müller-Thurgau. The latter is a real favorite in the tasting room, because it is off-dry and appeals to a broad spectrum of wine tasters.

www.montinore.com

A selection of wines from Hip CHICKS do WINE

regional events

Newport Seafood & Wine Festival □ February

Oregon's premier seafood and wine event highlights wineries and restaurants of the Pacific Northwest and offers a range of related activities.

www.newportchamber.org

Portland Rose Festival □ May–June

Two weeks of festivities in the city, including the largest floral parade in the United States.

www.newportchamber.org

International Pinot Noir Festival □ July

An international gathering of top Pinot producers and acclaimed chefs for a memorable weekend of extraordinary tastings, educational seminars, unforgettable meals, and celebrating together in Oregon wine country.

www.ipnc.org

The Bite of Oregon □ August

Wine lovers and foodies gather at this event showcasing local and national food, wine, chef demos and live entertainment.

www.biteoforegon.com

North Willamette Valley

The north Willamette Valley is the heart of Oregon wine country and the center of Pinot Noir production for the Pacific Northwest. Within the northern section of the vast Willamette Valley—which stretches from the Columbia River in the north past Eugene in the south—are six smaller American Viticultural Areas, or AVAs. Each of these is unique for its soil types, growing conditions and resulting wines, even though they are all basically within a 45-minute drive of each other.

This tour explores Chehalem Mountain near Newberg, the Yamhill-Carlton District around the towns of Yamhill and Carlton, the city of McMinnville (the unofficial capital of the northern Willamette) and the northern edge of the Eola-Amity Hills. The Dundee Hills are covered in Tour 18.

◀ Aerial view of WillaKenzie Estate in the north Willamette Valley

1 | Ponzi Vineyards

14665 S.W. Winery La., Beaverton, OR 97007-8773; (503) 628-1227

Dick and Nancy Ponzi share a strong entrepreneurial spirit. They founded their vineyard and winery in 1970 and have a well-earned reputation for producing some of Oregon's finest wines. The Ponzis launched BridgePort, Oregon's first microbrewery, in 1984 (they've since sold it) and opened the Ponzi Wine Bar in Dundee in 1998, followed by the Dundee Bistro in 1999. These two operations also feature competitors' wines.

The second generation of Ponzis is firmly in place, with three Ponzi children running the winery (Luisa Ponzi is the winemaker). In addition to Pinot Noir, Pinot Gris and Chardonnay, the winery crafts a dry white Arneis, from a rare Italian variety, and a dry Riesling that is available only at the winery.

www.ponziwines.com

2 | Chehalem

106 S. Center St., Newberg, OR 97132; (503) 538-4700

Harry Peterson-Nedry is one of the most cerebral folks you'll run across in Oregon wine country. A thoughtful man who quotes Latin phrases and writes fascinating articles on the art and science of winemaking, Peterson-Nedry also was one of the driving forces

behind the formation of the Chehalem Mountain AVA. He planted his first vineyard, 55 acres on Ribbon Ridge northwest of Newberg, in 1980 and launched his winery a decade later. He's also a partner in Stoller Vineyards in the Dundee Hills (and the Stollers are partners in Chehalem).

At the Chehalem tasting room in downtown Newberg, visitors can enjoy tasting Pinot Noir, Chardonnay, Pinot Gris, Pinot Blanc, Riesling and Gamay Noir.

www.chehalemwines.com

3 | Adelsheim Vineyard

16800 N.E. Calkins La., Newberg, OR 97132; (503) 538-3652

In 1971 David and Ginny Adelsheim bought the land to realize their dream of owning their own vineyard and winery. The vineyard was planted a year later, and the winery launched in 1978. The winery has expanded and now has 190 acres of vineyards, but the focus is still the same: to produce high-quality and distinctive wines. Pinot Noir is their specialty, from a number of exceptional single vineyards, though Adelsheim also

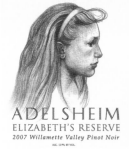

ADELSHEIM
ELIZABETH'S RESERVE
2007 Willamette Valley Pinot Noir

crafts Chardonnay, Pinot Gris and Pinot Blanc, as well as limited amounts of Syrah and a rare Auxerrois (an old French red variety better known as Malbec). The winery went through an extensive remodel in 2008 and unveiled a new tasting room in 2009.

www.adelsheim.com

4 | WillaKenzie Estate

19143 N.E. Laughlin Rd., Yamhill, OR 97148; (503) 662-3280

On a hill near the town of Yamhill, WillaKenzie is a marvelous—and maverick—producer of classic Pinot Noir.

Burgundian Bernard Lacroute purchased a cattle ranch in 1991 and began planting his vineyards a year later. His state-of-the-art gravity-flow winery was built in 1995, surrounded by 100 acres of vines that were thoughtfully planted without removing native fir trees.

The winery is named after the soil that is prevalent in the region, an ancient marine sedimentary type that would seem to be just about perfect for growing Pinot Noir.

In 2001 WillaKenzie became Oregon's first premium winery to switch to screwcaps, at first offering wines under corks as well for comparison. Today all of its wines are cork-free. WillaKenzie's beautiful tasting room provides several Pinot Noirs, Pinot Gris, Pinot Blanc, Gamay Noir and the unusual Pinot Meunier.

www.willakenzie.com

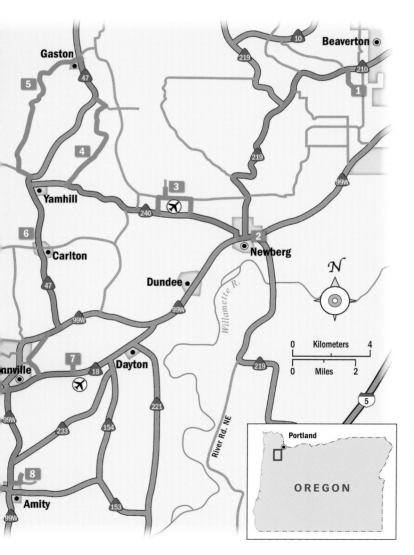

▲ WillaKenzie's magnificent oak tasting bar

▲ Visit Elk Cove for one of the most stunning settings in the Willamette Valley.

▲ The Cucina restaurant at Cana's Feast offers a range of food-and-wine events.

5 | Elk Cove Vineyards
27751 N.W. Olson Rd., Gaston, OR 97119; (503) 985-7760

In the northern corner of Yamhill County is one of Oregon's pioneer wineries. Joe and Pat Campbell launched Elk Cove in 1974, and their son Adam, who grew up on the farm and learned at the feet of the people who helped create and grow the Oregon wine industry, now runs the winery.

Elk Cove crafts some of the state's finest Pinot Gris, Pinot Noir, Pinot Blanc and Riesling. Of particular interest are Elk Cove's various vineyard-designated Pinot Noirs.

The winery is situated high in the hills above the small town of Gaston and is in one of the most beautiful settings in the Willamette Valley, making it a perfect location for weddings and other special events. The tasting room provides breathtaking views of the surrounding country.

www.elkcove.com

6 | Cana's Feast Winery
750 W. Lincoln St., Carlton, OR 97111; (503) 852-0002

Cana's Feast Winery, formerly known as Cuneo Cellars, is in an Italian-inspired building in the Yamhill County town of Carlton. Founder Gino Cuneo launched the winery in 1989 and moved it to its current location in 2001. In 2007 he left the winery to launch Gino Cuneo Cellars based in Dundee.

The beautiful building includes a tasting room, restaurant and two bocce ball courts. Unlike most Oregon wineries, Cana's Feast relies on grapes from Washington vineyards as well as Oregon fruit. Red wines are the focus here, especially from Italian varieties: Try the Nebbiolo, Sangiovese and Syrah.

www.canasfeastwinery.com

7 | Evergreen Vineyards
500 N.E. Capt. Michael King Smith Way, McMinnville, OR 97128; (866) 434-4818

If you want a chance to view history, then pay a visit to Evergreen Vineyards. This winery and aviation museum near McMinnville is home to the *Spruce Goose*, the famous wooden plane built by billionaire Howard Hughes in the 1940s.

In addition to enjoying this bit of American history up close, visitors will also be able to try some delicious wines. Evergreen Vineyards has more than 240 acres of vineyards and is also one of the country's largest hazelnut producers. The winery crafts Pinot Noir, Pinot Gris and Riesling and also makes a nonalcoholic sparkling juice from Pinot Noir.

www.evergreenvineyards.com

Amity Vineyards

18150 Amity Vineyards Rd., Amity, OR 97101; (503) 835-2362

Myron Redford is one of the real characters in Oregon wine country. The owner and winemaker of Amity Vineyards envisioned making great Pinot Noirs when he began planting his vineyard in 1971 and has not wavered from that path since.

Redford grew up in Seattle and happened into a job at Associated Vintners (now Columbia Winery) before moving to Oregon to make Pinot Noir. He was an early promoter of sustainable agriculture and eschews the use of new oak for crafting his wines. He made the first Gamay Noir in the United States in 1988 and was also the first winery to open a tasting room that featured competitors' wines as a way to promote the entire industry.

www.amityvineyards.com

findout more

- **www.bbyamhill.com**
  Bed-and-breakfast inns of Yamhill County.
- **www.yamhillvalley.org**
  Yamhill Valley Visitors Association.
- **www.willamettewines.com**
  Willamette Valley Wineries Association.

▲ The view down the valley from Amity Vineyards

Evergreen Vineyards' tasting room beyond the vineyards

CHARMING B&Bs AND CULINARY SPECIALTIES

One of the joys of wine touring in Yamhill County is the plethora of B&Bs. No fewer than 25 B&Bs dot the region, providing one of the greatest and most personal styles of lodging available. One of the most interesting is Abbey Road Farm near Carlton, whose rooms were created out of grain silos. The owners feature estate goat cheese as part of their delicious and extensive breakfast.

The restaurant scene continues to grow and mature. In McMinnville, Nick's is an upscale Italian café, while Bistro Maison specializes in traditional French bistro dishes. Top restaurants are also showing up in Carlton, Newberg and Dayton. Mushroom and truffle lovers should not miss the culinary artistry of the Joel Palmer House in Dayton.

TOUR 18
Dundee Hills

Since nearly its modern origins, the Oregon wine industry has been centered in the Dundee Hills in north Willamette Valley. Pioneers such as Dick Erath (Erath Vineyards), David Lett (Eyrie Vineyards), Susan Sokol Blosser (Sokol Blosser Winery), Cal Knudsen (Argyle Winery) and others planted Pinot Noir in the hills above the town of Dundee in the late 1960s and early 1970s. Their work drew others, most famously the Drouhin family of Burgundy, France, who took the leap of buying vineyards and opening a winery, effectively giving notice to the Old World that Oregon Pinot Noir was for real.

The region has gone by a few different names, including the Red Hills of Dundee, thanks to its red fractured basalt soil. Unlike Washington, which has very young soil, the dirt in the north of Willamette is ancient, going back millions of years. The red soil provides bright fruit in the Pinot Noirs and makes the Dundee Hills wines distinctive.

◄ Dense plantings of vines cover the little valleys and ridges of the Dundee Hills area.

1 | Duck Pond Cellars
23145 Hwy. 99 W., Dundee, OR 97115; (503) 538-3199

The Fries family has its feet firmly planted on both sides of the Columbia River, operating Desert Wind Winery in Washington (see page 54) and Duck Pond Cellars in Oregon. Its 325 acres of vineyards near Salem supply the grapes for its nicely priced Pinot Noirs and Pinot Grigio, which are supplemented by wines made with Washington grapes.

The winery opened in 1993 and produces more than 100,000 cases, making it one of Oregon's largest. The winery and tasting room—along the highway as one enters Dundee from Portland—is one of the most enjoyable stops on the Oregon wine trail.

www.duckpondcellars.com

2 | Argyle Winery
691 Hwy. 99 W., Dundee, OR 97115; (888) 427-4953 (ext. 233)

After Cal Knudsen ended his partnership with Dick Erath, he launched Argyle, on the highway in the town of Dundee. Since it opened in 1987, Argyle has grown to become one of the state's top-quality producers, with Texan winemaker Rollin Soles at the helm.

Argyle has carved a niche by crafting stunning sparkling wines using Chardonnay and Pinot Noir from estate vineyards as well as

▲ Duck Pond's tasting room makes an enjoyable stop along the Oregon wine trail.

from other top growers. The still Pinot Noirs are equally highly rated. Soles also has a passion for Riesling that is unmatched elsewhere in the state.

The winery is in a former hazelnut processing plant, hence the name Nuthouse for a line of Argyle's wines. The tasting room—which once served as Dundee City Hall—is reputed to be haunted by the ghost of a woman who committed suicide more than a century ago. Needless to say, a visit to Argyle should be fascinating, and nothing short of fun.

www.argylewinery.com

3 | Lange Estate Winery & Vineyards
18380 N.E. Buena Vista Dr., Dundee, OR 97115; (503) 538-6476

Former songwriter and singer Don Lange founded this winery in the Dundee Hills with his wife, Wendy, in the mid-1980s, and the pair have since gained a strong following for their elegant Pinot Noirs. Their son, Jesse, is the winery's general manager and crafts the wines alongside his father. He also oversees vineyard operations and is deeply involved in promoting the Dundee Hills.

Lange often gets overlooked because of the spotlight that shines so strongly on many of its neighbors, but the quality of its Pinot Noirs is superb and the winery is well worth a visit. The tasting room offers a panoramic view of the Cascade Mountains.

www.langewinery.com

▲ Erath Vineyards was one of the pioneer producers of Pinot Noir in Oregon in the 1970s.

4 | Erath Vineyards
9409 N.E. Worden Hill Rd., Dundee, OR 97115; (503) 538-3318

Dick Erath made the pioneering move to Oregon from California to make wine in the late 1960s. He planted his first vineyard in 1968 and by 1972 he produced the first wine in the Dundee Hills, launching Erath Vineyards at the same time. From 1975 to 1988, he partnered with Cal Knudsen to expand the operation and the winery was known as Knudsen–Erath. After he bought out Knudsen's share, the name returned to Erath.

The winery is one of Oregon's largest producers of Pinot Noir, with some great single-vineyard wines. For whites, it is hard to beat Erath's Pinot Gris and Pinot Blanc.

In 2006, Erath sold the winery to Ste. Michelle Wine Estates in Washington and then moved to Arizona to begin pioneering grape-growing all over again.

www.erath.com

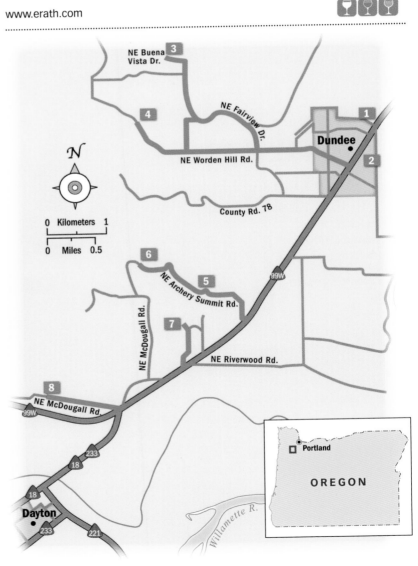

5 | Archery Summit
18599 N.E. Archery Summit Rd., Dayton, OR 97114; (503) 864-4300

High in the Dundee Hills above the towns of Dayton and Dundee is Archery Summit, a winery started by the late Gary Andrus that focuses on premium Pinot Noir.

The 100 acres of vineyards surround one of the state's first gravity-flow wineries—that is, the facility was built so that gravity rather than pumps are used to create the wines. The grapes come in at the highest level, then each step of the winemaking process is physically lower in the winery's multiple stories. Archery Summit was a trendsetter for gravity-flow wineries, which are now commonplace in Oregon. The winery was also one of the first Oregon producers to hit the $100-per-bottle price on a bottle of Pinot Noir.

The winery is open for tastings and tours of the caves where its wines are aged.

www.archerysummit.com

▲ Springtime at De Ponte Cellars

6 | De Ponte Cellars
17545 Archery Summit Rd., Dayton, OR 97114; (503) 864-3698

The Baldwin family purchased a vineyard of rare old head-pruned Pinot Noir grapes in the Dundee Hills in 1999 and launched De Ponte Cellars two years later. Isabelle Dutartre, classically trained in Burgundy, is De Ponte's winemaker. For the first few years, she commuted between her native France and Oregon but now lives full-time in nearby McMinnville. As well as Pinot Noir, De Ponte is known for its Melon de Bourgogne (a white grape of Burgundian origin now better known as the grape for Muscadet wine from France's Loire Valley).

www.depontecellars.com

AROUND AND ABOUT DUNDEE

The town of Dundee, about 45 minutes southwest of Portland, is a small town with a big appetite. It is home to a couple of wonderful restaurants: the Dundee Bistro and Tina's. The Dundee Bistro is owned by the Ponzi family (of Ponzi Vineyards fame) and boasts fresh local ingredients and a deep wine list. Tina's has been a favorite of winemakers since it opened in 1991.

One of the finest bed-and-breakfast operations in the region is the Black Walnut Inn & Vineyard, a B&B high in the hills above Dundee, with beautifully appointed rooms and delicious food.

7 | Sokol Blosser Winery
5000 N.E. Sokol Blosser La., Dayton, OR 97114; (503) 864-2282

Bill Blosser and Susan Sokol Blosser planted their vineyard in the Dundee Hills in 1971 and opened their winery in 1977. Today, their children, Alex and Alison, run the winery, and the operation has expanded to 87 acres of estate grapes and 85,000 cases of wine.

Their most famous bottling is a white blend called Evolution No. 9, which debuted in the late 1990s. It's a blend of nine grapes, including Müller-Thurgau, Riesling, Gewürztraminer, Pinot Gris and Chardonnay. It's a fun wine that tends to overshadow Sokol Blosser's more serious Pinot Noirs and Pinot Gris.

The winery exemplifies the push toward organic and sustainable growing practices. Sokol Blosser uses renewable energy in the winery. The new cellar, with a capacity of 900 barrels, features a chamber located underground to take advantage of the natural cooling properties of the soil.

www.sokolblosser.com

Sokol Blosser's new cellar has a living roof covered with wildflowers.

8 | Stoller Vineyards

16161 N.E. McDougall Rd., Dayton, OR 97114; (503) 864-3404

Look at the technical data of many top Oregon Pinot Noirs, and you might notice that many of them feature grapes from Stoller Vineyards. Bill and Cathy Stoller purchased land in the Dundee Hills in 1993 and began planting two years later. The estate wines, just Pinot Noir and Chardonnay, were first released in 2003 and have been well received by Pinotphiles since.

The winery is set on a hillside and has two guesthouses amid the vines—a picture-perfect setting for wine touring in Oregon. The Stollers are also partners in Chehalem, a winery in the nearby Chehalem Mountains AVA.

www.stollervineyards.com

findout more

- **www.dundeehills.org**
  The website of the Dundee Hills AVA, this is a terrific resource for wine touring, food and lodging.

- **www.oregonwine.org**
  Home of the Oregon Wine Board.

Neat rows of vines at Stoller Vineyards, a Pinot Noir specialist

South Willamette Valley

While the northern Willamette Valley tends to get most of the press for Oregon wine, the region just to the south also deserves credit and praise for raising the profile of the state's wine industry.

Starting with the Eola Hills near the capital city of Salem and stretching south to the university cities of Eugene and Corvallis, the central and southern stretches of the Willamette Valley provide wonderful opportunities for wine touring. This area tends to be quite a bit less crowded than the northern section, nearer to Portland. In fact, some of Oregon's largest producers (King Estate, Willamette Valley Vineyards and Silvan Ridge) are along this stretch, as is the state's oldest producer, Honeywood Winery.

◀ Planting a new vineyard at Witness Tree Vineyard. It takes four to six men abut two days to plant just 1 acre.

1 | Bethel Heights Vineyard
6060 Bethel Heights Rd. NW, Salem, OR 97304; (503) 581-2262

Bethel Heights is a story about family. Brothers Ted and Terry Casteel were educators in Washington State and Michigan and their families would spend their vacations talking about wine. In 1976 Terry and his wife moved to California so he could study winemaking; in 1977 the two families converged from the north and south to purchase land in the Eola-Amity Hills near Salem and began to plant wine grapes. Ted handled viticulture and Terry was the winemaker, though they worked together on all aspects of the estate.

The winery opened in 1984 and quickly gained a reputation for its elegant and complex Pinot Noirs. Today, Bethel Heights wines are revered amid New World Pinot Noir collectors. Terry's son Ben has inherited the winemaking mantle, crafting Pinot Noir, Chardonnay, Pinot Gris, Pinot Blanc and occasional Gewürztraminer and rosé. Take advantage of any special wines they may be pouring.

www.bethelheights.com

2 | Witness Tree Vineyard
7111 Spring Valley Rd. NW, Salem, OR 97304; (503) 585-7874

This winery on the eastern slope of the Eola-Amity Hills near Salem is named for a 250-year-old Oregon white oak tree that sits on the 100-acre estate. The tree was used as a boundary marker (a "witness") in 1854. The tree is beautiful to look at and is a nice walk through the vineyard from the tasting room. The winery started in 1987 and relies entirely on its 52 acres of estate grapes to craft multiple Pinot Noirs alongside Chardonnay, Pinot Blanc and a dry, apricot- and orange-blossom-scented Viognier.

www.witnesstreevineyard.com

3 | Redhawk Winery
2995 Michigan City Ave. NW, Salem, OR 97304; (503) 362-1596

Redhawk Winery, which launched in 1988, gained fame for its crazy labels, including Grateful Red, Punk Floyd and Great White. Since John and Betty Pataccoli purchased the winery in 2005, Redhawk has undergone a fair bit of change, including a remodeled winery and new tasting room.

The Grateful Red is the only one of the loony labels to remain (that's too good a name to give up), and continues to be a nicely priced Pinot Noir. Redhawk also offers several other Pinot Noirs, Pinot Gris, Chardonnay and a Bordeaux-style red blend called Redhawk Red.

www.redhawkwine.com

The ancient white oak tree at Witness Tree Vineyard has become quite a landmark.

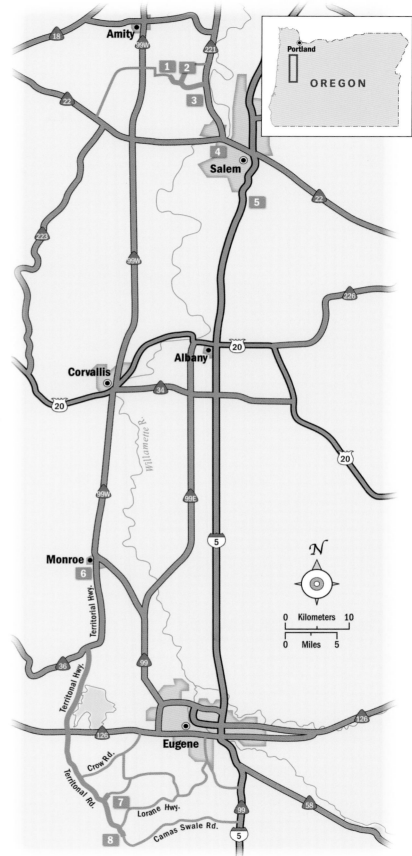

4 | Honeywood Winery

1350 Hines St. SE, Salem, OR 97302; (503) 362-4111

Honeywood is the Pacific Northwest's oldest winery, having opened in 1934, soon after Prohibition was repealed in 1933. This winery in the capital city of Salem crafts a dizzying array of wines—as many as 50 different bottlings, of which about a third are made with classic European wine grapes. The rest are made from fruit such as cranberries, blackberries, raspberries, honey, cherries, loganberries, marionberries ... well, the list goes on. The fruit wines tend to be on the sweeter side, and this makes Honeywood a real favorite at wine festivals and in its busy tasting room.

For those looking for the "serious wines," Honeywood also crafts Pinot Noir, Pinot Gris, Chardonnay, Cabernet Sauvignon, Syrah, Müller-Thurgau and more. It even produces a wine from Niagara, a grape native to the Americas that is similar in aroma and flavor to Concord (though white).

www.honeywoodwinery.com

5 | Willamette Valley Vineyards

8800 Enchanted Way SE, Turner, OR 97392; (503) 588-9463

In 1983, Jim Bernau purchased an old plum orchard near the tiny town of Turner, south of the capital city of Salem, with the vision of growing Pinot Noir in Oregon. By 1989, he was ready to launch Willamette Valley Vineyards. In 1997 Bernau and his stockholders purchased Tualatin Estate, an older vineyard in the northern

▲ Willamette Valley's vineyards are planted across the hills to make the most of the sun.

Willamette Valley. He also launched Griffin Creek, a label for grapes from the Rogue Valley. Combined, the wines made at Willamette Valley Vineyards make up one of the largest winemaking ventures in Oregon. The tasting room is a favorite stop for wine travelers.

Willamette Valley Vineyards crafts several styles of Pinot Noir and Chardonnay, crisp Pinot Gris and very good Rieslings.

www.wvv.com

6 | **Benton-Lane Winery**
23924 Territorial Hwy., Monroe, OR; (541) 847-5792

Steve and Carol Girard moved from their native California on a quest to make great Pinot Noir. They landed near the town of Monroe, where they planted their estate vineyard in 1988, and the winery—named for the two counties it straddles—was launched in 1992.

The winery produces two Pinot Noirs: a "standard" Willamette Valley bottling and a reserve wine called First Class, which is produced only in vintages the winemaker deems worthy. Benton-Lane also produces Pinot Gris and small amounts of Pinot Blanc. All of the wines are sealed with screwcaps.

www.benton-lane.com

7 | **Silvan Ridge**
27012 Briggs Hill Rd., Eugene, OR 97405; (541) 345-1945

This winery opened in 1979 as Hinman Vineyards, launched by Doyle Hinman and David Smith, and within a decade it had become Oregon's biggest winery; twenty years on it is still among the state's largest. The winery was sold in 1993, when its name changed to Silvan Ridge; it retains the name Hinman Vineyards as its value label.

2007
OREGON

Early Muscat
SEMI-SPARKLING

Silvan Ridge

Alcohol 6.4% by Volume

Meanwhile, in recent years Doyle Hinman has launched his own label, Five H, a family winery that focuses on Washington Riesling.

Through the years, Silvan Ridge has released a vast array of wines using grapes from Oregon, Washington and even California. Oregon highlights include Pinot Noir from the Willamette Valley and Cabernet Sauvignon and Syrah from the Rogue Valley. One of its most famous—and fun—wines is a semi-sparkling Early Muscat, a fizzy, low-alcohol, sweet wine that is a true crowd pleaser. The tasting room offers lovely views over rolling vine-covered hills.

www.silvanridge.com

8 | King Estate

80854 Territorial Hwy., Eugene, OR 97405; (541) 942-9874

No winery spreads the word about Oregon more than King Estate. Thanks to its broad marketing and distribution, King Estate is the de facto ambassador for Oregon Pinot Noir and Pinot Gris. Go into just about any fine restaurant across the United States, and chances are you'll find King Estate on the wine list.

King Estate was launched in 1991 by the King family. They built a beautiful winemaking facility atop a hill in the southernmost part of the Willamette Valley and surrounded it with vineyards. In recent years King Estate has converted its farming operations to be certified organic.

King Estate opened its château-style visitors center in 2005. The restaurant is open for fine dining at lunch and dinner, and the culinary team relies heavily on the estate's 30 acres of organically farmed fruits and vegetables.

King Estate is best known for its Pinot Gris and Pinot Noir, and it also crafts a delicious dessert wine, Vin Glacé—Pinot Gris icewine.

www.kingestate.com

AMENITIES AROUND WILLAMETTE

Traveling to and around the central and southern Willamette Valley and accessing its wineries is very easy if you use Interstate 5, which parallels the Willamette River from the Washington border south to Eugene. Once you exit the freeway, however, the back roads that lead to the wineries tend to be less traveled and more serene in nature.

Salem is about an hour south of Portland, and the Eola-Amity Hills are about 20 minutes to the west and north. Eugene is another hour south of Salem. For those looking to spend a bit of time on the Oregon Coast, the town of Newport is about an hour's drive west of Corvallis.

Visitors will find plenty of places to stay and eat. In Salem, Morton's Bistro Northwest gives a regional twist to bistro-style food, focusing on local ingredients and local wines. Eugene is a great place to seek out funky local restaurants, thanks to the nearby University of Oregon. SweetWaters on the River, the restaurant within the Valley River Inn, is as famous for its setting along the Willamette River as it is for its cuisine. The Sunday brunch is especially popular.

▲ The majestic winery at King Estate was built to resemble a French château.

Umpqua Valley

In 1961 Howard Sommer traveled north from the San Francisco Bay area and planted the first Pinot Noir in Oregon's modern winemaking history. The founder of HillCrest Vineyard, who passed away in the summer of 2009, was the man who first recognized the state's potential with the noble red grape of Burgundy. Ironically, he did so outside of the Willamette Valley, where Pinot Noir has become so famous.

The Umpqua Valley starts just south of the Willamette Valley and has gained momentum in recent years due to the ingenuity of wineries willing to plant grape varieties that were out of the mainstream just a few years ago. Today such grapes as Tempranillo, Albariño, Grüner Veltliner and Bastardo still are not huge names in the Oregon wine industry, but thanks to a few imaginative folks, the Umpqua Valley is now a much more fascinating region to visit.

◄ Henry Estate is famous worldwide for its pioneering system of vine trellising.

1 Brandborg Vineyard & Winery
345 First St., Elkton, OR 97436; (541) 584-2870

The tiny town of Elkton is pretty far off the beaten path; however, it is home to no fewer than four wineries. Terry Brandborg began his professional winemaking career when he set up a winery in the mid-1980s in the San Francisco area. In 2002 Terry and his wife, Sue, launched their winery in the Umpqua Valley. They specialize in Pinot Noir, Syrah, Pinot Gris, Pinot Blanc, Riesling and Gewürztraminer. Brandborg's style focuses on balance, elegance and restrained alcohol. Brandborg's tasting room on the main drag is spacious and includes live music on the weekends.

www.brandborgwine.com

2 Henry Estate Winery
687 Hubbard Creek Rd., Umpqua, OR 97486; (541) 459-5120

Five generations of the Henry family have farmed this land in the Umpqua Valley for more than a century, and they have grown wine grapes here since the early 1970s. Scott Henry III developed the Scott Henry trellis, a system for growing wine grapes that is used around the world. Henry Estate crafts a wide variety of wines, including Pinot Noir, Syrah, Cabernet Sauvignon, Chardonnay, Pinot Gris, Gewürztraminer and dessert Riesling. The winery grounds feature a beautiful garden and play host to an annual music concert.

www.henryestate.com

3 Spangler Vineyards
491 Winery La., Roseburg, OR 97471; (541) 679-9654

Pat and Loree Spangler bought the defunct La Garza Cellars in 2004 and have transformed it into one of the most decorated wineries in Oregon. The focus is on reds and whites from Bordeaux and Rhône varieties, though Spangler also crafts Chardonnay. Some of the estate Cabernet Sauvignon vines were planted in the late 1960s and early 1970s, making them some of the oldest in Oregon. The winery's beautiful grounds are available for special events, including weddings.

www.spanglervineyards.com

CHECK OUT THE STEAMBOAT INN

Roseburg is the biggest city in the Umpqua Valley and home to most restaurants and lodging. That said, there are a few B&Bs scattered throughout the region. Of particular interest is the Steamboat Inn in the town of Steamboat. It is famous not only for its accommodations and cuisine but also for fly-fishing tours on the North Umpqua River. Because winemakers love coming to the inn, visitors will find winemaker dinners scheduled throughout the year.

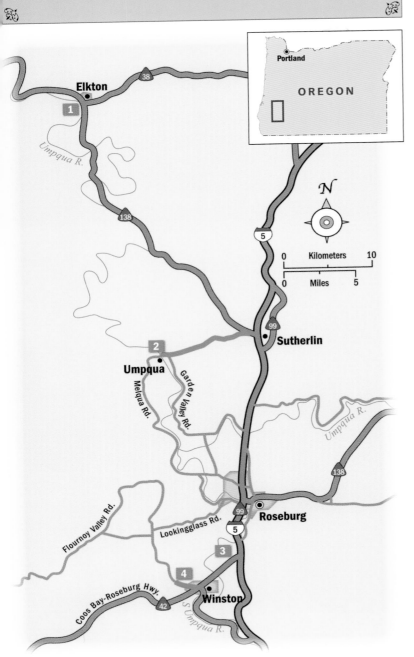

4 | Abacela Vineyards & Winery
12500 Lookingglass Rd., Roseburg, OR 97471; (541) 679-6642

Earl and Hilda Jones crossed the country from Florida to Oregon's Umpqua Valley because they recognized the region had the potential to grow great Tempranillo, the classic grape of Spain's Rioja region. They didn't stop with Tempranillo; they also planted Albariño, Bastardo, Dolcetto, Graciano, Touriga Nacional, Tannat and a host of others.

This might sound like one big science experiment, but the resulting wines are proving the Joneses correct. Even more, Tempranillo has enjoyed a surge of interest throughout the Pacific Northwest (even British Columbia), thanks to Abacela.

www.abacela.com

▲ The tasting room at Brandborg makes a friendly stopover in Elkton.

75

Rogue Valley

The Rogue Valley, home to the Rogue River and its famous whitewater rafting, is filled with back-to-nature opportunities, including the Oregon Caves and plenty of wilderness in the Siskiyou National Forest.

The valley borders California and is also Oregon's southernmost wine region. In fact, the wineries here have more in common viticulturally with Napa and Sonoma counties than they do with the Willamette Valley—the region is better known for Bordeaux, Italian and Rhône varieties than the Burgundy grapes of Pinot Noir and Pinot Gris grown in the north.

The Rogue Valley is part of the Southern Oregon AVA, which also includes the Umpqua Valley and Red Hill Douglas County appellations just to the north. And within the Rogue is the Applegate Valley. Visitors will also hear references to the Illinois and Bear valleys, which are unofficial designations within the Rogue Valley.

◀ The Rogue River is famous for its whitewater rafting and challenging fishing.

1 | Bridgeview Vineyard & Winery
4210 Holland Loop Rd., Cave Junction, OR 97523; (541) 592-4688

Beginning in 1986, Lelo and Bob Kerivan have built one of the largest and most successful wineries in Oregon. Legend has it that Bob traveled to Calgary, Alberta, prior to the 1988 Winter Olympics to bid on stainless-steel winemaking tanks that needed to be moved to make room for a ski jump. He and one other bidder were the only two to show up, so Bob acquired 270,000 gallons' worth of tanks for just 4 cents per gallon.

Bridgeview skyrocketed to fame with its sweet Blue Moon Riesling, in a distinctive blue bottle. That sole wine now makes up more than half of Bridgeview's production. Red wine lovers should try the Reserve Pinot Noir, Black Beauty Cabernet Sauvignon and Black Beauty Syrah. Thanks to the nearby Oregon Caves, Bridgeview is a popular destination, attracting over 200,000 visitors per year.

www.bridgeviewwine.com

▲ From Bridgeview Vineyard there are excellent views of the mountains of southern Oregon.

findout more

- **www.sorwa.org**
  Southern Oregon Winery Association.

- **www.oregonwine.org**
  Oregon Wine Board.

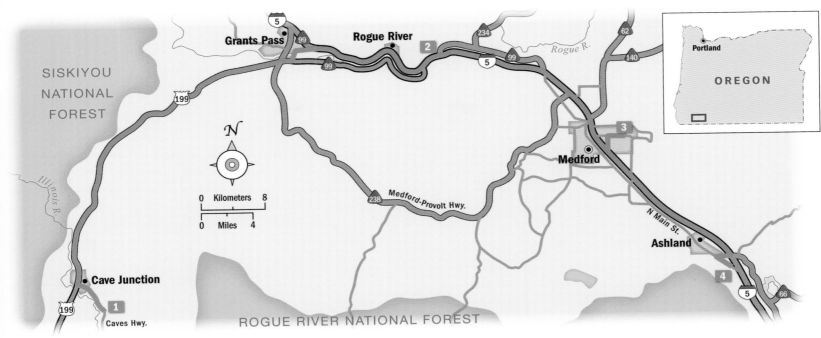

2 | Del Rio Vineyards
52 N. River Rd., Gold Hill, OR 97525; (541) 855-2062

Before Rob Wallace came to southern Oregon, he was a farmer in the Sacramento area of California. He now oversees one of Oregon's best vineyards. The 185 acres were planted in 1998, and produce 15 varieties, with the largest block dedicated to Syrah. When winemakers who normally focus on Pinot Noir discovered Wallace's grapes, they traveled south in droves and began crafting Del Rio Vineyard-designated Syrah, Cabernet Sauvignon and red blends.

Since 2005, Del Rio has produced wines under its own label. The focus is on high-quality reds (delicious Merlot and Bordeaux-style Claret), with a highly regarded Pinot Gris. The tasting room is at the foot of the vineyard, in the 1864 Rock Point Stage Hotel.

www.delriovineyards.com

3 | RoxyAnn Winery
3285 Hillcrest Rd., Medford, OR 97504; (541) 776-2315

Named for a dormant volcano that rises above the Rogue Valley, RoxyAnn crafts several styles of wines from estate grapes. The winery is at Hillcrest Orchard, which has been producing fruit for more than a century, and the tasting room is in a former stable. The focus is on warm-climate varieties, including Cabernets Sauvignon and Franc, Tempranillo, Grenache, Malbec and Syrah. In 2008 veteran California winemaker John Quinones joined RoxyAnn, and he continues crafting wonderfully balanced wines.

www.roxyann.com

4 | Weisinger's of Ashland
3150 Siskiyou Blvd., Ashland, OR 97520; (541) 488-5989

Deep in southern Oregon, just before one climbs into the Siskiyou Mountains and into California, is the artsy city of Ashland, home of the famous Shakespeare Festival as well as a small number of wineries. Overlooking Interstate 5 is Weisinger's, a superb producer of Bordeaux-style reds. Founder John Weisinger began to plant his vineyards in the late 1970s and launched his eponymous winery in 1988. For a dozen years he worked alongside his son Eric, who left in 2007 to travel the world as a consulting winemaker.

Next to the winery is a cottage that is available for wine travelers, a perfect place to stay while touring the valley.

www.weisingers.com

▲ The tasting room and shop at RoxyAnn Winery

Hopland & Redwood Valley

Mendocino County boasts far fewer vineyard acres and wineries than its neighbors, Napa and Sonoma, but in recent years has developed rapidly into a high-quality grape-growing culture. More than 80 percent of the grapes grown in Mendocino County leave the county for wineries in other regions, mainly Napa and Sonoma counties.

A 90-minute drive north of San Francisco puts you in the vicinity of Hopland. This is a thriving little community of shops, a brewery, and wineries worth touring. Farther up the road is warmer Redwood Valley, with a few more wineries to visit.

One vibrant wine-growing region is the antithesis of the typical tourist scene. Cloistered Potter Valley, at least 200 feet (61 m) higher in altitude than Redwood Valley and thus much cooler, has no tourism because it has no wineries. Its great potential is with cool-climate grape varieties—Riesling, Semillon, Sauvignon Blanc and Pinot Noir.

◄ Saracina Vineyards is a beautiful property in the hills near Hopland, with vines, olive groves and trails.

1 | Saracina Vineyards
11684 South Hwy. 101, Hopland, CA 95449; (707) 744-1671

John Fetzer was president of Fetzer Vineyards after the death of his father, Barney, who founded the large company. It was John who grew the brand from 200,000 cases to more than 2 million. When Fetzer was sold in 1992, family members were prohibited from using their name on succeeding wine projects, so John and his wife, Patty Rock, founded Saracina, taking the name from a farmhouse in Tuscany where they spent their honeymoon. The property covers 600 acres, with olive groves, a pomegranate orchard and bamboo garden populated with sheep, goat and other creatures.

Winemaker Alex MacGregor gets consulting assistance from brilliant winemaker David Ramey to create limited-production Sauvignon Blanc and sublime red wines.

www.saracina.com

▲ It took two years to carve out the rocky hillside and build the cellars at Saracina Vineyards.

2 | Graziano Family of Wines
13251 South Hwy. 101, Suite 3, Hopland, CA 95449; (707) 744-8466

One of the county's most proficient winemakers is Greg Graziano, who has four brands that focus on distinctly different wine styles. His attractive Hopland tasting room pours samples of all four brands:

Saint Gregory (Pinot Noir in a Burgundian style); Graziano (focusing on bold Mendocino Zinfandel); Enotria (Italian varietals from the Piedmont region) and Monte Volpe (Tuscan-style wines). Graziano is also the consulting winemaker for Naughty Boy in Potter Valley.

Next door to the Graziano tasting room is the tasting room of Guinness MacFadden, one of the most respected organic grape growers in the state, whose wines all come from his ranch in cool Potter Valley.

www.grazianofamilyofwines.com

3 | Jeriko Estate

12141 Hewlitt and Sturtevant Rd. (off Rte. 101), Hopland, CA 95449; (707) 744-1140

After the sale of Fetzer Vineyards in 1992, most of the 11 children of Fetzer founders Barney and Kathleen Fetzer remained in the business. Dan Fetzer founded Jeriko in 1997, growing all his grapes organically. The Jeriko Estate is a striking complex of California–Mediterranean-style buildings, some dating back to the late nineteenth century.

Since 2007, consulting winemaker George Vierra has made some improvements: Sangiovese is a highlight of the wide array of wines.

www.jeriko.us

4 | Mendocino Wine Co.

501 Parducci Rd., Ukiah, CA 95482; (707) 463-5350

John Parducci, one of the grand old men of the California wine business, made some of the finest wines in the county in the 1950s and 1960s.

Paul Dolan, formerly the winemaker for Fetzer Vineyards, acquired Parducci's winery (along with Tim, Tom and Tommy Thornhill, Jr.) and eventually founded the Mendocino Wine Co. in 2004. Dolan is one of the nation's leaders in organic farming, and the wines currently being made by winemaker Bob

Swain are sublime. The Parducci brand still lives on in a wide range of reds and whites, including Coro Zinfandel. Other wines come under various delightful labels, such as Tusk'n Red, Big Yellow Cab and Roselle.

www.mendocinowineco.com

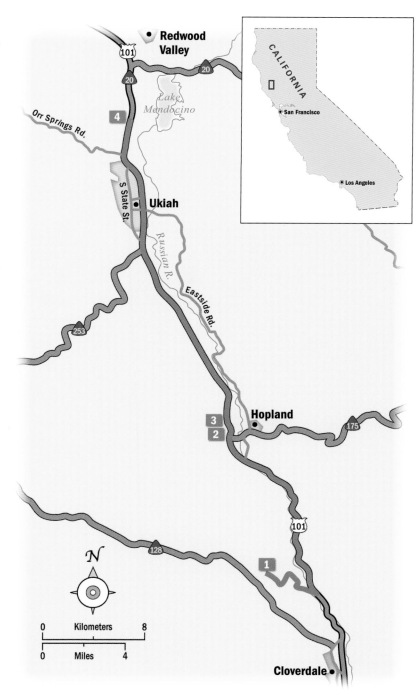

HOPLAND AMENITIES

One of the most delightful ways to taste Mendocino wines is to visit Sip Mendocino in Hopland, with a wide array that includes smaller, hard-to-get brands and older vintages (www.sipmendocino.com).

In Hopland, the best place to eat and stay overnight is Hopland Inn [(707) 744-1890]. The finest dining in the Ukiah area is Patrona Bistro and Wine Bar downtown [(707) 462-9181].

In search of Zinfandel

Zinfandel is the grape that California can truly claim as its own. It isn't actually Californian—North America has no native *Vitis vinifera* varieties—but there is no great European tradition of growing Zinfandel, and Californian wine makers have created their own styles rather than looking to the Pinot Noirs and Chardonnays of Burgundy or the Cabernet Sauvignons of Bordeaux for inspiration.

Widely planted throughout the state, Zinfandel is like no other variety from the Old World, in that it yields wines with an upfront fresh-berry aroma and flavor and a vibrancy and verve that few other grapes can match.

The earliest mention of Zinfandel in the United States is in the 1820s, when a nurseryman brought cuttings from Europe to Long Island, New York. Another nurseryman then took the vine to California in the 1840s.

California's first wine boom, in the 1880s, was based on Zinfandel, and some of the oldest vines still survive in Amador County, where Zinfandel was originally made as a cheap drink to slake the thirst of the area's gold miners. The grape was a favorite of Italian immigrant farmers in California in the years before Prohibition because it added exotic aroma, richness and sheer racy fruit to the blend when combined with other grapes. Carignan, with its rustic earthy flavors, was the workhorse grape used with Zinfandel; Petite Sirah added color and tannin to the blend; Barbera brought acidity; and Grenache was prolific.

Zinfandel was interplanted with other warm-climate varieties in the vineyard and these blends were known as a field blend or *mista nera* (dark blend). Such mixed plantings are rare today, but some are reputed to survive in some of California's oldest vineyards. When Prohibition ended, red wines were still made that way, but by the 1960s, varietal wines—wines made predominantly from single grape varieties—began to become more important.

Zinfandel hit its stride with some varietal wines made in the late 1960s. Sutter Home Winery pioneered a dramatic wine from the Deaver Vineyard in Amador County in the Sierra Foothills, which established a benchmark for the variety. At about the same time, winemaker Paul Draper at Ridge Vineyards in the Santa Cruz Mountains was looking at older vines of Zinfandel growing in Sonoma County (mainly at Geyserville), in inland Lodi and at warm Paso Robles. Half the Zinfandel currently growing in California is said to be more than 50 years old.

Sonoma County wine pioneer Joe Swan made some spectacular Russian River Zinfandels in the 1970s, and very soon after that, winemaker Joel Peterson at Ravenswood, also in Sonoma, was bitten by the bug and began to explore the possibilities of making wines using fruit from distinctive single vineyards.

Ridge and Ravenswood are generally the wineries credited with spurring the "vineyard-designated Zinfandel" quest, but

▲ Old Zinfandel vines are highly prized for their intensely flavored grapes.

inding the best places to grow Zinfandel was not an easy task. Some tiny vineyards located in hard-to-reach hilltop sites made spectacular wines, though usually in tiny amounts.

Zinfandel became so popular as a varietal wine that in 1991 author David Darlington published *Angels' Visits: An Inquiry into the Mystery of Zinfandel*, and soon thereafter an organization was formed to support the growing interest in the grape, called Zinfandel Advocates and Producers, or ZAP (www.zinfandel.org). A series of Zinfandel tasting events are staged early each year in San Francisco by ZAP, and attendance is in the thousands.

A serious investigation was launched to determine what Zinfandel really was. Where did it come from? Early DNA mapping efforts indicated a match with Primitivo of Southern Italy but scientists at UC Davis have now determined that Zinfandel is directly connected to a rare Croatian grape, Crljenak Kaštelanski.

To ripen fully, Zinfandel likes both warmth and a long growing season. Hot, sunny days and relatively cool nights provide ideal ripening conditions—which can be found in both Mendocino County and Sonoma County's Dry Creek Valley. Dry Creek Valley is famous for Zinfandel— in particular, old-vine Zinfandel, made from vines 50 to 100 years old, some older. These thick-trunked, gnarly old-timers produce tiny yields of intensely flavored, spicy grapes, and the wines made from them typically have aromas and flavors of wild raspberry and blackberry, black pepper, brown spice and bramble. "Old Vines" on a Zinfandel label still means something here. Dry Creek Valley Zinfandels range in style from crisp, dry rosés; to balanced, medium- to full-bodied table wines; to flamboyant, potent, jammy versions.

In the past decade, Zinfandels have been made that deliver high alcohol levels, and wines with as much as 18 percent alcohol by volume have been seen. Zin experts believe that 14 percent alcohol allows this grape to achieve perfect balance. Such wines are delightful with rustic Italian foods.

▲ Ripe Zinfandel grapes look as if they are starting to shrivel.

CORO MENDOCINO

Coro Mendocino is a red wine devised as a way to gain attention for the great growth in red wine quality in Mendocino County. It is based on two parallel concepts: the importance of terroir, or the sense of place that derives from a combination of soil, climate and exposure to the sun; and the best red grapes of the region.

Coro means "chorus" in Italian, and the wines are red blends comprising a minimum of 40 percent Zinfandel, and a maximum of 70 percent. The remainder of the blend is based on the philosophy of the winemaker.

Another local favorite, Petite Sirah, is a popular addition to the blends. Fetzer normally uses Syrah and Petite Sirah; Philo Ridge adds some Carignane. McDowell's Coro blend usually has some old-vine Syrah, while Pacific Star's Coro is more of an Italianate version, with some Dolcetto in the blend.

The Coro wines are all released at the same time, after aging for a minimum of one year in barrel and one year in bottle. All have essentially the same label design, and all are sold for about $35 a bottle. They represent a great vision of what Mendocino red wines are all about.

Two examples of Coro Mendocino, from Pacific Star and Fetzer

TOUR 23
Anderson Valley

This remote gateway to the Pacific Ocean is one of the state's less-traveled wine regions, but the Anderson Valley offers untold excitement for those who appreciate sublime wines—even without much Cabernet Sauvignon. This cooled-by-the-sea region isn't far from major cities: As the hawk flies, it's just 100 miles (160 km) to San Francisco. But the main road into the valley is winding Highway 128, north of Cloverdale, and the S-turn-laced road has little on it except woodlands and glens.

Boonville is the "city" at the heart of the valley; a small, charming burg with quaint shops and some great beer (Anderson Valley Brewing Co.). It was the heart of a dropout culture a century ago when the local lingo, *boontling*, was spoken as a way for residents to distance themselves from city folk (the *brightlighters*, in the argot of the language). Tasting rooms here are more casual than in many other regions, and the best of these (Navarro) is a statewide treasure.

◀ A tour at Navarro Vineyards includes meeting the resident farm animals.

1 | Goldeneye Winery
9200 Hwy. 128, Philo, CA 95466; (800) 208-0438

North of Boonville, heading toward the redwoods and the ocean, is the small, prestige property called Goldeneye, a project begun in 1996 by Dan and Margaret Duckhorn of Napa Valley fame.

Goldeneye was one of the first in Mendocino County dedicated to making top-rate Pinot Noir from the cooler, coastal regions. In recent years, its reputation has grown into cult status. As a result, visits are by appointment only, but well worth the effort—the wines are sensational, and loaded with cool-climate personality.

www.goldeneyewinery.com

▲ Roederer Estate chose its vineyard sites for their similar climate to Champagne, France.

ANDERSON VALLEY AMENITIES
Accommodations and dining in Anderson Valley are limited. The most charming bed-and-breakfast, the Anderson Creek Inn in Boonville, [(800) 552-6202], is as isolated as you'll find in the region, and hosts Grace and Jim Minton are delightful.

Best dining is at the roadhouse-style Boonville Hotel [(707) 895-2210], which also has accommodation.

2 | Scharffenberger Cellars
8501 Hwy. 128, Philo, CA 94566; (707) 895-2957

Just north of Goldeneye, across the road from the Philo Pottery Inn, sits a winery that has gone through a number of incarnations, including a period during which it was known as Pacific Echo.

Founded in 1981 by former grape-grower John Scharffenberger, later of chocolate fame, the property takes advantage of the valley's cool climate, which allows the Chardonnay and Pinot Noir grapes to ripen slowly and retain the critical acid levels needed to make great sparkling wines. As well as the Brut, Rosé and Crémant sparkling wines, there is a line of still wines sold only at the tasting room.

www.scharffenbergercellars.com

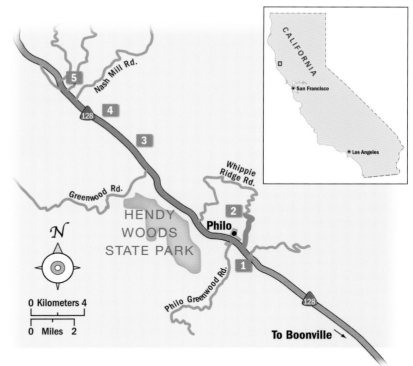

3 | Navarro Vineyards
5601 Hwy. 128, Philo, CA 95466; (800) 537-9463

Ted Bennett and wife Deborah Cahn founded Navarro in 1974 after falling in love with the French region of Alsace and its wines and seeking a respite from city life and a place that would do justice to Alsace grapes like Gewürztraminer and Riesling. They exceeded their wildest expectations.

The warm, popular Navarro tasting room just outside the small town of Philo has never charged for sampling its wines, which are served with superb knowledge of the region and its vines. Navarro's unique marketing system calls for most wines to be sold directly to consumers, either at the tasting room or through mail-order sales.

Winemaker Jim Klein, following a formula set out by Bennett, has crafted the wines for the last two decades. As well as unusual whites (sparkling Gewürztraminer and Dry Muscat), there are some sensational reds (Pinot Noir and Zinfandel). The owners' daughter, Sarah Bennett, a UC Davis viticulture graduate, is making huge contributions in the vineyards.

www.navarrowine.com

4 | Roederer Estate
4501 Hwy. 128, Philo, CA 95466; (707) 895-2288

The French influence in California is exemplified by this well-established property. Three decades ago, the Champagne house of Roederer decided to invest in California and began looking for the right place to plant grapes suitable for quality sparkling wine. Their consultant took several years to explore various sites,

finally deciding that cool Anderson Valley was the perfect place to emulate conditions in Champagne. The Chardonnay and Pinot Noir grapes are used here as they are in Champagne.

Unlike other California sparkling-wine houses, most Roederer wines use reserve wines (selected older vintages), which are added to the blends to make a more complex wine. Don't miss the superb L'Ermitage deluxe cuvée.

From the highway, the tasting room looks like a big farm building; inside it's modern, bright and cheery.

www.roedererestate.com

5 | Handley Cellars
3151 Hwy. 128, Philo, CA 95466; (707) 895-3876

Milla Handley was an assistant winemaker at Chateau St. Jean in Sonoma County when her late father, Raymond, acquired a vineyard in Dry Creek Valley. After six years in training at three wineries, Milla opened her own winery in Anderson Valley and today makes well over a dozen wines—white, red and sparkling—using grapes from both Dry Creek Valley and her own estate.

With its extensive range of wines, the Handley tasting room is one of the most interesting in the valley. Don't miss the Riesling, Gewürztraminer and Brightlighter White—a Gewürztraminer-based blend.

www.handleycellars.com

In search of Californian sparkling wine

It's made from the same grapes, using the same complicated method of production, but Californian sparkling wine is not Champagne, because it's not made in the chilly Champagne region of northern France. But despite the fact that most other nations are now restricted from using the term Champagne to refer to sparkling wine, the United States is not, and the word still occasionally pops up on labels—generally of inferior wine with bubbles.

While most of France's Champagne houses have been perfecting their craft for a century or more, California is, by contrast, a relative newcomer to fine bubbly. It's been just over 30 years since Schramsberg in Napa Valley and then, soon after, French-owned Domaine Chandon showed the world that top-rate sparkling wine could be made in California. Their success sparked interest in the potential of cooler regions, such as the Russian River Valley and Anderson Valley.

All the top producers use the grape varieties grown in Champagne (Chardonnay, Pinot Noir and Pinot Meunier) and the traditional method of production, in which the wine undergoes a secondary fermentation in the bottle, which creates the bubbles. This used to be known as the *méthode champenoise* but in deference to the French is now the "traditional method."

Top sparkling wines usually fall into one of the following categories: **Brut**, the most popular style, is a dry blend of Chardonnay, Pinot Noir and (sometimes) Pinot Meunier wines from two or more vintages—it can be white or rosé; **Blanc de Blancs** is made entirely from Chardonnay grapes; **Blanc de Noirs** is white sparkling wine made from black grapes. Many producers have a top-of-the-range **deluxe cuvée**; they may also make vintage-dated fizz in the best years.

Most California sparkling-wine producers have now settled on a fruit-driven style of wine, abandoning the quest to make imitation Champagne. They did this because they knew California was blessed with ideal weather conditions that produced bright, flowery-scented fruit. They have found a style that Americans seem to like and which befits the grapes they grow. It features a lot more fruit instead of the depth and complexity that are Champagne's hallmarks, so California focuses on brightness of youth rather than maturity.

▲ Sparkling wine is perfect for a festive occasion.

PICK OF THE FIZZ

The following are some of California's best sparkling-wine producers:

Domaine Carneros: The winery is a French investment (by the Champagne house of Taittinger). The Brut is sophisticated and the Le Rêve Blanc de Blancs a spectacular hit.

Domaine Chandon: The Champagne house of Moët & Chandon founded this Napa Valley project 30 years ago, and the winery's étoile is one of the more deeply flavored of the California sparklers.

Gloria Ferrer: Winemaker Bob Iantosca, blessed with new clones of Chardonnay and Pinot Noir, is making some dramatic bubblies. His regular Brut is reliable and tasty, and his rarer Blanc de Noirs is spectacular and worth seeking out.

Handley Cellars: Good Brut and Rosé from Anderson Valley.

Iron Horse: This family-owned property makes a huge array of limited-release wines, each of them superb, and none better than the Wedding Cuvée. The Russian Cuvée is a bit softer.

J Vineyards: Here the flavors are more lemony and grapefruity, using fruit from the cool Russian River area of Sonoma County. J Vintage Brut is one of the most stylish of California bubblies; the non-vintage version is also excellent.

Mumm Napa: Excellent producer with a house style that's more spicy than flowery. Deeply flavored Blanc de Noirs that's a bit fuller and works brilliantly with salmon, as well as a dramatic Blanc de Blancs.

Roederer Estate: Yet another French-funded project, with a drier, more complex wine than many listed here.

Scharffenberger: A Mendocino County project that seems to improve every year.

Schramsberg: California's original sparkling wine producer; its Reserve is sublime and its J. Schram is one of the finest and most complex wines on the shelf, though pricey.

▲ A selection of Schramsberg's sparkling wines

Dry Creek & Alexander Valleys

Healdsburg has become the jewel of northern Sonoma County's wine-producing crown. It's a base camp for those visiting the Dry Creek Valley and Alexander Valley regions, as well as the Russian River Valley (see page 90), with some 150 wineries in the city or just a short drive away. Wine lovers can find it all here—Sauvignon Blanc, Chardonnay, Merlot, Cabernet Sauvignon, Pinot Noir, Syrah, Zinfandel and more.

Dry Creek and Alexander Valleys are next-door neighbors and have similar soils and climates for grape-growing, with warm sun-splashed days during the growing season (March through October) and cool nights to refresh the vines.

The wineries are spread out, so expect to do some driving. Yet the scenery is gorgeous, the traffic usually light (watch out for cyclists), and there are enough places to grab a bite to eat or stock up for a picnic along the way.

◀ Dry Creek Valley is full of gentle hills and winding roads and is packed with vineyards.

1 | Dry Creek Vineyard
3770 Lambert Bridge Rd., Healdsburg, CA 95448; (800) 864-9463

One-quarter mile (400 m) from the junction of Dry Creek Road and Lambert Bridge Road is Dry Creek Vineyard, a must-stop for those wishing to sample a wide range of wines and share founder David Stare's passion for racy whites, inspired by those he enjoyed in France's Loire Valley.

Beginning in 1972, when California's premium wine industry was still in its infancy, Stare produced Sauvignon Blancs (labeling them as Fumé Blanc, as did Robert Mondavi) that were, and remain to this day, refreshing, crisp and citrusy on release, and remarkably age-worthy. Now in the hands of Stare's daughter, Kim Stare Wallace, and her husband, Don, Dry Creek Vineyard maintains its strength in Sauvignon Blanc and also specializes in Zinfandel, with bottlings from old vines and single vineyards. The range also includes Chardonnay, Cabernet Sauvignon, Merlot, Pinot Noir and a fruity-yet-dry Chenin Blanc from Clarksburg, in the Sacramento Delta region.

The gray stone winery and picnic area are welcoming, not at all ostentatious. The staff are friendly and knowledgeable, and one can't help but notice the nautical theme of the wine labels and tasting-room décor (David Stare is an avid yachtsman).

www.drycreekvineyard.com

▲ Dry Creek Vineyard was a pioneer in establishing Dry Creek Valley as a prime wine region in the 19

2 | Passalacqua Winery

3805 Lambert Bridge Rd., Healdsburg, CA 95448; (707) 433-5550

Walk across the street to Passalacqua and taste its Sauvignon Blancs, Zinfandels and Cabernet Sauvignons. The wines are available only at the winery and to wine club members. The deck has gorgeous views of Dry Creek Valley.

www.passalacquawinery.com

3 | Family Wineries of Dry Creek Valley

4791 Dry Creek Rd., Healdsburg, CA 95448; (888) 433-6555

Drive north on Dry Creek Road to this cooperative tasting room, where Collier Falls Vineyards, Dashe Cellars, Forth Vineyards, Lago di Merlo Winery and Vineyards, Mietz Cellars and Philip Staley pour their wines at the former Timbercrest Farms site. At the same address you will find Papapietro Perry Winery, producer of excellent Pinot Noirs, and the Dry Creek Olive Co., which presses its own olive oils.

www.familywines.com

4 | Sbragia Family Vineyards

9990 Dry Creek Rd., Geyserville, CA 95441; (707) 473-2992

Continue north on Dry Creek Road to Sbragia Family Vineyards, which lies at the base of the Lake Sonoma dam and has a panoramic view of Dry Creek Valley.

For more than 30 years, Ed Sbragia made the wines at Beringer Vineyards in Napa Valley, consistently winning high scores and Winemaker of the Year awards. Yet Sbragia lived in Healdsburg—taught to make wine there by his father, Gino—and has always called it home. So when he semi-retired from Beringer and founded his own brand, it was in the Healdsburg area.

Sbragia, together with his son, Adam, and Adam's wife, Kathy, produce some superior wines. Three Cabernet Sauvignons and one Chardonnay are from Napa Valley—vineyards Ed worked at for Beringer—yet the core lineup is from Dry Creek Valley: the crisp Home Ranch Sauvignon Blanc and Chardonnay; a smooth-textured Andolsen Vineyard Cabernet Sauvignon; the hearty Gino's Vineyard Zinfandel; and the energetic Schmidt Ranch Sauvignon Blanc, available only at the winery. Picnic provisions are available.

www.sbragia.com

5 | Preston Vineyards

9282 W. Dry Creek Rd., Healdsburg, CA 95448; (707) 433-3372

From Sbragia, go back down Dry Creek Road and turn right on Yoakim Bridge Road. Picnic tables on the courtyard welcome visitors, and amiable cats roam the grounds. The place is rustic and comfortable, like well-worn slippers; tolerate the shabby warning

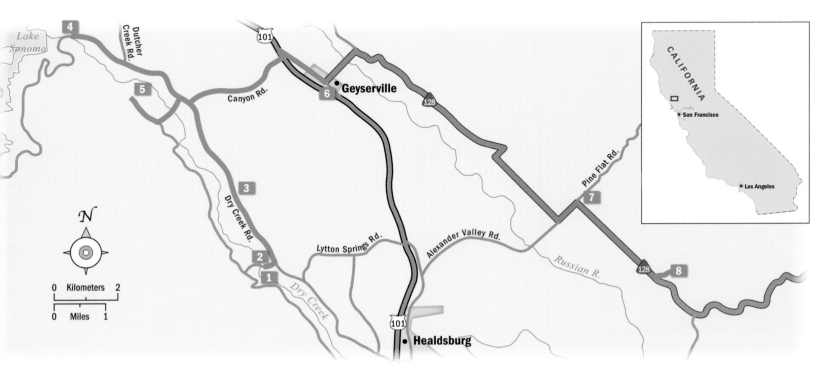

▲ Stonestreet Wines is just outside the pretty little wine town of Healdsburg.

▲ The low hills surrounding Alexander Valley produce grapes with intense flavors.

STOPS ALONG THE WAY

Close to the first two wineries on this tour, on Dry Creek Road, the Dry Creek General Store is owned by Gina Gallo, winemaker at Gallo Family Vineyards. Buy made-to-order sandwiches, salads, wine and other picnic fare. Eat inside or on the porch; don't be surprised if you find yourself seated next to a grower or winemaker.

In tiny Geyserville, eat at Diavola Pizzeria & Salumeria [21021 Geyserville Ave., (707) 814-0111, www.diavolapizzeria.com] with wood-fired pizzas, salumi (cured meats) and dishes such as Pork Cheek Ragu. Walk off your meal by visiting Bosworth's General Merchandise, an old-time hardware and western-wear store.

On the way back to Healdsburg, stop at the Jimtown Store [6706 Highway 128, (707) 433-1212, www.jimtown.com] for coffee, creative sandwiches and salads, and to browse the eclectic selection of antiques and old-fashioned candies and toys.

signs—against driving too fast on the gravel lane leading to the winery, against groups larger than eight, and against bringing other producers' wines into the picnic area—and this spot remains a friendly, comfy place to taste and relax. Don't miss Lou Preston's fabulous home-baked breads and the olive oil and other bounty from his organically farmed garden, which he sells at per-pound prices, far less than most stores in town.

Preston's range includes estate-grown Sauvignon Blanc, Viognier, Carignane, Zinfandel and Syrah, and on Sundays, Preston offers its Guadagni Jug wine, a blend of mostly Zinfandel and Carignane.

www.prestonvineyards.com

6 | Terroirs Artisan Wines
21001 Geyserville Ave., Geyserville, CA 95441; (707) 857-4101

From Preston, exit left (south) onto West Dry Creek Road, then make a left-hand turn onto Yoakim Bridge Road, then a quick jog along Canyon Road. Soon you'll be in Alexander Valley and the town of Geyserville.

Geyserville is named for the natural geysers on—what else?—Geyser Peak, which turn steam beds into energy for much of Sonoma County. Several tasting rooms are located here, and one of the best is Terroirs Artisan Wines in a sleek, airy space on the main drag, pouring the limited-edition wines of Godwin Family Wines, Hughes Family, Peña Ridge and Palmeri Wines, all made by wandering winemaker Kerry Damskey.

www.terroirsartisanwines.com

7 | Stonestreet Wines

7111 Hwy. 128, Healdsburg, CA 95448; (800) 355-8008

From Geyserville, drive east on Highway 128, across the Geyserville Bridge over the Russian River, and you're in the heart of Alexander Valley. Follow 128, turn left at the stop sign at Alexander Valley Road, and after the right-elbow bend make an immediate right into the driveway of Stonestreet Wines, where complex, age-worthy, mountain-grown Chardonnays and Cabernet Sauvignons are poured by knowledgeable staff.

www.stonestreetwines.com

8 | Hanna Winery & Vineyards

9280 Hwy. 128, Healdsburg, CA 95448; (800) 854-3987

Head south on 128 to taste Hanna's zesty Sauvignon Blanc and structured Merlots and Cabernet Sauvignons. The Mediterranean-style tasting room is warm and inviting, and the wraparound veranda is a great place to take in the view of Alexander Valley.

www.hannawinery.com

TASTING AND STROLLING IN HEALDSBURG

Healdsburg was known during Prohibition as the Buckle of the Prune Belt for its production of what are now fashionably called dried plums. Twenty years ago, Healdsburg was a small town populated mostly by farmers, ranchers, winemakers, schoolteachers and small-business owners who sold groceries, hardware, tack and feed, or a stiff drink. Locals can still get a beer and a shot at John & Zeke's Bar and Grill and B&B Lounge, yet today, Healdsburg is all about wine-tasting rooms and myriad restaurants, all eager to serve the thirsty and hungry visiting masses.

More than a dozen tasting rooms dot the streets surrounding the plaza, offering myriad tasting opportunities within easy walking distance. Hit Rosenblum Cellars for top-notch Zinfandels, La Crema for seductive Chardonnays and Pinot Noirs, Souverain for sturdy Cabernet Sauvignons and Merlots, and Gallo Family Vineyards—the E&J Gallo company's only tasting room in the United States.

▲ The veranda at Hanna Winery is a great place to sip wine and take in the view of Alexander Valley.

Russian River Valley

West of Santa Rosa and near the charming older town of Sebastopol, out where Gravenstein apples were once king, lies the intriguing region known as Russian River Valley, a cooler region of Sonoma County that seems to do well with a wide variety of grapes, notably the Burgundian varieties, Chardonnay and Pinot Noir. However, Russian River is also warm enough in some places (notably its northeast edge) that it can also ripen Bordeaux grapes such as Merlot and Cabernet Sauvignon, and some of California's best Zinfandels are produced where the Russian River meets the Dry Creek and Alexander Valleys .

Touring the region is a test of map-reading and global-positioning system expertise, since most roads are small, wineries are spread apart, and it takes time to get to the better ones. It's also a test of planning ahead, since there is only a handful of quality eateries in the region and many are not near wineries.

◀ The early morning mists are still clearing from Dutton Goldfield's vineyards.

1 | Dutton Goldfield

3100 Gravenstein Hwy N., Santa Rosa, CA 95401; (707) 568-2455

Dan Goldfield, who cut his winemaking teeth on Pinot Noir for some boutique producers, established a strong relationship with Steve Dutton, son of one of Sonoma County's pioneer grape growers, the late Warren Dutton. In 1998, they formalized their partnership and created this dramatic quality statement. Goldfield's brilliance is best seen with his Pinot Noirs and cool-climate Syrahs, wines of special merit. His Rued Vineyard Chardonnay is exceptional, as are the small lots of old-vine Zinfandel. All the wines are in strong demand.

Dutton Goldfield has just opened a new tasting room at the corner of Highway 116 and Graton Road, just a short distance from Graton and Sebastopol. The tasting room is homey and casual, with café tables, twin bay windows, a fireplace for winter use and a small wine library for visitors' use. An outside enclosed patio has picnic tables for use mainly in good weather. The next wineries on this tour are about 15 minutes north, along Westside Road.

www.duttongoldfield.com

▲ Near harvest time, vines are sometimes covered with netting to protect the grapes from birds.

2 | Gary Farrell Wines
10701 Westside Rd., Healdsburg, CA 95448; (707) 473-2900

On top of a hill, surrounded by forest, this iconic wine property has an amazing view of the Russian River Valley.

Balance is the key to all great wines, and Gary Farrell, who made his first wines in 1978 as a self-taught stylist, has always believed that. As winemaker for the former Davis Bynum Winery, Farrell slowly built his own brand and by the late 1990s had developed such a following that he was able to found his own stylish winery on Westside Road.

After a merger with a large wine company in 2004, Farrell eventually left to establish a new winery (Alysian), also on Westside Road, but he has a great working relationship with Susan Reed, who now makes the Gary Farrell wines. Included are superb Pinot Noirs, a sublime Sauvignon Blanc and rich Chardonnays.

www.garyfarrellwines.com

Early morning fogs high in the hills above Santa Rosa

THOSE FOGS

In the mornings the area west of Santa Rosa may appear a rather uninviting place to tour. The fogs rolling in off the Pacific last until about 11:00 a.m., even in summer, and have a dramatic cooling effect on what would otherwise be an extremely hot environment for quality grape-growing. The fog crawls over hilltops and settles in the low-lying spots overnight, and it keeps the ground cool. Cooling afternoon breezes, not to mention cold nights, also play their part, but it is the fog that defines the area's boundaries.

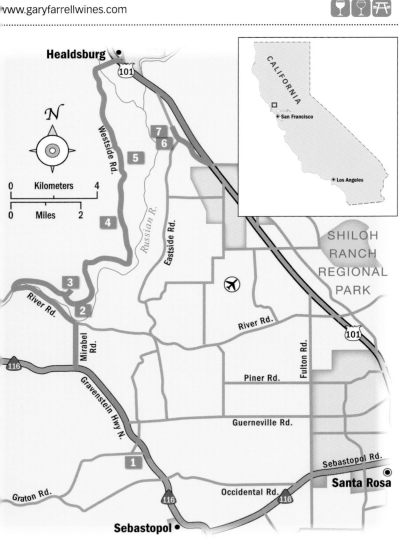

3 | Moshin Vineyards
10295 Westside Rd., Healdsburg, CA 95448; (707) 433-5499

Rick Moshin was a mathematics professor at San Jose State University when he founded this small property in 1989 to specialize in Pinot Noir. Today, with 28 acres of estate grapes, the winery makes some of the most flavorful yet delicate of Russian River Pinot Noirs by making use of a unique four-tier gravity-flow winery—built into the slope of

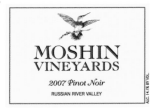

the land—that allows all juice to be processed without the harsh regimen of pumping. Tours of the winery are by appointment only.

www.moshinvineyards.com

Grape EXPECTATIONS

The Russian River Valley has become known for the quality of its Pinot Noir. Even though other grapes, such as Chardonnay and Zinfandel, do well here, Pinot Noir, in particular, benefits from the area's cool climate, especially in the vineyards along Westside Road to the west of Windsor, where the morning fogs and cool winds rolling in from the Pacific are particularly strong.

Russian River has 4,600 acres of Pinot Noir planted, nearly a fifth of all the Pinot Noir planted in the state. So lustrous is the connection between Pinot Noir and the Russian River Valley that high-profile Cabernet producers from the swankier Napa Valley, such as Phelps, Far Niente, Caymus, Araujo and Rudd, have all invested significantly in vineyards here.

The main attraction of Russian River Pinot Noir wines is that most of them do not have the dense color associated with the examples from warmer regions, like those from Santa Barbara. Indeed, if one single word defines the area's Pinots, it is "pretty."

▲ The winery at Hop Kiln is a handsome building dating from the early 1900s.

4 | Hop Kiln Winery
6050 Westside Rd., Healdsburg, CA 95448; (707) 433-6491

Founded in 1975, Hop Kiln began by making a wide array of red and white wines, but under new ownership since the mid-2000s, the property now specializes in delightful, cooler-climate Chardonnay and Pinot Noir, labeled HK, to distinguish them from Hop Kiln. The Hop Kiln brand is still being used for Sauvignon Blanc, Chardonnay, Grenache, Malbec and two proprietary wines, Big Red and Thousand Flowers.

The tasting room is set in a handsome California Historical Landmark, a stone hop kiln built in 1905. Gourmet foods, cheeses, bread and charcuterie are available to make your own picnic. The wines are also available at their superb sister property, the Kenwood Inn and Spa resort (www.kenwoodinn.com).

www.hopkilnwinery.com

5 | C. Donatiello
4035 Westside Rd., Healdsburg, CA 95448; (800) 433-8296

Chris Donatiello partnered with investment banker William Hambrecht in 2003 to convert one of Hambrecht's properties into a Chardonnay and Pinot Noir specialist, and the wines, using all estate-grown grapes, have proved to be excellent.

The modern tasting room is set above the road and gives a handsome view of the western Russian River Valley. An outdoor music concert series in summer evenings is free to visitors. There is also a fascinating organic aroma garden.

www.cdonatiello.com

RUSSIAN RIVER VALLEY AMENITIES

Rustic Russian River is an area of forests, creeks, glens and hills. As a result, most of the lodging is at hidden-among-foliage B&B locations, such as Vine Hill, Raford House, Santa Nella House and the Ferngrove Cottages.

For dining try Mosaic in Forestville, a small restaurant specializing in California cuisine with global fusion influences. There is a lovely outdoor seating area. A charming and casual spot where local winemakers love to dine is the Underwood in Graton. Under the same ownership as Underwood is Willow Wood Market Café, a casual market-cum-tables and a good bet for lunch.

6 | J Vineyards and Winery

11447 Old Redwood Hwy., Healdsburg, CA 95448; (707) 431-3646

From Healdsburg, drive south to the Arata Lane exit in Windsor. Turn right on Old Redwood Highway and continue under the underpass of Eastside Road; turn left into the next driveway. J Vineyards is on the left.

One of the most sybaritic Russian River wineries to visit in the area is this bright, modern building that was once dedicated to sparkling wine. Today, however, 60 percent of the wines made here are still wines, notably some terrific whites and some world-class Pinot Noirs, all made by winemaker George Bursick, who has worked in the industry for more than 30 years.

All tours and tasting should start with bubbly, among the best in the New World, and a special treat is the Bubble Room, with an optional hors d'oeuvres—graced mini meal.

www.jwine.com

7 | Rodney Strong Vineyards

11455 Old Redwood Hwy., Healdsburg, CA 95448; (800) 678-4763

Founded nearly 40 years ago by Rodney and Charlotte Strong, this was one of the first major wineries in the Russian River Valley. Rodney, a professional dancer by trade (he even danced at the Folies Bergère in Paris), was also a skilled blender. A large operation, it is adjacent to J Vineyards and Winery, and its handsome round tasting room looks into the fermentation bays.

Winemaker Rick Sayre and an expert crew of winemakers produce a diverse array of wines, most using fruit from the Russian River, with the Alexander's Crown Cabernet Sauvignon at the top of their list.

www.rodneystrong.com

findout more

- **www.rrvw.org**
  Russian River Valley Winegrowers official website, with maps, links to wineries and regional events listings.

- **www.russianriverinns.com**
  Information about lodging in the Russian River Valley.

regionalevents

California produces about 90 percent of all the wine made in the United States and about 98 percent of the country's world-class wine. As a result, there are literally hundreds of wine events for visitors to attend. The problem is that not many are advertised well, and may therefore fly under the radar—which is a shame. Imagine visiting a region and finding out after the fact that a major wine event took place. Look at the Wine Institute website for more details (www.wineinstitute.org; under Quick Links go to Lifestyle & Travel, then An Insider's Guide to California Wine Country).

Winter Wineland □ January

Over 100 wineries are represented at this Sonoma festival. Visitors partake in vertical tastings, food pairings, educational tours and more.

www.wineroad.com

Savor Sonoma Valley □ March

Meet local winemakers, connect with like-minded wine lovers, sample regional foods, listen to live music and, best of all, explore wines from 22 wineries throughout Sonoma Valley.   www.heartofsonomavalley.com

Anderson Valley Pinot Noir Festival □ May

This event boasts more than 40 wineries from the Anderson Valley region and offers gourmet nibbles, bites and music at Goldeneye Winery. Additional attractions include special tastings, seminars and food pairings.

www.avwines.com

Auction Napa Valley □ June

Indulge tastebuds at the world's largest wine charity event. Since 1981, the vintners of Napa Valley have joined together annually to offer regional wines and delectable food.   www.napavintners.com

Wine Country Film Festival □ July – August

The wine country's oldest and biggest celebration of world cinema offers a range of exciting events, including open-air film screenings, educational symposia, informal receptions, cooking demos, live entertainment and barrel tastings.   www.winecountryfilmfest.com

Sonoma Wine Country Weekend □ September

This epicurean event is a combination of two previously separate annual events: The Sonoma County Showcase of Wine and Food and the Sonoma Valley Harvest Wine Auction. The result is an unforgettable three days of wine, food and festivities.   www.sonomawinecountryweekend.com

Sonoma Valley

The charming town of Sonoma sits at the base of picturesque Sonoma Valley, its town square and older buildings reminiscent of yesteryear. Just east of the square lie a dozen or so wineries, where this tour begins.

Sonoma Valley actually starts well to the south, almost on the northern edge of the tidal estuary San Pablo Bay, an arm of San Francisco Bay. It then goes almost northwest toward inland Santa Rosa, Sonoma County's largest city. This is a major wine region that includes the spectacular subdistrict of Sonoma Mountain, with its gorgeous views; Bennett Valley, a small, cooler area to the west; and small pockets of "banana belt" warmth, where Cabernet Sauvignon ripens. The moderate climate of most of Sonoma Valley makes it a perfect location to grow a wide variety of grapes, and many of its wineries, though not as close to each other as the wineries are on Highway 29 in Napa, are close enough that you can easily visit a number of them in a short trip.

◀ The historic heart of Sonoma Valley north of Sonoma was once known as the Valley of the Moon.

1 | Gundlach Bundschu Winery
2000 Denmark St., Sonoma, CA 95476; (707) 939-3015

From Sonoma Plaza, take East Napa Street, then turn right at 8th Street East. Turn left at Denmark Street and follow it around to the gates of the winery.

The German founders of this old property, the Gundlach and Bundschu families, established a thriving wine business soon after Jacob Gundlach bought 400 acres of land—which he called Rhinefarm—at the feet of the Mayacamas Mountains in 1858. Gundlach–Bundschu was one of the dominant Californian wineries of the nineteenth century, with a huge warehouse in San Francisco, shipping wines all over the world. After the 1906 earthquake the family relocated to Sonoma where their vineyards were. In 2006 the Gundlach and Bundschu families gathered in San Francisco for a 100th reunion of the day when their ancestors' wine empire was destroyed by earthquake and fire.

Today, the sixth generation operates a charming old tasting room at Rhinefarm. A wide variety of wines grown on the large estate are showcased, including both new and old plantings. Don't miss the rich, velvety Merlot, the deeply fruity and chocolaty Cabernet Sauvignon and the vibrant Zinfandel.

www.gunbun.com

2 | Sebastiani Vineyards & Winery
389 4th St. E, Sonoma, CA 95476; (800) 888-5532

Just east of Sonoma Plaza is one of California's oldest continuously operating wineries. Founded in 1904 by Samuele Sebastiani, the winery survived through Prohibition. It was once much larger, with most of its production dedicated to inexpensive wines made from grapes grown in the hot San Joaquin Valley farther inland. In its heyday in the 1960s and 70s Sebastiani was one of the leading Italian-owned wineries in the state.

CHERRYBLOCK

SEBASTIANI

2004

CABERNET SAUVIGNON
SONOMA VALLEY

Following family squabbles, Sebastiani is now owned by William Foley. The lower-priced brands have been sold off and the winery has returned to its Sonoma County roots (literally). The result is a smaller range of wines for national sale, such as superbly balanced Chardonnay and Cabernet Sauvignon (the Cherryblock Cabernet is well regarded) and a popular Zinfandel. Some old standby wines such as Barbera are sold in the tasting room only. The tasting room features a collection of large hand-carved wooden wine casks.

www.sebastiani.com

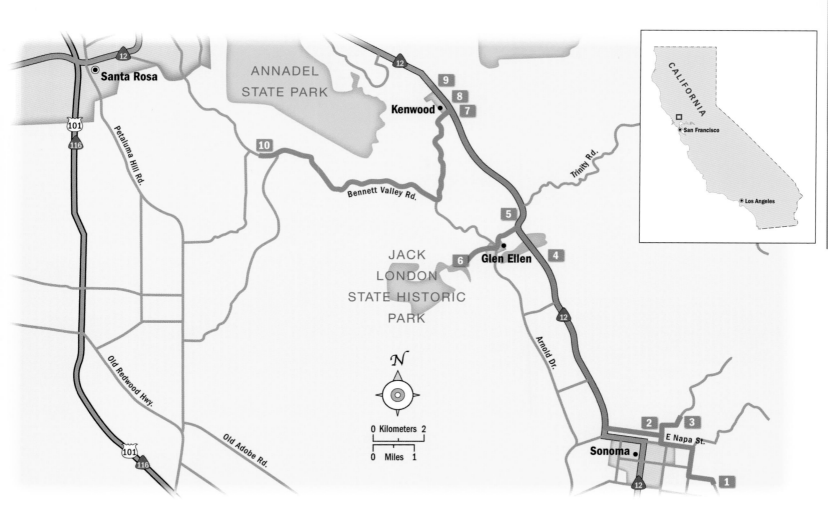

3 | Ravenswood Winery

18701 Gehricke Rd., Sonoma, CA 95476; (707) 933-2332

From Sonoma Plaza, take East Spain east to 4th Street, then go north less than a mile to Gehricke Road to find the property where Zinfandel advocate Joel Peterson founded his winery mainly to make that variety. Over the years, Zinfandel has remained the *raison d'être* for this bearded and passionate man, but Ravenswood has since become one of the premium brands of Constellation Wines, the world's largest wine company.

The winery now makes a huge array of fine wines, but the special lots of vineyard-designated Zinfandels are still the dominant features of this excellent project. Peterson also makes one of the more distinctive red blended wines in California, called Icon, an expensive but delightful Syrah-based Rhône-style blend.

www.ravenswood-wine.com

4 | Arrowood Vineyards & Winery

14347 Sonoma Hwy., Glen Ellen, CA 95442; (800) 938-5170

Take the Sonoma Highway north, into the heart of Sonoma Valley, and you will come to Arrowood Wines, founded by Richard Arrowood and his wife, Alis. Arrowood was the founding winemaker at Chateau St. Jean, just up the road in Kenwood, and in 1986, soon after its sale, Arrowood left to set up this handsome project.

Founded around Arrowood's Chardonnay and Cabernet Sauvignon, using grapes from famed Sonoma County vineyards, Arrowood also makes a number of special lots of wines, such as Côte de Lune Rouge, which features a high proportion of Grenache, Le Beau Mélange Syrah and an array of spectacular dessert wines. Arrowood is now owned by wine entrepreneur Jess Jackson, and though they are still affiliated with the winery, Richard and Alis are now pioneering new vinous ground with their Amapola Creek winery, located on a western slope of the Mayacamas range.

www.arrowoodvineyards.com

5 | Imagery Estate Winery
14335 Hwy. 12, Glen Ellen, CA 95442; (877) 550-4278

Joe Benziger, of Benziger Family Winery, opened Imagery in the late 1980s, intending to showcase wines from small vineyard sites. The vision evolved to focus on grape varieties that weren't in the mainstream.

The label concept has also evolved: each varietal gets a new label every vintage and the winery is a repository of original label artwork displayed as in an art gallery. The labels are as collectible as the wine. Don't miss the Barbera, Cabernet Franc, Malbec and Viognier.

www.imagerywinery.com

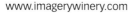

6 | Benziger Family Winery
1883 London Ranch Rd., Glen Ellen, CA 95442; (888) 490-2739

Members of the Benziger family moved from the East Coast to this Glen Ellen property in the early 1980s and there are now a dozen members of the family working at the winery. The Benzigers were one of California's earliest pioneers of biodynamic farming. The estate was converted in 2001 and today a tractor tour of the vineyard ($15 per person) is one of the highlights of a visit. Only small quantities of estate wine are produced, including excellent Sauvignon Blanc.

The winery is on the road that leads to the former utopian property of the writer Jack London, who wrote many of his famed novels here. Stop to view the remnants of Wolf House, within the Jack London State Historic Park. It was his prospective home, but was destroyed by fire before he moved in (www.jacklondonpark.com).

www.benziger.com

▲ At Kunde, in a scene typical of much of the Sonoma Valley, ancient California oak trees frame the vineyards.

7 | Kunde Family Estate

9825 Sonoma Hwy., Kenwood, CA 95452; (707) 833-5501

Sitting on the outskirts of Kenwood lies this unique venue. Located on the property of Kunde Family Estate are the stone ruins of the Dunfillan Winery, set in a beautiful, secluded 5-acre meadow surrounded by vineyards, mountains and majestic oak trees. Pioneer winemaker Captain J.H. Drummond made California's first varietally labeled Cabernet Sauvignon at Dunfillan well over 100 years ago. Louis Kunde bought the property in 1904, and the Kunde family became one of the largest grape-growers in Sonoma County. They built their winery—like an oversized local bungalow—in 1989 and started producing wine under their own name in 1990.

The winery is one of the best in the northern part of Sonoma Valley, with a wide array of fine wines by winemaker Tim Bell.

www.kunde.com

8 | Kenwood Vineyards

9592 Sonoma Hwy., Kenwood, CA 95452; (707) 833-5891

Just to the north of Kunde, Kenwood Vineyards was founded in the early 1970s by brothers Mike and Marty Lee and partner John Sheela. They modernized an old winery dating back to 1906, with the intention of making great wines from the heart of Sonoma Valley;

Kenwood Vineyards is a friendly place to visit, and the wines are outstanding.

their aim was accomplished with superb fruit such as that grown on Milo Shepard's Jack London Ranch (Shepard is the great-nephew of the famed writer). The Jack London Cabernet Sauvignon and Zinfandel and the Artist Series Cabernet Sauvignon have been the winery's flagships for more than 30 years.

After the Kenwood partnership sold the property to Korbel's Gary Heck, additional wines were added, including a superb, reasonably priced Russian River Valley Pinot Noir.

www.kenwoodvineyards.com

Joe Rochioli, Jr., is the second generation of the Rochioli family in Sonoma Valley.

THE HISTORIC HOME OF CALIFORNIA WINE

Sonoma Valley is, in fact, the place where California viticulture and winemaking began in earnest in the middle of the nineteenth century, with the first major planting of French *Vitis vinifera* grape vines under the guidance of Agostin Haraszthy, an iconic figure often called the Father of California wine.

Soon after that, the Italian families who also were the major workforce for the San Francisco fishing fleet made inroads into California winemaking, and names such as Sebastiani, Foppiano, Seghesio, Rochioli and Martini pioneered grape growing in Sonoma County.

9 | Chateau St. Jean

8555 Sonoma Hwy., Kenwood, CA 95452; (707) 833-4134

Founded in the early 1970s by two raisin farmers from California's Central Valley, this iconic property—now owned by Foster's of Australia—at the base of the western side of the Mayacamas Mountains remains one of the state's top wineries.

The handsome Spanish-style tasting room, approached via a mile-long driveway through the vineyards, offers a wide array of wines, notably some of Chateau St. Jean's famed vineyard-designated Chardonnays and Sauvignon Blancs, a delightful Riesling and Gewurztraminer and some terrific late-harvest wines.

The first winemaker, the man who put Chateau St. Jean on the map, was Richard Arrowood. One of his former assistants, Margo Van Staaveren, now heads up the stellar winemaking team.

www.chateaustjean.com

SONOMA VALLEY AMENITIES

The city of Santa Rosa is the largest in Sonoma County, with many amenities, but the town of Kenwood, 15 minutes away, has some pleasant surprises for the wine traveler. The luxurious Kenwood Inn and Spa is a gorgeous property hidden just off Highway 12, with restaurant, pools and spa. It is regularly chosen as a top resort by national travel magazines [(707) 833-1923, www.kenwoodinn.com].

Kenwood Restaurant & Bar offers classic California cuisine, either inside or on the sunny patio [9900 Sonoma Highway, (707) 833-6326, www.kenwoodrestaurant.com]. Cafe Citti is a no-frills Italian trattoria with sensational food at fair prices [9049 Sonoma Highway, (707) 833-2690, www.cafecitti.com].

▲ The graceful visitors' center at Chateau St. Jean, with the canyons of Sugarloaf Ridge rising up behind

The striking winery and tasting room at Matanzas Creek sit above the valley.

10 | Matanzas Creek Winery

6097 Bennett Valley Rd., Santa Rosa, CA 95404; (707) 528-6464

Founded by Bill and Sandra McIver, Matanzas Creek made an immediate impression with Chardonnay in the late 1970s, when California was only just starting to work out how to make the classic wine styles. In 2000 the winery was bought by former San Francisco attorney Jess Jackson, who has made significant changes in both winemaking and the vineyards.

The Bennett Valley subregion of Sonoma Valley is cool enough to grow Pinot Noir, and Matanzas Creek Sauvignon Blanc is highly acclaimed, but Chardonnay and Merlot remain the top wines of French-trained winemaker François Cordesse. The beautiful grounds include a huge lavender farm and gardens and a separate lavender sales room, making this a popular wine country destination.

www.matanzascreek.com

findout more

- **www.sonomawine.com**
  Sonoma County Vintners official site, with maps, links to wineries and regional events listings.

- **www.sonomacounty.com**
  Great source for lodging and restaurant information.

Vella Cheese Company has been making quality cheeses since the 1930s.

BREAD AND CHEESE

Sonoma County is home to far more than just wine. Once the home of a vast apple industry, it remains a vibrant culinary home for locally raised duck, lamb, turkeys and other "main dish" options.

But by far the most culinarily diverse aspect of Sonoma County (and Marin County, just to the south) are the artisanal breads and cheeses that are primarily sold locally. Many of the cheesemakers, in particular, have won praise from the likes of *The New York Times*, *San Francisco Chronicle* and food magazines.

One of the most historic is the Vella Cheese Company, which has been making cheeses in Sonoma since the 1930s, becoming famous for fresh and dry Monterey Jacks. Other cheesemakers who make splendid and unique cheeses are Spring Hill Cheese Co., Two Rock Valley Cheese, Bellwether Farms, Achadinha Goat Cheese, Laura Chenel's Chèvre, Petaluma Creamery, Sonoma Cheese Factory, Matos Cheese and Cowgirl Creamery.

Carneros

Carneros is the first major wine region that visitors encounter when they drive north from the San Francisco Bay Area. It's the rare California wine appellation that straddles two famous regions, Napa County and Sonoma County. You can crisscross between Napa and Sonoma and still remain in Carneros—Spanish for "ram," and a reference to the sheep that once ruled the grass-covered, gently undulating hills north of San Pablo Bay. The sheep are still here, and cows and goats, too, but much of the land is now carpeted in vineyards.

The area's cooling breezes, and Pacific Ocean fog and winds from the west, make Carneros ideal for growing Burgundian grape varieties Chardonnay and Pinot Noir, which are made into still and sparkling wines. Carneros has a casual, agrarian vibe. That's its charm (along with the wines), because it reminds you that winemaking is agriculture; without great grapes, great wines would not exist.

◀ The springtime flowering of mustard, used as a cover crop, is a glorious sight in the Carneros region.

1 | Truchard Vineyards
3234 Old Sonoma Rd., Napa, CA 94559; (707) 253-7153

From the city of Napa, take Old Sonoma Road southwest to Truchard for a tasting of wines that are crisp, elegant and age-worthy, as opposed to rich and potent. Tours of the winery and aging caves, as well as tastings, are offered by appointment only, so call ahead.

▲ Truchard Vineyards is worth a visit for its olive oil as well as for the top-quality wines.

Tony and Jo Ann Truchard have grown grapes on their property for more than 30 years, selling their fruit to other wineries. While several high-end producers continue to buy Truchard grapes, the family began making its own wines in 1989, after converting an old barn into a winery.

Truchard produces splendid Chardonnays and Pinot Noirs, as is to be expected in Carneros, and it also bottles Roussanne, Merlot, Syrah, Zinfandel and Cabernet Sauvignon, each with verve and backbone. And don't miss the peppery Truchard extra-virgin olive oil, made from olives grown on the property.

www.truchardvineyards.com

2 | Etude Wines
1250 Cuttings Wharf Rd., Carneros, CA 94559; (707) 257-5300

From Truchard, continue southwest on Old Sonoma Road and turn left (east) onto Highway 12/121, then right on Cuttings Wharf Road, to visit two of California's pioneering Pinot Noir producers.

Etude, founded by Tony Soter in 1982, is located in the former RMS distillery. Soter was the consulting winemaker for Napa Valley producers such as Araujo, Dalla Valle, Niebaum-Coppola, Spottswoode and Viader. He founded Etude to produce Carneros

Pinot Noir and Napa Valley Cabernet Sauvignon, sold the brand to Beringer Blass (now Foster's Group) in 2001, relocated to his native Oregon, but continues to work with Etude winemaker Jon Priest.

Make an appointment to experience Etude's Reserve Room Tasting, which includes samplings of the winery's Pinot Gris, Pinot Noir Rosé, Heirloom Pinot Noir, estate-grown GBR red blend (Merlot, Malbec and Syrah), Oakville Cabernet Sauvignon and Rutherford Cabernet Sauvignon. Grapes for these wines, and others in the Etude range, come from both Napa and Sonoma, giving tasters a broad view of different varietals and terroirs. If the tiny-production Temblor Carneros Pinot Noir is offered, accept in a heartbeat; it's focused and elegant.

www.etudewines.com

The entrance to Folio Winemakers' Studio

THE ART OF WINE

Some say winemaking is an art, others say it's a science, but most agree it's a combination of the two. Find both at Michael Mondavi's Folio Winemakers' Studio [1285 Dealy La., Napa, CA, (707) 256-2757, www.foliowinestudio.com]. It's home to several wine producers and their joint tasting room, as well as the Taste Gallery, which offers wine-and-food pairings, art exhibits and educational programs.

Artesa Vineyards and Winery [1345 Henry Rd., Napa, CA, (707) 224-1668, www.artesawinery.com] is worth a visit for its modern, set-into-the-hillside architecture, sculpture, artist in residence, and its Chardonnay, Pinot Noir, Merlot and Cabernet Sauvignon. The nearby di Rosa Preserve [5200 Sonoma Hwy., Napa, CA, (707) 226-5991, www.dirosaart.org] houses a vast collection of northern California art.

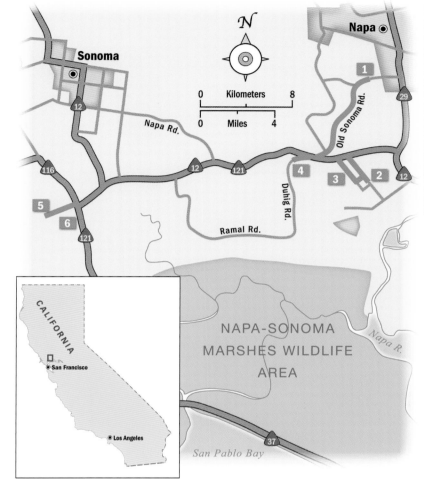

3 | Saintsbury
1500 Los Carneros Ave., Napa, CA 94559; (707) 252-0592

From Etude, backtrack left (north) on Cuttings Wharf Road and turn left on Withers Road. This will take you to Saintsbury's main entrance.

Welcome to the "Dick and Dave Show," as in Dick Ward and David Graves, founders and keepers of the Saintsbury flame since 1981. They met in 1977 while attending UC Davis, and after a misguided attempt to make and sell barrel-fermented Santa Barbara County Riesling, they zeroed in on Carneros as a perfect place to produce Pinot Noir and Chardonnay.

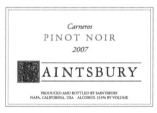

In the years since Saintsbury's founding, the Ward/Graves wines have gained depth and complexity, thanks in large part to the development of their Brown Ranch vineyard, planted to several Dijon clones from France. Saintsbury has branched out from

101

▲ Domaine Carneros is modeled after Champagne Taittinger's elegant château in France.

Carneros regional bottlings to vineyard-designed Pinot Noirs and Chardonnays, which include Pinot Noirs from the Lee, Toyon Farm and Stanly Ranch vineyards in Carneros, and one from the Cerise Vineyard in Mendocino County's Anderson Valley. Garnet Pinot Noir, blended from multiple vineyards, is fine value.

Open by appointment only. Visit Saintsbury not for touristy frills, but for bottle thrills.

www.saintsbury.com

4 | Domaine Carneros
1240 Duhig Rd., Napa, CA 94559; (800) 716-2788

Return to Highway 12/121 and turn left (west), driving the short distance to the French château-inspired Domaine Carneros. It's difficult to miss, because the impressive building dominates the landscape, as does the lush landscaping of the grounds.

Owned by Champagne's Taittinger family, Domaine Carneros was founded in 1987, when the French realized Carneros had a climate cool enough to grow the same grapes that go into Champagne:

Chardonnay, Pinot Noir and Pinot Meunier. Domaine Carneros's sparkling wines are produced with the same labor-intensive techniques used in Champagne, yet the wines have a sunny fruitiness to them that chilly Champagne cannot achieve, along with the yeasty complexity of fine Champagne.

Hike up the grand staircase and through the door; from that point, you will be pampered to whatever degree you wish. Enjoy founding winemaker Eileen Crane's bubblies (Vintage Brut, Brut Rosé Cuvée de la Pompadour and Le Rêve Blanc de Blancs Brut, plus limited-release wines available only at the winery) and Pinot Noir on the terrace or in the salon, with tastes or full glasses delivered to the table. Order cheeses and caviar to complement the wines, then sit back and soak in the panoramic views of the organically farmed estate vineyards. Take a tour and learn how traditional method sparkling wine is produced.

Domaine Carneros is the sort of winery where one intends to stop for 30 minutes and departs, happily, two hours later. Reservations are recommended for the peak months of June through October.

www.domainecarneros.com

5 | Schug Carneros Estate Winery

602 Bonneau Rd., Sonoma, CA 95476; (800) 966-9365

Continue west on Highway 12/121 across the Sonoma County line. At the intersection of Highways 116 and 121, go straight ahead to Bonneau Road and Schug Carneros Estate.

Walter Schug was raised in Germany's Rheingau region, the son of a vintner, and came to America to make wine—first at Joseph Phelps winery in Napa Valley, where he produced the flagship Phelps Insignia Bordeaux-style blend—and then to start his own winery, initially in Yountville, then in Sonoma Carneros.

Schug purchased 50 acres of grazing land to grow and produce Pinot Noir in 1990, and his commitment to making elegant, nuanced wines has never wavered. High scores from critics are nice but have never been his motivation; drinkability and compatibility with food are his mantras.

Today Schug is semi-retired, having turned over management of the business to his son, Axel, although Walter continues to consult. Pinot Noir remains the flagship wine—there are three different bottlings—yet the winery offers something for everyone, including Sauvignon Blanc, Chardonnay, Merlot, Cabernet Franc and Cabernet Sauvignon. And don't miss the delightful Rouge de Noirs Sparkling Pinot Noir.

Appointments to visit the winery, with its German-style post-and-beam architecture and underground barrel room, are not necessary, except for large groups. Special tours and tastings can be booked by prior arrangement. After visiting Schug, enjoy your picnic lunch at tables affording an expansive view of Sonoma Carneros.

www.schugwinery.com

6 | Gloria Ferrer Caves & Vineyards

23555 Hwy. 121, Sonoma, CA 95476; (707) 996-7256

From Schug, turn right (south) onto Highway 121 and immediately look to the right for the driveway to this sparkling and still wine producer, which is set attractively into the hillside, surrounded by 350 acres of grapevines.

Here, Sonoma grapes and Spanish culture commingle at a winery founded by the Catalan Ferrer family more than two decades ago. The Ferrers began making wine in Spain in the nineteenth century, and their California outpost continues the tradition of producing fine sparkling wines using the traditional method—meaning that the bubblies undergo a second fermentation in the bottle, with contact with the yeast cells, which enhances the complexity and ageability of the wines.

▲ Enjoy the Carneros's rural charm from Gloria Ferrer's deck set in the hills.

Take your glass to the deck to sip and take in the scenery. Wines poured on any given day vary, though Gloria Ferrer's finest include the Carneros Cuvée, Royal Cuvée and Brut Rosé. For those who prefer a slightly sweeter, fuller sparkler, try the new Va de Vi.

www.gloriaferrer.com

CARNEROS DELUXE

Where to stay and eat in Carneros? Myriad options exist close by in Napa and Sonoma, yet for a true Carneros experience—and a luxe one—there is the Carneros Inn resort [4048 Sonoma Hwy., Napa, CA, (707) 299-4900, www.thecarnerosinn.com]. The inn's Boon Fly Café [(707) 299-4870] is accessible to all—a great place to stop for coffee, juice and pastries in the morning, and casual lunches and dinners. Farm at Carneros Inn [(707) 299-4880] uses the bounty of local produce, seafood and meats in sophisticated, seasonal cooking.

findout more

- www.carneroswineries.org
  The website for Hospitality de los Carneros, an association of 25 wineries within the Carneros region, with links to member wineries.

- www.carneros.com
  Informative website of the Carneros Wine Alliance, an association of wineries and growers in the Carneros AVA.

Silverado Trail

Wine marketers call it "the road less traveled"; locals use it as an alternative north–south commute through Napa Valley, which is speedier than the busy Highway 29 that knifes through the valley. The Trail is 30 miles (48 km) long, running from the northeast edge of the city of Napa to Calistoga, along the base of the Vaca Mountains.

Many love the Trail for its slower pace and beautiful scenery, with just enough amenities to make a daylong wine explorer happy. Granted, lodging in the heart of the Silverado Trail route is limited to expensive resorts (with restaurants), such as Auberge du Soleil, Meadowood Napa Valley and Solage. Yet Napa city in the south and Calistoga in the north offer many choices in accommodations and are terrific starting points for a Trail blaze. And those crossroads between the Silverado Trail and Highway 29 mean that choices for lunch and lodging are just 10 minutes' drive away.

◄ The Silverado Trail got its name from the hillside silver mining that seemed so promising in the 1850s.

1 | HdV Wines
588 Trancas St., Napa, CA 94558; (707) 251-9121

The vineyards that produce the HdV wines are several miles away in Carneros, yet folks who prefer elegant, structured Chardonnays and Syrahs over ultraripe powerful styles can taste the former just 200 yards (183 m) west of the Silverado Trail, at HdV's winery. Be sure to make an appointment first.

Larry Hyde came to Napa Valley from California's Central Valley more than three decades ago and began developing Hyde Vineyards in Carneros, a cool region southwest of Napa. His planting of myriad clones and rootstocks, and meticulous farming to meet the needs of those who purchase his grapes, made Hyde a viticultural icon. That he's joined forces with his cousin, Pamela, and her husband, Aubert de Villaine, director of Burgundy's superstar winery Domaine de la Romanée Conti (DRC), can only result in success. And it has. The wines, made from Hyde Vineyards grapes, have a focus and finesse that aren't always found in Napa Valley Chardonnay and Syrah. Larry Hyde grows Pinot Noir for other wineries—why try to compete with DRC?

www.hdvwines.com

2 | Hagafen Cellars
4160 Silverado Trail, Napa, CA 94558; (888) 424-2336

Owner/winemaker Ernie Weir's wines—Cabernet Sauvignon, Chardonnay, Merlot, Pinot Noir, Sauvignon Blanc, Syrah, White Riesling, Zinfandel and Brut Cuvée sparklers—are as good as any you'll find in Napa Valley; that they are made according to Jewish dietary laws is a bonus for those keeping kosher, and a non-issue for non-Jews.

Hagafen is Hebrew for grapevine and these wines are well made and reasonably priced. The engaging Weir is usually behind the tasting bar, and he doesn't mention that his wines are kosher unless he's asked, because he wants them to be appreciated for what they are: delicious. Observant Jews will find that Hagafen wines bear no resemblance to sweet, grapey Manischewitz; no one else will even think to ask.

www.hagafen.com

3 | Clos du Val
5330 Silverado Trail, Napa, CA 94558; (800) 993-9463

In the early 1990s, consumers began to demand rich, fruity, opulent California wines, encouraged, no doubt, by influential wine critics who favored this style and by the wholesalers and retailers who used these critics' scores to recommend wines to their customers.

Yet since the early 1970s, when American John Goelet and French winemaker Bernard Portet founded Clos du Val in what would become the Stags Leap District, they have stuck to their guns in producing balanced, restrained Cabernet Sauvignons, Merlots, Pinot Noirs and Chardonnays that may not wow some critics upon release, but after a few years in the cellar, these wines develop into elegant, age-worthy, food-friendly bottlings.

Clos du Val—French for "small estate of a small valley"—has stayed true to its style and not chased critics' palates. In America, the pendulum seems to be swinging back to favoring less powerful, more balanced wines, and Clos du Val delivers just that. Taste the current-release wines, and for an additional fee, reserve and library wines. A demonstration vineyard is open to the public, and pétanque (a form of boules) courts are available.

www.closduval.com

4 | Stag's Leap Wine Cellars
5766 Silverado Trail, Napa, CA 94558; (866) 422-7523

The 1976 "Judgment of Paris" tasting, at which French wine experts tasted California wines against those from France, made Stag's Leap Wine Cellars famous. Founder/winemaker Warren Winiarski's 1973 Stag's Leap Wine Cellars' Napa Valley Cabernet Sauvignon finished first, ahead of first-growth Bordeauxs from Château Mouton-Rothschild and Château Haut-Brion, which shocked the world and instantly made California a wine region to be reckoned with.

Stag's Leap Wine Cellars' Cabernet Sauvignons have been the picture of balance and elegance ever since, improving in the cellar for 20 years or more. In 2007, nearing retirement, Winiarski sold the winery to a partnership of Ste. Michelle Wine Estates of Washington State and Tuscan winemaking icon Piero Antinori in 2007, but the stylistic beat goes on.

The tasting room is open daily, and various tasting options are offered, including Chardonnay and Merlot, as well as the famous Cabernet Sauvignons from the Fay and S.L.V. vineyards. The estate and cave tour tells the rich story of the winery and its place in California winemaking history. It's a winery not to be missed.

www.cask23.com

Clos du Val is renowned for classic, elegant wines.

5 | Shafer Vineyards

6154 Silverado Trail, Napa, CA 94558; (707) 944-2877

This is one of California's most famous producers, and its Hillside Select Cabernet Sauvignon is one of the most sought-after wines in America. The retail sales room is open to all, yet tastings are limited to those with appointments, so book ahead if you wish to taste and tour the winery.

Nestled in the volcanic hillsides of the Stags Leap District, Shafer was founded by John Shafer in 1972 after he left a career in the publishing industry. He bought the property and began replanting the existing vineyards, which dated to the 1920s. Shafer and his family, including winemaker son Doug, crushed their first Cabernet Sauvignon grapes in 1978 and began construction on their winery a year later.

In addition to the hard-to-get Hillside Select Cabernet Sauvignon, Shafer produces a lush One Point Five Cabernet Sauvignon, Merlot, and a rich yet racy Red Shoulder Ranch Chardonnay from Shafer's Carneros vineyard.

www.shafervineyards.com

6 | Robert Sinskey Vineyards

6320 Silverado Trail, Napa, CA 94558; (800) 869-2030

Drive through the stone-pillar entrance to this redwood-and-stone winery and enter a world of organic and biodynamic grape-growing, gardens abuzz with insect and bird life and, on most days, aromas of garden-sourced foods being cooked in the kitchen.

Rob Sinskey, who took over the winery from his father, Bob, in 1988, is best known for his Carneros Pinot Noir, Pinot Blanc and Pinot Gris wines, yet the winery and tasting room are located in the heart of the Stags Leap District appellation—Cabernet Sauvignon country—and Sinskey's Cabs are no slouches. All the wines are precise, elegant and meant to complement meals; those looking for ripe, ultra-rich, hedonistic wines should look elsewhere.

The aromas wafting from the kitchen might very well come from the hand of Rob Sinskey's wife, Maria Helm Sinskey, former chef at PlumpJack Café in San Francisco. She often prepares nibbles for visitors to enjoy when they taste the wines, while the gift-shop goods lean heavily to kitchen gadgets, cooking ingredients and cookbooks, including Helm Sinskey's *The Vineyard Kitchen: Menus Inspired by the Seasons*.

Several tasting and tour options are available, including a Cave Raider Tour (of the aging caves, naturally) and Culinary Tour, both by appointment. Walk-in visitors are welcome daily for the Flight of Fancy tastings.

A short detour on the Oakville Cross Road takes you to a row of wineries, including Groth, Gargiulo, PlumpJack, Rudd and Silver Oak, all within a mile or so of each other and producers of fine Cabernet Sauvignons. Screaming Eagle, maker of the most prized California Cabernet ($500 per bottle), is also in the neighborhood, yet visitors aren't allowed, there isn't a sign, and even if you find "Screagle," your chances of getting a taste are nil.

www.robertsinskey.com

Ancient Persia comes to the Napa Valley at Darioush.

A "QUINTESSENTIAL" EXPERIENCE

For a we're-not-in-Kansas-anymore (nor America) experience, visit Darioush [4240 Silverado Trail, Napa, CA, (707) 257-2345, www.darioush.com], Darioush Khaledi's replication of ancient Persepolis in his native Iran. Towering stone pillars, a stone amphitheater and palm trees create an oasis emerging from the vines.

Inside, taste Darioush's Bordeaux-style red wines, or make a reservation for the Quintessential experience—a visit to Khaledi's personal cellar, where you can select a bottle of first-growth Bordeaux from his collection and enjoy it with current-release Darioush wines and small tastes to complement the wines. Cost at time of publication: $300 per person.

7 | Mumm Napa
8445 Silverado Trail, Rutherford, CA 94573; (707) 967-7700

Mumm Napa, along with Domaine Carneros and Domaine Chandon, is a pioneer of high-end California sparkling-wine production. In 1983, the G. H. Mumm Champagne house established this Napa Valley outpost under winemaker Guy Devaux. The winery (then called Mumm Cuvée Napa) was completed in 1986, and since then, it's been known for its visitor-friendly hospitality, education and artistic programs.

Sip Mumm Napa's Brut Prestige, Brut Rosé, Blanc de Blancs and Prestige cuvées in the tasting salon or on the patio. Recently added is the Oak Terrace Tasting (by appointment only), a two-hour sit-down tasting of library wines that cannot be purchased in stores.

Guided tours are free, with knowledgeable hosts describing every step of the sparkling-wine production process. The fine art photography gallery features the work of local and international photographers—Ansel Adams's works have been shown here—and the retail shop has perhaps the most extensive selection of sparkling-wine service tools and gadgets anywhere in California.

www.mummnapa.com

8 | Quintessa
1601 Silverado Trail, Rutherford, CA 94573; (707) 967-1601

You'll need an appointment to tour and taste at this winery, which produces just one wine: the Bordeaux-style Cabernet Sauvignon blend called, naturally, Quintessa.

Yet don't let the single-wine thing stop you; the tour of the estate includes talks about the sustainably farmed vineyards, the curved, stone-fronted winemaking facility tucked into the hillside, and the underground aging caves. Tours end with a sit-down tasting of Quintessa and a canapé food pairing.

www.quintessa.com

9 | Duckhorn Vineyards
1000 Lodi La., St. Helena, CA 94574; (888) 354-8885

Founded in 1976 by Dan and Margaret Duckhorn, this winery is one of the most recognized in Napa Valley, thanks not only to its excellent Sauvignon Blanc, Merlot and Cabernet Sauvignon but also for the distinctive woodcut label depicting a duck on a marsh. The visitors' center displays the Duckhorns' vast collection of waterfowl

Traditional-method sparkling wines undergoing their second fermentation in bottle at Mumm Napa

▲ The estate house at Duckhorn Vineyards, where visitors can enjoy viewing the art collection

art, from paintings to decoys to sculptures. The traditional-style estate house has lovely grounds for visitors to stroll in.

Most of the grapes are grown on seven estate vineyards on the hillsides of Howell Mountain and alluvial fans on the valley floor. Three vineyard-designated Cabernets are produced (Monitor Ledge, Patzimaro and Rector Creek) and one Merlot (Three Palms Vineyard); the remaining wines are labeled under the Estate Grown and Napa Valley labels. The Decoy label is used for a red Bordeaux blend.

A number of tasting experiences and tours are available, some by prior arrangement only, including wine-and-food pairings, and the "Howell Mountain Experience" tour and tasting in that sub-appellation.

Paraduxx red blends are made at an attractive winery about 10 miles (16 km) back down the Silverado Trail. The Duckhorn's Goldeneye winery in Anderson Valley focuses on Pinot Noir.

www.duckhorn.com

10 | August Briggs Winery
333 Silverado Trail, Calistoga, CA 94515; (707) 942-4912

This is an unpretentious, welcoming place to try owner/winemaker August "Joe" Briggs's delicious Chardonnay, Pinot Noir, Petite Sirah, Syrah and Old Vine Zinfandel. If you're lucky, you may also get to taste the Pinot Meunier and Charbono, which are available only to wine club members.

With more than 20 years' experience, Joe has in-depth knowledge of his vineyard sources and uses grapes grown not only in Napa Valley but also in Sonoma and Lake County. Wine buffs will recognize such stellar vineyards as Frediani, Sinskey and Stagecoach on the labels, and Briggs delivers great quality for the prices he charges. August Briggs wines aren't cheap, but they are typically priced below that of his competitors.

While there are few frills, there is a casual Calistoga vibe here and a wine type for everyone. At publication time, August Briggs remained one of the few Napa wineries to pour complimentary tastes. Groups of five and larger are asked to make appointments, as this is a small, family-run winery.

www.augustbriggswines.com

11 | Chateau Montelena

1429 Tubbs La., Calistoga, CA 94515; (707) 942-5105

Come here for a taste of California winemaking history. Chateau Montelena's Chardonnay, Riesling, Zinfandel and Cabernet Sauvignon define the word elegant. The chateau, built in the late 1800s, was purchased by James Barrett, who released the first modern Chateau Montelena wines in 1972. The serene hillside setting, with its ivy-covered stone castle, Chinese gardens and Jade Lake, shouldn't be missed.

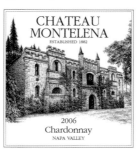

The 2008 movie *Bottle Shock*, based on Chateau Montelena's victory with its 1973 Chardonnay over French Burgundies at the famous "Judgment of Paris" tasting in 1976, doesn't do the winery justice, playing too loosely with the facts for the sake of entertainment. Yet Chateau Montelena is the real deal, a winery worth visiting, whether one has seen the movie or not.

Current release and library wine tastings are available; reservations are required for the latter.

www.montelena.com

▲ Chateau Montelena's setting is one of the most peaceful in the valley.

▲ The Estate Room at Chateau Montelena

Heart of Napa

What could be simpler than to travel one road and have more than 50 world-class wineries along the way? Such ease can be found on Highway 29, the main road through Napa Valley, where there are more tasting rooms, restaurants, gourmet food stores, boutiques, museums and art galleries than one could possibly visit in even a month. Highway 29 goes by various names—in St. Helena, it's called Main Street; south of St. Helena and in Rutherford, Oakville and Yountville, it's St. Helena Highway. Whatever the reference, it's always the yellow brick road to enological Oz, with dozens of Napa Valley's most recognized wineries just a left or right turn away … and it's difficult to get lost.

On weekends and during the commuter rush hour, traffic can get congested near St. Helena. But then, what's your rush? You're in wine country, where the pace is supposed to be slow. Just go with the flow and enjoy the scenery along the way.

◀ Beringer's original nineteenth-century Rhine House is now the winery's visitors center.

1 | Charles Krug Winery
2800 Main St., St. Helena, CA 94574; (707) 967-2229

This is Napa Valley's first commercial winery, founded in 1861 by Charles Krug and taken over by Cesare Mondavi in 1943. After Cesare's death, his sons, Robert and Peter Mondavi, carried on until Robert left in 1966 to found Robert Mondavi Winery. At the time of writing, Peter Mondavi (who turned 95 in November 2009) remained the winery chief, with sons Peter Jr. and Marc spearheading a winery and vineyard revitalization project that included new vine plantings and winemaking facilities.

The property is listed on the National Register of Historic Landmarks, and winemaking history abounds—from the tasting bars made from the original redwood tanks to the 2008 renovation of the historic carriage house and redwood cellar.

Stop for the history, stay for a tasting, or take a glass of racy Charles Krug Sauvignon Blanc or complex, very fairly priced, Cabernet Sauvignon to the grand lawn. Take a seat and enjoy the calm and beauty. Picnickers are welcome.

www.charleskrug.com

2 | Beringer Vineyards
2000 Main St., St. Helena, CA 94574; (707) 967-4412

No first-timer's visit to Napa Valley would be complete without a stop at Beringer, the oldest continuously operating winery in the valley (now part of the Foster's Group). Founded in 1876 by German immigrants Frederick and Jacob Beringer, it features gorgeously landscaped grounds; tunnels dug by Chinese laborers, which are still used to store wine; the Hudson House, in which Jacob lived; and the Rhine House, Frederick's Germanic mansion that is now the tasting room.

The range of wines is vast, the tasting and tour options extensive. Check the website for special tasting events throughout the year. There is something for everyone, from light, crisp white and blush wines to Beringer's famous Chardonnays and Cabernet Sauvignons from selected Napa Valley vineyards. On weekends, the winery offers retrospective tastings of Beringer Private Reserve Cabernet Sauvignon, its flagship red that has a tremendous following.

www.beringer.com

Charles Krug is one of Napa's most historic wineries.

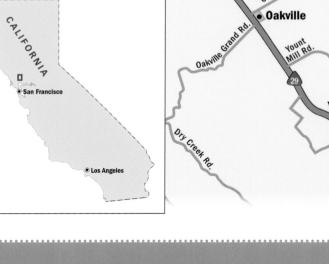

ST. HELENA AMENITIES

While in the St. Helena area, grab a wedge of cheese, a loaf of artisan bread, gourmet sandwiches, salads and other picnic items at the Sunshine Foods market.

The line moves fast at the original Taylor's Automatic Refresher, where burgers and fries get upscale tweaks, and two Cindy Pawlcyn restaurants—Cindy's Backstreet Kitchen (Cal-Med comfort food) and Go Fish (seafood and fabulous sushi)—are local favorites. For a sumptuous splurge, go to Terra, for Hiro Sone's Japanese- and French-influenced dishes. You'll likely be greeted by his wife and Terra co-owner Lissa Doumani, whose warm hospitality and decadent desserts keep residents and visitors alike coming back time and again. Great wine list, too.

Need a room? A good-value choice is the art deco-style El Bonita Motel, a single-story drive-to-your-door motor lodge that is comfortable, convenient, and has an old-school, kidney-shaped pool. The English Tudor–design Harvest Inn is far more upscale, surrounded by vineyards and offering quiet solitude and fireplaces in some rooms.

findout more

- www.legendarynapavalley.com
  Official tourist website with ideas for activities throughout the valley.
- www.napavintners.com
  Website for the wineries.
- www.napanow.com
  Lists all the major annual events.

111

3 | Spottswoode Estate Vineyard & Winery
1902 Madrona Ave., St. Helena, CA 94574; (707) 963-0134

Continue south on Main Street and turn right on Madrona Avenue to Spottswoode. Don't let the residential nature of the street fool you; there is indeed a winery up ahead, and a great one.

Some wine aficionados describe Cabernet Sauvignon as "masculine" and Pinot Noir as "feminine." Yet both varietals can be made in bold, tannic styles or as floral, elegant and caressing wines. At the 125-year-old Spottswoode Estate, the all-female team of owner Mary Novak, daughters Beth Novak Milliken and Lindy Novak, and winemaker Jennifer Williams produces Cabernet Sauvignons that are classic Napa Valley yet with a bit more restraint and elegance than many—not masculine, not feminine, but something in between.

Their wines have great structure and ability to age; while they are rich and enjoyable when young, the payoff comes at around 10 years old, when secondary layers emerge, including violets, potpourri, sea salt, soy and Indian spice, along with Cabernet Sauvignon's typical black cherry, cedar and forest-floor notes. Gender doesn't determine the wine style as much as the vineyard does. It's been farmed organically since 1985, and the wines reflect the personality of the site. Spottswoode is a special place, worth making an appointment ahead to tour the grounds, taste the wines (including a super Sauvignon Blanc) and meet the hospitable Novaks.

www.spottswoode.com

4 | Louis M. Martini Winery
254 St. Helena Hwy., St. Helena, CA; (800) 321-946

E&J Gallo purchased the winery from the Martini family in 2002, rescuing a historic yet struggling winery. Today, Louis Martini Winery thrives, with a broad range of well-made wines and a tasting room that resembles a trendy wine bar.

Founded in 1933, Martini made its name in Cabernet Sauvignon, Zinfandel and Barbera production. Its Monte Rosso Vineyard—not in Napa Valley but atop Sonoma Mountain—is one of California's most distinctive terroirs for Cabernet Sauvignon and Zinfandel, and Gallo proudly showcases those wines in its Napa tasting room, as well as

▲ Spottswoode is an architectural gem on the outskirts of St. Helena.

Chardonnay and Cabernet Sauvignon from Napa Valley. Several
tasting and tour options are available, and wines can be enjoyed
inside or on the shaded patio.

www.louismartini.com

5 | Frog's Leap Winery
8815 Conn Creek Rd., Rutherford, CA 94573; (707) 963-4704

Take a slight detour east from St. Helena Highway to Rutherford
Cross Road, then left on Conn Creek Road
to Frog's Leap, which bursts with flowers,
fruit trees, vegetable gardens and
grapevines from spring through fall.
Proprietor John Williams grows everything
sustainably and/or organically; the visitors
center is made partially from reclaimed
pickle vats and remnants of a piano
factory. The style of the wines places
varietal character ahead of rich flamboyancy, and the alcohol levels
(around 13.5 percent) are food-friendly.

A great place for kids to explore while the grown-ups taste
Sauvignon Blanc, Chardonnay, Merlot and Cabernet Sauvignon on
the porch overlooking the Mayacamas Mountains to the west.

www.frogsleap.com

The vineyards at Frog's Leap Winery are ablaze with flowering mustard in springtime.

Harvesting olives at Long Meadow Ranch

WHAT'S NEW IN ST. HELENA
Two new sites are worth a look. The first is Hall Wines [401 St. Helena
Hwy., St. Helena, CA, (707) 967-2626, www.hallwines.com]. It isn't
new, but it will appear to be so when construction is completed on
the $100 million Frank Gehry–designed visitors center and winery.
Gehry, designer of the Guggenheim Museum in Bilbao, Spain (and the
only architect to appear on TV's *The Simpsons*), created an "undulating
trellis" design for the roof of Hall Wines, allowing it to blend in with
the vineyards (and appease the neighbors). In 2003 Texas
businessman Craig Hall and his wife, Kathryn (a former ambassador
to Austria), purchased the winery, which began life in 1885 as the
Napa Valley Co-op and later became Bergfeld Winery. The Halls kept
the winemaking and tasting room going during construction of the
Gehry masterpiece, filling the visitor areas with artwork and a
sculpture garden, while pouring excellent Sauvignon Blanc, Merlot
and Cabernet Sauvignon wines in the tasting room.

Long Meadow Ranch Winery & Farmstead is another winery that
has tongues wagging in St. Helena, even though it's located in the
western hills in Rutherford. Ted and Laddie Hall and their son, Chris,
restored a 125-year-old farmhouse as a wine and olive-oil tasting
center and, in a barn behind the farmhouse, created Farmstead
restaurant, with a menu featuring ingredients the Halls produce
themselves by sustainable methods, including Highlands beef, eggs,
olive oil, vinegar, honey, fruits, vegetables and, naturally, Long
Meadow Sauvignon Blanc and Cabernet Sauvignon [738 Main St., St.
Helena, CA, (707) 963-4555, www.longmeadowranch.com].

7 | St. Supéry Vineyards & Winery
8440 St. Helena Hwy., Rutherford, CA 94573; (707) 963-4507

Return to Rutherford Cross Road and turn left (south) onto St. Helena Highway. Look to the left for the entrance to St. Supéry, a French-owned Napa Valley fixture.

Like most Napa Valley wineries, Cabernet Sauvignon and Merlot are mainstays at St. Supéry, yet Sauvignon Blanc is just as important here, with two different bottlings of the white varietal, plus a superb blended white wine called Virtú.

Before tasting the wines, head to the second-floor gallery for "Smell-a-Vision," a display that allows guests to smell and identify the various aromas found in wines. The gallery also features monthly art exhibits and a lofty perch from which to observe the day-to-day winemaking activities.

If hunger pangs hit, stop at the classic Oakville Grocery at the corner of Highway 29 and Oakville Cross Road for gourmet sandwiches, salads, breads, olive oils and other picnic provisions.

www.stsupery.com

▲ Ballooning is one of Napa's most popular attractions.

6 | Caymus Vineyards
8700 Conn Creek Rd., Rutherford, CA 94573; (707) 967-3010

From Frog's Leap, drive south on Conn Creek Road past Rutherford Cross Road; on your left, you'll see Caymus Vineyards, one of California's most famous Cabernet Sauvignon producers. The Wagner family, originally from France's Alsace region, has made wine here since 1915, with its Caymus Special Selection Cabernet Sauvignon highly sought after since its introduction in 1971. Splendid Zinfandels and the multi-variety white blend, Conundrum, add spice to the lineup. The tasting room is rancho-rustic and relaxed, and while appointments are required, the vibe is welcoming and casual.

www.caymus.com

▲ St. Supéry's historic Dollarhide Estate is high up on the eastern side of Napa Valley.

Domaine Chandon
1 California Dr., Yountville, CA 94599; (888) 242-6366

This sparkling wine house, founded by France's Moët Hennessy in 1973, has an outstanding restaurant, Etoile, so end your day by tasting Domaine Chandon's sparkling and still wines, followed by dinner at the romantic Etoile ("star" in French).

Park in the large lot, cross the bridge to the visitors' center, and find yourself in a secluded, soothing other world. Mature trees, spring-fed ponds and a field of mushroom-like rock sculptures add interest. Take a guided tour and discover how traditional-method sparkling wine is made, learn how to pair wines with food and sample Domaine Chandon wines in the salon or on the terrace.

Etoile blends French cooking techniques with local ingredients in a casually elegant dining room with a ceiling resembling the inside of a wine barrel. Walls are hung with artwork, and one all-glass wall shows off the grounds. Even without a restaurant, Domaine Chandon is a special stop.

www.chandon.com

▲ Domaine Chandon's Etoile restaurant makes a great dining choice after a day of wine touring.

Many wineries offer fun events for visitors, such as grape-stomping.

YOUNTVILLE AMENITIES

Yountville is named for George Yount, who planted the first wine grapes here in 1855. It's a dining mecca: Besides Etoile at Domaine Chandon (see above), Thomas Keller's restaurants—The French Laundry, Ad Hoc and Bouchon—are here, along with Redd (California cuisine), Bottega (Italian), Bistro Jeanty (French) and the venerable Mustard's (American). All are highly recommended, though you'll need a reservation well in advance at The French Laundry, a credit card that can take the punishment, and at least four hours to consume the meal. Keller's more casual Ad Hoc (American comfort food) and Bouchon (French bistro) deliver great tastes for a fraction of the cost (though without the theater).

At night, put your weary head on the luxurious pillows at the Villagio Inn & Spa [6481 Washington St., Yountville, CA, (707) 944-8877, www.villagio.com] and get a massage the next morning. Or book a room at the "green" yet luxe Bardessono Hotel [6526 Yount St., Yountville, CA, (707) 204-6000, www.bardessono.com], which has its own restaurant. Value-seekers should consider the many motor lodges in the city of Napa, just 10 minutes from Yountville.

Napa, Western Foothills

Growers and winemakers in the Rutherford and Oakville appellations of Napa Valley love to show off their benches—the gentle inclines between the valley floor and the Mayacamas Mountains, upon which world-class Cabernet Sauvignon grapevines are planted. These foothill benches, built up from sediment washed down from the Mayacamas range over the ages, are alluvial fans of gravelly soils and are superb for growing balanced Cabernet Sauvignons that are delicious to drink upon release and will also age gracefully.

Take this route and you'll discover the historical foundation for Napa Valley Cabernet Sauvignon and also taste distinctive Sauvignon Blancs, Merlots and Zinfandels. Several of Napa Valley's most famous vineyards are here, including Heitz Wine Cellars, Martha's and Bella Oaks vineyards in Rutherford and, the granddaddy of them all, To Kalon Vineyard, which is the source of grapes for the Robert Mondavi Winery.

◀ The Opus One winery, Oakville, with its impressive driveway entrance

1 | Provenance Vineyards

1695 St. Helena Hwy. S, Rutherford, CA 94573; (707) 968-3633

Tom Rinaldi, the founding winemaker at Duckhorn Vineyards (see page 107), left there after 20 years to join Provenance, finding the challenges of starting yet another winery invigorating. His wines—Sauvignon Blanc, Merlot and Cabernet Sauvignon—are beautifully balanced and classic representations of Rutherford and Oakville grapes.

The first wine, Rutherford Cabernet Sauvignon, was released in 1999 and since 2002 the winery has been located on the site of former Chateau Beaucanon in the heart of the Rutherford appellation. Check out the flooring, made from the staves of some 900 oak barrels, as you taste the wines (some options include wines available only in the tasting room). The best bottle is the age-worthy Oakville Beckstoffer To Kalon Vineyard Cabernet Sauvignon, which at time of publication sold for $75 a bottle (a typical price for top-notch Napa Valley Cab). Yet the Provenance Rutherford Cabernet Sauvignon is priced at approximately half that much and is a gem. White-wine lovers will thrill at Rinaldi's Sauvignon Blancs.

www.provenancevineyards.com

2 | Grgich Hills Estate

1829 St. Helena Highway, Rutherford, CA 94573; (800) 532-3057

There is nothing fancy or frivolous about the Grgich Hills tasting room, with its use of dark wood and the feel of a production wine cellar. The reason to stop is, quite simply, to taste the wines, particularly the deep, concentrated yet balanced Chardonnays and Cabernet Sauvignons.

Croatian immigrant Miljenko "Mike" Grgich, who founded the winery in 1977 with Austin Hills and his sister, Mary Lee Strebl, from the Hills Bros. Coffee family, produced the 1973 Chateau Montelena Chardonnay that won the Judgment of Paris tasting against French Burgundies. With that fame, he left Montelena to make wine for himself, and today Grgich's nephew Ivo Jeramaz is the winemaker, with Uncle Mike as consultant.

The wines, which include the classic Napa Valley Chardonnay, a rich barrel-fermented Fumé Blanc (Sauvignon Blanc), Zinfandel and Cabernet Sauvignon, are made from grapes grown organically and biodynamically, using no pesticides or herbicides. Call ahead to check when grapes are being crushed (usually September through October) to take part in Grgich Hills' harvest grape stomp, when visitors get a chance to crush grapes with their bare feet.

www.grgich.com

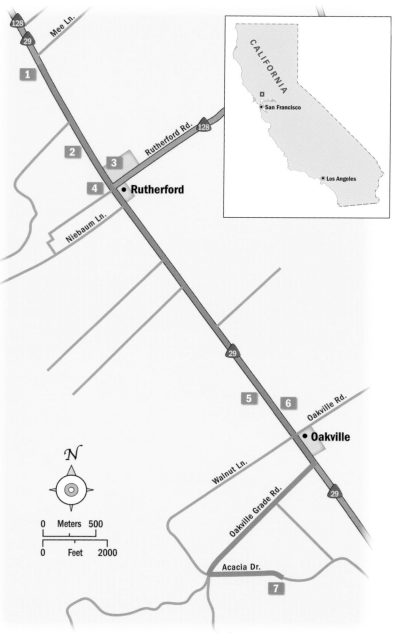

▲ Beaulieu set the style for Napa Cabernet Sauvignon at the beginning of the twentieth century.

3 | Beaulieu Vineyard
1960 St. Helena Hwy., Rutherford, CA 94573; (800) 373-5896

Consider crossing to the eastern side of Highway 29 to visit the tasting room of ivy-covered Beaulieu Vineyard. Now owned by wine-and-spirits giant Diageo, it produces wines from several Napa Valley appellations, yet its base has always been Rutherford, where founder Georges de Latour planted French rootstock on the ranch he bought in 1900. Later, he imported Russian-born Andre Tchelistcheff, who became the vineyard's enologist for four decades and mentor to many of Napa Valley's fledgling winemakers. The main tasting room offers current releases; the Reserve Room is the place to try BV's flagship Georges de Latour Private Reserve Cabernet Sauvignon, as well as other Reserve and older-vintage wines.

If you're hungry, eat where the locals eat: at the Rutherford Grill, which shares a parkling lot with Beaulieu. The menu is varied, but the roasted chicken is so popular that the restaurant makes extra to meet takeout demand. La Luna Market, also in Rutherford, is an ultra-low-key Hispanic market that has a fabulous taqueria in the back. The *carne asada burrito* is pure gut-busting pleasure.

www.bvwines.com

4 | Rubicon Estate
1991 St. Helena Hwy., Rutherford, CA 94573; (800) 782-4266

Long before film director/producer Francis Ford Coppola purchased the Inglenook estate in 1975, it was famous for its 1960s Cabernet Sauvignons, which continue to be pulled from collectors' cellars and enjoyed with 40 years of bottle age. Yet a series of corporate owner-ships reduced Inglenook to basically a jug-wine brand, until Coppola purchased the estate—including founder Gustave Niebaum's Victorian house—and set about restoring the property to its former grandeur, along with the replanting of vineyards. In 2006, the winery changed

its focus and its name, from Niebaum-Coppola to the Rubicon Estate. The signature wine, the high-end Rubicon, is a suave Cabernet Sauvignon–based Bordeaux blend; the Cask Cabernet Sauvignon and Edizione Pennino Zinfandel are also standouts.

Visitors pay $25 to visit the estate, which includes valet parking, a tasting and an optional tour. They also get a feast for the eyes and sense of nostalgia. The chateau/museum is filled with artifacts from Niebaum's early days on the property and Coppola's family, including his father's music career, movie memorabilia and artworks.

www.rubiconestate.com

....

5 | Robert Mondavi Winery

7801 St. Helena Hwy., Oakville, CA 94562; (800) 766-6328

If there is only one winery you visit in California, this is it. Not only is it extremely visitor friendly, it reflects the life work of the late Robert Mondavi, the person most responsible for showing the world that great wines can be made in California. Robert Mondavi thought so much of the Oakville Bench as a home for Cabernet Sauvignon that he established the Robert Mondavi Winery there in 1966. With its colorful history and iconic California Mission architecture, Robert

▲ Famous Napa wine pioneer Gustave Niebaum built this grand Victorian mansion at Rubicon.

▲ The neatly manicured rows of vines at Rubicon in the heart of the Rutherford Bench

Mondavi Winery is one of the most recognized wineries in the world.

Although it has been under corporate ownership since 2004, when the Mondavis sold the company to Constellation Brands, little has changed in the winemaking and visitor amenities. It remains, as it always has been, a source of education for those interested in wine, food, art, music and, as Robert Mondavi often said, living the good life. There are more opportunities for visitors than can be listed here. They range from standard tastings, to classes on wine-tasting basics, to walking tours and tastings in the cellars, to To Kalon Vineyard treks with a picnic lunch, to a sit-down lunch at the winery, with dishes paired to specific wines.

The Mondavi Reserve Cabernet Sauvignon from the To Kalon Vineyard is the wine to die for, yet the winery produces several other varietals, among them Fumé Blanc, Chardonnay, Pinot Noir and Merlot. It's one-stop shopping, with additional benefits.

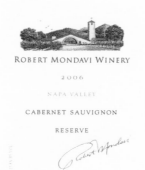

www.robertmondaviwinery.com

Opus One
7900 St. Helena Hwy., Oakville, CA 94562; (707) 944-9442

Exit Robert Mondavi Winery and look immediately to your right, to Opus One, a joint venture begun in 1980 by Robert Mondavi and Baron Philippe de Rothschild of Bordeaux's Château Mouton-Rothschild. It makes just one wine, the Cabernet Sauvignon-centric Opus One, and after years of VIP-only visitors, everyone can now tour the modern winery and taste the current-release wine. It might seem pricey to make an appointment to tour and taste just one wine (approximately $35), yet the Opus One experience is a rich one, detailing the history of the Mondavi–Rothschild partnership and showcasing architect Scott Johnson's three-level rotunda-style design that allows for gentle movement of wine via gravity flow, and the semicircular barrel room, where some 1,000 oak barrels, arranged in a single layer, appear to go on for infinity.

www.opusonewinery.com

Far Niente
1350 Acacia Dr., Oakville, CA 94562; (707) 944-2861

Far Niente—"without a care"—requires an appointment to visit, yet once you arrive, you'll have no worries about what's going on in the outside world. Take the guided tour through the lush gardens; the tri-level winery built into the hillside; and the vast aging caves, which were the first modern wine caves built in North America when excavation began in 1980; and the Carriage House, housing the late owner Gil Nickel's extensive classic car collection.

After the tour, taste the current releases of Far Niente's estate Chardonnay and Cabernet Sauvignon wines and perhaps an older library wine or two, paired with a local cheese. The tasting concludes with a sample of Dolce, a late-harvest dessert wine made in a style similar to the great Sauternes of Bordeaux.

www.farniente.com

▲ The Robert Mondavi Winery is one of the best-known landmarks in Napa Valley.

119

Napa, Western Highland

This is Napa Valley's most untouched wine route and one for lovers of big, powerful reds grown high above the valley floor. It also boasts the world-class sparkling wines of Schramsberg Vineyards and is ideal for those who enjoy winding roads, dramatic landscapes dotted with redwoods, oaks and wild blackberry vines. The Mayacamas Mountains separate Napa and Sonoma counties. The eastern Napa side includes, south to north, the Mount Veeder, Spring Mountain District and Diamond Mountain District appellations, which produce firmly structured, minerally wines that are worth the drive to taste and purchase.

Start in Napa (Mount Veeder), St. Helena (Spring Mountain) or Calistoga (Diamond Mountain) and go west into the Mayacamas. In stark contrast to Highway 29 and the Silverado Trail, there are no hotels, restaurants or gas stations, so fill up the tank and pack a picnic—or grab lunch in St. Helena or Calistoga.

◄ What the Western Highlands lack in amenities, they make up for in rugged beauty and stellar wines.

1 | Hess Collection

4411 Redwood Rd., Napa, CA 94558; (707) 255-1144

From Napa, take the Redwood Road up into the mountains. Keep an eye out for cyclists, who love the mountain roads, too. Seven scenic miles later you'll arrive at the Hess Collection on Mount Veeder, founded by Swiss businessman Donald Hess in 1978. The historic stone winery was originally built in 1903. From the terrace is a view straight into the Mayacamas range, a wild jumble of canyons and rocky outcroppings with steep patches of green vines.

Hess offers winery and vineyard tours daily and, by reservation, wine-and-cheese pairings. Estate wines include Hess's sturdy Mount Veeder Cabernet Sauvignon and Mount Veeder 19 Block Cuvée (a blend of Cabernet Sauvignon, Malbec, Syrah, Merlot, Petit Verdot and Cabernet Franc), as well as the classically made Mount Veeder Chardonnay. Single-vineyard wines from other Napa Valley AVAs are also available, including the Allomi Vineyard Sauvignon Blanc.

Come for the wines and stay for Hess's extensive collection of contemporary art. Admission to the art museum is included in the price of the tasting. Among the eye-popping exhibits are Franz Gertsch's huge, haunting portrait, *Johanna II*, and Leopoldo Maler's flaming Underwood typewriter.

www.hesscollection.com

▲ The Hess Collection of art features work by modern artists such as Andy Goldsworthy.

▲ Spring Mountain Vineyard's elegant Victorian house

2 | Spring Mountain Vineyard

2805 Spring Mountain Rd., St. Helena, CA 94574; (877) 769-4637

Next stop, the Spring Mountain District. From Highway 29 (also called Main Street) in St. Helena, turn left on Madrona Avenue and right on Spring Mountain Road, up the steep grade to Spring Mountain Vineyard. Many may recognize its elegant Victorian house, used in many scenes in the 1980s TV soap *Falcon Crest*. Today the house, vineyards and winery are owned by British businessman Jacob Safra and managed by Ron Rosenbrand and winemaker Jac Cole.

Named for the underground springs that burble to the surface on the property, Spring Mountain Vineyard was established by Tiburcio Parrott in the 1880s. It's now a merger of three separate properties— Miravalle, Chevalier and La Perla, each founded between 1873 and 1891—with an estate totaling 845 acres.

Spring Mountain's range of wines includes Sauvignon Blanc, Cabernet Sauvignon and small amounts of Syrah and Pinot Noir; the signature wine, the Elivette Cabernet Sauvignon-based blend, is rich, concentrated and long-lived.

Several tasting and tour options are offered, all by appointment. Don't miss the walking tour of the original estate and its vineyards, winery, caves and gardens.

www.springmtn.com

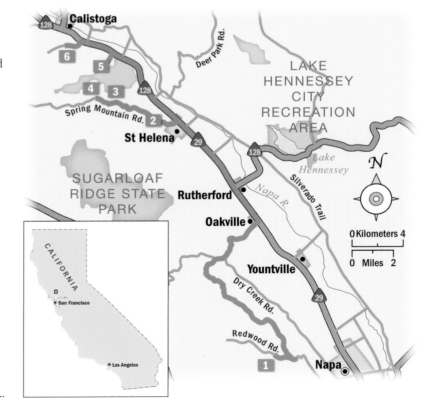

▲ Terra Valentine's highly ornate tasting room

3 | Terra Valentine
3787 Spring Mountain Rd., St. Helena, CA 94574; (707) 967-8340

Even remote Spring Mountain has its share of artworks, and Terra Valentine, just up the road from Spring Mountain Vineyard, is the place to see them. Founder Fred Aves made a fortune inventing accessories for automobiles and built a two-story stone winery on Spring Mountain, naming it Yverdon. Aves planted vineyards and made wine (apparently without great success) and was eccentrically creative in the stained-glass windows, grapevine-decorated spiral staircases, ornate doors and doorknobs, and other features of the winery that he crafted. Angus and Margaret Wurtele bought the property in 1999, renaming it Terra Valentine.

Tours and tastings are by appointment only; the stars are the Yverdon Single-Vineyard Cabernet Sauvignon and Wurtele Single-Vineyard Cabernet Sauvignon, and wine pairings with cheeses and chocolates.

www.terravalentine.com

4 | Pride Mountain Vineyards
4026 Spring Mountain Rd., St. Helena, CA 94574; (707) 963-4949

Even higher up on Spring Mountain Road is Pride Mountain, unique in the fact that half of its property is in Napa County and half in Sonoma County. Wines are produced from both regions and labeled as such. The crush pad is bisected by a brick inlay that defines the Napa/Sonoma County line, yet there is no question that this is Spring Mountain country, rugged and rocky, with dramatic vineyard plantings and a great view of Mount St. Helena.

Originally (and obviously) called Summit Ranch, the property was bought by the Pride family in 1989. Pride's use permit requires visitors to make appointments, though everyone who does so is welcome. Pride offers tastings of its outstanding Cabernet Sauvignons, Merlots, Cabernet Francs, Chardonnays and Viogniers, and a tour of the vineyards and the cool aging caves provides opportunities for visitors to enjoy the spectacular view at the top of the property.

www.pridewines.com

5 | Schramsberg Vineyards
1400 Schramsberg Rd., Calistoga, CA 94515; (800) 877-3623

Drive back down (east) Spring Mountain Road and reconnect with Highway 29, turning left toward Calistoga. Turn left on Peterson Drive and follow the signs to Schramsberg, where in 1965 Jack and Jamie Davies began restoring the 1862 ramshackle Jacob Schram property and producing sparkling wine. They employed the same techniques as those used in Champagne, and aged the wines in 2 miles (3 km) of caves dug by Chinese laborers employed by Schram.

Tastings are by appointment only, but this fascinating visit is well worth it, including a tour of the caves, which hold some 2 million bottles of bubbly; an educational discussion of how sparkling wine is made; and a formal tasting of several of the 8 to 10 sparklers made each year. Lush grounds and a lily pad, with its own metal-sculpture frog, surround the 120-year-old Victorian house that Jack and Jamie lived in until their deaths (his in 1998, hers in 2008). The youngest of their three sons, Hugh, is the Schramsberg president and oversees winemaking.

The Davies made traditional-method bubblies before the French Champagne houses opened their sparkling-wine houses in Napa Valley (Domaine Chandon, Domaine Carneros and Mumm Napa). They were the first winery in the United States to produce an all-Chardonnay blanc de blancs, and their wines have been served to presidents and by them—including Richard Nixon, who took the Schramsberg 1969 Blanc de Blancs to dinner in China with Premier Chou en-lai in 1972.

In 2001, Schramsberg began producing a Diamond Mountain District Cabernet Sauvignon from estate grapes, under the J. Davies label; it's become one of the finest red wines of the appellation.

www.schramsberg.com

Neat terraces of vines at Von Strasser, high up in the Diamond Mountain District

6 | Von Strasser Winery

1510 Diamond Mtn. Rd., Calistoga, CA 94515; (707) 942-0930

Return to Highway 29, turn left (north) and exit left on Diamond Mountain Road. As you leave the valley floor behind you enter the Diamond Mountain District high in the wild Mayacamas Mountain range that separates Napa and Sonoma valleys. Above the fog line Diamond Mountain enjoys long sunny days and has become renowned for its Cabernet Sauvignon.

The area is also home to the Von Strasser Winery, where Rudy von Strasser crafts Cabernet Sauvignons blended with heavy doses of Petit Verdot that are deeply colored, dense and tannic upon release. Like so many other mountain-grown Cabernets, they round out nicely after a few years of bottle age and keep improving for years.

Von Strasser typically makes six different Cabernet Sauvignons and one Zinfandel. They can be sampled by appointment at the winery's hospitality center, with a number of options available, including tours of the grounds and caves, and a wine-and-cheese pairing in the caves.

www.vonstrasser.com

Sparkling wine bottles in the Schramsberg cellars

Sierra Foothills

Even here in Amador County's Gold Country, where $13 million worth of shiny metal was mined, striking gold takes effort and luck. Fortunately, finding great old-vine Zinfandel requires neither. Savvy 49ers planted Zin, Carignane and Petite Sirah, plus a handful of Italian varietals. No Zin worshipper should miss this vine-studded shrine to the true roots of California's wine industry.

Just north of Sutter Creek is the Shenandoah Valley, near Plymouth. Here, at an altitude of 1,200 feet (365 m) in the Sierra foothills, red clay and volcanic soils give wines an earthy minerality that balances sun-baked fruit. Cool evening breezes help retain acidity. The region's current reputation is "Zin Heaven," but it's also a mecca for Mourvedre, Sangiovese and Barbera. Syrah is also rapidly gaining ground.

Most of the wineries do not charge tasting fees. They are very close together, so it's easy to overdo it. Pace yourself.

◄ From Karly Winery there are lovely views across the peaceful Shenandoah Valley.

1 | Bantam Cellars
10851 Shenandoah Rd., Plymouth, CA 95669; (209) 245-6677

From Highway 49 at Plymouth, take the Shenandoah Road exit and you'll come to Bantam Cellars on your left. Winemaker Garth Cobb, son of Karly Winery pioneer Buck Cobb (see right), makes vibrant Zinfandel and Italian varietals. New bottlings appear throughout the year: Look out for Cock of the Walk, a blend of old and new vine Zin aged in fine French oak, as well as vivacious Vermentino and Primitivo. Garth's wife, Jonna, raises bantam hens—and a few roosters—which provide the theme of the barn-style tasting room.

www.bantamcellars.com

2 | Vino Noceto
11011 Shenandoah Rd., Plymouth, CA 95669; (209) 245-6556

Almost next door, Vino Noceto is a Sangiovese specialist. The Hillside Sangiovese is worth the visit; Misto is a Sangiovese-based Chianti-style blend. Try the meaty Barbera or hearty Mistura, but don't miss Old Grandpere Zinfandel, from the oldest continuously farmed Zin vineyard in the country, planted in the 1860s.

www.noceto.com

3 | Karly Winery
11076 Bell Rd., Plymouth, CA 95669; (209) 245-3922

One of the five original wineries in the region, Karly offers old-fashioned hospitality and wine made in the same vein for 30 years by founder Buck Cobb, a former fighter pilot. The Pokerville Zin is a low-acid beauty for everyday quaffing. From 60-year-old Zinfandel vines blended with Petite Sirah, grown where Miwok Indians once stoked their campfires, Warrior Fires Zin delivers earthy charcoal and deep cherry. Deerhunter Zin packs a late-harvest punch. The monstrous Mourvedre is exceptionally smoky and peppery. An Orange Muscat, which they make in the style of an icewine, is an intense and zingy wakeup call for the palate. Fresh-baked bread and cheeses are a nice touch in the tasting room.

www.karlywines.com

4 | Cooper Vineyards
21365 Shenandoah School Rd., Plymouth, CA 95669; (209) 245-6181

For Cooper Vineyards turn right onto Shenandoah School Road, where you'll pass the Amador Flower Farm, a must-stop for lily lovers. Cooper Vineyards is a 60-acre operation with 15-plus varieties of grapes. The views in every direction are lovely. Everyone will find

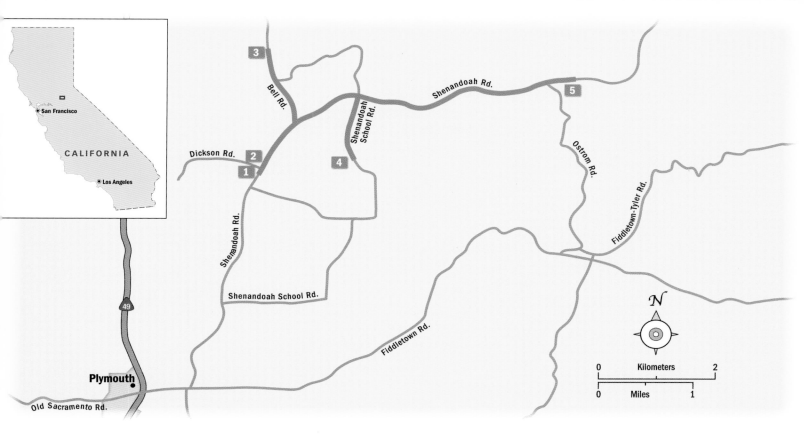

...mething to love at this spacious barrel-filled tasting room, with ...hairs to sit and enjoy the seemingly endless selection of well-made ...ines, along with nibbles of cheese and salami.

...Rhône whites demonstrate thoughtful winemaking—the Marsanne ...nectarines and honey, and the Roussanne is rich, creamy baked ...ears. Among the reds, Primitivo is bright and spicy, the Sangiovese ...pure cherry pie, and the Syrah is impressively packed with white ...epper. The Carignane wows with juicy fruity gum and red licorice, ...d the monstrous yet nimble Petite Sirah is a liquid blackberry-and-...ueberry cobbler.

...ww.cooperwines.com

Sobon Estate
14430 Shenandoah Rd., Plymouth, CA 95669; (209) 245-6554

...he plot is the site of one of California's oldest wineries, and the ...riginal winery houses a museum showcasing pioneer life in the ...800s. Zinfandels are sourced from various historic vineyards: Rich, ...usty blackberry Cougar Hill is from vines planted in 1928 on ...olcanic soils; Rocky Top, planted on granite in 1923, oozes ...spberry jam; Fiddletown hails from 100-year-old dry-farmed vines ...at create massive, long-lasting dusty cherry flavors.

...ww.sobonwine.com

▲ Picking grapes, here at Vino Noceto, is hard work.

Livermore Valley

Historic Livermore Valley is home to three of the oldest winemaking families in California—Concannon, Mirassou and Wente. Livermore also originated the most widely planted Chardonnay clone (Wente) in the United States and made the first varietally labeled Chardonnay (Wente, 1936), Sauvignon Blanc (1934) and Petite Sirah (1964).

A warm, red-friendly region, it is the only east–west valley in the state. Close enough to San Francisco Bay's cooling fog on the west end and far from it on the east end, Livermore can manage both Chardonnay with decent acidity and Sangiovese with hardly any. Strong suits include Petite Sirah, but look for cassis-laden Cabernet Sauvignon, zesty Zinfandel and righteous Rhônes.

◄ Vineyards surround the historic Ravenswood Historical Landmark in the heart of Livermore.

1 | Retzlaff Vineyards

1356 S. Livermore Ave., Livermore, CA 94550; (925) 447-8941

Begin your day in the Livermore Valley at Retzlaff Vineyards, next to historic Concannon, which was one of the valley's pioneer wineries back in the 1880s.

The first certified organic vineyard in the region, the Retzlaff estate was planted in the mid-1970s to Sauvignon Blanc, Chardonnay, Cabernet Sauvignon and Merlot, and nothing artificial in the way of herbicides or pesticides has ever been added, period. Unsurprisingly, the wines are as clean and spotless as you'd expect. Each label looks handwritten, and the fine Cabernets and Merlots are judiciously aged before release, some in French oak, some in American. These are the purest tasting wines in Livermore. There is even a Cabernet Sauvignon port, and a Zinfandel made from Napa Valley grapes.

Named for winemaker Bob Taylor's late wife, Gloria Retzlaff, the winery exudes country charm and genuine hospitality. One side of the barrel room is completely covered by a gargantuan Grey Riesling grapevine, a reminder of one of the early favorites that grew well in the Livermore Valley. Surrounded by enormous pepper trees, the grassy lawn is a delight to enjoy while relaxing in the Adirondack chairs.

www.retzlaffwinery.com

▲ Ready for a wine-tasting event in Wente's historic sandstone caves

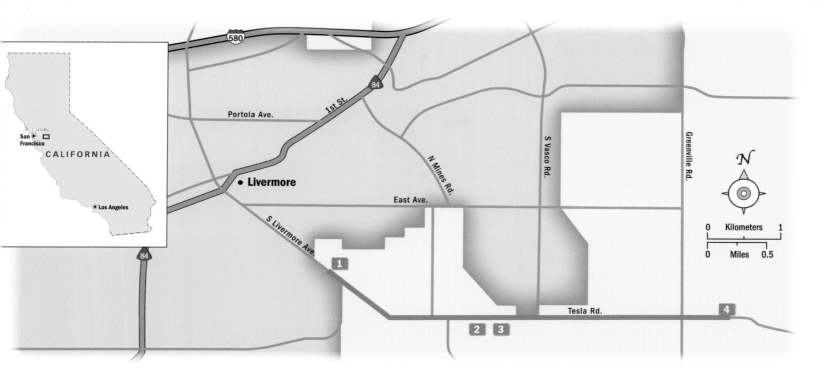

2 | La Rochelle Winery

5443 Tesla Rd., Livermore, CA 94550; (925) 243-6442

When you are driving down Tesla Road, tasting rooms abound, but some are better than others. An ideal place for a food-and-wine experience can be found at La Rochelle, a Pinot-lover's paradise, featuring tiny lot Pinot Noirs from the finest vineyards in the West. Here you'll experience a $20 seated tasting of outstanding Pinots, accompanied by a pairing platter of hand-selected artisan cheeses.

Owner Steven Mirassou, the fifth generation of his famous winemaking family to carry on the tradition, has two parallel passions: single-vineyard Pinot Noirs and boldly elegant Cabernet Sauvignons. He makes the latter under the Steven Kent label at the winery next door, where a superb pairing experience called The Table is available by reservation on weekends. His are the pinnacle of Livermore Cabernets.

www.lrwine.com

3 | Wente Vineyards

5565 Tesla Rd., Livermore, CA 94550; (925) 456-2300

Next stop on the tour is literally next door at historic Wente Vineyards, with beautiful refurbished grounds for lingering amid the stunning views of vine-covered hillsides. Fifth-generation winemaker Karl Wente's collection of wines are from the meticulously farmed estate vineyards in Monterey as well as in Livermore. Not to be missed are the top of the range Nth Degree Chardonnay and Pinot Noir. Wente's Small Lot lineup is impressive:

Unoaked Chardonnay lovers will appreciate Eric's Chardonnay (affectionately known as Big Daddy Eric's Chablis-style Chardonnay).

For a truly memorable taste of California wine history, arrange a one-hour private cave tasting experience at the Vineyard Tasting Room, 5050 Arroyo Road, about 5 miles (8 km) south of the Tesla Road estate [(925) 456-2405]. The Arroyo Road venue also houses a destination restaurant, golf course and big-name concerts in summer.

www.wentevineyards.com

4 | Bodegas Aguirre

8580 Tesla Rd., Livermore, CA 94550; (925) 606-0554

About 2 miles (3 km) down Tesla Road from Wente, you'll find Bodegas Aguirre, where winegrower and cardiac surgeon Dr. Ricardo Aguirre, who hails from El Salvador, makes powerful Petite Sirah and bold Bordeaux varietals and blends.

Don't miss the Estate Trio, a mouth-filling blend of Cabernet, Merlot and Petite Sirah, or the Castello Nuovo, a popular blend created by the doctor for his daughter's wedding. The good doctor also serves up some ravishing and memorable Cabernet Franc. The winery's distinctive label was created by a Picasso disciple.

www.bodegasaguirre.com

Poetic Cellars

Santa Cruz Mountains

The Santa Cruz Mountains grape-growing region encompasses nearly half a million acres, from Half Moon Bay in the north to Mount Madonna in the south. The climate is ideal for Burgundian varieties, and nearly 1,500 acres of primarily Chardonnay and Pinot Noir have thrived here since Paul Masson brought cuttings from France in the 1800s. Nearly half of the 70-plus bonded wineries make Pinot Noir. The high-altitude vineyards also produce Cabernets and Merlots of immense structure and intensity.

Your options are wide open if you visit on a weekend: Most wineries here are not open weekdays. Begin from Los Gatos, gateway to the Santa Cruz Mountains, and either return to this lovely gem of a town with a distinctly Old World flair, or continue southward to Monterey Bay. There, you can bed down in the cool, retro Santa Cruz, or the Greek isle–style seaside getaway, Capitola.

◄ The Santa Cruz Mountains are just high enough to allow sea fogs to spill over their tops.

1 | Burrell School Vineyards
24060 Summit Rd., Los Gatos, CA 95033; (408) 353-6290

Head south (toward Santa Cruz) on Highway 17 from Los Gatos and begin your day at the old red schoolhouse (built in 1890). The iconic bell tower is on your right on Summit Road, about 4 miles (6.5 km) from Highway 17, and about 15 minutes from Los Gatos.

Here, at a 1,600-foot (488-m) elevation, winemaker Dave Moulton crafts wines with school-themed names, including Teacher's Pet Chardonnay, Principal's Choice Pinot Noir, Honor Roll Merlot, Spring Break Syrah and Detention Zin. Top-of-the-line Valedictorian is a Bordeaux-style red blend. Decks off the tasting room provide tranquil views of the vineyards and massive fog-enveloped redwood forests descending to the sea. This spot was named Best Place for a Picnic by both *Sunset* magazine and the *San Francisco Chronicle*.

www.burrellschool.com

2 | Loma Prieta Winery
26985 Loma Prieta Way, Los Gatos, CA 95033; (408) 353-2950

Continue on Summit Road for about 5 miles (8 km) to reach the spectacular Loma Prieta Winery, the highest in the region at 2,300 feet (700 m). A bird's-eye view of the Pacific Ocean and

Monterey Bay awaits, and when the fog lifts, the shining sands of Capitola sparkle below. The patio is a great spot for lunch, accompanied by a glass of Loma Prieta's award-winning Pinot Noir.

Owners Amy and Paul Kemp have created a sun-drenched oasis in the shadow of Loma Prieta Mountain, where the 1989 Bay Area earthquake originated. The label depicts Bodo the magician, flying over Loma Prieta (which means "praying woman"), with a glass of Pinot in hand. At the mountain's base is a jagged red line depicting the earthquake fault. There are no faults in the well-made wines, which include Cabernet, Pinotage and Viognier, as well as Pinot Noir.

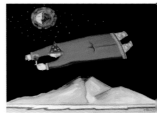

www.lomaprietawinery.com

3 | Silver Mountain Vineyards
Silver Mountain Dr., off Miller Cut Off, Soquel, CA 95063; (408) 353-2278

Third stop should be Silver Mountain, on Miller Cut Off, down Soquel–San Jose Road, with glorious views across Monterey Bay. Proprietor Jerold O'Brien is one of the patriarchs of winemaking in

regionalevents

Pinot Paradise □ March

This Pinot Noir-exclusive event allows visitors to discover the wines from the many producers in the region and engage in seminars, VIP tastings and more.　　　　　www.scmwa.com

Vintners' Festival □ April

The ever popular Santa Barbara festival invites visitors to meet member vintners, taste wines and enjoy food and music in a relaxed outdoor environment.　　　　　www.sbcountywines.com

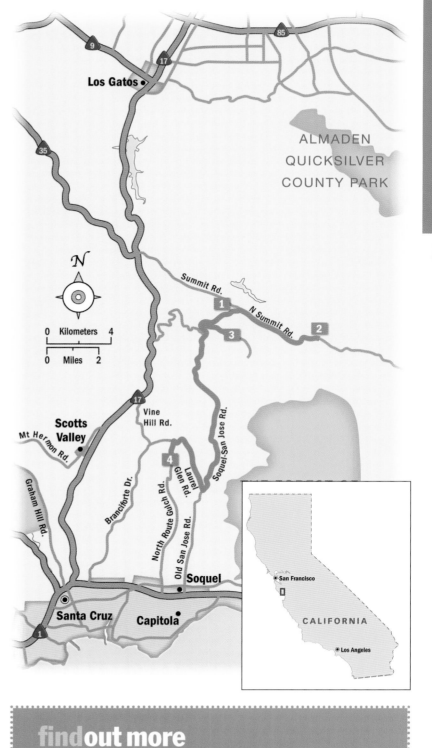

he region. His "triple-green" project uses solar power to make the winery self-sufficient in energy and collects rainwater from the massive winery roof. Jerold's organically grown Chardonnay is ntense and haunting, and his Pinots, crafted by winemaker Tony Craig (who also makes Sonnet wines here), are exemplary. Open aturday afternoon by appointment or visit the new tasting room, art of the Surf City Vintners Group on the west side of Santa Cruz ity [(831) 466-0559].

ww.silvermtn.com

Poetic Cellars

5000 N. Rodeo Gulch Rd., Soquel, CA 95073; (831) 462-3478

Make your final winery stop of the day at Poetic Cellars, just off aurel Glen Road from Soquel–San Jose Road. Winemaker Katy ovell puts poetry in the bottles and her partner, Joseph, adds lyrics o the labels. Katy is a classical flautist and textile artist; in the winery er forte is Mourvedre and Petite Sirah. She weaves beautiful blends ke Mantra, an edgy, fragrant combination of Mourvedre, Syrah and angiovese; and Quatrain, a rich and playful mélange of Merlot, infandel, Syrah and Petite Sirah. Enjoy a glass of Santa Cruz Mountains Chardonnay or Pinot Noir as you relax beneath old oak ees in this tranquil mountainside setting—ideal for weddings.

ww.poeticcellars.com

findout more

- www.scmwa.com
  The website of the Santa Cruz Mountains Winegrowers Association.

The Real Monterey

It is often said that wine tastes best where it's made, like eating a peach right off the tree. If a road trip suits your style, welcome to Monterey wine country, John Steinbeck style. This is one of the few places on the planet where you can see fields of asparagus, romaine and broccoli right next to vineyards. The Salinas Valley in Monterey is America's salad bowl. It also provides aromatic whites to wineries statewide where Riesling, Sauvignon Blanc and Gewürztraminer are off limits.

The Santa Lucia Highlands, a 40-mile (64-km) mountain ridge topping out at 2,300 feet (700 m) along the eastern edge of the Salinas Valley, are renowned for plump extracted Pinots, while the benchlands produce ethereal Pinots and apple-crisp Chardonnays.

Of the 18,000 acres of vineyards in Monterey, 5,200 are in the beautiful, windswept Santa Lucia Highlands along the crop-flanked Salinas River. The area has a haunting, rugged beauty.

◀ The dry, parched hills along the eastern side of the Salinas Valley

1 | Paraiso Vineyards

38060 Paraiso Springs Rd., Soledad, CA 93960; (831) 678-0300

From Highway 101, take the Arroyo Seco Road exit and go straight to where the road becomes Paraiso Springs. Take a right at Foothill (you'll see the Paraiso sign) and turn up the driveway.

Marvel at the quietude that surrounds you here at the southern end of what the locals call "the Santa Lucia bench" above the Salinas River valley. Admire the immaculate vineyards of pioneer winegrower Richard Smith, who back in 1973 named this place "paradise." The maritime climate here, where the wind is always blowing, is perfect for Pinot Noir—Paraiso's flaghip varietal—and Chardonnay. Clinging to the steep hillsides, cool-climate Syrah translates the chill winds that meet the sun-warmed valleys into delightfully spicy white pepper. Safe from the buffeting breezes, enjoy the vista from the country cottage-style tasting room and recharge with elegant Eagles' Perch Chardonnay, ponder a Pinot, savor a Syrah, then refresh with racy Riesling.

www.paraisovineyards.com

▲ Having fun with friends and family at Pessagno Winery

2 Hahn Estates

37700 Foothill Rd., Soledad, CA 93960; (866) 925-7994

Go left out of Paraiso onto Foothill Road. The colorful rooster on the sign (*hahn* is rooster in German) points the way to Hahn Estates' tasting room, in a spectacular setting overlooking the vineyards, between the Salinas Valley and the mountains. Here you'll enjoy a wide selection of Smith & Hook brand wines, along with the well-made Hahn Estates wines (don't miss the Merlot). Step up to the Lucienne range of single-vineyard beauties crafted from estate fruit: Doctor's Vineyard Pinot Noir is the prescription for perfection.

www.hahnestates.com

3 Wrath Wines

35801 Foothill Rd., Soledad, CA 93960; (831) 678-2212

At the intersection of River Road and Foothill, you'll find Wrath Vineyards. Winemaker Sabrine Rodems crafted wines under the San Saba label for years and is now guiding Wrath on its new path to small-lot greatness (Syrah and Pinot Noir stand out). Arrange an appointment to taste the full Wrath lineup; you can taste San Saba wines, including the well-structured Merlot, without a fee.

www.wrathwines.com

4 Pessagno Winery

1645 River Rd., Salinas, CA 93908; (831) 675-9463

Continue on River Road to the welcoming rustic-style tasting room of Pessagno. Winemaker Steve Pessagno is a local legend. Using grapes from some of the best vineyards in the Central Coast region, his Chardonnays and Pinot Noirs are as big as his handshake and his smile. He likes his oak and is not afraid to use it when the fruit can stand up to it.

www.pessagnowines.com

ON A MISSION

If history is your thing, don't miss Mission Soledad on Fort Romie Road. Step back in time—all the way to 1791—when it became the 13th mission in California. Alone in the windswept fields, with the towering mountain wall to the west, you'll understand why Soledad means "place of sorrows."

▲ You can't miss the entrance to Hahn Estates.

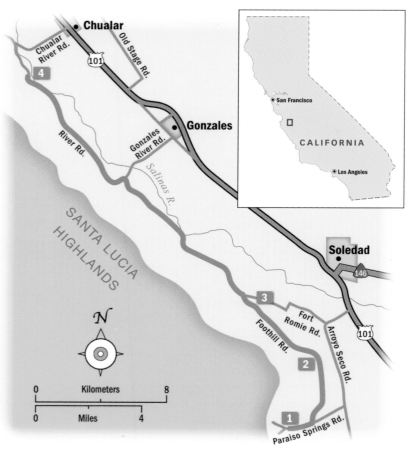

Edna Valley

Far from the crowds and the massive heat of the Paso Robles region to the northeast lies the Edna Valley—about 5 miles (8 km) east of the Pacific Ocean. Blessed with frequent morning sea fogs and constant sea breezes, the 8-mile (13-km)-long valley runs northeast to southwest under the watchful eye of dormant volcanoes known as the Seven Sisters. Ancient marine soils lend distinctive minerality to Chardonnay and Pinot Noir, the dominant plantings here. The scenery is rural and stunning, but a nearby airport will have you occasionally turning your eyes skyward.

Make the town of San Luis Obispo your anchor if you like eclectic dining and accommodation; go for Arroyo Grande if your preference is more casual and country-western. If you're coming from the south, exit at Traffic Way and take Bridge Street through old Arroyo Grande, where you can grab coffee, pastries or picnic fixings.

◄ Edna Valley is one of the coolest grape-growing regions in California's central coast.

1 | Kynsi Winery
2212 Corbett Canyon Rd., Arroyo Grande, CA 93420; (805) 544-8461

Head up Corbett Canyon Road to Kynsi, a family-run operation where the parched, windswept landscape has the wistful feel of an old Western. If you're lucky, you may catch a glimpse of the real-life barn owl portrayed on the label. The winemaking philosophy here is one of minimal intervention, and the resulting Pinot Noirs and Syrah are precise and highly acclaimed.

www.kynsi.com

2 | Chamisal Vineyards
7525 Orcutt Rd., San Luis Obispo, CA 93401; (805) 541-9463

Take Tiffany Ranch Road, where you'll admire the handsome horses and magnificent gates of the manicured ranches. From Tiffany Ranch, go left on Orcutt Road to Chamisal (formerly Domaine Alfred), home of impeccable estate Chardonnays and exquisite Pinots that really define the region's terroir. Initially planted in 1973, this was the first vineyard in Edna Valley. A few straggly Cabernet and Merlot survivors guard the gate, but the bulk of the 80-acre vineyard

▲ Like most wineries in the Edna Valley, Chamisal specializes in Chardonnay and Pinot Noir.

s Chardonnay and Pinot, with some lovely Pinot Gris, Grenache and Syrah. Seek out the Califa designates, an Indian word meaning "the prettiest one." Picnic here for the high, lonesome views.

www.domainealfred.com

3 | Edna Valley Vineyard

2585 Biddle Ranch Rd., San Luis Obispo, CA 93401; (805) 544-5855

From the knolltop tasting room, a fabulous perspective on the area's geography, as well as a demonstration vineyard, await you. The spacious, crowd-friendly facility with lots of retail is well-stocked with picnic supplies. Dine outside among the trees and revel in the unrivaled views of the volcanic peaks to the north. Estate-grown Chardonnay is the focus here, but the lineup offers group-pleasing variety across reds and whites.

www.ednavalleyvineyard.com

4 | Claiborne & Churchill

2649 Carpenter Canyon Rd., San Luis Obispo, CA 93401; (805) 544-4066

Named for husband and wife Claiborne Thompson and Fredericka Churchill, the winery was founded in 1983 to produce fruity but dry Alsace-style wines. For expertly made aromatic whites, especially the Dry Riesling and Gewürztraminer, Claiborne & Churchill is still the standard of measure, but every wine here is worth trying, and many are unavailable outside the winery. The Pinots hang like magic on your palate, and the dessert wines are divine. The winery and tasting room are housed in an environmentally friendly straw bale building, which provides perfect insulation.

www.claibornechurchill.com

5 | Tolosa

4910 Edna Rd., San Luis Obispo, CA 93401; (805) 782-0500

Named for the San Luis Obispo Mission de Tolosa, this winery and vineyard just before the airport is an impressive enclave of stainless steel. Oceans of tanks in the cellar are visible through the glass wall of the modern, chic tasting room, where you can navigate a sea of Pinots and good Chardonnays. Tastings on weekends feature wine-and-cheese pairings. The beautifully rendered 3-D map of their 800 acres of local vineyard plantings is a lesson in the area's topography.

www.tolosawinery.com

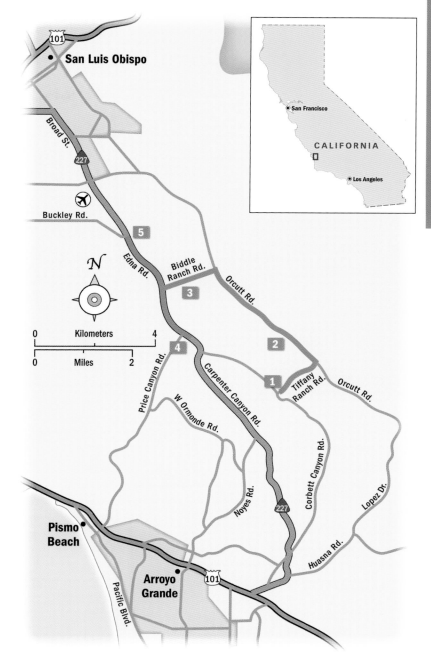

findout more

- **www.slowine.com**
  Website of the San Luis Obispo Vintners Association, with information on wineries (including all those on this tour), wine-related events, accommodation and places to eat.

Santa Maria Valley

This windswept benchland bisected by the Sisquoc and Santa Maria Rivers is rich in crops. Squash is grown at the southern end, broccoli, cauliflower and strawberries are to the north, closer to the town of Santa Maria. Once the morning fogs have burned off, you get a magical combination of consistently sunny days with cool temperatures because of the maritime breezes. Hence, Santa Maria Valley produces excellent Chardonnay and Pinot Noir, as well as some enticing Bordeaux blends. Traveling along narrow and windy Foxen Canyon Road requires concentration, so admire the scenery with caution.

You can get the essence of this unique place by visiting a handful of small family-run wineries, where you'll probably see the winemaker or his daughter tending the bar; the larger ones to the south (Fess Parker and Zaca Mesa) are more commercial, as are the wines.

◄ The winery at Kenneth Volk Vineyards overlooks the Tepusquet Creek.

1 | Foxen Winery
7600 Foxen Canyon Rd., Santa Maria, CA 93454; (805) 937-4251

Start with Foxen, a 20-minute drive up Alisos Canyon from 101. You'll see centuries-old cactus at the gateposts of the original ranchos, with ancient oaks amid seas of row crops. Foxen has two tasting rooms: 7600 Foxen Canyon Road is the all-solar newer one, featuring bountiful Burgundies (legendary Bien Nacido Block 8 Pinot Noir) and head-turning Rhônes. Upgrade your tasting fee to include the Bordeaux-style wines at the original old wooden shed at 7200, where you may spy owners Bill Wathen and Dick Doré, who began making wine here in 1985. The anchor on the label pays homage to Dick's great-great grandfather, a sea captain, who used it as his cattle brand. Before leaving, you may want to purchase a T-shirt that reads: "If you don't know Foxen, you don't know Dick . . . or Bill."

www.foxenvineyard.com

2 | Rancho Sisquoc Winery
6600 Foxen Canyon Rd., Santa Maria, CA 93454; (805) 934-4332

Next stop should be Rancho Sisquoc, a 37,000-acre ranch on the banks of the Sisquoc River. You'll pass the historic San Ramon Chapel that graces the winery's label. Amble down the gravel driveway past fields of cauliflower and lowing cattle, and you'll be warmly welcomed in the beautiful old barn. Founded in 1972, this is one of the region's original wineries. The wide selection of primarily estate-grown wines will tempt you to linger over lush Chardonnay, crisply made Riesling and sassy Sylvaner, oozing of spicy peaches and lime. Rancho Sisquoc is the only California winery to grow

SANTA MARIA AMENITIES

Santa Maria Valley is known as California's barbecue capital, and a number of local restaurants specialize in the authentic Santa Maria BBQ. This heralded feast features prime sirloin, about 3 inches (7.5 cm) thick, cooked over red-oak coals and seasoned with salt, pepper and garlic. Standard accompaniments are salsa, green salad, Pinquito beans and toasted French bread with melted butter. Add a bottle of Santa Maria Valley wine—you'll be in Santa Maria heaven.

Historic Santa Maria Inn [(800) 462-4276] was built to satisfy the lodging needs of Hollywood guests on their way to Hearst Castle. Stay in one of 30 star rooms named for greats like Gloria Swanson, Gregory Peck and Doris Day. There is also an on-site dining and tap room, where John Wayne put back a few beers.

...ylvaner. Don't miss the Sisquoc River Red, award-winning Cabernet and muscular Malbec. Cellar Select Meritage is a smooth-as-silk Bordeaux blend aged in French oak.

www.ranchosisquoc.com

3 | Riverbench Vineyard

6020 Foxen Canyon Rd., Santa Maria, CA 93454; (805) 937-8340

Continue on Foxen Canyon to Riverbench, surrounded by the third oldest Chardonnay and Pinot Noir vineyards in the Valley, planted in 1973. The tasting room is in a restored 1920s house by the river; it's a great place to relax with a bottle of Riverbench's perfectly balanced estate Chardonnay and a French-style picnic while drinking in the view. World-class Pinots invite your contemplation. All the wines are made in limited quantities, with some exclusive to the tasting room.

www.riverbench.com

4 | Kenneth Volk Vineyards

5320 Tepusquet Rd., Santa Maria, CA 93454; (805) 938-7896

Across the river, on Tepusquet Road, you'll find Kenneth Volk's winery, producing a cornucopia of well-made wines from nearby vineyards, including Bien Nacido Pinot Noir, Mourvedre from Enz, plus some righteous Cabernets from the Westside of Paso Robles. Unoaked Jaybird Chardonnay is a delight. Winemaker Ken hasn't met too many grapes he doesn't like. He aims to encourage more people to appreciate heirloom varieties such as Negrette and peppery Cabernet Pfeiffer.

www.volkwines.com

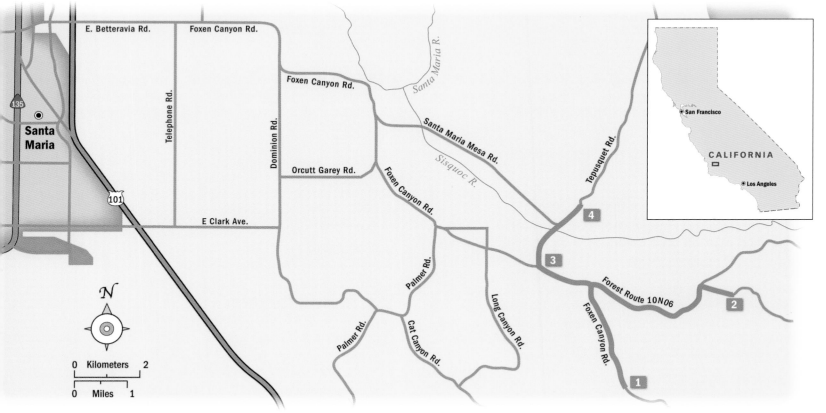

▲ You might catch a glimpse of the fermentation process if you visit a winery during the crush.

135

A Stroll in Los Olivos

To the north of Santa Barbara, the Santa Ynez Valley's spectacular setting between two mountain ranges (Sierra Madre and Santa Ynez) and two rivers makes it a sweet place to grow the Rhône varietals of Syrah, Roussanne and Grenache. Sufficient warmth in some spots ripens the red Bordeaux varieties of Cabernet Sauvignon and Merlot. Fields of peppers nestle between palatial horse ranches, and vineyards share manicured hillsides with lavender. The town of Los Olivos in the heart of the valley is a perfect place to begin unfolding this many-faceted region.

Turn off Highway 154 at Grand Avenue to downtown Los Olivos. Here time stops, literally. None of the clocks on any of the buildings seem to be working, so you might as well just go with the timeless flow. Salute the flagpole in the middle of the Mayberry-perfect town center as you find a shady place to park. You won't need your car.

◀ Los Olivos in the heart of Santa Barbara wine country is a relaxing place to do some wine tasting.

1 | Carhartt Winery
2990A Grand Ave., Los Olivos, CA 93441; (805) 688-0685

Begin with a visit to the tiniest tasting room in America, at 300 square feet (28 m²). Carhartt combines farmer Mike Carhartt's passion for growing fruit with wife Brooke's love of making small lots of wine. Syrah, Merlot and spicy Sangiovese are the standout wines.

www.carharttvineyard.com

2 | Daniel Gehrs
2939 Grand Ave., Los Olivos, CA 93441; (805) 693-9686

Stroll down to Heather Cottage, Daniel Gehrs's historic tasting room and gift shop. Dan has been making wine for more than 30 years: After founding Congress Springs (now Savannah-Chanelle) in the Santa Cruz Mountains, he worked at nearby Zaca Mesa and started his own label in 1990. Delirio is Dan's fruit-packed blend of Sangiovese, Cabernet and Merlot. The varietal Cabernet Franc, from Mission Estate near the old Santa Inés mission, is blueberries and perfume in a glass. Pinot Noir and aromatic whites such as Riesling and Chenin Blanc are made in limited quantities.

www.danielgehrswines.com

3 | Longoria Wines
2935 Grand Ave., Los Olivos, CA 93441; (866) 759-4637

Another quaint building—originally a machine shop dating back to the early 1900s—houses Longoria's tasting room. Behind the building is a small patio and garden, where you can relax while enjoying the wine. One of the pioneers of the region, Rick Longoria, began the label in 1982.

Check out the prodigious lineup here: Standouts are Pinot Grigio, Albariño, Clover Creek Syrah, Lovely Rita Pinot Noir, Fe Ciega Pinot Noir and the Blues Cuveé, which features a different musician on the label each year. Evidence, a striking Bordeaux blend, bears Rick's mantra: "I submit this wine as evidence you don't have to go to France to find a grand cru...."

www.longoriawine.com

4 | Carina Cellars
2900 Grand Ave., Los Olivos, CA 93441; (805) 688-2459

Carina Cellars is a recent addition to the Los Olivos wine scene. This is serious Syrah territory, where you can delight in the voices of different vineyards all tuned by the same winemaker. Rhône blends Clairvoyant, Sibylline and "7 Percent" combine Syrah with

▲ Dramatic benchlands tower over the vineyards of Santa Ynez Valley near Los Olivos.

Mourvedre, Grenache or Viognier. Iconoclast is a blend of Cabernet Sauvignon and Syrah made in very small amounts. The wines are serious, but the atmosphere is cordial, with a smack of irreverence that appeals to the youthful crowd.

www.carinacellars.com

5 | Stolpman

2434 Alamo Pintado Ave., Los Olivos, CA 93441; (805) 688-0400

Truly distinguished wines can be found at Stolpman's tasting room just off the town center. The gorgeous chandeliers set the scene for high-class wines made in a carefully crafted style reflective of serious grape-tending. The estate vineyard is 160 acres and was planted in the early 1990s. The Roussanne is elegant and strong, the Sangiovese racy, while the Hilltops Syrah smolders with white pepper and roasted jalapeños.

www.stolpmanvineyards.com

LOS OLIVOS AND SANTA YNEZ AMENITIES

The Santa Ynez Inn at Santa Ynez, 4 miles (6.4 km) south of Los Olivos, is a modern interpretation of a fabulous Victorian mansion, with a health spa tucked behind a wedding-ready garden. Gourmet dinners and phenomenal breakfasts keep you fueled for adventure.

For lunch in Los Olivos, grab a sandwich at Country Market and sit outside with the fountain burbling in the background. Wine Country wine shop is a great option for tasting in Los Olivos, typically offering wines from small high-end wineries with no tasting rooms.

For dinner, Los Olivos Café & Wine Merchant has locally sourced, flavorful food and an impressive list of local wines. It was featured as a location in the movie *Sideways*.

find out more

- **www.sbcountywine.com**
  The website for the Santa Barbara County Vintners' Association has links to more than 100 wineries, plus touring maps, dining and lodging, and wine-related events.

- **www.losolivosca.com**
  The website for Los Olivos town.

Temecula

To most Americans, the phrase "wine country" means Napa Valley; to the sophisticated it may also mean Sonoma County or even Santa Barbara. Many other regions of California have prime growing conditions, but one region that the experts, as late as 1972, said was not right for planting fine wine grapes for table wine was the area known as Temecula Valley.

This narrow swath through the southern Riverside County hills offers a perfect harmony of climate and well-drained soils to create a new wine country. Just 60 miles (97 km) north of San Diego and 90 miles (145 km) southeast of Los Angeles, the area is cooled by ocean breezes that come in from the southwest. Today the region draws thousands of visitors every weekend. Touring the wineries here is easy since nearly all are located on Rancho California Road. Most are within a 3-mile (5-km) radius and all are hospitable.

◀ Sip sparkling wine while ballooning over the breathtaking Temecula Valley.

1 | Hart Winery

41300 Avenido Biona, Temecula, CA 92591; (951) 676-6300

Drive east on Rancho California Road from the freeway. After 3 miles (5 km) you'll find this winery on the left. Schoolteachers Joe and Nancy Hart were among the first to blaze the Rancho California Road trail, founding their winery here when the area was still brush and undeveloped rocky ridges.

Today Hart remains small, unaffected by the development of homes and wineries around it, and white-bearded Joe continues to make some of the best wines in the region, both reds and whites.

www.thehartfamilywinery.com

2 | Maurice Carrie Winery

34225 Rancho California Rd., Temecula, CA 92591; (951) 676-1711

The winery, in the style of a Victorian farmhouse, has attractive picnic grounds. Winemaker Gus Vizgirda is crafting some stellar wines, including refreshing picnic-style whites, such as Sauvignon Blanc, Chenin Blanc and unoaked Chardonnay. The range also includes red, semisweet and sweet wines.

www.mauricecarriewinery.com

▲ Vine-based treatments are on offer at the GrapeSeed Spa at the South Coast Winery, Resort and S

3 | South Coast Winery, Resort and Spa

34843 Rancho California Rd., Temecula, CA 92591; (951) 587-9463

A couple of miles farther down Rancho California Road is by far the most sophisticated winery operation in the area, owned by developer Jim Carter. Carter's winemaker, Texas-reared Jon McPherson, makes an astounding array of excellent wines, both whites and reds, with dessert and sparkling wines recently added to the line. He earned the winery the title of Best Winery in California for its showing in 2008 and 2009 at the California State Fair.

The spacious tasting room has beamed ceilings and a terrace where you can sip your wine. Don't miss the superb gift shops—and the Vineyard Rose Restaurant is the best in the area.

www.wineresort.com

4 | Wilson Creek Winery & Vineyards

35960 Rancho California Rd., Temecula, CA 92591; (951) 699-9463

Ken Wilson's handsome courtyard-graced property, one of the earlier developments along Rancho California Road, now sits within proximity of many neighboring wineries. The friendly tasting room offers a large range of wines, and the elegant Creekside Grille restaurant is an added attraction.

www.wilsoncreekwinery.com

TEMECULA AMENITIES

Accommodation on offer varies from the sophisticated South Coast Winery, Resort & Spa (see left) and Temecula Creek Inn [44501 Rainbow Canyon Road, (951) 676-5631], to Loma Vista Bed and Breakfast [33350 La Serena Way, (951) 676-7047].

For casual but elegant dining, try the restaurant at the South Coast Winery, Resort & Spa (see left) or Wilson Creek Winery (see left), or Carol's Restaurant (lunch only, Wed.–Sun.) at the Baily Winery [33440 La Serena Way, (951) 676-9243].

A sunrise hot-air balloon flight makes a memorable start to your day's tasting. Reserve your flight with A Grape Escape [(800) 965-2122, www.hotairtours.com] or California Dreamin' [(800) 373-3359, www.californiadreamin.com].

findout more

- www.temeculawines.org
  The website of the Temecula Valley Winegrowers Association includes winery listings and information to help you make the most of your visit.

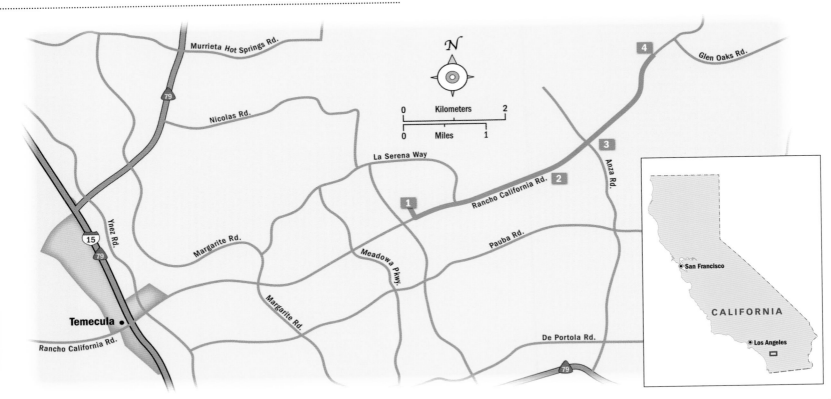

Western Colorado

One of America's greatest natural-beauty states is Colorado, with the Grand Canyon and the Grand Mesa, towering mountains, streams, forests and clean cities. The quality of the wines here is startlingly high given the industry's relative youth. Literally dozens of Coloradoans are trying to change the viticultural common wisdom by planting grapes and making excellent wine despite numerous problems such as cold nighttime temperatures.

Roughly 90 percent of Colorado grapes come from the western high plains, from the Grand Valley AVA at Grand Junction and the West Elks AVA 50 miles (80 km) south around Hotchkiss and Paonia. What makes the "vineyard" areas look odd is the barren moonscape cliffs surrounding the patches of green on which nothing, not even scrub brush, will grow. Most Colorado wines are sold in tasting rooms, and this is the best way to taste and buy the better ones.

◀ Terror Creek has the highest-altitude vineyards in the United States.

1 | Two Rivers Winery & Chateau
2087 Broadway, Grand Junction, CO 81503; (970) 255-1471

Bob and Billie Witham founded Two Rivers in 1999, and the handsome winery building—located near the the two entrances to the Colorado National Monument—is now a destination for great wines as well as a site for weddings, social events and outdoor concerts.

The winery makes a stellar array of wines, from a floral Riesling to dark reds, and a superb blended wine, the Vintner's Blend. This is one of the longest-lived wines in the state. Winemaker Tyre Lawson crafts wines of elegance and European character, such as the Burgundian Chardonnay.

www.tworiverswinery.com

2 | Plum Creek Cellars
3708 G Rd., Palisade, CO 81526; (970) 464-7586

A giant "Chardonnay Chicken" adorns the front entrance to this attractive property founded in 1984 by Doug and Sue Phillips. The vineyards were planted near Paonia in 1980, and today the winery is one of the most respected in the region. A great deal of credit for that reputation is the work of winemaker Jenne Baldwin, who makes a series of exceptional wines, including superb Cabernet Sauvignon, Cabernet Franc, Sangiovese, a terrific Riesling and a stylish Palisade Rosé. The large, inviting tasting room plays host to numerous hospitality events.

www.plumcreekwinery.com

3 | Canyon Wind Cellars
3907 North River Rd., Palisade, CO 81526; (970) 464-0888

Norm Christiansen established this stylish hacienda-designed winery on one of the best vineyard sites in all of Colorado and hired Robert Pepi of the Napa Valley to be consultant for the remarkable project.

The winery and its vineyards, literally adjacent to the Colorado River, produces superb Cabernet Sauvignon, which is grown in cobbly soils on the high desert that typically is raked by afternoon winds. The wines are stylish and world-class and also include Pinot Gris, Chardonnay (both oaked and unoaked) and a delightful Sauvignon Blanc.

www.canyonwindcellars.com

4 Black Bridge Winery

15836 Black Bridge Rd., Paonia, CO 81428; (970) 527-6838

Situated between the Grand Mesa and the Gunnison National Forest in Paonia, Lee Bradley's winery was one of the first in the state to grow grapes for fine wine back in 1977, long before Colorado had a recognized wine industry. Because the vineyards are located on the cool north fork of the Gunnison River, cooler-climate varieties, such as Pinot Noir and Chardonnay, were particularly successful. Starting in 2005, the winery began to produce wines under its own brand.

The Black Bridge tasting room is also where visitors can taste the hard-to-get wines of Alfred Eames Cellars, Jack Rabbit Hill and other local wineries.

www.blackbridgewinery.com

5 Terror Creek Winery

17445 Garvin Mesa Rd., Paonia, CO 81428; (970) 527-3484

Probably the highest-altitude winery in the United States is Terror Creek, at more than 6,400 feet (1950 m) above sea level. The altitude brings cold weather that slows the ripening of the grapes, one of the reasons that the Alsace-styled whites, such as Riesling and Gewurztraminer, are so distinctive. Joan Mathewson, owner and winemaker, trained in Europe, where she developed a sense of the best style for such wines. Terror Creek is one of the top wineries in the West Elks area which has Colorado's best potential for cool-climate grapes.

www.terrorcreekwinery.com

▲ Barren moonscape cliffs tower over the vineyards in western Colorado.

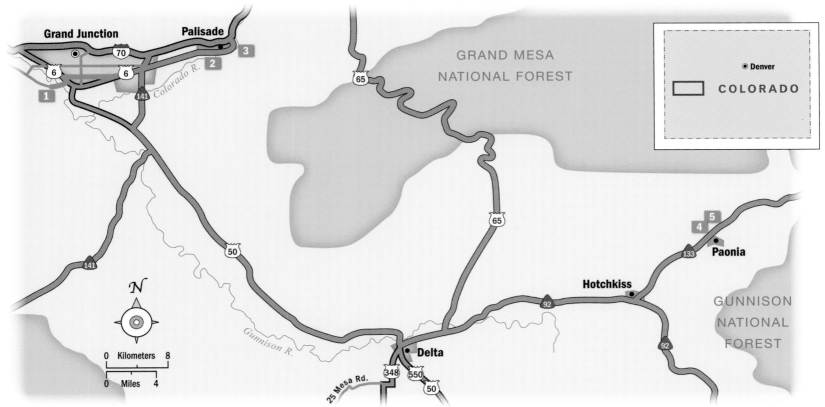

Denver/Boulder Area

The three wineries in this tour may be city-based, but their wines are among the best in the state. Almost all of Colorado's winemakers get their fruit from the two vineyard areas in the western high plains of the state covered in Tour 40.

Just a bit east, the Continental Divide rises up toward Aspen and other ski resort areas, where altitudes rise to 14,000 feet (4,267 m) and more, and the land only dips some 300+ miles (480+ km) later to the relatively low-lying "mile-high" Denver and Boulder areas, which are both in the so-called Front Range. The Front Range gets so cold in winter that no *vinifera* grape vines can survive the low temperatures.

To visit wineries with vineyards planted nearby requires a four-hour drive from the Denver/Boulder area to reach the Grand Valley and West Elks AVAs along the Colorado River and the North Fork of the Gunnison River.

◄ The mountains surrounding Denver drive the local wineries to source their grapes from farther afield.

1 | Balistreri Vineyards
1946 E. 66th Ave., Denver, CO 80229; (303) 287-5156

This small family-owned operation, founded by John Balestreri, is located in an industrial area outside of downtown Denver and makes remarkably fine red wines, notably an award-winning Petite Sirah. To make wines as naturally as possible, the winery adds no sulfur dioxide and does no fining or filtration.

One of the more popular wines is a Little Feet Merlot, using grapes that were foot-stomped by children at the winery's annual harvest party held in October.

www.balistreriwine.com

2 | BookCliff Vineyards
1501 Lee Hill Rd. #17, Boulder, CO 80304; (303) 449-9463

Just south of the Pearl Street Mall, this small operation gets its fruit from family-owned vineyards planted nearly two decades ago in DeBeque Canyon, facing the cooling Colorado River and underneath the BookCliff escarpment in western Colorado. Cool evening breezes prevent frost and provide moderate growing temperatures for the vines.

▲ Vineyards near Grand Junction provide grapes for the urban wineries of Denver and Boulder.

Owners John Garlich and his wife, Ulla Merz, began the winery in 1999, and early reviews were excellent. A wide array of stylish wines, including Merlot and Cabernet Franc reds and Riesling and Viognier whites, is available in the friendly tasting room. There are are also various red and white dessert wines, including ones from Orange and Black Muscat.

www.bookcliffvineyards.com

3 | Boulder Creek Winery

6440 Odell Pl., Boulder, CO 80301; (303) 516-9031

Don't be put off by the mundane setting of this winery, which is located in an industrial park. Local regulations make it nearly impossible to establish a winery unless it is in a city-approved industrial zone.

Set up in 2003, Boulder Creek is owned by Mike and Jackie Thompson and their son, Will. Jackie is one of Colorado's most innovative winemakers. She uses a number of time-consuming techniques to make sublime red wines with some of the best tannin

▲ Jackie Thompson of Boulder Creek Winery is one of Colorado's most innovative winemakers.

structures you will ever see. All fruit is trucked in cold from vineyards in the western part of the state. The hospitality and wine knowledge at Boulder Creek are superb, and the wines are among the best in Colorado.

www.bouldercreekwine.com

findout more

- **www.coloradowine.com**
  Everything you need to know about Colorado wine, including wine trails and links to the wineries.

- **www.winesofcolorado.com**
  Taste the wines from more than 40 Colorado wineries. Located south of Denver at the entrance to the Pikes Peak region.

Central Region

Missouri was once a huge and important wine-shipping and -producing state. But a key problem with most of the Midwest was that it often fell victim to Canadian Clipper winds. Cold winters, with their large annual snowfall and subzero temperatures, can destroy grape vines. Moreover, high humidity during most growing seasons, as well as potentially excessive rainfall and moist temperatures, can cause rot.

As a result, much of the Midwest has relied on the hardier grapes of Native American grape varieties or the newer, French-American hybrids, many of them developed in upper New York.

From the 1960s, however, plant scientists were developing techniques that can deal with climate-related issues as they relate to certain less extreme regions. And in places like Michigan (notably on the Old Mission Peninsula and the Leelanau Peninsula), Riesling and other planted grapes challenged the old order and made superb world-class wines.

In addition, grape transportation systems grew more sophisticated in the 1980s, and consequently many wineries contracted to buy grapes from warmer climes and were able to make excellent wines literally thousands of miles from the fruit's related vineyards.

Meanwhile, in states such as Texas, more diligent attention to former viticultural problems, such as rot, have helped to create booming wine industries in regions that had almost none even 20 years ago.

▲ Vineyards on Old Mission Peninsula, Michigan

Old Mission Peninsula

Just outside Traverse City, a skinny finger of land juts northward into Lake Michigan. For about 22 miles (35 km) one main road (M-37) rides the spine of Old Mission Peninsula to dramatic bay views on each side. Vineyard rows sweep dramatically toward the shore, alternating with orchards, pastures and the occasional old red barn. This agricultural area used to be mostly planted with cherries, but today wine grapes are a close second.

Old Mission is home to six wineries, located here largely for a micro-climate that in winter is formed from warmed lake air masses that blanket the peninsula and help produce its acclaimed Rieslings, Gewürztraminers and other wines. All six wineries have tasting rooms. The peninsula's one notable fine-dining restaurant is the Bowers Harbor Inn at 13512 Peninsula Drive, a Victorian mansion looking out over a lovely cove. The best travel months are May through November.

◄ Early fall is a stunning time to visit this part of Michigan when the leaves turn yellow and red.

1 | Peninsula Cellars
11480 Center Rd., Old Mission Peninsula, Traverse City, MI 49686; (231) 933-9787

Head north on M-37 to the red-roofed nineteenth-century school-house, which is the tasting room of Peninsula Cellars—one of the early breakout wineries of northern Michigan to become known nationally through competitions for both its Rieslings and its Gewürztraminers. It has won a prestigious Jefferson Cup as well as top honors in other national contests. Particularly worth trying are the Manigold Vineyard Gewürztraminer, the Select Riesling and the Pinot Blanc, often compared with their Alsace counterparts for dryness, floral character and acidity.

The winery itself is in another location and is not open to public tours. The rustic and charming tasting room and store is right on the main road north.

www.peninsulacellars.com

2 | Chateau Grand Traverse
12239 Center Rd., Traverse City, MI 49686; (231) 223-7355

Continue up M-37 a mile or two until vineyards appear on the left and begin sloping down toward the bay. In the middle sits this winery's inn, which welcomes overnight guests. The winery itself, a practical industrial building of no particular distinction, is on the right. But Chateau Grand Traverse is of huge significance to the wine history of the area and is now the state's third-largest winery.

In 1974 it was the first to go full-bore into Riesling and then other *vinifera* grapes. This winery also led the way on Gewürztraminer, Chardonnay and, later, Pinot Grigio and Pinot Blanc—with the understanding that, despite what some experts and scientists said, they would survive the harsh winters.

www.cgtwines.com

3 | Brys Estate Vineyard & Winery
3309 Blue Water Rd., Traverse City, MI 49686; (231) 223-9303

Head back to the M-37 and go north again a few miles, then turn right at St. Joseph Catholic Church. Down the road sits a lovely restored old farm homestead and a series of rehabbed outbuildings. Since 2004 this relative newcomer has been showered with more than 130 medals in national competitions, including a Jefferson Cup. The winery makes Merlot, Pinot Noir and Cabernet Franc; and in whites, Chardonnay, Pinot Grigio, Riesling, Pinot Blanc and Gewürztraminer.

Owners Walt and Eileen Brys are gracious, and don't be surprised to find them on hand at the luxurious stone-and-mahogany tasting room that ranks as one of the nicest around.

www.brysestate.com

4 | Bowers Harbor Vineyards

2896 Bowers Harbor Rd., Traverse City, MI 49686; (231) 223-7615

Farther north and to the left of the M-37, tucked away into the gently sloping vineyard, is this pretty, scenic little winery on a picture-perfect piece of land—slightly up the grade from a hook-shaped cove known as Bowers Harbor. In 1985 the Stegenga family bought the 43-acre property dotted with tall oak and beech trees as a working farm, complete with animals. In 1990 they began converting it to a vineyard. Today the horse barn is the tasting room, and among the prettiest on the peninsula. In addition to superb cold-climate Chardonnays, zesty Pinot Grigios and bright citrus Rieslings, this winery is well worth the stop for its location.

www.bowersharbor.com

5 | Chateau Chantal

15900 Rue de Vin, Traverse City, MI 49686; (231) 223-4110

Atop one of the highest points on the peninsula sits this imposing modern turreted winery and guest inn; it has views of both bays, perhaps the most dramatic panorama in the region. It is also the home of its owners, the Begin family, who make several excellent wines.

Founders Robert and Nadine Begin are a story of their own—a Catholic priest and a former nun who married and had a daughter, Chantal, for whom the winery is named. In the summer and fall, the winery holds cooking classes and an evening of jazz and wine on the terrace as the sun sets in the west. All the main rooms, the tasting room and the great hall are built for the views—as are the 11 guest rooms and suites, the price of which includes breakfast.

www.chateauchantal.com

6 | Two Lads Winery

16985 Smokey Hollow Rd., Traverse City, MI 49686; (231) 223-7722

If there is a winery whose mere appearance reflects the bright future of the wine industry here, it is Two Lads, the newest addition to the peninsula's wineries. The dramatic architecture of the winery is almost museum-like, with its contemporary structure of stone, steel

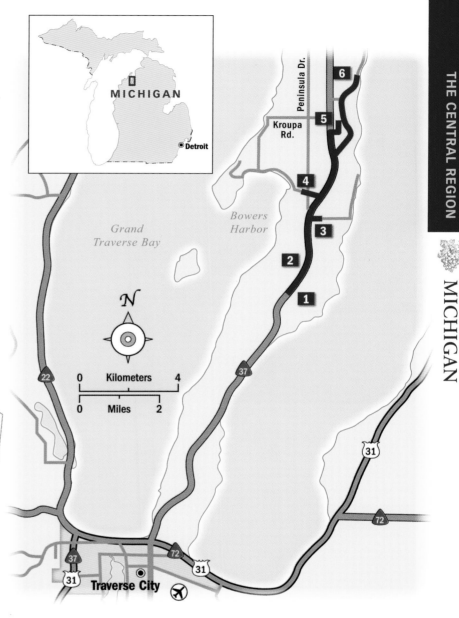

and poured concrete, fronted by soaring glass panels. The sleek and modern tasting rooms look ready to hang a selection of modern art.

Gravity-flow techniques in the winery handle the juice and wine gently in order to maximize aroma and flavor. Most importantly, the wines are excellent examples of improving new regionalism and cold-climate character—especially the reds, which until lately had not been given much chance in Michigan. Try the bold, aggressive Cabernet Franc, which reminds many of Chinon, Bourgueil and other Loire Valley reds made from the same grape variety.

www.2lwinery.com

TOUR 43
Leelanau Peninsula

The larger Leelanau Peninsula, starting around Traverse City, the vacation hub for Chicago and Detroit, is home to 17 wineries. Summer homes and little lake cottages dot the shoreline, and boat docks jut out into the gently lapping lake. The inland areas are rolling hills that used to be cherry and peach orchards, but in the 1980s much of that land was converted to grape-growing for an exploding wine industry.

By the 1990s the Leelanau—like Old Mission Peninsula (see Tour 42)—began to see a future in agritourism. Fancy tasting rooms sprouted and are now the backbone of the local economy. In August the new Traverse City Film Festival, championed and chaired by filmmaker Michael Moore, has become a jammed event, causing hotel shortages and long waits for tables. Several summer food-and-wine conferences and gatherings also draw large crowds.

◄ Left Foot Charley makes for an enjoyable visit while in Traverse City.

1 | Left Foot Charley
806 Red Dr., Traverse City, MI 49684; (231) 995-0500

This winery is a must-visit for all wine enthusiasts to this part of Michigan—and not just for its wines—though it's technically slightly outside the Leelanau in Traverse City, near M-22, the coastal road to all the other wineries in the peninsula.

Owner-winemaker Bryan Ulbrich stunned wine experts around the country with the high standard of his Rieslings and dry Gewürztraminers when he was at Peninsula Cellars on Old Mission Peninsula (see Tour 42). Now he's drawing the same attention at this winery for his Pinot Blancs, among others.

Left Foot Charley—Bryan's childhood nickname—is in a most unusual setting: an urban redevelopment project on the lovely grounds of a 63-acre park of mature trees and walkways. Its Italianate chateau-like stone-and-brick buildings, with slate roofs and cupolas, were once the state's premier mental hospital. It was abandoned in the 1960s and almost torn down and is now called The Village at Traverse City Commons. The winery is located in the old hospital laundry, while the sleek glass-fronted tasting room can be found in Building 53 nearby. Café Leftique on the same site serves a selection of freshly cooked dishes.

www.leftfootcharley.com

2 | L. Mawby Vineyards
4519 S. Elm Valley Rd., Suttons Bay, MI 49682; (231) 272-3522

Follow the languid coast road along the eastern shore of the peninsula several miles to Suttons Bay, and make a short detour to what is now the largest producer of traditional-method sparkling wine in the Midwest, at 100,000 bottles a year. It's a simple and unpretentious place, reflecting the personality of owner Larry Mawby, godfather of the northern Michigan industry and revered locally for decades for his bubbly. If Champagne-style wines from Michigan seem odd, consider that the climate and soil of the Leelanau are far closer to Champagne than California. The result is crisp, mineral, lean and citrus sparkling wines, with much depth and complexity, and Mawby is the one who led the state to them.

International renown came Mawby's way when Tom Stevenson, a noted British wine writer, launched his *Wine Report 2006* with a note about Mawby. Try the top cuvées: Blanc de Blancs, Talismøn and Cremant. His second label—not made by the traditonal method—includes the popular Sex, a rosé, and Wet, made from Pinot Gris, which began as something of a joke but have become fast sellers.

www.lmawby.com

3 | Black Star Farms

10844 E. Revold Rd., Suttons Bay, MI 49682; (231) 944-1270

A few miles farther north, you will see what looks like a horse farm and manor house straight out of Kentucky blue-grass country. Black Star Farms still has horses and a stable, plus a winery, an impressive tasting room, a distillery that make brandies, a luxury inn and a cheese creamery. It is truly another must-see stop.

Black Star was the first winery designed specifically for agri-tourism by the owner and former president of Hiram Walker, Don Coe, and his wife, Marylou. (Black Star also has a tasting room and a second winery at the foot of Old Mission Peninsula.)

All of winemaker Lee Lutes's wines are worth trying, especially his clean, light Be Dazzled sparkling. If you like spirits, don't miss the Pear Brandy (with the pear in the bottle) or the superbly smooth Red Grape Grappa.

www.blackstarfarms.com

4 | Forty-Five North Vineyard and Winery

8580 E. Horn Rd., Lake Leenlanau, MI 49653; (231) 271-1188

Heading up M-22 again and left onto C-204, the road follows the gentle roller-coaster hills toward Lake Leelanau and to an exciting new winery that lies on the 45th parallel.

Located on an undulating parcel of land that ends at the lake, Forty-Five North has gathered high praise since its first vintage in 2007, largely because of the skill of winemaker Shawn Walters and the faith and investment of owner Steve Grossnickle.

It is still a work in progress. A new tasting room—a post-and-beam barn hand-hewn by Amish builders in Ohio and reassembled on the site—opened in the fall of 2009.

One of the wines, a Pinot Noir rosé, stunned the judges at the Pacific Rim (California) wine competition in 2009, leading to a demand that a new "best of rosé" category be created just so that it could be awarded to the wine. Other medal-winning wines include dry Riesling, Pinot Blanc, late-harvest sweet Vignoles and a superb dry Sparkling Cherry Wine.

www.fortyfivenorth.com

5 | Bel Lago Vineyard and Winery

6530 S. Lake Shore Dr., Cedar, MI 49621; (231) 228-4800

From Forty-Five North continue south to the western arm of Lake Leelanau for a pleasant half-hour ride south toward Cedar, and the gentle slopes of Pinot Noir vines at Bel Lago. The winery and tasting room are modest compared to some others, but what you get is some of the best wines in the Leelanau Peninsula and beautiful views across the lake by which to sip them. The property has sweeping vistas of the majestic lake and views all the way to the distant opposite shore.

Winemaker Charlie Edson makes superb wines—do not miss his traditional-method sparkling wines and his Alsatian-style, full-bodied Gewürztraminer—but what really distinguishes him is his work seeking the right Pinot Noir clones that will do well in Michigan. At one point, he had trial plots of more than 30 different Pinots in the vineyard. Today he makes one of the best versions in the state. His Auxerrois, a French white grape from Alsace not seen too much in this country, is impressive, too.

www.bellago.com

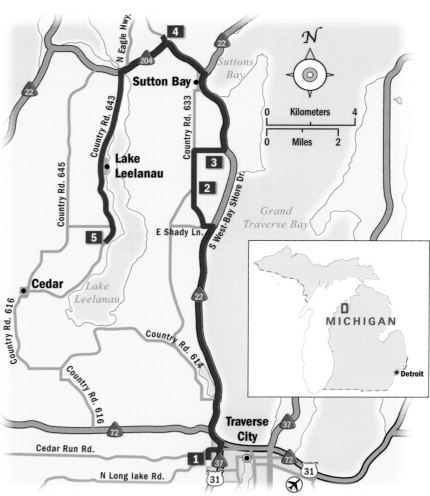

Southwest Michigan

This area of Michigan has more connection to Chicago, about a 90-minute drive away, than to Detroit, the state's largest city, three hours east. The vineyards here hug the coastline of Lake Michigan, which has long been a weekend playground and beach-cottage area for Chicagoans seeking brief refuge from the oppressive summer city heat. Other than a swatch of hilly country that follows the St. Joseph River, the terrain here is largely flat, a blend of farmland and the occasional rural industrial complex.

The 18 wineries of southwest Michigan are spread all over the region, from Muskegon down to the Indiana border, and from Grand Rapids down to Kalamazoo. Eight of the wineries are closely located around the Buchanan and Baroda areas, and others are fairly close to the major east-west interstate highway, I-94.

◄ The warm air masses from Lake Michigan make winemaking possible in such a northerly region.

1 | St. Julian Winery
716 S. Kalamazoo St., Paw Paw, MI 49079; (269) 657-5568

Just north of Interstate 94 in Paw Paw is the St. Julian winery. It all began nearly 90 years ago, when a young Italian immigrant named Mariano Meconi arrived in Windsor, Canada, and opened his first wine operation there. After Prohibition ended in the United States in 1933, Meconi moved to Detroit and in 1936 to Paw Paw, where St. Julian, named after the patron saint of Meconi's native village in Italy, remains today under the direction of his grandson, David Braganini. St. Julian is now the 36th largest winery in the country, producing 100,000 cases a year.

Over the years, it has evolved from making the popular sweet fruit and fortified wines from native American grapes and hybrids, to a multi-tiered wine business. While fruit wines such as blackberry and sparkling peach are still part of its portfolio, St. Julian also makes serious premium table wines, led by an excellent line of *vinifera* wines under the Braganini Reserve label, including Merlot and Cabernet Sauvignon.

The winery offers a range of daily wine tours and there is a large tasting room with charming outdoor seating around a fountain and stone courtyard.

www.stjulian.com

▲ St. Julian is one of Michigan's historic wineries and is still going strong today.

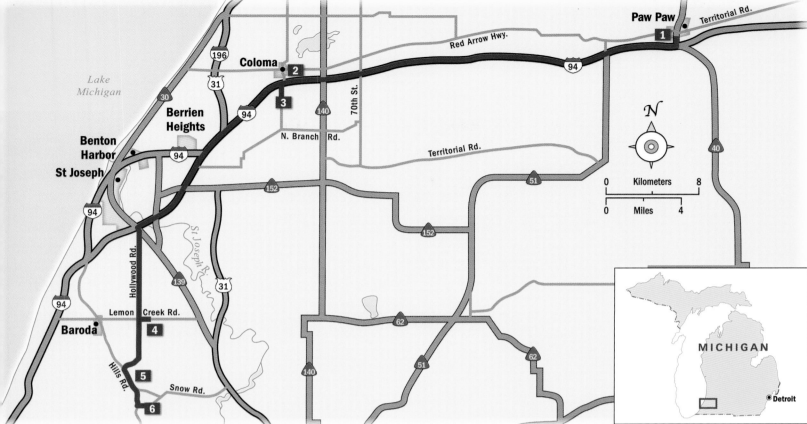

2 | Karma Vista Vineyards
6991 Ryno Rd., Coloma, MI 49038; (269) 468-9463

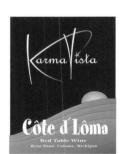

Head west on Interstate 94 to the Coloma exit and follow the road toward Lake Michigan. Launched in 2002, Karma Vista is one of the newer wineries in the area to produce award-winning wines. Karma Vista makes upward of 5,000 cases yearly and has a tasting room in the middle of the vineyard.

The Herman family have been fruit growers in the southwest area for 150 years, and their vines straddle the new and older delineations of Michigan wine. Joe and Sue Herman, the current generation, grow hybrids—Seyval Blanc and Vidal—along with *vinifera* grapes such as Sauvignon Blanc and Pinot Gris. Seyval Blanc and Vidal are blended with Riesling into a white wine called Starry, Starry Night. In reds, there are hybrids—such as Foch, de Chaunac, Chancellor and Chambourcin—as well as the native American Concord grape, and like most other wineries here in southwest Michigan, they also grow Pinot Noir, Merlot and Cabernet Franc. Côte d'Lôma is a red blend of Cabernet Franc, Chancellor and Chambourcin, which is almost totally dry.

www.karmavista.com

3 | Contessa Wine Cellars
3235 Friday Rd., Coloma, MI 49038; (269) 468-5534

This winery, a chalet structure perched on a hill looking down the freeway, is just south of Interstate 94 at the Coloma exit. Owner and winemaker Tony Peterson comes from three generations of fruit growers and winemakers. His father, Duane, started making rhubarb wine in the 1980s and developed it into Peterson & Sons, which became the best-known fruit winery in the state.

So it was a logical next step for son Tony to open Contessa and follow the trend toward *vinifera* grapes. Contessa is part of what's known as the Lake Michigan Shore AVA, or appellation, which benefits greatly from warm air masses from the lake, which hover inland during winter and protect vines from harsh freezes.

www.contessawinecellars.com

4 | Domaine Berrien Cellars & Winery
398 E. Lemon Creek Rd., Berrien Springs, MI 49103; (269) 473-9463

The ride over to this modest, simple, fairly recent winery run by owners Wally and Katie Maurer—he makes the wines—takes you through beautiful countryside. And while the winery itself isn't anything fancy, what the Maurers are doing with wine makes it worth the visit. Domaine Berrien is one of those striving, young Turk

▲ The restaurant at Tabor Hill enjoys views over the vineyards to Lake Michigan.

wineries gaining recognition for surprisingly good reds. Some of Maurer's Syrahs, such as his 2002 and 2007, are great examples of well-made cold-climate red wines, more like a northern Rhône Valley red. Other wines include Merlot and Cabernet Franc, by far his steadiest and most distinctive red.

www.domaineberrien.com

5 | Round Barn Winery, Distillery & Brewery

19083 Hills Rd., Baroda, MI 49101; (800) 716-9463

The winding Red Arrow Highway leading to this winery is one of the most scenic in southwest Michigan. It reminds many of New England as it stretches above the St. Joseph River, then heads sharply up tree-

▲ The massive old round Amish barn at Round Barn Winery

covered two-lane roads and catapults down toward grassy hillside farms. Around one of those turns and up a skinny gravel driveway is Round Barn, one of the most scenic and wide-ranging operations around, not just a winery but also a distillery and a brewery.

Rick Moersch, owner and winemaker, is a seminal figure in the wines of this area. Like Larry Mawby in the north (see page 148), Moersch was one of the first true believers that Michigan could make fine traditional-method sparkling wine. After all, not every season here gets the same sunshine and ripening as California, and it's more similar to the cool climate of the Champagne region.

Moersch first grew small plots of Chardonnay and Pinot Noir in the 1980s, when he was a young winemaker at nearby Tabor Hill winery. He left in 1991 to develop Round Barn, so named for a massive old round Amish barn that he had dismantled in Indiana and rebuilt here.

Moersch has pioneered making distilled fruit spirits, eaux de vie and brandies, and even has a luxury vodka called DiVine, made from selected grapes. The winery also makes a range of very good red and white wines from *vinifera* grapes.

www.roundbarnwinery.com

Tabor Hill Winery & Restaurant

185 Mount Tabor Rd., Buchanan, MI 49107; (800) 283-3363

The Upton family, owners of Tabor Hill, actually made their mark producing washing machines and refrigerators at a small local company they founded nearby, which they named Whirlpool. Launched in 1968, Tabor Hill is the second oldest winery in the area. It has been upgraded over the years and is now home to a state-of-the-art winery with a large tasting room. It is one of the most pleasant places to visit in the area, not least because it is one of the only wineries that has a full-service restaurant with a view facing westward over the vineyard to the lake and distant dunes.

Veteran winemaker Mike Merchant has long been respected for his skill with whites and the development of a very successful sparkling-wine program started by Rick Moersch of Round Barn (see facing page) in the 1980s. But Merchant has also been at the forefront of growing *vinifera* reds, which many believed, incorrectly, would not survive here. Tabor Hill Cabernet Francs tend to be lean and sinewy in character, very much in the Loire Valley style. But of all the wines they make, the wonderful, unusual dry white Traminette, which has a lovely perfume and bracing acidity—it's a derivative of Gewürztraminer—is very much worth trying.

www.taborhill.com

▲ Checking a barrel sample at Tabor Hill

findout more

- www.michiganwines.com
  The official Michigan wine industry site, including maps of the wine regions with winery locations.

Southern Wisconsin

The Badger State has a wine-growing history at least from the mid-nineteenth century, which is when Agoston Haraszthy, a Hungarian entrepreneur, started to build a cellar in Prairie du Sac. He smelled good summer weather but didn't smell the vine-killing winters. He left for California and later made history there. What followed were mainly fruit growers—cherries and apples—until the 1970s, when Bob Wollersheim's zeal (see below) sparked a revival of vineyard planting and serious winemaking. The vast majority of the vineyards are planted with hybrids that can survive the harsh winters, with Foch, Frontenac, Marquette and St. Croix among the big reds and St. Pepin, Edelweiss, La Crosse, Frontenac Gris and La Crescent leading the whites.

Today Wisconsin has three dozen wineries, spanning the four corners of the state. This tour takes in three winery visits over the two southernmost regions, starting in Milwaukee.

◄ Cedar Creek Winery is located in an old wool mill in the attractive town of Cedarburg.

1 | Cedar Creek Winery

N70 W6340 Bridge Rd., Cedarburg, WI 53012; (800) 827-8020

A 15- to 20-minute drive north from Milwaukee to Cedarburg brings you to Cedar Creek Winery. It rests in a great old limestone wool mill whose cellars are perfect for wine aging and storage. Now owned by the Wollersheims (see right), the wineries share the same philosophy (and winemaker): Buy from out of state any grapes that don't grow well in a cold climate and use grapes from their own vineyards that do, i.e., hybrids. The tasting room is small but well stocked, and kids will love the nooks and crannies of the old stone property. Before or after the visit, take an hour or so just to walk around the town: If you're from the big city, it's great medicine.

Recommended wines from their purchased grapes include Unoaked Chardonnay, a crisp, clean, dry wine in the French Chablis vein; Pinot Grigio (off-dry) with tangy, grapefruity overtones; and Waterfall Riesling, huskier in style than a German version but still with good, under-ripe apple character. The Vidal, light and off-dry, makes a welcome aperitif. Of the homegrown wines, the Old Mill Red, from the Foch grape, is light, tangy and Beaujolais-like, whereas the Hillside Red, also from Foch, is aged in American oak barrels to give a robust full-bodied wine.

www.cedarcreekwinery.com

2 | Wollersheim Winery

7876 State Rd. 188, Prairie du Sac, WI 53578; (800) 847-9463

Cedar Creek is at the eastern end of the Glacial Hills region. The 95-mile (153-km) drive west to Wollersheim will give you a great view of the area's rolling hills, highlighted by the Kettle Moraine State Forest. Unless you're in a great hurry, avoid US 94 and take the more scenic Route 60.

Wollersheim is at the eastern end of the so-called Driftless region, one of the few areas not affected by the grinding and gouging of the glaciers. Bob Wollersheim's career "drift"—from developing satellites—was a leap of faith and courage. In 1972 he bought the old stone winery near the Wisconsin River and moved his family next door. After a while, he hired a French winemaker, Philippe Coquard (who eventually married Bob's daughter, Julie). The original winery (see top photo) was built in 1858 by a German immigrant and has been augmented by tasteful additions that can accommodate the army of visitors. Even if you do not like wine, the beautiful tree-covered setting will bring your heart rate down.

Coquard uses both purchased grapes (from Washington, mainly) and the estate's 23 acres' worth, plus other Wisconsin-grown grapes, for his 20 or so wines—most of which are available to try in the bustling tasting room. The Prairie Fumé (Seyval Blanc) is his standout, off-dry white. Try also the Chardonnay aged in French oak. For the reds, Prairie Sunburst is a Maréchal Foch-based, unoaked, soft and dry Beaujolais-style wine, while Domaine du Sac is a fuller, mildly oakier interpretation of the Foch grape.

www.wollersheim.com

3 | Weggy Winery

30940 Oak Ridge Dr., Muscoda, WI 53573; (608) 647-6600

Weggy (pronounced "WEH-gee") Winery is a 45–60-minute hike west from Prairie du Sac to the town of Muscoda ("Mus-uh-DAY"). "I call my husband Weggy," says Marlys Weglarz; hence, the winery name. This is one of those way-out-here-in-the-country wineries, but the trip is worth it. Staying on Route 60 all the way brings you through winding roads and gorgeous scenes of rock outcroppings, ever-forests and the placid Wisconsin River, where you can rent canoes and play on the sandbars. On the way, you can stop at Frank Lloyd Wright's Taliesin Preservation in Spring Green (www.taliesinpreservation.org).

Rustic in setting, the small tasting room can accommodate a lot more people than you might expect to see this far out—the Mississippi River and Iowa are less than 40 miles (64 km) to the west. But Marion and Marlys Weglarz, who live in Naperville, Illinois, and commute back and forth, attract visitors from Milwaukee,

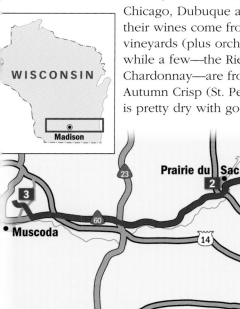

Chicago, Dubuque and Minneapolis. Most of their wines come from their 16 acres of vineyards (plus orchards for the fruit wines), while a few—the Riesling, Pinot Noir and Chardonnay—are from Michigan fruit. The Autumn Crisp (St. Pepin and La Crosse grapes) is pretty dry with good tangy appley flavors

▲ A visit to Weggy Winery makes a pleasant day out in the country.

and a long refreshing finish. The Vanilla Oak doesn't hit you with splinters as some oak-aged wines do, but it is quite dry and well-balanced. The Semi-sweet Riesling has an appley, non-cloying flavor. The Weggy Red (from Wisconsin-grown St. Croix grapes) is a good light-and-fruity red along the lines of a Beaujolais. Their Apple & Blackcurrant wine is deliciously tangy and spicy.

Finally, if you are interested in visiting more wineries, you can head north to Vernon Vineyards at Viroqua. Or head south into far northwestern Illinois and check out Galena Cellars (near Galena) or Massbach Ridge Winery (10 miles/16 km south of Elizabeth).

www.weggywinery.com

findout more

- **www.wiswine.com**
The Wisconsin Winery Association website with links to the wineries.

- **www.dnr.wi.gov/org/land/parks/specific/kms**
The Kettle Moraine State Forest's southern section is about one hour's drive east of Madison and comprises more than 20,000 acres of glacial hills, kettles, lakes and forest.

Northern Illinois

Although the state has been growing grapes for more than a century, Illinois is better known for grain. A big problem was the winter cold, which prevented the use of *vinifera* grapes, such as Chardonnay and Cabernet, that are so familiar to California wine drinkers. The other was pesticide sprays, especially 2-4-D, which devastates vines.

Today, while the Prairie State is no Napa Valley, vine acreage has grown to about 1,200 acres and around 80 wineries. Growers have learned how to better cope with the cold and plant mainly hybridized grapes that are better acclimatized. Chardonel, Vignoles, Traminette, Vidal and Cayuga are predominant white grapes, while Chambourcin, Frontenac, Foch, St. Croix, Léon Millot and Norton are the leading reds. Because Americans are not as familiar with these grape names, many winemakers label them with proprietary names. But just ask, and they'll tell you. This tour visits four wineries west of Chicago and could easily be done in a long, leisurely day.

◄ Lynfred Winery is the state's largest and an easy drive from Chicago.

1 | Lynfred Winery

15 S. Roselle Rd., Roselle, IL 60172; (630) 529-9463

Lynfred Winery is less than an hour's drive from the center of Chicago in the pretty suburb of Roselle. The ride is über-urban but very convenient. Fred Koehler founded the winery in 1975 in a small building, which has grown into a major presence at Roselle and Irving Park roads. Inside the modern tasting room, you'd think you were in Napa or Sonoma (or maybe along the Rheingau, with its German touches). There is a long, winding tasting bar, or you can enjoy glasses of wine in the various nooks inside and outside the premises. A few years back, they built a small collection of gorgeous bed-and-breakfast rooms. Of course, there's also a store where you can buy wine, as well as bread, cheese, spices and wine-related knick-knacks of all sorts.

There are no vineyards, but there is a great winery tour helping visitors to understand the sometimes confusing winemaking process. Koehler buys grapes from California, Washington and Michigan, as well as from Illinois, and from the beginning has shown a knack for turning other folks' fruit into well-made wines (very early on, a Chardonnay he made from Napa grapes won two back-to-back wine competitions for Best of Show). His current Chardonnay is still winning medals, and the Fumé Blanc, Viognier and Gewürztraminer are favorite dry whites; the Vidal Blanc is delicious and only slightly sweet. The dry reds are very reliable, with the Merlot a current standout.

Don't overlook the fruit wines. The (Montmorency) Cherry is spectacular, but also check out the Strawberry and Rhubarb wines.

www.lynfredwinery.com

2 | Prairie State Winery

217 W. Main St., Genoa, IL 60135; (815) 784-4540

From Roselle, the trip to Genoa ("jen-OH-a"), a classic small Midwestern town, is 45 minutes west. The drive is still urban but not aggressively so, and you may see an eagle, a hawk or a hayfield on the way. Right in town on Main Street (Hwy. 72) sits the Prairie State Winery, established in 1999 by Richard and Maria Mamoser. The winery boasts a small vineyard a few miles west, which they planted about 12 years ago, mainly with Foch but also with some Niagara and St. Pepin grapes.

Most of their wines, "Illinois-grown only" it is stressed, come from vineyards located farther south, from Springfield onward, which is where 60 percent of the state's acreage lies.

When touring, explore beyond your favorite wines by trying a new grape variety at each visit.

The owners, Terrie and Alexandra (Lex) Tuntland, have filled the winery with—among other things you'd expect—two harvesters and an antique car. They farm 12 acres of grapes but grow 1,000 acres of corn and soy as well. The vineyard is some distance from the farmhouse and is protected by a swatch of pine trees. Terrie grows around 30 different grape varieties, mainly hybrids but a few natives.

The Tuntlands, along with partners Clem and Anne Stiely, opened the winery in 1998 and use only their own fruit for their wines. Together they share backgrounds in chemistry, agriculture and social sciences (they are retired teachers) and apply these skills, along with others learned at the hands of vineyard and winery experts. It's still a work in progress and a great way to see a winery and vineyard in evolution.

The wines are works in progress as well. If oaked wines are to your taste, try the Wine Dog White (based on Chardonel grapes). Instead of using barrels, wood bars are used to infuse the wine in stainless-steel drums—something more commonly done the world over than you'd suspect. The Waterman White (a blend) is a clean, very tangy and concentrated, fairly dry wine. The Royal Red (de Chaunac) is dense and similar to a southern Rhône, although tarter. The Waterman Red (Frontenac) is a little sweeter but has a nice cranberry-like character. Lex's favorite, the Niagara, is a wine for the sweet-toothed.

www.sunsetwines.net

Prairie State makes about two dozen wines, including some fruit wines. The grape-based wines are usually given proprietary names, although the very respectable Cabernet Franc sports its own name; it's more in the leaner, northern Italian style than a Napa interpretation. The Chambourcin Reserve also waves its own flag: It's tangier up front and may remind some of Beaujolais. The State Red (based on Foch) is Rhône-like in flavor with just a hint of sweetness. Similarly, very slightly sweet-tinged is the Recession Noir, full of cranberry and pomegranate-like flavors that linger and linger. The State White is a great tangy-tart aperitif wine made of Vidal Blanc, while the Prairie White is a Seyval Blanc, a mildly sweet wine that recalls a good Riesling. The Oak Savanna (Chardonel) lives up to its name. Aside from the small tasting bar, there is a small shop for foodies, including the richest-looking fudge in the state.

www.prairiestatewinery.com

Waterman Winery (Sunset Wines)
11582 Waterman Rd., Waterman, IL 60556; (815) 264-3268

The next drive, 30 minutes south of Genoa to the Waterman Winery, a mix of small-town rural and flat-out farm country. The winery is a modern building alongside a great old barn.

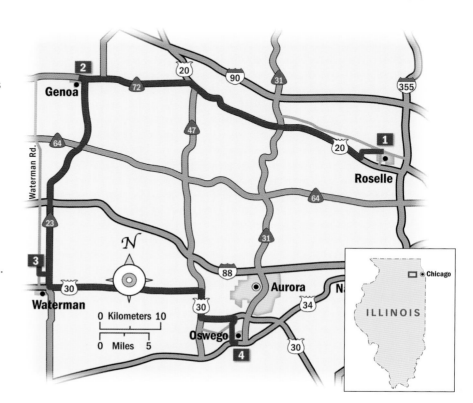

157

The Shawnee Hills of southern Illinois

PREFER THE SOUTH?

With a deeper history of wine-growing, the Shawnee Hills area of southern Illinois may seem the more logical short tour to take—unless you're from Chicago. However, if you live anywhere from St. Louis to Indianapolis or the Ohio River Valley of Indiana, you'll probably prefer this tour. The concentration of the 18 wineries lies between Carbondale and Cobden in a 15 x 20-mile (24 x 32-km) square, with most wineries just a few miles from one another. And it's right off US 57. It's 400–800 feet (120–250 m) higher than in the north; it wasn't ground down by the glaciers that smoothed out the north. This also makes for longer "hang time" for the grapes (increasing the flavors and colors). The hillier, more dispersed vineyards work against the cross-crop pesticide problems that had long plagued the north.

▲ Fox Valley Winery has a friendly tasting room for visitors.

4 Fox Valley Winery

5600 Rte. 34, Oswego, IL 60543; (630) 554-0404

The last of our quartet has us heading back to Chicago from Waterman; along 23 South to 34 East, then toward Oswego and Fox Valley Winery—all small-town urban driving. Built in 2007, this winery is more like Lynfred, in that it's a fully equipped tasting room and sales floor, but with more of a Nordic than German feel.

Fox Valley was founded by the Faltz Family in 2000 with the original winery in Sandwich (now closed) and vineyards in Sheridan, 20 miles (32 km) southwest of Oswego. For the most part, they use Illinois-grown grapes (the exception being their California-based Big Terra brand) and produce about 30 wines.

Their Chardonnay (from their own grapes) is Chablis-like (crisp and lean, with little or no oak) and lingers well on the palate. The Vidal Blanc recalls a moderately sweet Chenin Blanc-based Loire wine. The Vignoles is very aromatic, off-dry and pineappley. Of the reds, try the Chambourcin, sort of a Rhône–Burgundy style with more tang. The RA Faltz Vintner Reserve—a Norton, Chambourcin and Cabernet Franc blend—is a leathery, tangy dry red with hints of old-fashioned Zinfandel in the flavor.

www.foxvalleywinery.com

findout more

- **www.illinoiswine.org**
Information on Illinois wine including links to wineries. The state's 80 or so wineries are organized into six wine trails.

regionalevents

Taste the Passion □ February
Special wine pours and a decadent chocolate treat at each Michigan winery.
www.lpwines.com

Lake Michigan Shore Wine Festival □ June
Locally produced wine varietals from Michigan's top wineries with live music, food and fun in the sun on beautiful Weko Beach, MI.
www.miwinetrail.com

Traverse City Film Festival □ Late July—August
Hugely popular film festival run by filmmaker Michael Moore. Free nightly films along the waterfront. **www.traversecityfilmfest.org**

Wine Days of Summer □ August
Celebrate the season with a souvenir wine glass and wine and food pairings at wineries across Michigan. **www.pioneerwinetrail.com**

Lake Geneva Wine Festival □ September
The lush lanscape of Lake Geneva, WI, sets the backdrop for this entertaining event with tastings, demos, luxury auctions, seminars and more. **www.lakegenevawinefestival.com**

Cedarburg's Wine & Harvest Festival □ September
This Wisconsin festival boasts a winery and food booth, farmers market, live music and arts arena along with other special events.
www.cedarburgfestivals.org

Vintage Illinois □ September
Northern Illinois' premier wine festival. At Starved Rock State Park.
www.vintageillinois.com

Illinois Wine & Art Festival □ September
This popular regional wine & art event offers wine tasting from over a dozen leading Illinois wineries and local artist performances.
www.wineandartfestival.com

Oktoberfest □ October
In the heart of Missouri Wine Country, Hermann celebrates its German heritage with four weekends of local wines and beers, and brats on the grill.
www.visithermann.com/special_events/oktoberfest

Missouri River

Less a trail than a few wineries clustered near Highway 70 in the middle part of the state, the Missouri River Wine Trail nonetheless has several pretty wineries perched along the Missouri River's banks.

One of these wineries, Les Bourgeois, offers one of the top experiences for winery visitors in any state. The sunset viewed from Les Bourgeois's restaurant and bar is a common experience for many University of Missouri students, graduates and teachers as well as smart winery tourists. In the beauty of the fall foliage, perhaps the wine tastes even better.

This tour begins west of St. Louis in Rocheport, a beautiful little town with antique stores and an entry onto Missouri's famous cross-state biking trail, the Katy Trail: The portion between Rocheport and Boonville is easily the prettiest part of this trail. If you're visiting the area solely by car you could easily reverse the order and start at Kansas City.

◀ Fall is a beautiful time of year to visit the Missouri River Wine Trail.

1 | Les Bourgeois Vineyards
14020 West Hwy. BB, Rocheport, MO 65279; (573) 698-2133

Les Bourgeois is easy to find from Highway 70: Look for the Rocheport exit (Exit 115 on Route BB), turn north, and you'll spot the winery. It's very rustic and simple, so it's worth going another mile north to their Blufftop Bistro, which offers very good lunch and dinner; for most central Missourians and tourists, watching the sunset over the Missouri River from the restaurant or from the nearby "A-frame," the winery's original building, is a must-do on a summer or fall evening.

With Missouri's French legacy, the name Les Bourgeois is ideally suited for a Missouri winery. The winery takes its name from its owners, the Bourgeois family, who have gone from strength to strength since their first vintage in 1985. Winemaker Cory Bomgaars has elevated his craft in the last several years, and their wines are among the most reliable in the state. The Norton can stand proudly alongside any other, while Les Bourgeois Chardonel is often the best the state has to offer.

www.missouriwine.com

2 | Cooper's Oak Winery
96-A W. Jones St., Higbee, MO 65257; (660) 456-7507

The trail to Cooper's Oak Winery heads north away from Rocheport on Highway 240 for 11 miles (18 km) and then on State Highway H for another 15 miles (24 km). Turn right at Highway B, go for 1.5 miles (2.5 km), and look for the sign as you enter the town of Higbee. The Kirby family produces solid Chambourcin and Norton, as well as a few dessert wines, and the family also owns A & K Cooperage, maker of American white oak barrels—Silver Oak Cellars in Napa Valley is their largest customer. That's well worth a visit, though you'll need to call ahead to make an appointment. The wine cellar also shares space with the historic town jail.

www.coopersoakwinery.com

3 | Baltimore Bend Vineyard
27150 Hwy. 24, Waverly, MO 64096; (660) 493-0258

Head west toward the city of Waverly; you can go across country through Marshall or go back to Interstate 70 and head north at Concordia on Highway 23. Travel 15 miles (24 km), and when you reach Highway 24 (just before you get to Waverly), go west for 5 miles (8 km), where you'll see Baltimore Bend Vineyard.

The "Bend" is a bend in the Missouri River, and though Baltimore Bend isn't an official part of the Missouri River Wine Trail (the same is true for the remainder of the wineries on this tour), it's a pretty spot along the river. Two sweet wines in particular are worth your attention: Sweet Beginnings and Last Minute. Try also the dry reds, Cynthiana and Chambourcin, as well.

www.baltimorebend.com

4 | Stonehaus Farms Winery

24607 N.E. Colbern Rd., Lee's Summit, MO 64086; (816) 554-8800

Back on Highway 70, head west toward Kansas City, and when you reach Blue Springs—just under 40 miles (64 km) from Concordia—go south on Highway 7 for 6 miles (10 km). When you come to the town of Lee's Summit, look for Colbern Road. Go west for just over a mile (2 km) and you'll see the signs for Stonehaus Farms.

The winery has been around since 1997 but has recently jumped forward in wine quality. In particular, you should taste their Traminette, their Vignoles and their fun and sappy Chambourcin.

www.stonehausfarms.com

5 | Inland Sea Winery

1600 Genessee, Suite 160, Kansas City, MO 64102; (888) 984-9463

A true city winery, Inland Sea breaks the mold in its choices of grapes, as well as its location. You'll first want to call to make an appointment; they're a very small operation. Go through downtown Kansas City, along Interstate 70, take Interstate 670 through the downtown area, and toward Kansas. The last exit is Genessee Street; take it south under the highway a couple of blocks to the winery.

Owner Michael Amigoni has eschewed hybrid grapes, choosing instead to focus on classic European grapes such as Cabernet Sauvignon, Merlot, Cabernet Franc and especially Petit Verdot. Since few growers here believe these grapes can thrive in the harsh climate, the Amigonis must grow many of their own grapes in a vineyard an hour east at Warrensburg. It's tempting to taste everything here—but don't taste too much, because it's still a small family project and the Amigoni family needs to have a bit left to sell!

www.inlandseawines.com

6 | Jowler Creek Vineyard & Winery

16905 Jowler Creek Rd., Platte City, MO 64079; (816) 858-5528

Take Highway 29 north (in the direction of Kansas City International airport) and head to Platte City, about 30 miles (48 km) north of Kansas City. When you reach Platte City, take the exit for Camden Point (Missouri Highway E), go east for half a mile (800 m), then south on Elm Grove Road for 1.3 miles (2 km).

Jason and Colleen Gerke have thrown themselves into the wine business. They planted their first 250 Norton vines in the spring of 2004 and have expanded the vineyard several times since then. They began making wine commercially in 2005. They've quickly shown themselves adept at Norton, Chambourcin, Traminette and Vignoles. They have a very nice dessert Vignoles and a well-balanced fortified Norton called Nort.

www.jowlercreek.com

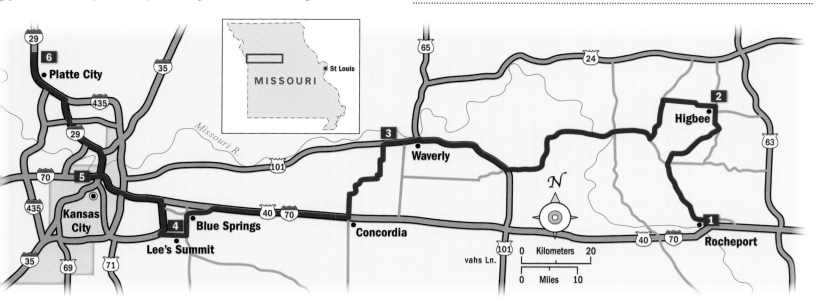

Hermann Wine Trail

Hermann's origins offer a dramatic example of nation-building as practiced in the nineteenth century. In 1836, an émigré group in Philadelphia created the German Settlement Society, a philanthropic society looking to build a German community in America. They chose a chain of hills along the Missouri River for their New Germany and offered free tickets to any Deutschlander wishing to trek across an ocean and a continent to build their paradise. Tailors, farmers and blacksmiths were chosen, but vintners and grape-growers were prized above all. The town prospered for decades, but the philanthropy dried up and Prohibition abruptly ended the careers of the vintners.

Winemaking began again in 1965, when the Held family reopened their winery at Stone Hill. Hermann is now home to seven successful family-owned wineries, and the town continues to celebrate its German heritage year-round.

◄ Hermann is one of the prettiest towns in Missouri.

1 | Hermannhof Winery
330 E. First St., Hermann, MO 65041; (800) 393-0100

From Interstate 70, it's a 14-mile (23 km) drive south on Highway 19 (Exit 175) to reach sleepy little Hermann, though on some festival days it can be downright raucous in town.

Just after you cross the Missouri River, turn left on Highway 100 (First Street), where sits Hermannhof Winery, a remarkable, restored edifice. Wine, however, may have been a second thought in 1848 when the first of the many cellars were built there. Beer was more important, though, in truth, any alcoholic beverage was useful back then; people needed something good and healthful to drink other than water, and wine and beer lasted a lot longer than grapes or grain. Beer and wine production increased; by the 1900s the town of Hermann was producing the equivalent of more than 1 million cases of wine annually. But Hermannhof's brewing and winemaking equipment were sold off when Prohibition arrived in 1919.

In 1974, the Dierbergs bought and refurbished the winery. The family also owns a prestigious grocery group in St. Louis and some great Pinot Noir property in California's Santa Barbara region. They expanded the winery and vineyard area, now totaling 300 acres, but Hermannhof retains historically important vineyards, including those once owned by pioneer Julius Ruediger, perched on bluffs high above the Missouri River.

They have a very pretty inn, and the grounds are picnic-perfect on a sunny day. Check out the local sausages and cheeses available in the store, as well as their Vidal Blanc, Vignoles and Traminette wines. The Dierberg family also has ownership in the nearby Tin Mill Brewery, and the beer is dandy.

www.hermannhof.com

2 | Stone Hill Winery
1110 Stone Hill Hwy., Hermann, MO 65041; (573) 486-2221

Heading back down Highway 19, turn right on Highway 100 (going west) and follow the signs up the Old Stone Hill Highway. At the top of the hill, you'll find Stone Hill's picturesque home vineyard (planted solely with Norton) and its Historical Register mid-nineteenth-century buildings, including the Vintage Restaurant, built inside the original stable and carriage house. The conservatory and the winery's three tasting rooms are each worth a visit, but if the weather's cooperative, you should take in the pretty views from outside in any direction you gaze.

The underground cellars are beautiful and date back to 1847, the beginning of Stone Hill's long preeminence among American wineries. For a time, it was the second-largest winery in the United States, and

A display of local farm produce and flowers at the attractive Stone Hill Winery

163

▲ Stone Hill's picturesque home vineyard

today it's the second largest in Missouri. Like others in Missouri, Stone Hill closed at the onset of Prohibition, and the Held family reopened the winery in 1965.

Under the tutelage of chief winemaker David Johnson, who joined Stone Hill in 1970, the winery has, until recently, dominated State Fair competitions. And while St. James Winery (see facing page) produces more wine, no winery has greater visibility outside the state than Stone Hill. Johnson continues to oversee great fortified wines: The Norton Port and the Cream Sherry are world-class wines. And Stone Hill Norton, Chardonel, Traminette, Vidal Blanc, Vignoles and Seyval Blanc are as good as anything produced in the state.

www.stonehillwinery.com

3 | Adam Puchta Winery
1947 Frene Creek Rd., Hermann, MO 65041; (573) 486-5596

Another 2.5 miles (4 km) down Highway 100 (turn left onto Frene Creek Road) brings you to Adam Puchta Winery. While a handful among America's more than 6,000 wineries can boast of nineteenth-century origins, none of them has the family-owned longevity of the Puchtas, who have been making wine continuously since 1855. Ancestor Adam Puchta dug gold in California and dodged wild beasts in Nicaragua, but he also made wine on this land, including a wine he called Riefenstahler, from the Catawba grape. It was named after his wife, who later died in childbirth.

Prohibition killed his wine business in 1920, though the family saved most of the equipment and continued to make enough wine to keep the neighborhood happy. It wasn't until 1990, however, that

the winery began creating commercial wine again. Today Adam Puchta's winery is stronger than it's ever been.

Great-great-grandson Tim Puchta has been running the show for years and he has one of Missouri's most sought-after brains in the wine business. Tim's got a stable of Nortons: not simply content to make a big table red, he has a Norton Port (actually two of them), two table Nortons, and a Norton he splashes with a bit of berry juice (called Berry Black). The last one is fun, and the rest are serious.

His sweet and tasty red Riefenstahler (named, of course, for great-great-grandma) is a wildly popular tourist wine. The Traminette is tangy and perfumed, as the grape can be at its best. Tim's Chardonel, Vignoles, and Vidal Blanc wines have balance and pretty fruit as well.

www.adampuchtawine.com

4 | Heinrichshaus Vineyards & Winery
18500 State Rte. U, St. James, MO 65559; (573) 265-5000

Officially, the Hermann Wine Trail covers only those wineries in and around Hermann. But if you continue south, after about 50 miles (80 km) you'll reach another area with an illustrious, if less-known, wine history, around the college town of Rolla. Heinrichshaus Winery is on Highway U. It's a small and quiet place, but the Grohe family has offered quality Norton (or Cynthiana as it is called locally) for decades; these days you should taste their Traminette, Chambourcin, Vidal Blanc and the semi-sweet Vignoles.

www.heinrichshaus.com

HISTORIC HERMANN
Hermann, one of the prettiest towns in Missouri, still celebrates its German heritage, and there are more than 110 buildings on the Historic Register in and around the town. The Tin Mill Brewing Company continues Hermann's brewing heritage, producing Germanic pilsners and utilizing German hops. One of the Dierbergs of the Hermannhof Winery (see page 162) is a co-owner. The Hermann Farm and Museum (www.hermannfarm.org) is a National Landmark and working farm and was the home of George Husmann, one of the true heroes of early American viticulture.

Among the many festivals, OktoberFest is celebrated on weekends throughout October (the original Weinfest was first celebrated back in 1848), and Hermann is decked out in its finest array. Maifest is an old-fashioned German celebration of spring in May and sees an outdoor beer and wine garden, and there are lots of activities for kids and grown-ups.

5 | St. James Winery
540 Sidney St., St. James, MO 65559; (800) 280-9463

Head back to Interstate 44, then go west, and just before you get to the town of St. James, you'll see St. James Winery; you can't miss it.

Jim and Pat Hofherr started the winery in 1970, but things really took off when the second generation finished their studies in California and brought back new practices to the area. St. James is now Missouri's largest winery. They farm more than 300 acres of vineyards in Missouri and Arkansas and produce 130,000 cases of wine from 15 different varieties. Pat is the public face of the winery, while her sons carry on the hard work behind the scenes.

The Hofherr's Norton (sometimes labeled as Cynthiana) is always full and rich; the Chambourcin and Vintner's Select Vignoles are very good, too, though nearly everything in their portfolio is worth a taste. They make a prodigious amount of dessert wine (some hybrids handle the dessert style in some ways better than the better *vinifera* grapes), so look for the Chardonel Dessert, Norton Dessert and Late Harvest Chardonel.

www.stjameswinery.com

▲ A bridge over the Missouri at Hermann

find out more

- **www.missouriwine.org**
  The official site of Missouri wine with links to the wineries.

- **www.missouriwinecountry.com**
  Travel guide to Missouri wine country, with maps and trails.

- **www.hermannwinetrail.com**
  Information on visiting the Hermann wine country.

- **www.visithermann.com**
  Local information, including the town's many festivals.

Missouri Weinstrasse

An elision of Missouri's French and German ancestry, the Weinstrasse ("Wine Street") is a neighborhood with great and even famous real estate. Three of Missouri's top wineries are on the Weinstrasse, but the trail's fame rests upon the Augusta AVA (American Viticultural Area).

The AVA concept defines all of America's famous wine-growing areas (including the Napa Valley): The very first AVA approved by the federal government was Augusta (all the way back in 1980). Be sure to tell your Napa Valley friends about that; it makes them crazy.

The Weinstrasse is less than an hour's drive from St. Louis, but that's not why some of the wineries along the route are well known; instead, they have earned their fame with great wine and remarkable longevity, and the scenery's pretty, too.

◄ Located on a bluff above the river, Montelle Winery enjoys sweeping views over the Missouri River Valley.

1 | Montelle Winery
201 Montelle Dr. (at Hwy. 94), Augusta, MO 63332; (636) 228-4464

Driving west out of St. Louis, pick up state highway 94 toward the town of Augusta. Just 1.5 miles (2.5 km) east of town, you'll reach the turnoff for the Montelle Winery. The driveway takes you to a bluff above the Missouri River, overlooking the charming little town of Augusta. The Klondike Café offers good food, and in nice weather it is lovely up here.

Clayton Byers founded Montelle in 1970, making him a pioneer within the Missouri wine community. Tony Kooyumjian bought the winery in 1998. He is one of the stars of Midwestern winemaking (see Augusta Winery, facing page), and his ability to fashion delicious wines from hybrid grapes is, for many, the best evidence that hybrids have a great future in the wine marketplace. At Montelle, he makes a wonderful Cynthiana (the local name for the Norton grape) and first-rate Chambourcin, Seyval Blanc, Vignoles, Chardonel, port and icewine, as well as good red and white blends. He also makes an excellent peach brandy eau-de-vie and a not-to-miss Framboise.

www.montelle.com

2 | Mount Pleasant Winery
5634 High St., Augusta, MO 63332; (800) 467-9463

Leaving Montelle Winery, continue to Augusta and look for signs to Mount Pleasant Winery. This winery deserves much of the credit for establishing the Augusta AVA back in 1980. The Dressel family has shepherded the winery since 1966 and, despite a few lapses in judgment and a generational change, continues to improve a program that has been excellent for decades. The winery grows 16 different grape varieties on its 85 acres. It's just an example of how the Dressels can be vexing to anyone expecting them to follow the well-worn path. For one, they grow *vinifera* vines; a Pinot Noir vineyard was recently planted on a bluff above the Missouri River. Owner Chuck Dressel explains that the vineyard is windy enough to mitigate hot temperatures, and the air movement tends to keep the temperature above the point where Pinot Noir dies in winter.

Mount Pleasant has had far more success with hybrid grapes— their gentle, lemony Rayon d'Or is the world's best version of a grape that nearly a century ago some thought might be ideal for France's Loire Valley. Their other whites (a Vidal Blanc called Cuvee Blanc and a semi-sweet Vignoles) are pretty and they've been famed for port for decades. The wines are all solid and sometimes exciting.

www.mountpleasant.com

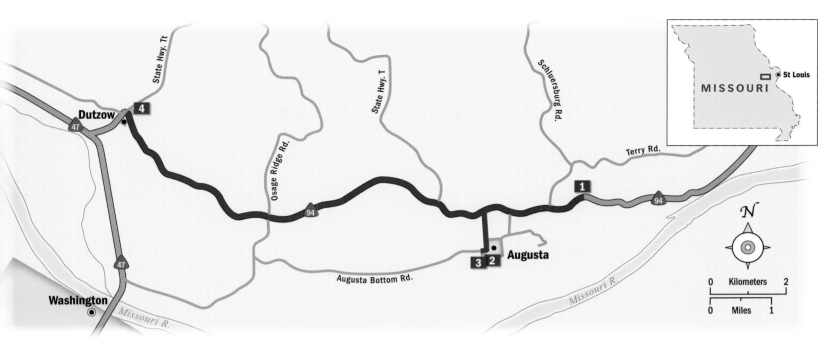

3 | Augusta Winery
5601 High St., Augusta, MO 63332; (888) 667-9463

Almost next door to Mount Pleasant is Augusta Winery, headed up by Tony Kooyumjian (Augusta shares Tony with Montelle Winery, see facing page), arguably Missouri's top winemaker. Especially in the last five or so years, Tony has bested every other winemaker in the state of Missouri, whether with his wines at Augusta or at Montelle. His touch extends to every grape in the Missouri arsenal: brilliant Chambourcin, elegant (yes, elegant) Norton, tangy Vidal Blanc, complex Vignoles, aromatic Traminette, wonderful icewine and rich port. Tony does it all.

Augusta Winery isn't one of those places with acres of beautiful refurbished structures. However, it has a very pretty beer-and-wine garden open weekends between May and October, often featuring live musical entertainment, and it's a nice place to sit if you're in the mood to taste some of Missouri's best wines. Indeed, Tony's wines represent the best examples of most of these grapes anywhere in the world.

www.augustawinery.com

findout more

- **www.explorestlouis.com**
  With St. Louis this close to the tour, you may want to stay in St. Louis and consider a day trip to the Augusta AVA . This site gives you plenty of options.

- **www.augustamissouri.org**
  Check out this site for local information.

4 | Blumenhof Vineyards & Winery
13699 S. Hwy. 94, Dutzow, MO 63342; (800) 419-2245

Get back on Highway 94 and head 7.5 miles (12 km) west. Just before the town of Dutzow, you'll see the winery sign. The Blumenberg family opened the winery in 1986, though the vineyards date back to the 1970s. In the last few years, the wines have become more consistently tasty; their semisweet Vignoles and Valvin Muscat are particularly delicious. Visitors should also check out their Norton (called Original Cyn), as well as the off-dry Rayon d'Or and Femme Osage (a very good Traminette), and Missouri Weinland (an off-dry Vidal Blanc).

www.blumenhof.com

▲ Visit Augusta Winery to try a wide range of excellent Missouri wines.

Route du Vin

Southern and southeast Missouri have historically been the poorest and least populous parts of the state. Wineries are often playthings of the rich and urbane, and they succeed best when they are convenient and close to large urban areas. So while southeast Missouri has a wealth of German and French heritage, its wine fortunes have lingered behind the rest of the state. Only recently has it sprouted a crop of wineries, but some of the most interesting projects in the state are happening along the Route du Vin. Having lagged behind, wineries here know that they need to catch up and build projects that will attract tourists.

The tour begins in the town of Sainte Genevieve, about 50 miles (80 km) downriver from St Louis. This is the oldest French settlement west of the Mississippi, dating back to the 1730s, and it still has a certain sleepy charm. The tour then progresses south through the rolling hills toward Farmington.

◀ Chaumette Vineyards' tasting bar and restaurant is located right in the middle of the vineyards.

1 | Sainte Genevieve Vineyard
245 Merchant St., Sainte Genevieve, MO 63670; (573) 883-2800

Make your way to Merchant Street in the historic district of town and you'll see the refurbished, turn-of-the-century house that is Sainte Genevieve Winery. The Hoffmeister family started the winery in 1983, but the wines have recently improved under winemaker daughter Elaine's care. The focus is on fruit wines, in particular strawberry, cranberry and a particularly tasty Christmas plum wine.

www.saintegenevievewinery.com

2 | Cave Vineyard
21124 Cave Rd., Sainte Genevieve, MO 63670; (573) 543-5284

Head south out of town on Highway M. Once on Highway P, turn left on Cave Road. Cave Vineyard is a small, new winery named for the cave that came with the pretty property. The Strussione family purchased it in 1995, and planted 14 acres of vineyards in 2001. Be sure to taste their vibrant Chambourcin, and the Traminette and Norton are well made, too. Their young Vignoles vines will soon be part of the portfolio here.

www.cavevineyard.com

▲ The patio at Crown Valley Vineyards is a busy place in fine weather.

3 | Chaumette Vineyards
24345 State Rte. WW, Sainte Genevieve, MO 63670; (573) 747-1000

Continue on Cave Road for a little more than 1 mile (2 km) and then go right on Saline Creek Road for about 4 miles (6.5 km). Turn right on State Route WW (also called Highway Y) and travel farther for another mile. Chaumette's 310 acres lie within the pretty Saline Creek Valley and the winery has a spa, private villas and a full-service restaurant, the Grapevine Grill, which utilizes local products.

The winery has just taken on winemaker Mark Baehmann from Mount Pleasant (see page 166). Up to now, the Chambourcin has been their best offering, but Baehmann is crafting two Nortons (one with French oak and one with American oak), and the Chambourcin program is likely to go the same way.

www.chaumette.com

4 | Crown Valley Vineyards
23589 State Rte. WW, Sainte Genevieve, MO 63670; (866) 207-9463

Just a half mile (800 m) north of Chaumette Vineyards on State Route WW is a remarkable property called Crown Valley Vineyards. Crown Valley's scope is on a scale unknown in Missouri: Opened in 2000 but built on a farmstead created in 1984, Crown Valley just keeps growing. Today it includes a large winery with wines from local, regional and out-of-state vineyards, as well as a brewery, bistro, full-service restaurant, dance hall, golf course, tiger sanctuary…well, you get the idea.

Perhaps because the winery has taken to blending a bit of out-of-state juice with some of their wines, the wines have shown some inconsistencies of late. Nonetheless, they can be relied upon for solid Norton (the Norton Museum), tasty Riesling, a delightful fortified wine (Fine Old Vintage Museum) and a very pretty Chardonel Brut sparkling wine. This property just has to be seen to be believed.

www.crownvalleywinery.com

▲ The tasting room and patio at Twin Oaks is a peaceful spot among the vines.

5 | Twin Oaks Vineyard & Winery
6470 Hwy. F, Farmington, MO 63640; (573) 756-6500

Continue north on Highway WW for 1 mile (2 km) and look for the sign for Highway Y and Highway F. Take a left onto that road (the two highways are the same at this point) and drive just over 10 miles (16 km) until you see the signs for Twin Oaks. It's a small place with a delightful patio above a tranquil lake. The Hudson family have filled the winery with movie memorabilia. For the moment, the Two Brothers (a soft rosé blend of Catawba and Concord) is their most impressive wine, but this is a Missouri winery to watch in the future.

www.twinoaksvineyard.com

High Plains

Welcome to Lubbock and the Panhandle of Texas! The High Plains region is the premier grape-growing area in Texas. Quality grapes are necessary for quality wine, and here dramatic shifts between day and nighttime temperatures make for intensely flavored grapes. It's dry, hot and sunny in the daytime, with enough elevation and wind so that it's cool at night.

Driving into the Lubbock sunset feels like the set of a John Wayne movie with tumbleweeds, dust and wind. This Lone Star State prairie experience bears no comparison to other wine trails—its wine bars are essentially modern saloons. The pace is slower as you experience cowboy culture and the beauty of the desert and plateaus. Discover museums and cafés that reflect the heritage and spirit of the pioneers. May through October are ideal months to visit.

◀ The flat, high-altitude Texas High Plains is one of the state's premier vineyard areas.

1 | Pheasant Ridge
3507 E. County Rd. 5700, Lubbock, TX 79403; (806) 746-6033

Pheasant Ridge is one of the earliest pioneers of commercial winemaking in Texas, planting its first vineyards in 1979. Owner Bill Gipson is proud to say that all the wines are estate grown from their 50-acre vineyard. The tasting room, which is in the middle of the vineyard, is located in the barrel room with all the wonderful smells and aromas of the wines fermenting.

Pheasant Ridge wines are more typical of the styles of France than of the United States. Reds are big and bold but delicately balanced and full of fruit. Pheasant Ridge's largest sellers are the Cabernet Sauvignon, Proprietor's Reserve blend of Cabernet, Merlot and Cabernet Franc, and the dry Chenin Blanc.

www.pheasantridgewinery.com

2 | McPherson Cellars
1615 Texas Ave., Lubbock, TX 79401; (806) 687-9463

What used to be the Coca-Cola bottling plant in the historic Depot District of Lubbock is now a place to relax and enjoy a glass of wine, either in the tasting room surrounded by artwork from local artists or outside in the bamboo-lined courtyard. Owner Kim McPherson founded the winery in 2000, following in the footsteps of his father, "Doc" McPherson, a pioneer in the Texas wine industry. Kim's West Texas friendly opinion is: "Plant to the land. The High Plains aren't Napa. Cabernet Sauvignon here is smooth and full with soft tannin, but it isn't going to have the same deep richness Napa Cabernets have. Put Sangiovese and Tempranillo in the ground—they love the heat and so do the Rhône varietals."

▲ The courtyard at McPherson Cellars in the historic Depot District of Lubbock

Water-pumping windmills

Kim makes delicious Viognier that has flavors of pear, peach, melon and citrus, and a fabulous Sangiovese that is dry and soft, with cherry, plum, spice and a whiff of oak. It is also worth trying the red Tre Colore, a blend of southern Rhône varietals, or the Rosé of Syrah–Grenache.

Kim's wife, Sylvana, owns La Diosa, a Bohemian-style tapas bar, bistro and winery just around the corner on 17th Street, with a variety of Texas wines on offer. Her homemade La Diosa Sangria is also a bestseller with customers.

www.mcphersoncellars.com

PLENTY TO DO IN LUBBOCK

On the north side of Lubbock, between Pheasant Ridge and McPherson Cellars in the Depot District, is the Silent Wings Museum in the old terminal at the Lubbock Airport. It chronicles the history of World War II's military glider program and displays more than 10,000 items, such as aircraft, vehicles, weapons and personal effects.

Still in the Depot District, the Buddy Holly Center chronicles the life and music of the Lubbock native, as well as other musicians.

The 14-acre National Ranching Heritage Center near Texas Tech University houses more than 30 restored ranch structures, from chuckwagons to log cabins and Victorian homes.

One of the most fascinating visits is the American Wind Power Center and Museum, slightly east of downtown. See the collection of more than 90 iconic American-style water-pumping windmills, new and old, and think open air, wind space, life and freedom.

Fun places to eat include the Stars and Stripes Drive-In Theater in North Lubbock, a 1950s café with a specialty that's not to be missed—the "famous" Chihuahua sandwich of two crispy corn tortillas, homemade chili, pimento cheese, shredded cabbage, onions and jalapeño pepper. Just south of the airport, stop at County Line Restaurant for juicy barbecue and flavorful steaks.

Two B&Bs offer a place to rest: Woodrow House, across from the University, and Broadway Manor (built in 1926), close to the Depot District.

▲ Dry air and constant wind are characteristics of the High Plains.

3 | Llano Estacado
3426 E. FM 1585, Lubbock, TX 79404; (800) 634-3854

Founded in 1976, Llano Estacado was the first bonded winery in Texas to open its doors after the repeal of Prohibition. In 1977 production was 1,300 cases; today it is the state's largest premium winery, producing more than 100,000 cases annually. Determination and consistency are driving forces at Llano. As one of the wineries credited with Texas's current wine renaissance, they have an understanding of what it takes to keep Llano moving forward. Winemaker Greg Bruni and President and chief operating officer Mark Hyman make an unbeatable team.

Llano made a real mark on the world wine scene in 1986, when they won a Double Gold at the San Francisco Wine Competition for their 1984 Chardonnay. The fact that Texas produces wine was no longer a secret. Over the years, Llano expanded its team of growers beyond the High Plains into the Hill Country and far West Texas, so Texas fruit is now used for almost all its wines. The growers, meanwhile, are finding the varieties that best suit their region.

Llano Estacado's range currently comprises around 30 wines. The top red, Viviano, is a "super-Tuscan" blend of Cabernet Sauvignon and Sangiovese. Its new sibling, Viviana, is an aromatic white. Signature White and Signature Red are perfect "house wines."

www.llanowine.com

▲ Llano Estacado's tasting room offers 30 different wines.

4 | Cap*Rock

408 E. Woodrow Rd., Lubbock, TX 79423; (806) 686-4452

Cap*Rock is a must-see for the ambience, the beauty and the architecture of its mission-style building, which is unlike anything else in the High Plains and perhaps in Texas. The name refers to the geological formation of the High Plains.

Cap*Rock's 2008 Viognier, full of stone fruit, melon and honeysuckle flavors, was a first for Texas—a wine made from organically grown grapes from a vineyard in West Texas. Alas, in the next growing season the vineyard suffered huge rainfall and more bugs than normal, so the vines had to be sprayed. The current vintage will be non-organic. Texas does not yet have an association to monitor organic and sustainable vineyards.

Cap*Rock has none of their own vineyards, and the majority of grapes currently come from California, but general manager Phillip Anderson says that they are looking to plant 27 acres behind the winery and also to sign more contracts with local growers, since there are thousands of acres planted within 45 minutes of the winery. For now, sip the Palo Duro Canyon White and the Red.

www.caprockwinery.com

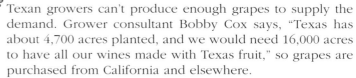

Grape EXPECTATIONS

Texan growers can't produce enough grapes to supply the demand. Grower consultant Bobby Cox says, "Texas has about 4,700 acres planted, and we would need 16,000 acres to have all our wines made with Texas fruit," so grapes are purchased from California and elsewhere.

In the 1980s and 1990s, growers planted more vines than they had money for, so the Texas Department of Agriculture stepped in to support the state's $1.35 billion wine industry, offering grants for growers to increase grape acreage. The High Plains area has been a major beneficiary of state support and now sells grapes to wineries throughout Texas.

Texas soils and climatic conditions are very varied and support a diverse list of grape varieties. Cabernet Sauvignon does well in both the Hill Country and the High Plains; Tempranillo and Sangiovese (for red wines) and Viognier (whites) are new Texan stars. Rhône varieties such as Syrah, Grenache and Mourvedre are at home in the High Plains.

▲ Visitors to Lubbock should pay a visit to Cap*Rock to see its grand mission-style winery.

Dallas

Visiting urban wineries is a bonus for wine lovers if you are heading to metropolitan Dallas with its modern architecture, culture and high-end shopping. Wine fans can fly into Dallas/Fort Worth International and begin tasting at La Bodega Winery, which has wine bars at Terminals A and D for sampling its own and other Texas wines.

The Dallas/Fort Worth area is considered the heart of North Texas. Approximately 370 acres of grapes are grown in the North Texas area, but few of those grapes are used by the urban wineries. La Bodega and La Buena Vida source many of their grapes locally, but other urban wineries have to look farther afield to meet demand, with vineyards in other parts of the state—they may also source grapes from California and elsewhere.

◄ The thriving city of Dallas offers the visitor urban wineries as well as myriad culinary events.

1 | Times Ten Cellars

6324 Prospect Ave., Dallas, TX 75214; (214) 824-9463

In the Lakewood area, 10 minutes from downtown Dallas, three entrepreneurs opened Times Ten Cellars in 2005. They opened a second facility, in Fort Worth, in 2009. A stop at either location combines the experience of a winery visit, where you can see the fermentation tanks and barrels, with the ambience of a wine bar, where a mix of high and low tables and soft couches encourage staying a while. No snobbery here—whether the customer is clad in shorts or a tuxedo, the staff are trained to take the mystery out of ordering and enjoying wine.

The selection of wines is large, with Cabernet Sauvignon being the bestseller, closely followed by Sauvignon Blanc and the unoaked Chardonnay. Enjoy your own mini class by choosing a taste of four wines. The staff will explain the characteristics of each wine, where it is produced, and answer questions such as which foods it will complement. Wines from other Texas wineries are available at the wine bar.

Many of the grapes come from California, but Times Ten also owns 8 acres in the high desert mountains near Alpine, 500 miles (800 km) west of Dallas, planted mainly to Tempranillo and Syrah, with some Grenache, Mourvedre and Petite Sirah, which are used in the Cathedral Mountain Vineyard red blend. Vintners are discovering that these varietals do well in parts of Texas that are drier, have more sun and cool down at night.

▲ The wine bar at Times Ten Cellars

www.timestencellars.com

DOWNTOWN DALLAS AMENITIES

For a panoramic view of the city, eat at Nana, a fine dining restaurant on the 27th floor of the Hilton Anatole. You'll also get great food at Craft in the W Hotel. Restaurants abound at Victory Park, where the American Airlines Center has entertainment and is home to the Dallas Mavericks and Dallas Stars. In the Lakewood area to the east, Gloria's on Greenville, serving Latin American food, is a great lunch spot, while York Street restaurant and its chef/owner Sharon Hage will provide you with a dinner you may never forget.

On the western edge of downtown is the Sixth Floor Museum, with an interactive history of President John F. Kennedy's life. If time permits, walk through the original Neiman Marcus on Main at Ervay—it's a Dallas icon. While downtown, check out the Nasher Sculpture Center, Meyerson Symphony Center and the Dallas Museum of Art. The Dali Wine Bar is nearby, at 1722 Routh Street. Times Ten Cellars is only 2 miles (3 km) from the Dallas Arboretum (a 66-acre botanical preserve), or take a 10-mile (16-km) walk around White Rock Lake.

Stay overnight at Daisy Polk Inn or The Corinthian (both B&Bs).

▲ Cookery demonstration at the popular Dallas Wine and Food Festival

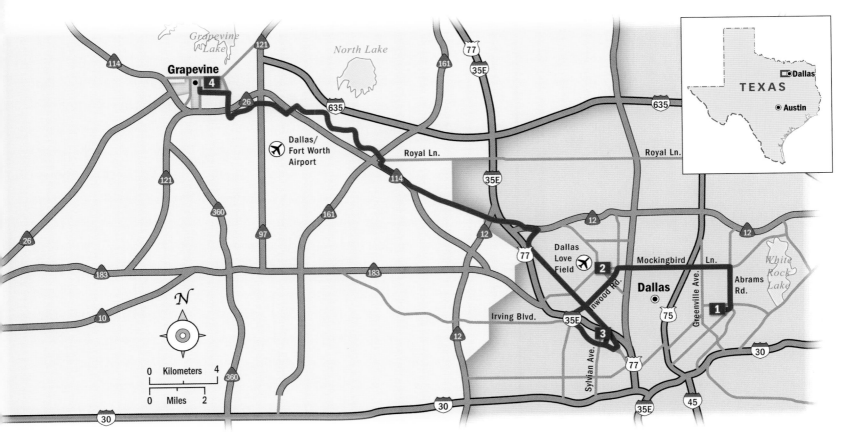

2 | Fuqua Winery
3737 Atwell St., Suite 203, Dallas, TX 75209; (214) 769-1147

Very close to Love Field is a boutique winery that is all about the wine. Fuqua produces small-lot, handcrafted wines. Visitors receive personal attention from winemaker Lee Foster Fuqua or his wife, Julia.

Fuqua has been a prolific winemaker for more than 13 years, and his dedication has resulted in the production of many award-winning wines. In 2009, the 2006 Fuqua Tempranillo was awarded a Double Gold medal at the San Francisco International Wine Competition. His Texas Red Reserve is a Tempranillo–Cabernet blend sourced from the Texas High Plains, and he makes a Pinot Noir and Chardonnay from California grapes.

Fuqua is both a winery and a wine bar, with a few wines from Italy and France. It is located behind a Home Depot, so a crowd congregates in the parking lot and they all descend at once. Lee Fuqua says, "I'm happy to open anything I have for anyone who asks. On a weekend, we will have 10 to 12 bottles open at once. If a bottle isn't finished, we take it home." The winery hosts three to four tasting parties each week and has over 5,500 visitors each year.

www.fuquawines.com

3 | Inwood Estates Vineyards
1350 Manufacturing St., Suite 209, Dallas, TX 75207; (214) 902-9452

Behind the Hilton Anatole on Interstate 35, the hotel serves as a landmark for Inwood Estates, a really different type of winery. It is actually in a warehouse, where all the bottling and labeling is done by hand. Inwood Estates produces beautiful, expensive wines that you absolutely must experience.

Owners Dan and Rose Mary Gatlin, believing that Texas wines are heavily influenced by the terroir, first planted a small vineyard on the property where they lived in Dallas. Today their success is based on plantings of vines spanning the state. Tempranillo and Cabernet Sauvignon are from far west Texas, near the New Mexico border; Palomino and Chardonnay are grown 80 miles (129 km) east of Dallas.

After years of experimenting with various grape varieties, Dan realized that Spain's hot-weather grapes would produce well in Texas. Palomino, a white variety primarily used for sherry production in southern Spain, has a honeyed-melon aroma and a rich, dense texture—so dense that it needs to be blended. Chardonnay is the

right companion, lending complexity yet thinning out the mouthfeel of the Palomino. The Tempranillo-Cabernet is a full-bodied inky blend that is perfect for a Texas steak or wild-game dinner.

www.inwoodwines.com

4 | La Buena Vida Vineyards
416 E. College St., Grapevine, TX 76051; (817) 481-9463

Gina Puente-Brancato became so enamored with the wine business when she created La Bodega Winery at Dallas/Forth Worth airport that her company bought La Buena Vida in 2006. La Buena Vida, which means "the good life" in Spanish, is located in what was once a college and then a church in the Grapevine historic district. The winery was purchased from Texas wine-industry pioneer Dr. Bobby Smith, who founded La Buena Vida in Springtown, 45 miles (72 km) away. Gina says, "Dr. Bobby remains the primary winemaker for our winery, producing Merlot, Cabernet Sauvignon, Chardonnay, Viognier, Sweet Ruby—a blend of Texas Cabernet, Ruby Cabernet

▲ Tasting wine at Fuqua Winery

and Merlot—and Sweet Amber, made from barrel-aged late-harvest Chardonnay. Dr. Bobby's ports can stand tall with any in the world."

Under its new owners, La Buena Vida has undergone a significant facelift. Spanish-tiled fountains, shady patios, waterfalls and lush landscaping create an ambience of "the good life." The vineyard in Grapevine is just two rows, to give visitors an idea of how grapes are farmed. Wine-tasting classes and concerts are well attended. If you cannot get to the airport (see below), La Bodega's wines are available to taste here.

La Bodega Winery, located at the Dallas/Fort Worth International Airport (DFW), halfway between the two cities, houses the world's first and only bonded winery in an airport. It is not an on-site working winery, but a wine bar serving wine from its own winery and more than 30 premium wines made in Texas, as well as several international wines for the taster to compare and contrast. You will need an airline ticket before you visit, and, whether you are arriving or departing, you must have been cleared by security at any of the airport's five terminals.

When Gina Puente-Brancato joined the family business in 1991, her father operated three newsstand/gift shops at the airport. By 1995, after realizing that there were certain incentives to make the nearby town of Grapevine the wine capital of Texas, Gina created La Bodega out of part of a family newsstand.

Today La Bodega has two locations at the airport, in Terminal A, Gate 15, and Terminal D, Gate 14. The grapes for its wines—which include a blackcurranty Cabernet Sauvignon and a crisp, citrus Chardonnay with a hint of oak—are grown near Lubbock, Texas. Wines are offered by the taste, glass or bottle, and a wide selection of wine-related gifts is sold in both stores. La Bodega is an oasis for wine lovers, or for anyone who is just plain curious about Texas wines: Try Aero Port, from Lenoir, a native Texas grape.

www.labuenavida.com

▲ The town of Grapevine is a draw for wine-loving tourists.

IN GRAPEVINE

The town of Grapevine, 2 miles (3 km) west of DFW airport, is a tourist destination with more than 100,000 visitors a year. The historic downtown area has a laid-back feel, with bohemian shops, wine bars and eateries. Nine wineries have tasting rooms here. Some stops to make are Cross Timbers, located in an old farmstead built in the 1870s; Su Vino, where you can create your own wine; D'Vine Wine, with more than 30 wines in production; and Homestead, in a fully restored Victorian-era home. For chili, chicken or fried steak, don't miss Willhoite's on Main Street. Garden Manor B&B in the historical district is close to many tasting rooms.

findout more

- www.txwines.org
Find out about the wine regions of Texas, its wineries and many festivals.

- www.grapevinetexasusa.com
Information on visiting the town of Grapevine.

- www.dallasfoodandwinefestival.com
Five days of entertainment and events focused on the pleasures of the table. You can take in dinner and a movie, catch a rising star, enjoy the best of Texas, learn how to entertain with style and taste world-class award-winning wines and cuisine.

TOUR 53
Hill Country

The Texas Hill Country is the second most popular destination for wine tourism in the United States—behind Napa Valley. Within a triangle formed by the colorful historic cities of Austin and San Antonio and the charming country town of Fredericksburg, two dozen wineries are waiting to give visitors a taste of Texas hospitality with their delicious wines. It is about an hour's picturesque drive from one of these three towns to the next.

The Hill Country is best discovered by getting off major highways and seeing Texas alive with wildflowers, lakes, ranches and family-run antique shops. Be sure to taste authentic smoked barbecue, Czech *kolaches* (filled pastries) and German sausage. Whether stopping to "remember" the Alamo in San Antonio or two-stepping at a legendary dance hall in Gruene or Luckenbach, the dress code calls for comfort, ranging anywhere from jeans and boots to motorcycle chic.

◄ The log cabin at Becker Vineyards is now furnished as a delightful B&B for visitors.

1 | Torre di Pietra
10915 E. Hwy. 290, Fredericksburg, TX 78624; (830) 644-2829

From Fredericksburg take Highway 290, pass Grape Creek Vineyards, known for its Muscat Canelli. Next door is Torre di Pietra, where the large tasting room is often packed with visitors. While owner Ken Maxwell was working on his business plan, he got excited when he analyzed the demographics of people who visit the area. "No question, the Fredericksburg area is the best place in Texas to have a winery. Texans support Texas products."

Although this location opened only in 2004, the Maxwell family has been making wine in Texas for 100 years. They now own 80 acres of vineyards in the region, and most of the 5,000 cases of wine they produce every year are from estate-grown grapes.

On Saturday afternoon, you can enjoy live music on the piazza at Torre di Pietra while sipping Dirty Girl Chardonnay, Carignane, Claret or a sweet wine. Primitivo—almost identical to California's own Zinfandel grape—is their bestseller. Several wines are offered in single-serve (6-ounce) bottles, which is unique to this winery. While there why not feast on CKC Farm's fresh goat cheese, Uncle John's quail sausage and wine-infused chocolates, as well as enjoying some wine-tasting?

www.texashillcountrywine.com

2 | Becker Vineyards
464 Becker Farms Rd., Stonewall, TX 78671; (830) 644-2681

Richard and Bunny Becker are still in disbelief that Becker Vineyards has brought such unexpected fame and fortune. Richard says, "We started out as an estate winery growing all our grapes and producing 1,500 cases in 1995. Today we have contracts with 12 growers from Fredericksburg to Mason, San Angelo, Lubbock and the High Plains near the New Mexico border." In 2009 they produced 80,000 cases.

Becker owns about 100 acres of vines on a property in Stonewall and another 50 in Ballinger. Because of the uncertainties of Texas weather, with late freezes and hailstorms, it is best not to have all your grapes in one basket.

Richard praises his winemaker, Russell Smith, describing him as "a genie in the bottle." The Malbec was Bunny's idea. She said, "Argentina is hot like Texas, and they make wonderful Malbec." She's been proved right. Other best-selling wines are the Claret, Cabernet Sauvignon Newsom Vineyard, Cabernet Sauvignon Reserve Brenda Canada Vineyard, Prairie Rotie (a Rhône-style blend) and Grenache. Be sure to buy a bottle of the popular Viognier, too.

The newly enlarged tasting room offers in-depth wine tasting, tours of the winery, or a more relaxed experience with a glass of wine on the shady porch with snacks from the deli. On weekends, enjoy a picnic lunch under the trees while listening to music.

Three acres of lavender fields behind the winery is a breathtaking sight. In April and May the scent of lavender is everywhere and culminates with the annual Lavender Festival that includes vendors selling plants and products along with cooking demonstrations. Red poppies and bluebonnets now surround the lavender fields, making potpourris of color. Artichoke plants are the newest addition for beauty and consumption, if the deer don't eat them first.

Becker has an authentic log cabin, The Homestead, used as a B&B. Nearby Rose Hill Manor is a charming luxury inn with a gourmet restaurant.

www.beckervineyards.com

3 | Texas Hills Vineyard
878 Ranch Rd. 2766, Johnson City, TX 78636; (830) 868-2321

You know you're in Texas when a medal-winning wine is called Kick Butt Cab. Toro de Tejas (the bull of Texas) is made from Tempranillo. Sweet, well-balanced Orange Moscato is another favorite at the horseshoe-shaped bar in the intimate, friendly tasting room.

Gary and Kathy Gilstrap, with son Dale Rasseft, work to protect the environment by using as few chemicals as possible in the vineyards. The winery and tasting room were built by digging down to solid rock and pouring a concrete footing as a base for the 24-inch (61-cm)-thick walls, using a technique formerly called

▲ Red wine varieties are flourishing in Texas, and growers cannot keep up with the demand.

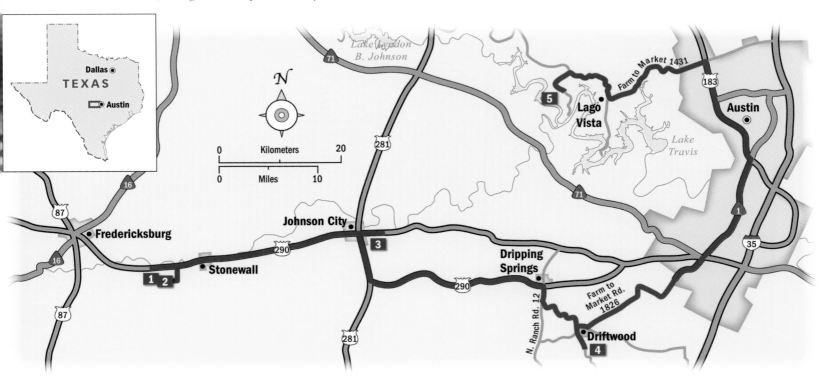

"rammed earth." With no windows and only two doors in the winery, the temperature remains constant.

Gary is proud to say that all of their grapes come from Texas, with about 40 percent from their own vineyard. The popular Kick Butt Cab is 100 percent Cabernet Sauvignon from Newsom Vineyard in the High Plains.

If you have camping in mind (tent or RV), Pedernales Falls State Park is nearby.

www.texashillsvineyard.com

▲ Picking grapes at Texas Hills Vineyard just outside Johnson City

4 | Mandola Estate Winery

13308 FM 150 W, Driftwood, TX 78619-9274; (512) 858-1470

The Hill Country's Italian heritage has been brought to life through the Tuscan-style architecture of Mandola Estate Winery. Texas is duly represented by the lush landscaping using Texas native plants that are, importantly, deer-resistant. The grounds are perfect for strolling.

Damian Mandola, the iconic Houston chef, opened the winery in 2006 in partnership with Dr. Stan Duchman after enough Mandola wine was produced to serve in the tasting room. Making long-term contracts with growers in the Hill Country and High Plains, and asking them to plant something they had never heard of, was tricky. Damian wanted Italian varietals such as Vermentino, Montepulciano, Dolcetto, Nero d'Avola and Aglianico, as well as Sangiovese and Pinot Grigio. Another passion is Rhône wine, so he planted the popular Viognier and Syrah.

Dave Reilly, operations chief, says, "As the vineyard grows, we grow. My job is to let the varietal speak for itself . . . with no overwhelming oak in a more elegant style."

Trattoria Lisina, the restaurant at the winery, is the inspiration of Lisa Duchman and Trina Mandola. Upscale casual in a rustic setting, it serves Mandola wines and a large Italian wine portfolio at reasonable prices. High ceilings and big windows lend a beautiful spaciousness to the restaurant, which is open for lunch and dinner. Watch for a cooking school to open.

Other options for lunch or dinner nearby include barbecue at Salt Lick, outside of Driftwood. Customers have walked past the open pit of meats smoking here since 1967 and still come in droves. Bring your own wine, and it's cash only. For a gourmet meal in an unlikely setting, Creek Road Café in Dripping Springs is hopping, even during the week.

For an overnight stay, Blair House Inn B&B is only a few minutes' drive to the south, at Wimberley.

www.mandolawines.com

5 | Flat Creek Estate

24912 Singleton Bend East Rd., Marble Falls, TX 78654; (512) 267-6310

On the road to the north shore of Lake Travis is Flat Creek Estate, owned by Rick and Madelyn Naber. Madelyn describes the ambience of the tasting room as "Texas comfortable with a Tuscan flair." The Nabers' goal is to use all Texas fruit—weather permitting. Of the 80 acres of Flat Creek Estate, 20 are vineyards, which usually provide grapes for half of their annual production of 10,000 cases. Contracts with growers supply the rest.

The elegant, dry Pinot Blanc, fruit-forward Pinot Grigio, Super Texan Sangiovese and Mistella (a dessert wine made from unfermented Muscat Canelli grapes and grape brandy) are favorites in the tasting room. The Bistro is open for lunch Friday, Saturday and Sunday and for "First Saturday" wine classes and dinner.

www.flatcreekestate.com

▲ The Bistro at Flat Creek Estate

THINGS TO DO IN AUSTIN

Austin's outdoor soul is Zilker Botanical Garden and the adjacent Barton Springs Pool, west of downtown. Walk the scenic urban trail around Lady Bird Lake, or climb the 100 steps to the top of Mount Bonnell for the sweeping panorama. Visit the state capitol, built of local "sunset red" granite.

Party at the restaurants and bars on Sixth Street and listen to some of the best blues and jazz anywhere. For barbecue, try the brown-sugar-and-coffee-rubbed brisket at Lamberts on Second Street, or go for Tex-Mex at Matt's Famous El Rancho on South Lamar Boulevard.

regional events

Savor Dallas □ March

Big fun and big flavors at this annual international experience of wine, food, spirits and the arts.   www.savordallas.com

Texas Hill Country Wine & Food Festival □ April

The oldest and largest wine and food festival in Texas, held in and around Austin. Includes speakers from all over the world, cooking classes, tastings and a gala auction.   www.texaswineandfood.org

Dallas Wine & Food Festival □ April

Tastings, demonstrations, live music and lots more over a 5-day period at landmark settings in and around Dallas.

www.dallaswineandfoodfestival.com

New World Wine & Food Festival □ May

Promotes San Antonio as a premier wine-and-food destination, with wine and food seminars and tastings and a glamorous black tie masquerade.

www.nwwff.org

Austin Wine Festival □ May

Three-day celebration of Texas wine with over 30 wineries taking part.

www.austinwinefestival.com/index.html

GrapeFest □ September

Uncork the fun in the town of Grapevine. A carnival for the kids, with live music and food and wine tastings.   www.grapevinetexasusa.com

Fredericksburg Food & Wine Fest □ October

A celebration of Texas food, wine and music. Specialty booths, food court and fun for all.   www.fbgfoodandwinefest.com

Original Terlingua International Chili Championship □ October

This spicy event boasts a revered barbecue cook-off and live music each night, plus many other activities.   www.chili.org

Eastern Region

Grape-growing along the Eastern Seaboard of the United States has always been a tricky proposition. For one thing, in the South, where temperatures are more moderate, humidity creates rot, and winter problems (cold) can kill most *vinifera* vines. Florida has a different problem: It isn't cold enough for grape vines to "hibernate," as they should. As a result, the success for early East Coast winemakers came in New York with Native American grapes and the fruit muscadine, which often makes an assertively scented, sweet wine.

The Finger Lakes of upstate New York grew the most grapes early on, little of it *Vitis vinifera*, until the 1970s when Dr. Konstantin Frank, an experiment-oriented German winemaker, led efforts to plant the *vinifera* varieties. His voice was strong enough to energize plant scientists, who developed systems for ripening certain grapes in the colder climates and for avoiding some cold-related issues. As a result, throughout the upper East Coast region, entire wine industries sprang up with superb wines being made in New York (especially in Finger Lakes and Long Island), New Jersey, Pennsylvania, Virginia, Ohio, and later in Canada at Nova Scotia and Ontario.

New York eventually developed a worldwide reputation for its Rieslings, from dry to sweet. Moreover, East Coast red wines (though notably lighter in weight than those of California) were designed nicely to work as an accompaniment to food.

▲ Vineyards on the west side of Lake Keuka, New York State

Annapolis & Gaspereau

From the air, this area of gently rolling hills looks like a patchwork quilt of orchards, vineyards and vegetable fields, with forests occupying the less-favored high ground. Dubbed "Canada's first breadbasket," the Annapolis Valley runs from Wolfville to Annapolis Royal, between a rugged escarpment to the north and a parallel range of mountains on the south. The two mountain ranges, separated by 6 miles (10 km), offer shelter from offshore winds. The region has the warmest temperatures in the province and moderately low rainfall.

The Gaspereau is a comparatively small area of steep slopes and immense charm that runs east of the Annapolis Valley. A good time to visit is during the five-day Apple Blossom Festival (end of May) or the Harvest Festival at Sainte-Famille Wines (in early October) in Falmouth. The town of Windsor, where you'll find the eighteenth-century Fort Edward, is the eastern gate to the Annapolis Valley.

◄ The Annapolis Valley is a gently rolling landscape of orchards and vineyards.

1 | Domaine de Grand Pré
11611 Hwy. 1, Grand Pré, NS, B0P 1M0; (902) 542-1753

Traveling from Halifax on Highway 101 west, take Exit 10 and turn right onto Highway 1. Travel approximately half a mile (1 km) west and look for the first winery on your tour, Domaine de Grand Pré, on a hill to your right, just past the road for the Grand Pré National Historic Site.

Founded in 1978, the winery claims to be the oldest in the Nova Scotia province. But you wouldn't know it by its appearance. Hans Peter Stutz bought the property in 1994, closed it down for four years, and spent several million dollars replanting the vineyards and constructing a showplace winery and cellar. During the vast reconstruction, Stutz sent his son Jürg to the Wädenswil wine school in Switzerland to learn winemaking. Three years later, in 1999, Jürg returned for his first crush. Stutz officially reopened the dazzling complex as Domaine de Grand Pré in 2000. It resembles a small, very tidy, and elegant wine hamlet.

Since then, the winery has become a magnet for tourists and has many special events on offer. The beautifully landscaped site includes cobblestoned walkways inlaid with giant grape leaves, as well as an art gallery, which is below the tasting room and looks onto the wine cellar. There is also a fine restaurant serving lunch and dinner. The Pergola is an ideal spot to sit with a glass of wine and take in the luxurious ambience. Try the Vintner's Reserve Foch, Seyval Blanc, Vidal and New York Muscat Icewine. Stutz also makes an excellent cider.

www.grandprewines.ns.ca

▲ Many wineries make great venues for celebratory parties.

▲ L'Acadie is best known for sparkling wine.

2 | L'Acadie Vineyards

310 Slayter Rd., Gaspereau, RR#1 Wolfville, NS, B4P 2R1; (902) 542-8463

Leaving Grand Pré, take Grand Pré Road south, then turn right at Gaspereau River Road. Drive 2.5 miles (4 km), then turn left on Slayter Road. Bruce Ewert is an expert sparkling-wine producer,

A CLIMATIC SURPRISE

Midway between the equator and the North Pole, Nova Scotia is an unlikely wine-growing region. It may surprise you to learn that St. John's, Newfoundland, is Canada's third warmest city in winter, ranking just below Victoria and Vancouver in mean temperature. Look at a map and you will see that most of the Maritime provinces are located farther south than British Columbia.

Apart from Prince Edward Island, this province has the smallest number of wineries of any established wine region in Canada, but it is fiercely proud of them. Wherever you go, you will find the local wines displayed on lists in hotels as elegant as the Blomidon Inn in Wolfville and in the smallest guesthouses along the Evangeline Trail (Highway 1), which runs through the Annapolis Valley.

Grape EXPECTATIONS

Nova Scotia's most widely planted grape, L'Acadie Blanc, is unique to the province, apart from small plantings in New Brunswick. Although it was bred in Ontario's Horticultural Research Institute at Vineland Station in 1953, it never caught on with Niagara growers. L'Acadie is a winter-hardy early-ripening grape that's perfect for short growing seasons. It can survive in temperatures down to −23.8°F (4.5°C).

Roger Dial, the pioneer of the Nova Scotia wine industry, made the first wine from this variety in 1975. Like Austria's signature white grape Grüner Veltliner, L'Acadie Blanc can be made in a range of wine styles: from light and bone-dry without oak, to richly expressive fruit buttressed with vanilla oak flavors, to off-dry and dessert wines.

having honed his craft in Australia, California and British Columbia before settling in the Gaspereau Valley to create Nova Scotia's first organic winery. The winery building, constructed with environmentally friendly geothermal heating and cooling, was opened in May 2008. In addition to traditional-method sparkling wines, Ewart and his wife, Pauline Scott, offer a range of table wines, including L'Acadie Star, which was awarded a double gold medal and Best of Category award for its first vintage (2007); they also make organic cider. You can book a reservation to stay at L'Acadie's vineyard-side cottages.

www.lacadievineyards.ca

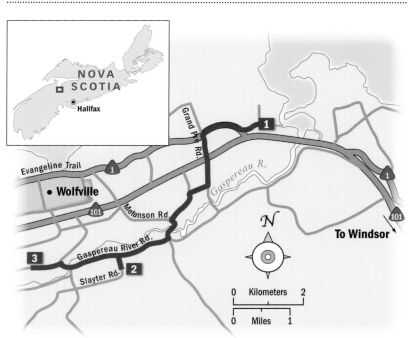

▲ Machine harvesting at Gaspereau Vineyards

3 | Gaspereau Vineyards

2239 White Rock Rd., Gaspereau, NS, B4P 2R1; (902) 542-1455

Drive back to Gaspereau River Road, turn left, and in 1.2 miles (2 km), cross the bridge over the river and you will see Gaspereau Vineyards. It is the smallest winery in the province and is owned by Hans Christian Jost, who also owns the largest winery in Nova Scotia, Jost at Malagash (see opposite). The winery produces 2,000 cases a year.

In 1996 Jost planted a 37-acre vineyard on a former apple orchard and built a small red barn of a winery here. He believes that the Gaspereau Valley has the greatest potential of any area of Nova Scotia for growing grapes—and he may well be right. The soil here varies markedly between the lower south-facing slope nearer the winery, consisting of loam (where De Chaunac, L'Acadie, New York Muscat and Lucy Kuhlmann are planted), and the warmer, upper part that is mainly clay loam and slate (which is good for Chardonnay, Ortega, Riesling and Vidal). A walk to the top of the vineyard rewards you with a breathtaking view of the entire valley. Try winemaker Gina Haverstock's Riesling, Rosé and Ortega Icewine.

www.gaspereauwine.com

findout more

- www.winesofnovascotia.ca
Learn more about Nova Scotia's wineries, wine festivals and other events.

Fall is a beautiful time of year to visit the Nova Scotia vineyards.

NOVA SCOTIA, CANADA'S FIRST VINEYARD

Nova Scotia has a legitimate claim as being the site of Canada's first vineyard. In the spring of 1633, a high-ranking French naval officer, Isaac de Razilly, chosen by Cardinal Richelieu to reclaim Acadia for France, set up the French outpost Fort Ste.-Marie-de-Grâce (now LaHave). In the following year de Razilly wrote: "I have planted some vines as they do in Bordeaux which come along very well … Vines grow here naturally. The wine made from these has been used to celebrate mass." By the mid-nineteenth century there was a thriving commercial production of table grapes on family farms in the Annapolis Valley and along the South Shore. Evidence of this still remains in the 150-year-old vine at the Miller Point Peace Park near Bridgewater.

TOUR 55
Malagash Peninsula

No visit to Nova Scotia for the wine lover would be complete without a diversion to the Malagash Peninsula, a 90-minute drive from Halifax. This remote area, which runs from the Cumberland Basin to Pictou and Merigornish Island, is the unique domaine of Jost Vineyards (pronounced "Yost"), the second winery to be opened in the province (in 1984) and now the largest.

This area is a bird-watcher's paradise and, incidentally, the home of Canada's first salt mine, dating back to 1918 (the Malagash Salt Miners' Museum is well worth a visit). The Malagash Peninsula is on the same latitude as Alsace in France and enjoys exceptionally warm summers with cooling breezes from the Northumberland Strait. The Eagle Tree Muscat produced by Jost will remind you of a Muscat wine from Alsace.

◄ Jost Vineyards overlooking Northumberland Strait

1 | Jost Vineyards
48 Vintage La., Malagash, NS, B0K 1E0; (800) 565-4567

The province's biggest winery, Jost Vineyards, is approximately a 2-hour drive north of Halifax on Highway 102. Jost boasts a 35,000-case production, and you see the Jost label in virtually every restaurant, hotel and licensed B&B in the province. Jost makes more than 30 different wines, and it would take you five weeks at a bottle a night to try them all!

Hans Christian Jost farms 45 acres of vines, some of which date back to 1978, which is when his parents, Hans Wilhelm and Erna, established the vineyard on the Malagash Peninsula overlooking the Northumberland Strait.

The Jost winery is a wood-paneled complex that sits at the foot of the vineyard; the Vintage Loft upstairs sells local crafts, books and food products. Jost's enthusiasm for Nova Scotia wines is infectious—as you'll discover when you visit his winery. Look for the following wines: Eagle Tree Muscat (dry white); Leon Millot and Maréchal Foch Reserve (reds); Muscat Icewine and Vidal Icewine.

www.jostwine.com

2006
RESERVE
MARECHAL FOCH
NOVA SCOTIA
JŌST
VINEYARDS
RED WINE
VIN ROUGE
750 ML
11.8% ALC/VOL
PRODUCT OF CANADA / PRODUIT DU CANADA

TOUR 56
Île d'Orléans

This perfect little island about 3 miles (5 km) downstream from downtown Quebec is perhaps better known for its cideries than its wineries, and two are featured on this tour. Forty-two miles (67 km) around, the island is chock-full of nineteenth-century churches, restaurants serving traditional Quebec dishes, roadside fruit stands, sugar bushes and orchards, chocolate factories and cheese producers.

Île d'Orléans, where the Vandal-Cliche grape was first propagated, also boasts the most northerly red-oak stand on the continent, Canada's oldest golf course (1868) and its oldest chapel. A bridge at the eastern end of Quebec City takes you onto the island. All the wineries are located along one road, the Chemin Royal, so they are easy to find.

◄ Vignoble de Sainte-Pétronille is located at the western tip of the Île d'Orléans.

1 | Vignoble de Sainte-Pétronille
1A Chemin du Boût-de-l'Île, Ste-Pétronille, QC G0A 4C0; (418) 828-9554

Sainte-Pétronille sits high above the St. Lawrence River at the western end of Île d'Orléans, with a magnificent view of Montmorency Falls and the graceful bridge to the island. The winery boasts the first commercial planting of renowned grape breeder Joseph Vandal's newly developed crossing, Vandal-Cliche, the first hybrid that did not need winter protection. This grape is widely planted in Quebec and produces a white wine with a fruity, almost grapey, character.

The winery began in the basement of the elegant Normandy-style house, with its green roof and large covered verandas. The house looks as though it has been there for two centuries, but Louis Denault and Nathalie Lane built it as recently as 1991. Winemaking is a parallel career for Denault, who also builds bridges and other major construction projects. He now produces five wines and a Mistelle (Pineau des Charentes-style fortified grape juice); try the Réserve du Bout de l'Île (white) and Cuvée Ste-Pétronille (red). The views from the vineyard alone are worth the visit—it's a photographer's dream as you look toward Montmorency Falls—and when you're there, have a meal in the bistro.

www.vignobleorleans.com

2 | Vignoble Isle de Bacchus
1071 Chemin Royal, St-Pierre, Île d'Orléans, QC G0A 4E0; (418) 828-9562

Within walking distance as you travel east along Chemin Royal is Vignoble Isle de Bacchus—the original name given to the Île d'Orléans in 1535 by the French explorer Jacques Cartier, who was the first European to map the Gulf of Saint Lawrence. He named it Isle de Bacchus because of the abundance of wild grapevines he found growing up the trees. Donald Bouchard, a retired lawyer who owns the property, planted the original vineyard in 1982; there are now three parcels of vines covering 25 acres, producing around 35,000 bottles a year.

The stainless-steel fermentation tanks were originally located in the cellar of the magnificent eighteenth-century stone house, and the tasting room was in the kitchen below the main rooms. The living area of the house has maintained its historic integrity, with its stone walls, open fireplace and old timbers. This historic home is licensed as a B&B, and it makes a wonderful base for touring.

In 2007 the family built a new winery and barrel cellar. Call ahead to arrange a tour of the winery and vineyards. Their table wines are based on blends of grapes, for greater complexity: Try Le 1535 (dry white) and Le Saint-Pierre (rosé).

www.isledebacchus.com

3 | Domaine Steinbach

2205 Chemin Royal, Saint-Pierre de l'Île d'Orléans, QC G0A 4E0;
(418) 828-0000

Continuing your leisurely drive east, you will soon come to Domaine Steinbach. Claire and Philippe Steinbach came to Quebec from Belgium in 1995 on a one-year sabbatical and fell in love with Île d'Orléans. Entranced by its pastoral landscape, they never left. They bought an old apple orchard two years later and transformed it into a biodynamic farm producing a range of ciders and vinegars, as well as a variety of mustards, preserves, jellies, terrines and "confits" made from the ducks and geese they raise on the property.

You can sample this country fare from the outdoor terrace while enjoying a magnificent view of the St. Lawrence River. No wine is made here, but there's a delicious ice cider called Cristal de Glace.

www.domainesteinbach.com

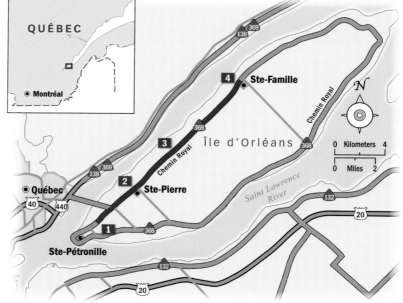

Only winter-hardy grape varieties can survive the winters in Quebec.

SURVIVING THE WINTER

If you've ever spent a winter in Quebec City, you may shake your head in disbelief that this region actually grows grapes. The mercury can drop to –40°F (4.5°C) in winter—too cold even for icewine, because the grape bunches simply disintegrate.

Although it is the newest vineyard area in the province, its history dates back to the founding of French Canada. Ever since Jacques Cartier discovered wild grape vines on the Île d'Orléans, the image has excited Québécois winegrowers. But past experiments failed because those early growers did not have the benefit of winter-hardy varieties that could withstand polar temperatures. The growers can make wine only from winter-hardy varieties that they can keep alive from one year to the next, and the flavor profiles may not be what you are used to. The wines are lean and tart, but they work well enough if you select your accompanying dishes carefully.

4 | Domaine de la Source à Marguerite

3788 Chemin Royal, Ste-Famille, QC G0A 3P0; (418) 952-6277

Progressing east, you will arrive within a few minutes at Domaine de la Source à Marguerite. Conrad Brillant, a retired banker, purchased this farm, with 34 varieties of apples, on Île d'Orléans in 2001. He decided to add wine to his flourishing cider business and, in 2002, planted a vineyard behind the orchard. Brillant also has an experimental plot of Gamay and Pinot Noir planted on a slope with a great view of the Laurentian Mountains that runs down to the river. You'll find the winery in a large renovated barn located right on the Chemin Royal.

In addition to the apple products, the farm grows pears, raspberries, plums and cherries. You can buy the fresh fruit, juices and jams, along with the range of fermented products in the cider salesroom, an old wood barn across the road from the winery. The tasting room, offering wines, a variety of ciders and Mistelles, is currently located here as well. Given its scenic location, this winery is an ideal picnic spot. Try the ice cider.

www.domainemarguerite.com

find out more

- www.laroutedesvins.ca/en/
  Follow Quebec's first signed 75-mile (120-km) Wine Route.
- www.bonjourquebec.com/qc-en/routevins0.html
  Official tourist site of the government of Québec.

Cantons-de-l'Est

The first settlers in the eighteenth century called this scenic part of Quebec "Eastern Townships," a name that was later translated to French as Cantons-de-l'Est. A 45-minute drive south from Montreal, it's a region of covered bridges, affluent towns and villages with solid Victorian brick houses, elegant Normandy-style châteaux and fieldstone barns. The antique stores along the route may distract you from your dedicated pursuit of the wineries, as will the shops that sell locally made pâtés, cheeses, sausages and chocolates.

Dunham, at the crossing of the Richelieu and St. Lawrence Valleys, was the first township to be developed in the 1790s. This charming town is the unofficial wine capital of Quebec. The gravel slopes of the surrounding hills offer a longer, relatively frost-free growing season. The best time to visit is the late fall, when the maple trees are turning color.

◄ The winery and terraced vineyards are a spectacular sight at Chapelle Ste. Agnes.

1 | Vignoble de La Bauge
155 des Érables, Brigham, QC J2K 4E1; (450) 266-2149

Southeast of Farnham, the wine route on Highway 104 takes you to La Bauge (which translates as "the wild boar's lair"). Is this a winery or an animal park? There is something of a circus atmosphere, with its range of caged and free-range animals and exotic birds vying for the visitor's attention alongside the wines. A covered wagon will take you through the vineyard and the exotic animal reserve, where you will see Texas longhorns, Peruvian llamas, Himalayan yaks, Australian emus, European deer, South American nandous, Japanese sikas, red deer and the wild boar that give the property its name. The wild boar pâté and smoked venison sausages can be purchased in the wine shop—and consumed at the picnic tables. They are products of the farm's extensive woodland acreage. (You can buy a license to hunt with a crossbow on the property, if that's your taste, and they'll even help prepare and transport your meat.)

The vineyard, a quick walk from the charming village of Brigham, is on the south side of the Appalachian foothills on land that was once the Champlain Sea. Among the 10 or so table wines and fortified wines made here, try Les Patriarches (red), Le Solitaire (dry white) and Novembre, a late-harvest dessert wine.

www.labauge.com

2 | Domaine des Côtes d'Ardoise
879 Bruce St. (Route 202), Dunham, QC J0E1M0; (450) 295-2020

Traveling east from La Bauge toward Cowansville, turn south on Highway 139 and then south on 202 to arrive in Dunham. A mile or so beyond the town is Domaine des Côtes d'Ardoise.

"Ardoise" means slate in French and refers to the soil of Dr. Jacques Papillon's horseshoe-shaped vineyard, set in a perfect natural amphitheater. It was the first vineyard to be planted in the modern era of Quebec wines (in 1980), and it happens to be on the first hill you see as you drive south from Montreal. Protected by trees, the vineyard rises behind the weathered, ivy-covered old barn built in 1945, where you can taste the wines.

Forty sculptures by Canadian artists are set in the grounds and in the vineyard—with pride of place, at the highest point, going to a huge Montreal butterfly. If you're interested, you can buy them here from the artists. It's worth taking a whole afternoon to enjoy the art, taste the wines and sample the restaurant's food (or your own). There is also a covered terrace in the picnic area. Recommended wines: Seyval Carte d'Or (semi-dry white) and two wines from the Vidal grape—Givrée d'Ardoise Blanc (icewine) and Douceur d'Ardoise (late-harvest white wine).

www.cotesdardoise.com

3 | Vignoble de l'Orpailleur

1086 Bruce St. (Route 202), Dunham, QC, J0E 1M0; (450) 295-2763

Virtually within sight of Domaine des Côtes d'Ardoise is Quebec's largest and most venerable winery, Vignoble de l'Orpailleur. First planted in 1982, the owners decided on the name l'Orpailleur (the gold panner) after a poem in which growing wine in Quebec was likened to panning for gold.

The original wood house has been expanded in colonial style to include a restaurant and a wine shop. From its lookout tower on the second floor, you can see a commanding view of the surrounding vineyards. Inside the original house is an exhibition of wine culture through the ages, complete with a collection of antique corkscrews. If you visit only one winery in Dunham, this one will give you the complete Quebec wine experience and a history lesson as well. In September, l'Orpailleur sets off fireworks to mark the beginning of the grape harvest—courtesy of one of the owners, Frank Furtado, who puts on firework displays across Canada. Recommended wines: L'Orpailleur Elevé en Futs de Chêne, L'Orpailleur Blanc, L'Apérid'or (mistelle, or fortified grape juice) and Vin de Glace (icewine).

www.orpailleur.ca

4 | Chapelle Ste. Agnès

2565 Chemin Scenic, Sutton, QC, J0E 2K0; (450) 538-0303

It is advisable to book ahead to visit this winery located near the Quebec/Vermont border; its spectacular architecture, historic artifacts and sweet wines should not be missed. There are country back roads that will take you from Dunham to Route 139, but to enjoy the scenery, return to Cowansville, take the 104 to West Brome to Route 139, then head south, past Sutton; at Abercorn turn east on Rue des Eglises for the winery.

The proprietor, Henrietta Antony, owns the largest fine antiques store in Montreal. She has invested millions of dollars to create 18 terraces of vines that descend down to an ornamental lake. She has also built a gem of a Romanesque chapel consecrated to Sainte Agnès, a thirteenth-century Bohemian saint. "I wanted to inspire people," says Antony. Her son John is the assistant winemaker to consultant Christian Barthomeuf, and together they produce Quebec's most costly wines, mostly icewines, including a Gewurztraminer at $150 that rivals a fine Sauternes. A tour of this spellbinding winery, with its magnificent stone cellar, costs $25, including a tasting; try the Geisenheim and Vidal icewines.

www.vindeglace.com

THE EASTERN REGION

QUEBEC

QUEBEC'S WINTER WINE: ICE CIDER

Quebec makes almost as much cider as it does wine. It's a cottage industry whose history goes back to the province's first settlers from Normandy and Brittany in the seventeenth century.

Those early pioneers brought cider with them but soon found that the conditions around Montérégie were ideal for growing apples. As a result, cider-making has been a venerable and venerated occupation in Quebec. Today the range of styles made is impressive—from dry, to sweet and sparkling, to fortified. But none is more cherished than ice cider or *cidre de glace* in French.

What is ice cider? Think of icewine and replace the frozen grapes with frozen apple juice, and you have ice cider. You get the same honeyed sweetness and racy acidity in ice cider as you do in icewine, but it tastes of apples, of course, rather than the more concentrated peach and tropical fruit flavors found in icewine. Today, there are around 50 commercial producers but most are very small scale.

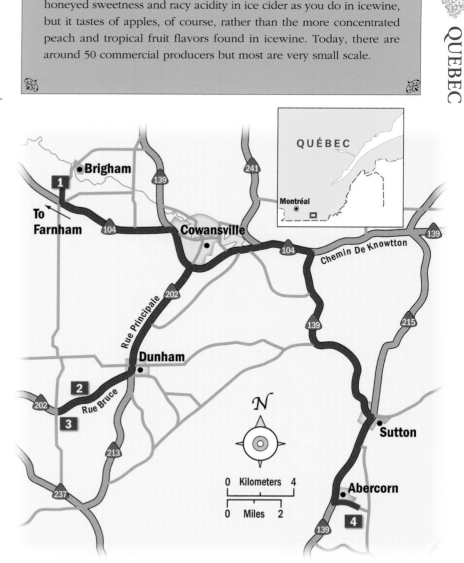

Prince Edward County

Prince Edward County, an island jutting out into Lake Ontario, might seem an unlikely wine region, but the limestone soil has attracted growers who seek to produce the wine lovers' Holy Grail: Pinot Noir. This is a landscape of undulating pastureland and charming villages with stone farm houses, pioneer barns and handsome Victorian mansions. Wellington, a town with a village feel, boasts one of the oldest homes in Ontario, dating back to 1786. The town overlooks one of the greatest natural beach areas in Canada, Sandbanks Provincial Park—a great place to take a break from wine touring and have a picnic.

This tour takes you through the villages of Cherry Valley and Milford to the coast road that runs east along Prince Edward Bay. Your final destination is a cidery, but if you proceed a little further you can visit the Fifth Town Artisan Cheese Company, an environmentally responsible producer of fine goat and sheep milk cheeses.

◄ Sandbanks is one of Canada's finest beaches and makes an excellent picnic spot on this tour.

1 | Norman Hardie Winery
1152 Greer Rd., Wellington, ON K0K 3L0; (613) 399 5297

The Norman Hardie winery is a contemporary New Age barn with a metal roof and redwood-stained pine siding that melds into the surrounding farmscape. Hardie's two-story home is connected to the winery by a breezeway. The building is judiciously situated on a steep slope, allowing for a gravity-flow operation and a barrel chamber to be carved out of the hillside. Remnants of the exposed rock in the cellar show the meter-deep band of solid limestone that runs through the property—ideal base soil for growing Pinot Noir.

Norman Hardie's winemaking experience in South Africa, New Zealand and Burgundy, where he studied at the University of Dijon, shows in the finely structured, richly flavored wines he's making here since the 2004 vintage—especially in the Chardonnay and Pinot Noir.

His years spent working as a sommelier and restaurant manager at the Four Seasons Hotel in Toronto guarantee a warm welcome to winery visitors.

www.normanhardie.com

▲ The Norman Hardie Winery gives a warm welcome to its visitors.

2 | Rosehall Run Vineyards
1243 Greer Rd., RR1, Wellington, ON K0K 3L0; (613) 399-1183

Dan Sullivan became a professional winemaker after winning many amateur competitions, including the Best Wine in Canada 2001 for his 1999 Chardonnay; gold medal in Intervin's Amateur Division competition for his 1999 Baco Noir; and Best Chardonnay 2003. His winning ways continued at Artevino, the wine competition for PEC wineries. Sullivan bought this picturesque 150-acre farm property in 2000 and planted 15 acres of *vinifera* vines, including 7 acres to four different clones of Pinot Noir. In 2009 he built a new winery that resembles a contemporary barn; he had to blast 20 feet (6 m) down through layers of limestone to create the county's largest gravity-flow barrel cellar. In addition to Chardonnay and Pinot Noir, Dan has planted "a smattering of Ehrenfelser and Chardonnay Musqué."

www.rosehallrun.com

3 | By Chadsey's Cairns Winery & Vineyard
17432 Loyalist Pkwy., Wellington, ON K0K 3L0; (613) 399-2992

Take Loyalist Parkway south and follow it east. By Chadsey's Cairns is on the left. Ira Chadsey (1828–1905) was an eccentric Loyalist and professed atheist, who settled this 200-year-old farm and fenced in its boundaries with a series of 14 cairns built of fieldstone and interspersed with Victorian metal posts. In 1995 Richard Johnson bought this historic property overlooking Wellington Bay, near Picton, and planted his vineyard four years later.

All four historic barns on the property are part of the winery operation—the former horse barn is now the winery, and a beautifully proportioned old red-brick Quaker meeting hall has been transformed into the wine shop. In addition to 20 acres of vines, Johnson and his wife, Vida, keep a flock of Cotswold sheep and other farm animals. The pioneer cemetery on the property, with gravestones dating back to 1805, is a treat for amateur genealogists. Recommended wines: Gewürztraminer and Riesling.

www.bychadseyscairns.com

4 | The Grange of Prince Edward
990 Closson Rd., Hillier, ON K0K 2J0; (866) 792-7712

Turn right onto Loyalist Parkway, then turn right at Danforth Road; you should arrive at Closson Road in about 15 minutes.

Robert Granger and his wife Diana lovingly restored the 1875 farmhouse, barn and Trumpour's sawmill. They landscaped the grounds around the creek that runs through the property, creating two pond sites. The imposing barn, which dates back to 1826, now houses the winery. The open-plan tasting room, with its handsome

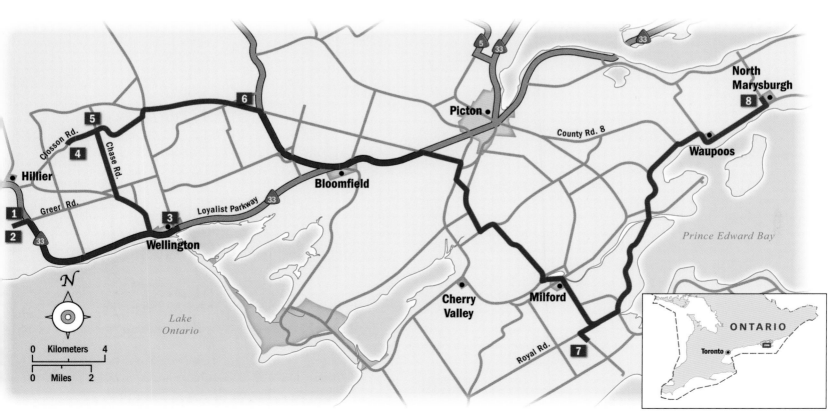

▲ The barrel room at Huff Estates Winery

▲ Hand-pressing grapes at Long Dog

maple bar and fieldstone fireplace, is located in the former hayloft and is furnished with local Canadiana pieces. The barrel cellar is below in the old milking stalls. The Grangers' daughter, Caroline, a former Dior model and actor, came home from Paris to run the vineyards, having taken a two-year course in vineyard management at Loyalist College in Belleville. Winemaker Jeff Innes' Cabernet Franc and Trumpour's Mill Pinot Noir are well worth trying.

www.grangeofprinceedward.com

5 | Closson Chase Vineyards
629 Closson Rd., Hillier, ON, K0K 2J0; (613) 399-1418

The partners couldn't decide on what to call their winery, so they looked at the nearest cross streets, Closson and Chase. The self-contained winery is housed in a magnificent 130-year-old double milk barn that has been cleverly renovated. Sheets of Plexiglass sheath the walls and maintain the integrity of the old structure, with all its gaps between the boards, while ensuring comfort inside.

The small tasting room, with its tin-sided bar, is an ideal spot to enjoy the only two wines Deborah Paskus makes here—Pinot Noir and Chardonnay. But what wines! Paskus is known for her intense, Burgundian-style Chardonnays and Pinot Noirs produced from low-yielding grapes fermented in the best French oak barrels. The winery's evocative labels, based on shipping flags, were designed by the renowned Newfoundland artist David Blackwood. The colors are re-created in the stained glass at the main entrance to the winery.

www.clossonchase.com

6 | Huff Estates Winery
2274 County Rd. 1, Bloomfield, ON K0K 3L0; (613) 393-5802

Turn right onto Closson Road and drive 2 miles (3 km). Turn left at County Rd 2 and after 525 feet (160 m) turn right at Scoharie Road; continue for 3.75 miles (6 km). The modern industrial building is set back from the road at Huff's Corners (named for Lanny Huff's ancestors, who settled here as United Empire Loyalists in 1825).

An 8-acre vineyard (one of the three owned by Huff, totalling 43 acres) leads up to the winery, which sits on top of Mount Pleasant, one of the highest points in Prince Edward County. Its position allows for a gravity-feed operation to the barrel cellar below.

Huff was the first winery in the region to grow Merlot (at the South Bay vineyard, close to Lake Ontario). To make his wines, Lanny Huff hired the young Burgundy-trained winemaker Frédéric Picard, who produces award-winning Chardonnay, Caberne' Merlot and Gamay. You can purchase a light lunch on the patio.

www.huffestates.com

7 | Long Dog Vineyard & Winery
104 Brewers Rd., Milford, ON K0K 2P0; (613) 476-4140

From Huff Estates, take Highway 62 south, then go east along Loyalist Parkway, turn right at Sandy Hook Road and head south toward Milford. Take County Road 10 south, turn right at Royal Road, then left onto Brewers Road.

▲ The County Cider Company in Waupoos is worth a visit for the view alone.

James Lahti, an IMAX film producer, bought the farm as a country retreat in 1997. It turned out that the land had terroir similar to that of Burgundy and so when Lahti planted the first 1,200 vines in 1999 he chose the Burgundian varieties of Pinot Noir, Chardonnay and Pinot Blanc and also Gamay, Beaujolais' red grape. Buried behind the first Pinot Noir vine he planted are the ashes of "Otto the Wonder Dog," a wire-haired dachshund that gives the winery its name of Long Dog. The current dachshunds-in-residence are Bella and Fanny. Since 2000 a further 18,000 vines have been planted and the first wines were sold in 2004.

Lahti operates Long Dog out of two barns dating back to 1860 and 1870. Both have been marvellously restored. The larger of the two—a former horse stable with a silver-painted roof—houses a series of old milk tanks purchased for fermenting his Pinot Noir. The smaller building used to be a pig barn ("I call it the Swinery," he says).

Long Dog is a complete estate winery using only its own grapes, one of the few that does not resort to bringing in fruit from Niagara. All the wines are pressed by hand in small presses as shown in the photograph on page 194. The Chardonnay, Pinot Gris and Pinot Noir are particularly recommended.

www.longdog.ca

findout more

- **www.tastetrail.ca**
  Suggested routes and information about visiting restaurants, wineries, cideries, breweries and food producers.

- **www.thecountywines.com**
  Places to eat and stay, plus wine information.

- **www.pecwinetours.com/van.html**
  Guided winery tours with someone else to do the driving.

8 | County Cider Company
County Road 8, RR 4, Picton, ON K0K 2T0; (613) 476-1022

From Long Dog, return to Royal Road and turn right. Turn left at County Road 13 toward Waupoos. Pick up County Road 8 and follow it east until you come to Bongards Cross Road.

The family farm has been growing apples here since 1850 and boasts the largest orchard of European cider apples in Canada, producing 1,600 tons of 14 different varieties a year. The restored limestone tasting room and patio restaurant (with its wood-fired oven), surrounded by an orchard and vineyard, have a commanding view of Waupoos Island and Prince Edward Bay. In addition to the range of ciders, including a peach-flavored product and an award-winning ice cider, the County Cider Company also produces wines—Chardonnay and Pinot Noir, made by its winemaker Jenifer Dean. The view alone is worth the visit.

www.countycider.com

Hugging the Lake

Ontario is a Huron name that means "great lake." Lake Ontario is the smallest of the Great Lakes, but it contains one of the world's great wonders: Niagara Falls. The Niagara River that feeds the falls is bordered by the Niagara Parkway, one of the most scenic drives in the province, which winds past endless vineyards and elegant homes. The road leads up to Queenston Heights and Niagara Falls, offering spectacular views along the way. En route, check out the Butterfly Conservatory at the Niagara Parks Commission site.

From Queen Elizabeth Way, the prettiest drive is to take Exit 47 (Ontario Street) and drive along Lakeshore Road to your first winery, Konzelmann Estate, which should take about 15–20 minutes.

◄ This tour leads past vineyards up to Niagara Falls.

1 | Konzelmann Estate Winery
1096 Lakeshore Rd., Niagara-on-the-Lake, ON L0S 1J0; (905) 935-2866

The door to Herbert Konzelmann's winery on the lip of Lake Ontario is a replica of the one that graced his German great-grandfather Friedrich Konzelmann's winery in his native Württemberg. In 1958 Herbert joined the winery Friedrich had created in Stuttgart in 1893, working there until he emigrated to Canada. On a visit to Niagara, he was so impressed with the potential for grape-growing that he took soil samples back to Germany in margarine containers for analysis.

Four years later he relocated his family to Niagara-on-the-Lake and purchased a farm on the shore of Lake Ontario, a 3-minute drive from the town. Given his German background, Konzelmann makes excellent for Riesling, aromatic and dessert wines and he is constantly experimenting with new varieties.

www.konzelmann.ca

▲ The winery at Konzelmann

2 | Strewn Winery
1339 Lakeshore Rd., Niagara-on-the-Lake, ON L0S 1J0; (905) 468-1229

Continue along Lakeshore Road for a few minutes until you arrive at Strewn, on your right. Winemaker Joe Will took over an abandoned fruit cannery built in the 1930s and transformed it with great flair and taste into a winery and restaurant. Strewn also includes a cooking school run by his wife, Jane Langdon. Joe calls his top wines Strewn Terroir, and he makes them only if he feels the vintage has delivered the right quality. The same sense of the land is reflected in the name of the restaurant, Terroir La Cachette. With its rustic interior and extensive outdoor patio, the restaurant-cum-wine bar serves a Provençal menu and is a favorite stopping place for winery visitors—especially cyclists who enjoy the pastoral ride along Lakeshore Road.

www.strewnwinery.com

3 | Peller Estates Winery
290 John St. E., Niagara-on-the-Lake, ON L0S 1J0; (905) 468-4678

Continue along Lakeshore Road, through Niagara-on-the-Lake, and on to Mary Street; turn right on Mississauga Street and then turn right onto John Street. There's an excellent restaurant called Niagara Stone Grill in the small shopping mall here (238 Mary Street in the Garrison Plaza). The Peller family built an impressive new château-style winery in 2001, set in a 25-acre vineyard. They own another 120 acres off site and also buy from 22 contracted growers. The building has cellars worthy of a Hollywood movie set and the restaurant, in a magnificent chandeliered dining-room, looking out onto the vineyard, is one of the best in the peninsula. You can also eat on the outdoor terrace. If you dine here, start with a glass of Ice Cuvée sparkling wine (spiked with icewine) and order a bottle of the Signature Cabernet Franc to complement the local produce.

www.peller.com

4 | Lailey Vineyard
15940 Niagara Pkwy., Niagara-on-the-Lake, ON L0S 1J0; (905) 468-0503

A short drive south along the Niagara Parkway will take you to Lailey Vineyard, on your right. In 1970 Donna Lailey and her husband, David, bought 20 acres of farmland from David's father. They planted *Vitis vinifera* varieties, and over the years, they have turned the property into one of Ontario's finest vineyards.

After growing grapes here for 25 years, Donna decided to open her own modern winery. She was inspired by the success of the winemakers to which she sold her fruit, who consistently won medals in local and international competitions. Now Lailey's winemaker, Derek Barnett, makes top-flight Chardonnays and richly extracted Cabernet Franc and Cabernet Sauvignon from the grapes grown on the estate.

www.laileyvineyard.com

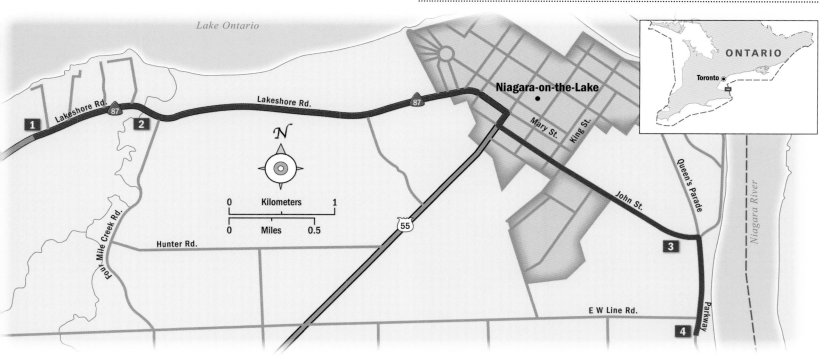

Niagara-on-the-Lake

There is a cluster of wineries around the town of Niagara-on-the-Lake, which makes wine touring in this area very convenient. The first three wineries listed are located on Niagara Stone Road as you drive into the town from Queen Elizabeth Way. Give yourself time to explore the historic town that was first settled at the end of the American Revolution by Loyalists coming to Upper Canada. You can take a horse-drawn carriage around the Old Town or stroll along Queen Street shopping for antiques and locally made food products. Don't miss Fort George, the scene of several battles during the War of 1812.

Established in 1962, the annual Shaw Festival (June–October) presents plays by George Bernard Shaw and his contemporaries in three distinctive theaters, all within walking distance of each other. For more information, see www.shawfest.com.

◀ The outdoor amphitheater at Jackson-Triggs puts on food, wine and musical events throughout the year.

1 | Southbrook Vineyards

581 Niagara Stone Rd., RR4, Niagara-on-the-Lake, ON L0S 1J0; (905) 641-2548

You can't miss Southbrook as you drive down Highway 55 to Niagara-on-the-Lake from Queen Elizabeth Way. You'll see a wall 670 feet (205-m) long and painted fuchsia or periwinkle blue, depending on the light. The ultra-modern winery behind was designed by Jack Diamond, the same architect who created Toronto's opera house. This elegant building, all glass and polished wood, is as stunning to the eye as its wines are appealing to the palate. The winery is the first in Canada to be certified as biodynamic. In the vineyard, the rows between the vines are kept grass-free by grazing sheep (who themselves have to be organically raised to qualify the winery as biodynamic). Owners Marilyn and Bill Redelmeier have created a series of wines under the Poetica label, which features poems by Canadian poets. Winemaker Anne Sperling's Triomphe wines (red and white) are just that. Sample them with a slice of pizza from the outdoor wood-burning oven.

www.southbrook.com

▲ The ultra-modern winery at Southbrook Vineyards

2 | Stratus Vineyards

2059 Niagara Stone Rd., Niagara-on-the-Lake, ON L0S 1J0; (905) 468-1806

Continuing down Highway 55 (Niagara Stone Road) past Hillebrand Estates, on your right, through the town of Virgil, past Pillitteri Estates on your left (great country produce here) and Joseph's Winery on your right, you will arrive at Stratus. The winery houses the most sophisticated winemaking equipment in the province, governed by a rigorous Old World winemaking philosophy: The finished wine is a blend of the best barrels, sometimes of different

The heart of Niagara wine country is the historic town of Niagara-on-the-Lake.

grape varieties (as in Bordeaux) or different clones of the same grape (as in Burgundy). J-L Groux, a Loire Valley native who trained in Burgundy and Bordeaux, is the winemaker. The winery is 100 percent gravity fed for the grapes and the wines, to ensure the gentlest handling at all phases of production. Stratus is one of the few Canadian wineries that use large French oak vats rather than stainless-steel tanks to ferment their grapes. The flagship wines are simply labeled Stratus Red and Stratus White. Wines not selected for the Stratus label go into a second label, called Wildass.

www.stratuswines.com

3 | Jackson-Triggs Niagara Estate Winery

2145 Niagara Stone Rd., Niagara-on-the-Lake, ON L0S 1J0; (905) 468-4637

You can see Jackson-Triggs from Stratus; it's the neighboring winery. The imposing modern building that houses the Jackson-Triggs winery covers 47,000 square feet (4,366 m²). It looks like an airline terminal at first glance, but architecture buffs will be fascinated by its reverse-trussed roof and harmonious use of glass, wood, cement board and stone. An outdoor ramp leads the visitor up to the catwalk that crosses the building, affording a bird's-eye

regionalevents

Niagara Ice Wine Festival □ January

Icewines take center stage at this Niagara event. A gala evening toast, chestnut roasts and unique ice bars make it a memorable occasion.

www.icewinefestival.com

The Shores of Erie □ September

This international wine festival combines regional wines with fine cuisine and live entertainment.

www.soewinefestival.com

Taste! □ September

Regional cuisine and locally brewed wines and ciders reign supreme at this Prince Edward County event.

www.tastecelebration.ca

199

view of the stainless-steel fermentation and storage tanks. Below ground, the vast vaulted barrel room with its stone arches resembles the crypt of a latter-day cathedral. The wines to taste are those from the Delaine Vineyard and the Proprietors' Grand Reserve series. If you're there in the summer, you can enjoy the musical entertainments performed in the outdoor amphitheater.

www.jacksontriggswinery.com

4 | Inniskillin Wines

1499 Line 3 Rd., Niagara Pkwy., Niagara-on-the-Lake, ON L0S 1J0;
(905) 468-2187

Inniskillin is a short drive beyond the town of Niagara-on-the-Lake, along the picturesque parkway. Unlike the first three wineries of this tour, Inniskillin has a more historic presence. The barn, built in the 1920s and inspired by the architect Frank Lloyd Wright, contains the shop and tasting room. A smaller, adjacent barn, part of the self-guided tour, is now a museum. Think of Inniskillin and you think icewine. Under the winery is a room dedicated to icewine, where you can watch a video on how this "gift of winter" is made and admire some of the oldest vintages available in Canada.

www.inniskillin.com

5 | Château des Charmes

1025 York Rd., Niagara-on-the-Lake, ON L0S 1J0; (905) 262-4219

Continue along Niagara Parkway to Queenston, then turn right onto York Road until you arrive at Château des Charmes. The French heritage of Paul-Michel Bosc is evident in the magnificent Loire-style château that is the home of Château des Charmes. There is a sense of grandeur here as you enter the main door and see the curved staircase and the well-appointed tasting room on the ground floor. There is also a state-of-the-art winery.

With his wife, Andrée, and two sons, Paul-André and Pierre-Jean, Bosc has created an impressive portfolio of wines in the French style, based on four separate vineyards, totaling 279 acres. Along the way, he has introduced several new French varieties to the province, such as Aligoté, Viognier and Savagnin, and, from his original vineyard he has developed a new clone of Gamay (Gamay Droit).

A dedicated equestrian with his own horse-breeding stable, Bosc named his flagship Bordeaux blend Equuleus. This winery excels in sparkling wines, Chardonnay, Late Harvest Riesling, Riesling Icewine and Bordeaux-style reds. Enjoy the outdoor Vineyard Courtyard, where you can eat lunch and sample their impressive wines, with the romantic rose gardens just beyond. There is also a wine boutique and tasting bar.

www.chateaudescharmes.com

▲ Château des Charmes is a leading producer in the Niagara region and also boasts a grand winery.

In search of icewine

Not since New Zealand hijacked the Sauvignon Blanc grape in the 1970s and '80s has one country so successfully dominated the international market with a wine style. Eiswein is a German invention that dates back to the late eighteenth century, when a freak drop in temperature froze the late-harvest grapes in Franken before they could be picked. Today true vine-frozen icewine (eiswein) is made in many countries—Germany, Austria, the Czech Republic, Hungary, Luxembourg, New Zealand, Romania, Slovenia, Switzerland and New York State—but it is Canada that has co-opted icewine and made it its own. Originally made from Riesling and Vidal, winemakers are now using other varieties, both white and red.

The harvesting of grapes for icewine is a particularly polar experience because the berries must remain frozen as hard as marbles until they reach the press. This means a sustained temperature of at least 18°F (7°C). Because of desiccation—and the fact that the ice has been left behind in the press—winemakers get only about one-fifth the amount of juice they would normally harvest. But this juice is unique: Highly concentrated in both sugar and acidity, it gives flavors of honey, peach, apricot, mango and caramel when fermented.

Because of its intense sweetness and balancing acidity, icewine makes a dessert all by itself, but you can match these wines with fruit-based desserts or pâtés (especially with foie gras), spiced Asian appetizers or blue cheeses. If you're pairing wine with desserts, the wine should be sweeter than the dish, which is why fruit-based desserts go so well. Icewine is also excellent paired with cake, chocolate-dipped strawberries and candied fruits.

▲ Frozen grapes ready for picking

▲ Picking the frozen grapes to make icewine is a tough job.

Jordan Valley

An hour's drive from Toronto, or 20 minutes from Niagara Falls, this tour will take you from lake level up to one of the most elevated wineries in the province—Flat Rock Cellars—at 500 feet (150 m) above Lake Ontario, from which point you can see the skyscrapers of Toronto on a clear day. This is a zone of peach and cherry orchards on the flat ground, which give way to vineyards as the land slopes up to the escarpment. You can feel the difference in temperature from the lakeshore as you move inland. As you climb the escarpment again, you can experience a sudden dip in the mercury.

You will want to spend time walking the main street of picturesque Jordan Village, just off Queen Elizabeth Way, where you'll find art-and craft-galleries, shops and a local museum all within a few hundred yards. This village is an ideal spot for a leisurely visit or perhaps for an overnight stay at the luxurious Inn on the Twenty.

◀ View of the skyscrapers of Toronto from the Flat Rock vineyards

1 | Creekside Estate Winery
2170 Fourth Ave., Jordan, ON L0R 1S0 (905) 562-0035

From Jordan Village, head for 4th Avenue and drive a little over 1 mile (2 km) to the winery. Tag-team winemakers Craig McDonald (a former winemaker at Penfolds and Coldstream Hills in Australia) and Rob Power have won more medals for their products at Creekside than you can imagine. You can relax on the deck and enjoy a glass of wine with lunch prepared in the open kitchen from all local products in season.

Creekside made an early mark with its Sauvignon Blanc and its flagship Laura's Blend, which is named for the owner, Laura Jensen, and now renamed Laura Red and Laura White. The Bordeaux-style Laura Red could easily be mistaken for a claret. The Laura White, mainly from Sauvignon Blanc, resembles a Bordeaux Blanc. Don't miss the Creekside Shiraz, Australia's icon grape.

www.creeksidewine.com

2 | Cave Spring Cellars
3836 Main St., Jordan, ON L0R 1S0; (905) 562-3581

Return to Jordan Village, where they are lucky enough to have a winery right on the main street—along with one of wine country's best restaurants. Cave Spring, in Jordan Village, is housed in a gracious, long, gray-stone building—originally an apple warehouse—that dates back to 1871. The entire enterprise—winery, restaurant and luxury inn on the other side of the street—has its foundation on 175 acres of benchland vineyards, planted in 1978 by Len Pennachetti and his father. They discovered the original site by scouting the area in a small plane.

Spend some time here and spoil yourself with lunch at the bright and airy Inn on the Twenty. Winemaker Angelo Pavan's CSV Riesling and Chardonnay are not to be missed.

www.cavespring.ca

3 | Flat Rock Cellars
2727 Seventh Ave., Jordan, ON L0R 1S0; (905) 562-8994

Drive south along Main Street, which becomes 19th Street, and continue until you get to 7th Avenue; turn left and you will soon arrive at Flat Rock Cellars. Set high on the escarpment into the side of a hill, lawyer Ed Madronich's striking contemporary winery—two

▲ The state-of-the-art winery at Flat Rock Cellars uses gravity to move the grapes and wine around.

4 | Henry of Pelham Family Estate Winery
1469 Pelham Rd., St. Catharines, ON L2R 6P7; (905) 684-8423

The Speck brothers—Paul, Matthew and Daniel—run this winery with its 150 acres of vineyards; the property has been owned by their ancestors since 1794. The original owner was Nicholas Smith, whose son Henry (after whom the winery is named) built a coaching inn in 1842. This historic building is now the tasting room, wine store and the Coach House Café.

The Specks were in the vanguard of planting *vinifera* grapes in Ontario back in the early 1980s. Their winemaker, Ron Giesbrecht, has gone from strength to strength, producing some of the best wines in the province, including an intense, flavorful Baco Noir, a signature wine for Henry of Pelham. Giesbrecht's top wines are the Speck Family Reserve Chardonnay, Pinot Noir and Cabernet-Merlot blend. There is also a delicious sparkling wine. Don't miss the art gallery in the coaching inn, where sales and tastings with Canadian cheeses are conducted.

www.henryofpelham.com

six-sided spaces linked by a bridge over a five-story gravity-flow facility in concrete, steel, wood and glass)—has a commanding view of the 75-acre vineyard. The wine shop, on two levels erected on enormous steel legs, has a 360-degree windowed panoramic view. The winery gets its name from the huge flat rocks that were excavated from the site to put drainage tiles under each row of vines. The geothermal heating and cooling system, involving 15,000 feet (4,570 m) of piping, is just one of the innovative technologies in this space-age facility.

Flat Rock was the first winery in Ontario to commit its entire portfolio of wines to screwcap closures, including its Icewine (a world first). Winemaker Marlize Beyers produces an excellent Riesling, Chardonnay and Pinot Noir.

www.flatrockcellars.com

Beamsville-Vineland

A 90–minute drive west from Toronto along the Queen Elizabeth Way, with its occasional glimpses of Lake Ontario, will take you into the heart of the Niagara Peninsula, with its signposted wine route. The most prominent feature on this tour is the Niagara Escarpment—a limestone cliff that stretches from Grimsby to St. Catharines, following the shoreline of Lake Ontario. In this rural stretch, you'll find farms and vineyards and redbrick Victorian houses surrounded by beautiful gardens. The sub-appellation known as the Beamsville Bench is a narrow strip of land, like a step on the escarpment, where vineyards and woodlands proliferate.

The four wineries selected for this tour are within easy driving reach of each other. If you have the time, you could also visit Thirty Bench and Hidden Bench wineries, both of which make very good wines.

◀ The approach to Malivoire Wine Company's main entrance is through its beautiful rock gardens.

1 | Peninsula Ridge Estates Winery
5600 King St. W., Beamsville, ON L0R 1B0; (905) 563-0900

From Queen Elizabeth Way, take Exit 68; at the lights turn left onto King Street and drive for about 1 mile (2 km). Perched on the hill, the Victorian farmhouse of Peninsula Ridge is now a sophisticated restaurant, and the retail store and tasting bar are housed in a tastefully restored 1855 post-and-beam barn. The coach house that stands behind the farmhouse is used for private and corporate events. Not to be missed is the magnificent, L-shaped, underground cellar.

Winemaker Jamie Evans has just taken over from the winery's longtime Burgundian-trained winemaker Jean-Pierre Colas. Try Peninsula's Chardonnay and Sauvignon Blanc and the red Meritage blend Arcanum.

www.peninsularidge.com

2 | Malivoire Wine Company
4260 King St. E., Beamsville, ON L0R 1B0; (905) 563-9253

Turn right out of Peninsula Ridge onto King Street and drive about 2 miles (3 km) to a lane on your right, which will take you up to Malivoire. Martin Malivoire's original company made special effects for the movie industry, but his passion for wine led him to open a

winery. His state-of-the-art facility is unique: three attached Quonset huts set on a hillside with a 32-foot (10-m) drop to allow a gravity-fed operation. The wine is gently moved along at each stage, from crush to tank to barrel, without the use of pumps. The entranceway, with its local stone pillars and rock gardens, softens the utilitarian lines of the winery. Malivoire wanted to produce the best rosé in Canada, and with his Ladybug Rosé he has achieved that goal. The best wines here come from the Moira Vineyard, named for Malivoire's wife and planted with Chardonnay and Pinot Noir.

www.malivoire.com

3 | Tawse Winery
3955 Cherry Ave., Vineland, ON L0R 2C0; (905) 562-9500

Continue east on King Road for about 1.5 miles (2.5 km), turn right on Cherry Avenue and drive up the hill. Investment banker Morey Tawse is a serious Burgundy collector, and when he decided to get into the wine business, he spared no expense creating a small, elegant winery with the most modern equipment on the Lakeshore plain. The winery's sloped roof, reflected in an ornamental pond, suggests the height within that allows for a gravity-fed operation on six levels, together with three barrel-aging cellars. While the primary focus is Chardonnay, Tawse's winemaker Paul Pender also produces small amounts of Cabernet Franc, Pinot Noir and Riesling. Make an appointment to visit; even the most jaded palate will be impressed.

www.tawsewinery.ca

4 | Vineland Estates Winery

3620 Moyer Rd., Vineland, ON L0R 2C0; (905) 562-7088

Return to King Street and drive east for 1 mile (1.5 km) to Victoria Avenue and then turn right. Continue uphill and turn right onto Moyer Road. The winery is down on your left. Vineland Estates, with its distinctive stone tower, is one of the handsomest and best-sited wineries in Ontario, with extensive vineyard holdings stretching over 275 acres. From its large cedar deck, diners can see across the undulating St. Urban vineyard to Lake Ontario and the Toronto skyline in the distance. The 1845 farmhouse was redesigned as a tasting room and restaurant, and the historic stone carriage house has been restored for functions. The restaurant, which specializes in local food products, is a destination on its own. The wine boutique, with its magnificent wood bar and upstairs loft, houses the best wine store in Niagara. Winemaker Brian Schmidt and his brother Allan before him have made Riesling the signature variety here, whether in dry, off-dry, sparkling or late-harvest and icewine styles. Vineland also has the challenge of selling one of Canada's most expensive wines, a magnum of Cabernet-Merlot priced at $140 a bottle.

www.vineland.com

findout more

- **www.winesofontario.ca**
  The official guide to the wineries of Ontario: event calendar, travel ideas, learn about food and wine, meet the winemakers, and explore the wine regions.

- **www.laileyvineyard.com/bandb.html**
  Bed-and-breakfast in the Niagara Peninsula.

- **www.niagarawinefestival.com**
  Information on the many wine festivals.

- **www.niagaraonthelake.com**
  Official tourist information for the whole Niagara region.

- **www.wineriesofniagaraonthelake.com**
  Information on the more than 20 wineries nestled below the Niagara Escarpment.

- **www.shawfest.com**
  Bringing great theater to life in Niagara-on-the-Lake every June through October.

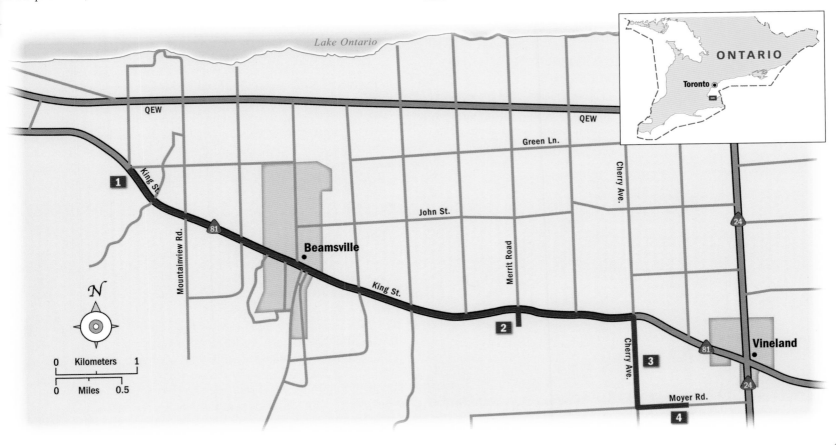

Tour 63
Niagara Region

The Niagara Wine Trail in the United States starts very close to one of the world's great wonders, Niagara Falls. The Niagara region, which straddles the border of New York and Ontario, Canada, has become recognized as one of the world's finest cool-climate wine-growing areas. The Niagara River, flowing between the two Great Lakes Ontario and Erie, the "lake effect" weather they produce, and the Niagara Escarpment's limestone soil add up to ideal growing conditions.

There is a wide variety of wineries in the region, producing wines ranging from fruit wines to wines from Native American grape varieties and classic European varieties. This diversity derives from the region's long history as a major region for growing apples, cherries, pears and other fruits, including Concord grapes used for both grape juice and wine, and the more recent discovery that classic European *vinifera* grape varieties can also grow very well in this climate.

◀ The winery at Arrowhead Springs is built into the hillside to make full use of natural earth cooling year-round.

1 | The Winery at Marjim Manor
7171 East Lake Rd., Appleton, NY 14008; (716) 778-7001

The Niagara region is a major fruit belt, and The Winery at Marjim Manor is located right in the middle of it. Owner Margo Bittner and her husband, Jim, first created the Marjim name in a previous life as dairy farmers. Their son Kevin is the winemaker, and daughter Janet handles sales and marketing, making this a true family farm. The fruit for their wines comes from nearby Singer Farms, where Jim is a partner.

The large 1800s mansion, originally called Appleton Hall, is built of bricks imported from Italy and includes an enclosed wraparound porch. Although created as a farm house, it later became a summer retreat for the Sisters of St. Joseph convent. The house supposedly has resident ghosts, with more details described in the tasting room.

www.marjimmanor.com

▲ The nineteenth-century mansion at Marjim Manor

2 | Arrowhead Springs Winery
4746 Town Line Rd., Lockport, NY 14094; (716) 434-8030

Duncan Ross takes wine and the environment very seriously, as is evident by his winery. The winery is built into a hillside, so the temperature in the barrel room remains between 55° and 60°F (13° and 16°C) year-round, avoiding the need for additional cooling and the energy it requires.

Reclaimed timber, used radiators and lighting fixtures, renewable bamboo flooring and durable Vermont slate also reflect the commitment to environmental

responsibility. Even the bottles, corks and labels are selected on that same basis. Similar care is taken in the vineyard, which includes Cabernet Franc, Cabernet Sauvignon, Chardonnay, Merlot and Syrah.

www.arrowheadspringsvineyards.com

3 | Niagara Landing Wine Cellars

4434 Van Dusen Rd., Lockport (Cambria), NY 14094; (716) 433-8405

Niagara Landing Wine Cellars is surrounded by vineyards established in the late 1800s and farmed by three generations before the winery opened in 1998. Reflecting the mix of grape varieties grown, much of its production is with Native American grapes, which yield aromatic, fruity, mouth-filling wines, though European varietals such as Cabernet Sauvignon are also featured. The gift shop and gallery features work by local artists, as well as little-known facts about the Niagara region and its daredevils.

www.niagaralanding.com

4 | Warm Lake Estate

3868 Lower Mountain Rd., Lockport, NY 14094; (716) 731-5900

The Niagara Escarpment runs for more than 650 miles through the Great Lakes region and one of its unique features from a viticultural perspective is the limestone-rich soil from the Jurassic period, similar to that underlying the most famous Pinot Noir vineyards in Burgundy's Côte d'Or, France. The soils are so similar that two large Burgundian producers have purchased land here. Pinot Noir is the sole focus of Warm Lake Estate and the passion of Michael Von Heckler, who is one of the joint owners.

Warm Lake's 55-acre Pinot Noir vineyard is the largest planting of the variety east of the Rocky Mountains and represents more than 20 percent of New York's total.

The cellar store is open daily for wine tasting, and personally guided barrel tastings and winery and vineyard tours are available. The wine-tasting room includes a deck, and the Toronto skyline across Lake Ontario may be seen by a remote camera.

www.warmlakeestate.com

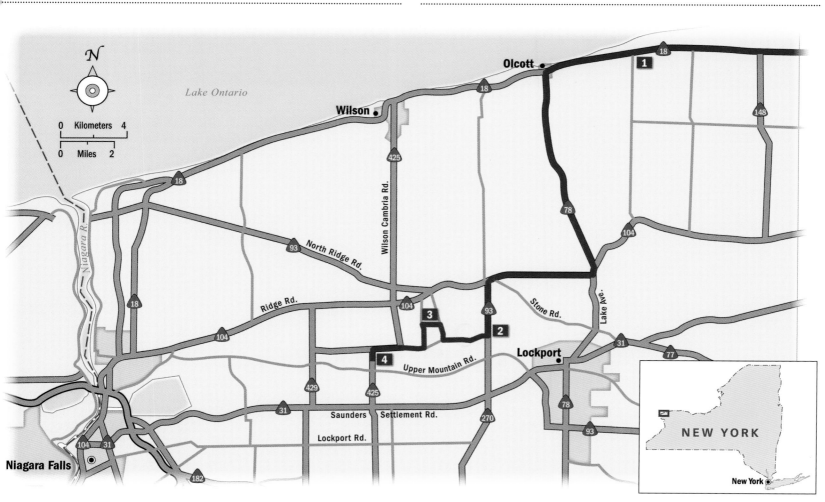

Lake Erie Region

The Lake Erie region is the largest grape-growing area in the eastern United States, including parts of New York, Pennsylvania, and Ohio along the southern shore of Lake Erie. The region benefits from well-drained gravel and shale soils, long hours of summer sunlight, the "lake effect" weather produced by Lake Erie, and the Allegany Plateau—a ridge of hills parallel to the south shore of Lake Erie, which traps those beneficial effects.

The vast majority of grapes grown in this region are Concord, used for grape juice, and a drive past the vineyards in the fall provides a luscious aroma. Regional wines include a wide range from traditional Native American grape varieties, as well as French-American and *vinifera* varieties.

◀ Vineyards hug the shoreline on the eastern shore of Lake Erie.

1 | Johnson Estate Winery

8419 W. Main Rd., Westfield, NY 14787; (716) 326-2191

Established in 1961, Johnson Estate is the oldest estate winery in New York State and is located on a farm where the Johnson family have tended the vineyards for over a century. Growing all its grapes enables the winery to control every aspect of production, and the winery proudly labels its bottles, "grown, vinified, and bottled in the Chateau Tradition."

The winery itself was at one time a cold-storage facility for apples, which were plentiful on the property until the 1960s, when Frederick S. Johnson, the second generation, removed all the fruit trees and Concord grapevines. He replaced them with various French-American grape varieties, as well as the Native American grapes Delaware and Ives.

www.johnsonwinery.com

2 | Woodbury Vineyards

3215 S. Roberts Rd., Fredonia, NY 14063-9417; (716) 679-9463

The Lake Erie wine region southwest of Buffalo is a large strip of east-to-west vineyards nestled between that Great Lake and the Allegheny Mountains, which in combination create a microclimate ideal for growing grapes and other fruit. The Woodbury fruit farm was established a century ago, and the winery opened in 1979.

Located just a few minutes from Interstate 90, Woodbury Vineyards reflects the diversity of grape varieties and other fruits that flourish in the region. Classic European varieties like Chardonnay, Cabernet Franc and Riesling are joined by French-American varieties such as Seyval and fruity Native American offerings like Niagara, along with a selection of fruit wines, including Blueberry, Cherry, Cranberry and Strawberry. The winery and tasting room at Fredonia are set in a rustic apple orchard with a delightful picnic pavilion with views over the vineyards to Lake Erie.

www.woodburyvineyards.com

3 | Liberty Vineyards

2861 Rte. 20, Sheridan, NY 14135; (716) 672-4520

A visit to Liberty Vineyards is akin to tasting a rainbow of different flavors. While the winery is one of the newest in the Lake Erie region the vineyards date back 100 years, and the wine selection celebrates the diversity of the region since it was established.

The white wine selection ranges from the Native American variety Diamond to the Cornell variety Traminette (which reflects its

Gewurztraminer parentage with refreshing spiciness) and Pinot Grigio. Its selection of rosé blends carry fanciful names like Cool Cat, Cat Noir, and Reds, Whites & Blues; and reds include European classics like Cabernet Sauvignon and Pinot Noir supplemented by the new Cornell variety Noiret.

The staff in the light, airy tasting room also offer recipes using the wines, as well as recommended food pairings for them.

www.libertywinery.com

4 | Merritt Estate Winery

2264 King Rd., Forestville, NY 14062; (888) 965-4800

The land on which the Merritt Estate Winery sits has been in the Merritt family since the late 1800s. The winery wasn't established until 1976, however, after the passing of the Farm Winery Act, which made it easier to have a small winery in New York State and sell direct to the public.

The winery is run by Bill Merritt and his son Jason, who produce a wide range of wines, from classic *vinifera* reds such as Merlot, Cabernet France and Pinot Grigio to red and white icewines and late-harvest wines.

www.merrittestatewinery.com

▲ The tasting room at Liberty Vineyards

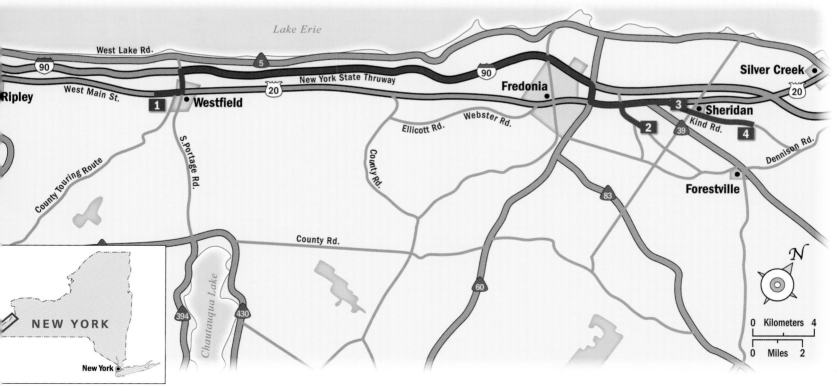

Canandaigua Lake

Due to its proximity to Rochester as well as its natural beauty, Canandaigua Lake has some of the highest prices for lake frontage in the country, comparable to Lake Tahoe. A cruise on the *Canandaigua Lady* paddlewheel boat includes views of several lakeside mansions owned by the region's corporate titans.

At the lake's south end is the charming village of Naples, whose population multiplies from about 5,000 to 100,000 during each fall's Naples Grape Festival, which features Concord grape pies. On the north end in the city of Canandaigua, the New York Wine & Culinary Center promotes New York wines, foods and agriculture through tastings, seminars and a fine restaurant.

◀ It is easy to see why the name Canandaigua means "The Chosen Spot" in the Seneca language.

1 | Casa Larga Vineyards

2287 Turk Hill Rd., Fairport, NY 14450; (585) 223-4210

Casa Larga Vineyards offers a touch of country in the city. It sits high on a hillside with a view of the Rochester skyline, just a few miles from the largest shopping mall complex in the area. The Colaruotolo family created Casa Larga in the 1970s before the area was widely developed, and now the vineyard and winery serve as an oasis of rural charm.

The family's involvement in the construction business is reflected in the large, elegant, Italian-style building, which includes a beautiful tasting room and gift shop, large rooms for weddings, and a deck overlooking the vineyard. There are several festivals during the year, including grape stomping in September and an ice festival in February. While Casa Larga produces a broad range of wines, it has become famous for its Fiori delle Stelle icewines, which are made from grapes that freeze on the vine, producing a luscious golden nectar. There are currently two icewines, from Cabernet Franc and Vidal.

www.casalarga.com

▲ Casa Larga Vineyards in winter

▲ The New York Wine & Culinary Center has plenty to offer food and wine lovers.

2 | New York Wine & Culinary Center
800 S. Main St., Canandaigua, NY 14424; (585) 394-7070

In 2006, a new facility opened along the Canandaigua lakefront which brings together New York wines, foods and agriculture in a warm, friendly setting. The New York Wine & Culinary Center is a partnership among Constellation Brands, the New York Wine & Grape Foundation, Rochester Institute of Technology and Wegman's Food Markets—a unique blend of wine company, trade association, educational institution and food retailer.

There is no admission fee, and the center offers something for everyone. There are wine seminars and cooking demonstrations in the Wine Spectator Educational Theater, a direct cooking experience in the Viking Range Hands-On Kitchen, constant wine-and-beer tastings in an elegant tasting room, and a fine restaurant featuring local products in its seasonal menu. The center was intended to be a gateway rather than a destination, and it's the perfect starting point for exploring the wonderful world of New York wine and food.

www.nywcc.com

3 | Arbor Hill Grapery
6461 Rte. 64, Naples, NY 14512; (585) 374-2870

The grapery is located in the tiny town of South Bristol, just north of Naples, and has a distinct New England feel to it. While most wineries stick to just wine, Arbor Hill goes well beyond a line of fine and unusual wines to offer many other grape products. John and Katie Brahm created Arbor Hill in 1987 in one small building that has now grown into a complex of antique buildings, which serve as retail shop, bistro and production area. John's training at Cornell and a 23-year career at nearby Widmer Wine Cellars prepared him well for grape and wine production. He has consistently been on the

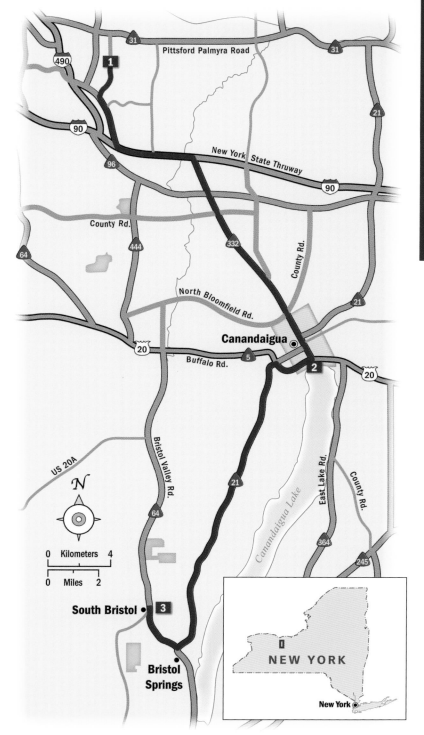

forefront of producing new or unusual varieties, like Cayuga White and Traminette, developed by Cornell University, and a little-known grape called Vergennes. There are also award-winning gourmet food products, like Brahm's Wine Syrups.

www.thegrapery.com

Keuka Lake

The jewel of the Finger Lakes, Y-shaped Keuka Lake is anchored by the charming village of Hammondsport at the south end, then forks into east and west branches leading to Penn Yan and Branchport on the north ends. Keuka Lake is the cradle of the Finger Lakes wine industry, with the first vineyard planted in 1829, the first winery opened in 1860, and the origins of the "*vinifera* revolution," which led to the region's current reputation for world-class Rieslings and other classic European styles of wine.

Before Prohibition in the early 1900s, the hillsides were covered with vineyards, with large boats transporting the grapes to Hammondsport for processing into wine that was loaded onto trains for distribution throughout the country. When Prohibition ended in 1933, the historic wineries in Hammondsport reopened and reestablished Keuka Lake as the center of the industry.

◀ Many of Keuka's wineries offer magnificent views of vineyards, the lake and the Bluff (peninsula).

1 | Bully Hill Vineyards

8843 Greyton H. Taylor Memorial Dr., Hammondsport, NY 14840; (607) 868-3490

"Wine with laughter" is one of the phrases you'll see on corks from the wines of Bully Hill, reflecting the philosophy of the late Walter S. Taylor and his wife, Lillian, that wine should be fun. That attitude also penetrates the tasting room, where hosts engage visitors and help them to loosen up while enjoying a journey through the many wines Bully Hill produces. The winery also has several gift shops, and a fabulous restaurant featuring some of the best and most reasonably priced food in the Finger Lakes. Lillian Taylor, an intuitive chef, creates the recipes and is very proud to feature local foods, including some grown in Bully Hill's own gardens.

www.bullyhill.com

▲ Bully Hill Vineyards overlooking the lake

2 | Heron Hill Winery

9301 County Rte. 76, Hammondsport, NY 14840; (800) 441-4241

Heron Hill Winery has a 30-year history of producing elegant, cool-climate Chardonnays and Rieslings, as well as offering a spectacular setting for enjoying the wines on a slate hillside high above Keuka Lake. Owner John Ingle has had a commitment to living and farming sustainably for many years. Partly because of the spectacular view, combined with the winery's unique architecture, Heron Hill was named in 2009 by *Travel & Leisure* magazine as having one of the top 10 tasting rooms in the world.

www.heronhill.com

▲ The gazebo makes a perfect spot to sample the wines of Dr. Frank's.

Country provides a relaxed family-friendly ambience with hayrides through the vineyards, wine and food festivals, and a broad selection of award-winning wines from many different grape varieties. Among the most popular are the Foxy Lady series of sweet fruity wines, but Hunt Country is also noted for its elegant Pinot Gris and Riesling, as well as for its luscious late-harvest wines and icewine.

www.huntwines.com

3 | Dr. Frank's Vinifera Wine Cellars
9749 Middle Rd., Hammondsport, NY 14840; (800) 320-0735

The roots of today's thriving New York wine industry are planted in the soil high above Keuka Lake at Dr. Frank's Vinifera Wine Cellars. In the 1950s, the German-born Russian émigré started the "*vinifera* revolution" by combining vision, experience and determination to prove that the delicate European (*Vitis vinifera*) grape varieties such as Riesling and Pinot Noir could survive and thrive in the Finger Lakes region. Today nearly all of the 100-plus Finger Lakes wineries produce *vinifera* wines, and the region has become world famous for the quality of its Riesling wines.

Fred Frank, the third generation to continue the commitment to excellent wines, including a pleasant Chateau Frank fizz, has assembled a talented international team of winemakers and expanded the tasting facilities to accommodate the ever-increasing number of visitors who come to sample the wide range of wines while drinking in the beautiful view of Keuka Lake. You can even try Rkatsiteli, an obscure Georgian grape variety.

www.drfrankwines.com

4 | Hunt Country Vineyards
4021 Italy Hill Rd., Branchport, NY 14418; (800) 946-3289

Hunt Country Vineyards is a family-run farm winery combining the passions of Art and Joyce Hunt: grapes, wine and horses. Located on a Century Farm owned by the Hunt family for over 100 years, Hunt

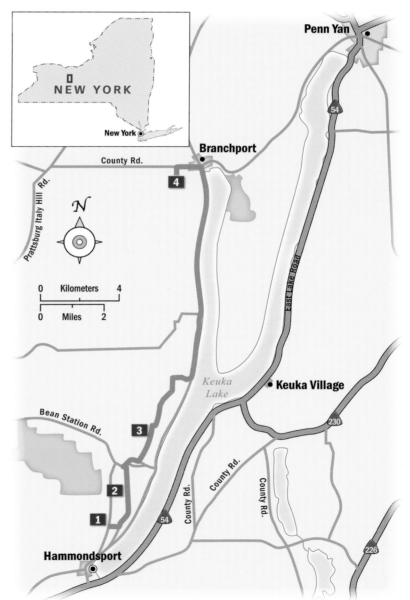

213

TOUR 67
Seneca Lake

Seneca Lake is by far the deepest of the Finger Lakes, more than 600 feet (183 m) deep where the U.S. Navy has a sonar testing facility, and there is great variation in terrain from north to south due to the movement of the Ice Age glaciers. Most of the Finger Lakes freeze entirely or partially in winter but due to its depth, Seneca never does. The vineyards on the southeastern slopes are called the Banana Belt, because of the lake's temperature-moderating effects in winter.

At the north end of the lake, the New York State Agricultural Extension Station, operated by Cornell University, is one of the world's foremost grape-research facilities, which has been vital in improving the quality of New York wines. The charming village of Watkins Glen is at the south end, where the annual Finger Lakes Wine Festival is held each July. Seneca Lake has the region's highest concentration of wineries, now numbering about 50.

◀ Seneca Lake is the largest and deepest of the Finger Lakes, as well as being the second longest.

1 | Lamoreaux Landing Wine Cellars
9224 Main St. (Rte. 414), Lodi, NY 14860; (607) 582-6011

One of the more spectacular settings in the Finger Lakes is that of Lamoreaux Landing Wine Cellars, on the east side of Seneca Lake. The impressive Greek Revival building overlooks acres of vineyards and vistas encompassing more than 25 miles (40 km) of Seneca Lake.

Owner Mark Wagner comes from a family of grape growers and shifted the emphasis from traditional Native American and French-American varieties to the classic European grapes, like Chardonnay and Riesling. His own grape-growing experience and vision for the future immediately paid off when Lamoreaux's 1991 Riesling wine won a gold medal and the Deinhard Trophy for Best New World Riesling at the New World International Wine Competition in 1993.

www.lamoreauxwine.com

2 | Wagner Vineyards, Winery & Brewery
9322 Main St. (Rte. 414), Lodi, NY 14860; (607) 582-6450

Bill Wagner is a true pioneer in the New York wine industry. A long-time grape grower, he started his own winery shortly after the 1976 Farm Winery Act was passed, allowing direct sales to consumers; opened the Ginny Lee Café (named for his granddaughter) once

▲ The impressive winery at Lamoreaux Landing Wine Cellars

▲ Long, dry, sunny days are just what the winemaker needs at harvest time.

wineries were allowed to have restaurants; and opened the first and only brewery attached to a winery. He also designed the unique octagonal winery building, which now hosts more than 100,000 visitors each year. With 250 acres of grapes and 50,000 cases of wine produced each year, Wagner has become one of New York's largest wineries, but the wines are still estate grown, using their own fruit. Both the Ginny Lee Café and Wagner Valley Brewing offer views of the vineyards while sampling the homegrown products.

www.wagnervineyards.com

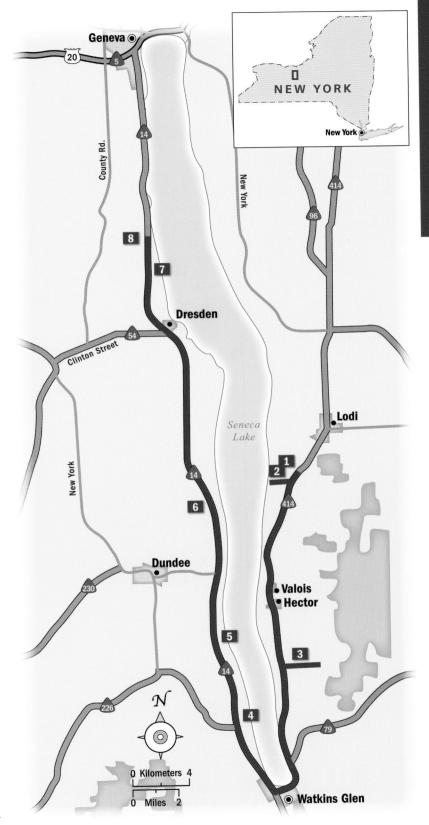

3 | Red Newt Cellars & Bistro

3675 Tichenor Rd., Hector, NY 14841; (607) 546-4100

Debra and Dave Whiting *are* food and wine: Deb makes the food; Dave makes the wine. For anyone looking for a taste of "local," Red Newt is the place. Deb is a self-taught chef who began a gourmet cheesecake business, graduated into upscale catering, and now runs one of the most popular restaurants in the Finger Lakes. Her passion for local products translated into being president of Finger Lakes Culinary Bounty, an organization of regional food producers, restaurants and consumers.

Dave had a similar evolution on the wine side, working at several award-winning Finger Lakes wineries before launching his own Red Newt line of wines to accompany Debra's exceptional food. The range of wines now numbers more than a dozen—be sure to try the stunning aromatic Riesling, Gewurztraminer and Pinot Gris, and the superb Syrah, a rarity in the Finger Lakes region.

www.rednewt.com

4 | Lakewood Vineyards

4024 Rte. 14, Watkins Glen, NY 14891; (607) 535-9252

"Family farm" best describes Lakewood Vineyards, not just because of the family that owns it but also the family-friendly atmosphere, with a play area for kids just outside the tasting room. Visitors always meet one or more members of the Stamp family: Bev (matriarch and business manager), Liz (tasting-room manager), Dave (vineyard manager), Chris (winemaker) and others, who always offer a warm welcome. With 70 acres of vineyards sloping toward Seneca Lake, Lakewood is a relatively large producer with a diversity of wines to suit many tastes. Chris Stamp is an iconoclastic winemaker who enjoys trying the new and unusual—for example, White Catawba, Crystallus (a blend of Cabernets Sauvignon and Franc) and Glaciovinum (icewine made from frozen Delaware grapes), which often turn into favorites among visitors and wine experts alike.

www.lakewoodvineyards.com

5 | Glenora Wine Cellars

5435 Rte. 14, Dundee, NY 14837; (607) 243-9500

Glenora Wine Cellars is one-stop shopping for the wine-and-food lover who also enjoys a nice place to stay. A consistent pioneer in the Finger Lakes wine industry, Glenora became Seneca Lake's first winery in 1977, experimented with different grape varieties throughout the years, created a popular summertime jazz concert series, opened a restaurant, and established a luxurious 30-room inn.

From 5,000 cases in 1977, Glenora has grown to 45,000 and hosts more than 85,000 visitors annually. Like Wagner (see page 214), this is another relatively large winery with a spacious and efficient tasting

▲ A visit to Glenora Wine Cellars offers something of interest to all food and wine lovers, along with a spectacular setting.

room, along with a restaurant and luxury inn, so the visitors are scattered among them. It's the experience that never closes, except on Christmas Day; the winery, Veraisons Restaurant, and the Inn at Glenora are all open 364 days a year.

www.glenora.com

6 | Hermann J. Wiemer Vineyard
3962 Rte. 14, Dundee, NY 14837; (607) 243-7971

Hermann Wiemer's roots extend deeply into the German wine business in the famous Mosel region, where his mother's family had more than 300 years of winemaking history and his father headed the Bernkastel Agricultural Experiment Station, overseeing the replanting of Mosel vineyards after World War II. So it's no surprise that Riesling was his passion or that he helped put the Finger Lakes on the world's wine-growing map.

Housed in a converted barn, the winery is now owned and run by Hermann's longtime winemaker Fred Merwarth, whose wines have won numerous top awards at major wine competitions and received national recognition by the media. While Riesling of different styles remains the focus, several other classic European wines and sparkling wines are also produced.

www.wiemer.com

▲ Fox Run Vineyards, overlooking Seneca Lake

find out more
- www.fingerlakeswineries.org
  Map and guide to all the wineries in the Finger Lakes.
- www.senecalakewine.com
  Seneca Lake Winery Association.

7 | Anthony Road Wine Company
1020 Anthony Rd., Penn Yan, NY 14527; (800) 559-2182

At Anthony Road Winery several members of the Martini family are actively involved in the business. John and Ann Martini began growing grapes in 1973 on a 100-acre farm overlooking Seneca Lake and opened the winery in 1990, with their four children involved in different aspects at different times.

In 2009 the Anthony Road 2008 Semi-Dry Riesling won the coveted Governor's Cup trophy at the New York Wine & Food Classic, topping more than 800 other wines for the best-of-show award. That Riesling, and other Anthony Road wines, reflect the combination of vineyard work by son Peter Martini and German-born winemaker Johannes Reinhardt. A special feature of the winery is a popular garden designed to emphasize the point that food and wine come from the earth, not from the store.

www.anthonyroadwine.com

8 | Fox Run Vineyards
670 Rte. 14, Penn Yan, NY 14527; (315) 536-4616

Housed in a spectacularly renovated Civil War-era dairy barn with a panoramic view of Seneca Lake, Fox Run Vineyards is widely recognized as a leader in the region for wine quality, friendly atmosphere, and food-and-wine pairing. The barn served as a winemaking facility starting in 1993 until three years later, when a separate production building was built at the top of the hill overlooking 55 acres of vineyards sloping down to the lake.

Now the main building includes an elegant tasting room, a popular café open for lunch and afternoon snacks, and a barrel room for special tastings. Fox Run is also famous for its Garlic Festival held each summer in early August, which draws thousands of garlic (and wine) lovers.

Winemaker Peter Bell is well known for award-winning Riesling and other aromatic white wines, but he also makes some outstanding reds, such as Cabernet Franc, Lemberger and Pinot Noir and various blends, including Meritage.

www.foxrunvineyards.com

Cayuga Lake

Stretching more than 30 miles (48 km), Cayuga Lake is anchored on the south by the college town of Ithaca and on the north by Seneca Falls, home to the 1848 Women's Rights Convention, and now to the National Women's Rights Museum and Hall of Fame. While most wineries are located on the lake's west side, the eastern shore has attracted new wineries as well. The Cayuga Wine Trail, established in 1983, was the first in the United States and set the standard for tourism-friendly information and events.

The charming city of Ithaca combines big-city attractions—art, culture, fine restaurants—and small-city charm in a region so well known for its spectacular waterfalls that the local tourism agency's slogan is, "Ithaca is gorges." Those waterfalls and the steep hillsides at the south end of Cayuga Lake show how the Ice Age glaciers pushed the earth southward before retreating and forming the lake.

◄ Ithaca's own winery, Six Mile Creek, enjoys panoramic views down the valley.

1 | Six Mile Creek Vineyard
1551 Slaterville Rd., Ithaca, NY 14850; (607) 272-9463

Visitors to Ithaca, home of Cornell University and Ithaca College, need not venture far to visit a vineyard and winery, since Six Mile Creek is right at the eastern edge of the city. Roger and Nancy Battistella began planting a vineyard in 1982 and opened the winery five years later. The 6-acre vineyard produces Chardonnay, Riesling, Cayuga White and other white wine varieties, while red wine grapes are purchased from other growers.

Production is kept small, at about 4,000 cases annually, so close attention can be focused on all the wines. Recently the product line has been expanded to include a wine-based Vodka, Limoncella (styled after a popular Italian liqueur from the island of Capri) and Grappa, distilled from the alcohol remaining on the grape skins.

www.sixmilecreek.com

2 | King Ferry Winery
658 Lake Rd., King Ferry, NY 13081; (315) 364-5100

Peter and Tacie Saltonstall operate the vineyards and winery at King Ferry, along the east side of Cayuga Lake, on land that has been in the family for decades. Their Treleaven brand of wine, named after

▲ Award-winning wines in the tasting room at Six Mile Creek Vineyard

the Treleaven Farm, which includes 27 acres of vineyards, specializes in Chardonnay but has also become well known for high-quality Rieslings.

Peter serves as the head winemaker, focusing on Burgundian-style Chardonnay. He uses techniques such as harvesting the grapes by hand, barrel fermentation and aging the wine in 100 percent French oak casks to produce a rich, round, complex style. Tacie is the business manager—and resident artist, whose works adorn the tasting-room walls.

www.treleavenwines.com

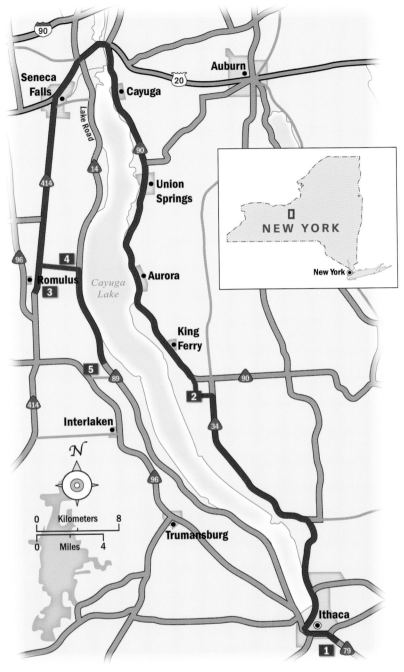

▲ Grape harvesting at King Ferry Winery

3 | Swedish Hill Vineyards

4565 Rte. 414, Romulus, NY 14541; (315) 549-8326

A visit to the tasting room here makes it clear that this is among New York's most decorated wineries in terms of medals won in wine competitions throughout the country. Swedish Hill produces a very broad selection of wines, and nearly every wine has won gold medals in competitions in California and other states. Swedish Hill also won the prestigious Governor's Cup, as well as Winery of the

Year, at the 2008 New York Wine & Food Classic. The winery has also grown from just 1,300 cases at its 1986 start-up to more than 60,000 cases today, making it one of New York's largest producers.

The Peterson family also owns the nearby Goose Watch Winery, which specializes in unusual wine types, such as Diamond, Traminette and Lemberger and these wines have added to the large stash of medals.

www.swedishhill.com

4 | Knapp Vineyards Winery & Restaurant
2770 Ernsberger Rd., Romulus, NY 14541; (800) 869-9271

Knapp Vineyards Winery & Restaurant has been an industry leader since its opening in 1984. It planted the first Cabernet Franc vines in the Finger Lakes region, planted some of the first *vinifera* vines on the shores of Cayuga Lake, opened the first winery restaurant on Cayuga Lake and was the first winery on the East Coast to operate an alembic pot still for the production of brandy. Knapp has shown steady growth, from just 500 gallons initially to more than 36,000 today, with distribution expanding proportionately.

The gift shop includes gourmet food items, and the Vineyard Restaurant features locally focused, eclectic cuisine on a patio shaded by a vine-covered trellis overlooking gardens and vineyards. There is even a cottage for rental right on the shores of Cayuga Lake.

www.knappwine.com

Cayuga Lake

NATIVE AMERICAN LEGEND

The Finger Lakes got its name from a Native American legend of the Iroquois nation claiming that the many lakes reflected the handprints of the Great Spirit. Indeed, all of the lakes have Native American names, like Canandaigua (The Chosen Spot), Cayuga (Boat Landing), Keuka (Canoe Landing) and Seneca (Place of the Stone), which are the major lakes of today's Finger Lakes wine region.

▲ At Knapp Vineyards grapes are used to produce brandy as well as wine.

regionalevents

Long Island Wine Camp □ March, April, June

At last, a camp designed for adults! This very special event includes accommodations, savory gourmet meals, tastings and even a case of wine to take home with you!　　　　　www.liwines.com

Bounty of the Hudson □ July

Enjoy regional wines, foods, farm fresh produce and culinary workshops in this fun-filled Hudson Valley event. Location varies.

www.shawangunkwinetrail.com/swtevents.html

Finger Lakes Wine Festival □ July

More than 70 wineries, breweries and regional artisans come together at one location. Music, culinary classes and more are also on offer.

www.flwinefest.com

Pride of New York Harvest Festival □ November

This three-day extravaganza includes award-winning beers, wines and food products from growers and producers from across the state.

www.harvestfestny.com

5 | Hosmer Winery

6999 State Rte. 89, Ovid, NY 14521; (607) 869-3393

Like many Finger Lakes winery owners, Cameron and Maren Hosmer began as grape growers who sold their fruit to large wineries before deciding to take the next step of controlling the quality of the final product themselves. That decision has paid off, with the winery growing from 2,500 cases in 1985 to over 20,000 today, and the reputation for quality widespread in New York State and beyond. Cameron is also a well-known consultant with a laser-based system for planting vineyards, so not surprisingly the 60 acres at Hosmer are perfectly aligned. The winery is in a renovated barn that also includes a consumer-friendly tasting room. Riesling and Cabernet Franc are Hosmer specialties, and its rich and fruity Raspberry Rhapsody is one of its most popular offerings.

www.hosmerwinery.com

findout more

- www.cayugawinetrail.com
Information on regional events and visiting the wineries.

Hudson River Region

In 1609, explorer Henry Hudson sailed north from Manhattan toward the Adirondack Mountains, discovering a river and region that has been a key part of American history and commerce. A couple of centuries later, French Huguenots were delighted to discover vineyard-covered hillsides, only to learn that their wild grapes made terrible wine.

The Hudson Valley has branded itself the "Roots of American Wine," boasting the nation's oldest vineyard at Benmarl Winery and oldest continuously operating winery at Brotherhood. Yet the region is also experiencing a renaissance, with new wineries opening on both sides of the river. The main vineyard areas are around the city of Poughkeepsie on the east side (grouped into the Dutchess Wine Trail) and on the west side, from New Paltz down to Marlboro (the Shawangunk Wine Trail).

◀ The tall cliffs along the Hudson River help make the climate suitable for grape-growing.

1 | Clinton Vineyards

450 Schultzville Rd., Clinton Corners, NY 12514; (845) 266-5372

Clinton Corners is a community so small that you'll miss it if you blink, which is what makes Clinton Vineyards so charming. Nestled in the rolling hills of Dutchess County, the 30-year-old farm winery exudes a warm and personal atmosphere in a historic Dutch barn surrounded by a pond, gardens, woods and a vineyard as part of a 100-acre landscape.

When artist Ben Feder first purchased the former dairy farm, he decided to plant only Seyval Blanc grapes, which produce a dry white table wine as well as a traditional method sparkling wine. All the wines are estate bottled, made with grapes from the 15-acre vineyard and truly hand-crafted.

In recent years his wife, Phyllis, has expanded the offerings to include pure fruit wines from both red and black raspberries and blackberries and even a blackcurrant cassis, with names like Romance, Embrace and Desire. Clinton Vineyards is proof that "small is beautiful."

www.clintonvineyards.com

▲ The historic Dutch barn at Clinton Vineyards

2 | Millbrook Vineyards & Winery

26 Wing Rd., Millbrook, NY 12545; (845) 677-8383

Millbrook Vineyards & Winery has been a leader in the regional wine industry for decades. Owner John Dyson, a wine lover who also owns vineyards in California and Italy, has proved his belief that delicate European grape varieties can grow in the region. The 130-acre estate includes a 30-acre vineyard planted with several different grape varieties, leading up to the winery and tasting room located in a restored barn. The location, 90 minutes from both Albany and New York City, has made Millbrook a popular destination for wine lovers.

www.millbrookwine.com

3 | Stoutridge Vineyard

10 Ann Kaley La., Marlboro, NY 12542; (845) 236-7620

Stoutridge Vineyard is a new state-of-the-art winery on land that has been planted with grapevines and fruit trees for more than 200 years. This area was the principal supplier of fresh fruit to New York City during the nineteenth century. Opened in 2006, the winery sits where vineyards were planted in the 1700s; a winery opened in 1902 (later closed due to Prohibition), and a bootleg distillery operated on the site until 1956.

The winery is built into a hillside, with the wine cellars underground to maintain constant, cool temperatures without requiring energy. Solar energy is used exclusively to power the winery, with waste heat from its stills used to heat the building in the winter through a radiant floor system. The wines are made with minimal processing to preserve the character of the fruit, and they are available for sale only at the winery.

www.stoutridge.com

4 | Brotherhood, America's Oldest Winery

100 Brotherhood Plaza Dr., Washingtonville, NY 10992; (845) 496-3661

With its first recorded vintage in 1839, Brotherhood claims to be the oldest continuously operating winery in the United States. Begun by French Huguenot Jean Jacques, Brotherhood still uses the cellars he created in 1839 and was the first winery to offer tours of its cellars. The winery is on both the national and New York State Registers of Historical Places.

Brotherhood is also a modern winery, offering a wide array of wines, as well as facilities for picnics, live concerts and even a grape-stomping series during the fall harvest. Located in Washingtonville, only an hour north of New York City, Brotherhood winery provides a convenient way to visit the world of wine, past and present.

www.brotherhoodwinery.net

▲ The new winery at Stoutridge Vineyard

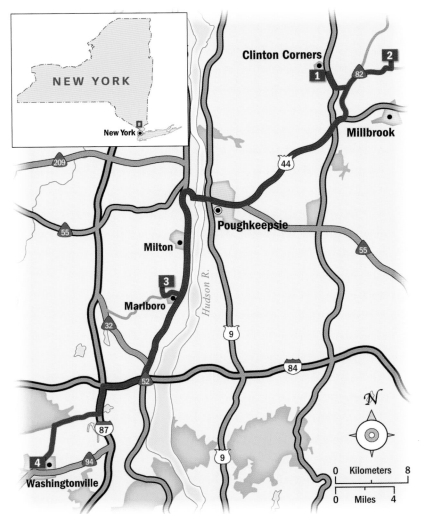

Long Island

Eastern Long Island, New York State's newest wine region, has earned an international reputation in the short time since the first grapes were planted in 1973. With about 3,000 acres of vineyard and 50 wineries, Long Island benefits from a maritime climate, abundant sunshine and a long growing season conducive to classic red varieties like Cabernet Sauvignon and Merlot.

Long Island begins right across the East River from Manhattan, but the wine region is located about 75 miles (120 km) east, where the island divides into the North Fork and the Hamptons, the tiny playground of the rich and famous. The vast majority of wineries are conveniently located along two major routes on the North Fork, and the striking architecture of many wineries provides visual pleasure to accompany the taste of fine wines.

◀ The vineyards on Long Island benefit from a sunny, maritime climate and a long, mild growing season.

1 | Pellegrini Vineyards

23005 Main Rd., Cutchogue, NY 11935; (631) 734-4111

Located in Cutchogue, New York State's sunniest town, Pellegrini Vineyards is a visual feast—with the stunning winery, the elegant barrel room underneath, and the manicured vineyard with a gazebo overlooking the vines that is a popular site for weddings.

The artistic bent of owner Bob Pellegrini is matched by that of his Australian winemaker, Russell Hearn, who has been with the winery since it started out in 1991. His judicious use of oak produces wines where the fruit is enhanced rather than masked. Pellegrini specializes in Merlot which seems to do well in Long Island's climate but also offers an eclectic range of wines, including Chardonnay, Petit Verdot and Finale, a luscious dessert wine created with frozen Gewurztraminer and Sauvignon Blanc grapes.

www.pellegrinivineyards.com

▲ An old vineyard truck belonging to Castello di Borghese

findout more

- www.newyorkwines.org
  The "Wine Country" section has extensive information for planning a trip.
- www.liwines.com
  Information on Long Island wines.

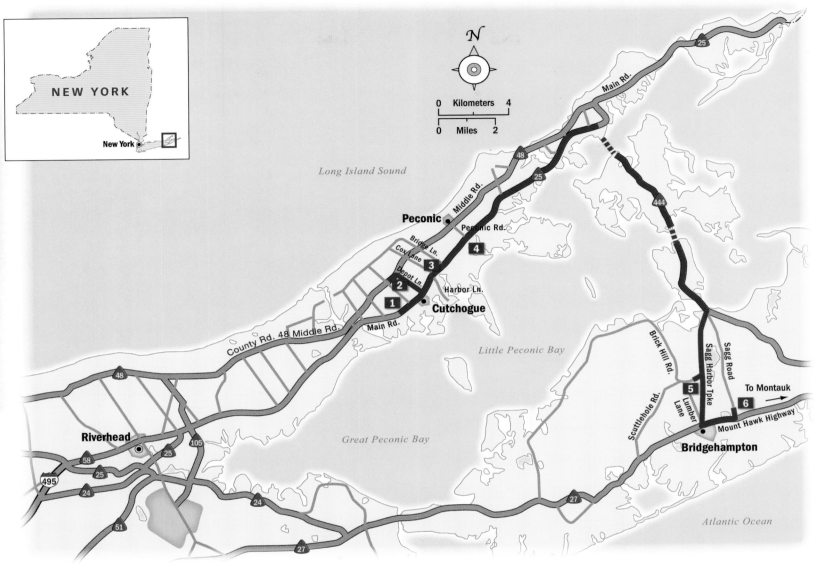

2 | Castello di Borghese

17150 Rte. 48 (Sound Ave. and Alvah's La.), Cutchogue, NY 11935;
(631) 734-5111

The roots of the Long Island wine industry are planted in this vineyard, which began in 1973 as Hargrave Vineyard. Since 1999, the Castle of the Borgheses has been owned by Italian Prince Marco and Princess Ann Marie Borghese from Philadelphia. While preserving the property's heritage, the Borgheses have added their own touches by expanding the vineyard, redesigning the tasting room and creating a relaxed setting for visitors to sample wines. The winery is also very involved in the arts, and hosts events throughout the year to highlight the connection between art and wine.

www.castellodiborghese.com

3 | Bedell Cellars

36225 Main Rd., (Rte. 25), Cutchogue, NY 11935; (631) 734-7537

Bedell Cellars dramatically illustrates that wine is art through its wines, labels and winery. The owner, Michael Lynne, was the executive producer of the *Lord of the Rings* film trilogy and is very active in the fine-arts world in New York City. An international winemaking team produces award-winning blends, which are named Taste, Gallery and Musée, and presented in elegant bottles with labels created by famous artists. The focus on fine art is reinforced in the tasting room and housed in a renovated old potato barn with contemporary art on the walls. Outside, a large grand tasting pavilion built of mahogany features expansive views of Bedell's vineyards.

www.bedellcellars.com

▲ Raphael's magnificent tasting room

4 | Raphael

39390 Main Rd., (Rte. 25), Peconic, NY 11958; (631) 765-1100

The entrance of Raphael winery, named after the father of owner John Petrocelli, Sr., provides a first visual glimpse of the European-style elegance that permeates the entire operation, from the architecture of the buildings to the wines and even a "Renaissance Room" for special events.

One of Long Island's most experienced winemakers, Richard Olsen-Harbich was instrumental in custom-designing the tank room and cellar, where he concentrates on producing world-class Merlot in the tradition of great Bordeaux châteaux. In addition to Merlot, Raphael produces a consistently stunning Sauvignon Blanc, as well as Chardonnay, Cabernet Franc and other wines.

www.raphaelwine.com

▲ Looking over Riverhead Great toward Peconic Bay, with Little Peconic Bay beyond

5 | Channing Daughters

1927 Scuttlehole Rd., Bridgehampton, NY 11932; (631) 537-7224

Located in Bridgehampton on Long Island's south fork, also known as the Hamptons, Channing Daughters offers diversity, creativity and quality, which forms the foundation for a wide array of different wines. The property includes a 25-acre vineyard, small winery and tasting room.

Channing Daughters grows more different grape varieties than any other winery on Long Island, uses several combinations of stainless-steel and oak barrels for fermentation and aging, and creates 26 different wines, mostly unique blends. All grapes are hand-picked, and the red grapes are stomped by foot and punched down by hand in the Old World tradition. Channing Daughters also features a unique Sculpture Garden Vineyard, where the vines share space with various sculptures.

www.channingdaughters.com

6 | Wölffer Estate Vineyard

139 Sagg Rd., Sagaponack, NY 11962; (631) 537-5106

It is hard to envision former potato fields where Wölffer Estate now stands as a manicured European-style chateau between the tiny towns of Easthampton and Southampton.

Created by the late Christian Wölffer, the winery is a tasteful blend of European features: Tuscan architecture with outside walls of ocher, Provençal blue shutters, tall French doors and an antique stained-glass window from Germany. Leading up to the winery's massive front doors are impeccable grounds with conifers, junipers and hemlocks, and a coin-filled fountain overlooking the immaculate vineyards. Like Mr. Wölffer, winemaker Roman Roth is German-born and employs classical styles of winemaking in the winery's high-vaulted cellars. Wölffer Estate has released limited quantities of Long Island's most expensive wine, Premier Cru, a red wine priced at $125 per bottle.

There are also magnificent riding stables on the estate, from where you can ride out into the Hamptons (turn right from the winery onto Sagg Rd., then turn right onto Narrow Lane East).

www.wolffer.com

▲ A wedding table laid out in the vineyards at Wölffer Estate

Northern Ohio

The southern rim of Lake Erie is also the northern border of Ohio—a flat, vast stretch that arcs from Toledo, through Sandusky, Lorain, Cleveland and over to the Pennsylvania border. Along one of the most-traveled east–west truck-laden turnpikes in the country (the conjoined interstates 80 and 90), endless miles of farmers' fields yield to cities and the occasional silent, hulking wreck of America's past industrial might. This is part of what they call the rust belt.

But before industry, it was also wine country all the way back to the 1850s, due to an ideal combination of soil and climate. In the winter, warm lake air drifts to hold back icy, frigid masses that would otherwise destroy the vines, while excellent soil conditions lend extra minerality and vigor to the wines. Many of the wineries on this tour straddle the mid-section of those two interstates, beginning just south of Toledo and heading east, a stretch that is slightly less than a two-hour drive.

◀ The Marblehead lighthouse at Sandusky on the shores of Lake Erie

1 | Hermes Vineyards & Winery
6413 Hayes Ave. (Rte. 4), Sandusky, OH 44870; (419) 626-8500

Travel Interstate 80/90 to the exit at Route 4 and head north to this 30-acre winery owned by David Kraus, a practicing psychiatrist in Manhattan for two decades whose family has owned this farm for seven generations. Kraus's maternal ancestors—the German Hermes family—immigrated here and bought the property to plant Mosel-like wines in the 1850s. Then, for generations, it produced other agricultural products.

In 2002, after looking for land in Long Island, Kraus rediscovered his own farm and replanted it with *vinifera* vines in 2002, convinced that great cold-climate European vines would thrive here because of the long growing season created by the moderating influence of the lake.

Today, Kraus focuses on the red grapes of Spain, Italy and the Rhône Valley of France: Mourvedre, Barbera, Nebbiolo, Sangiovese, Syrah, Merlot, Tempranillo, Cabernet Franc and Cabernet Sauvignon, as well as several whites, such as Chardonnay, Sauvignon Blanc, Gewürztraminer and Riesling.

Hermes has a modest tasting room and store at the winery that operates daily.

www.hermesvineyards.com

▲ Along this route, away from the busy interstates, are many peaceful vineyards.

2 | Firelands Winery

917 Bardshar Rd., Sandusky, OH 44870; (419) 625-5474

Perhaps no winery holds more history than this Ohio gem. Firelands dates back to the 1870s, when a German émigré and stonecutter began building a winery out of the local limestone, along with a massive pavilion for visitors. He called it Golden Eagle, and it eventually claimed to be the largest winery in the country—California became a state in 1850 and had almost no wine production at the time. Golden Eagle hosted American presidents and travelers from Buffalo, Detroit and Cleveland.

The winery was purchased from the founder by the original winemaker, Peter Lonz (also a German), and handed down to his son George. Over the years, a series of fires destroyed one version after another of the winery and grand hotel on the property. Today, the Lonz name adorns a line of wines, which are central to the Firelands portfolio.

Since 1979, the wines have been made by Italian native Claudio Salvador, who trained in northern Italy. Firelands pioneered the conversion to European *vinifera* grapes in the area, creating a reputation as a premier winery.

In the past decade, new plantings of grape varieties—such as Chardonnay, Pinot Noir, Cabernet Sauvignon, Riesling and Pinot Grigio—have won top honors in some of the most prestigious competitions in the country and have earned Ohio much of its recent reputation.

www.firelandswinery.com

▲ Checking the clarity of the wine in the barrel room of Firelands Winery

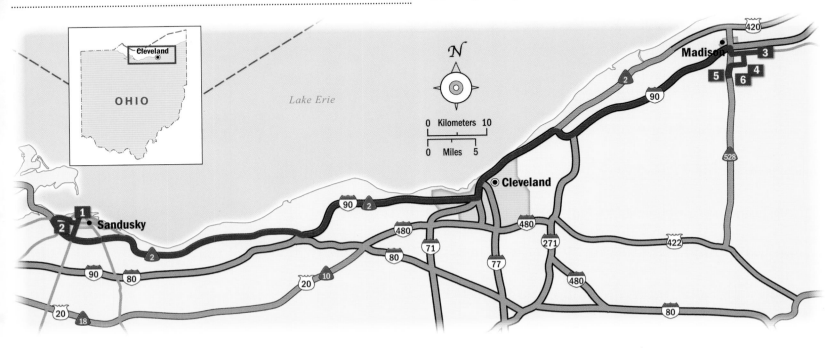

Concord grapes

3 | Ferrante Winery and Restaurant
5585 State Rte. 307, Harpersfield Township, Geneva, OH 44041; (440) 466-8466

This large modern estate houses its own Italian restaurant and is located a short distance inland from Lake Erie in Geneva, south of Interstate 90. The small but impressive tasting room, winery and lunch stop make Ferrante a worthwhile trip.

The Ferrante family, now into its third generation of winemaking in Ohio, began the winery in 1937. Like all the wineries of the Midwest, Ferrante made wine from native American and French hybrid grapes. It still does, but it began to plant European grapes in the 1980s and now makes exceptional cold-climate whites, such as Chardonnay, Riesling and Gewürztraminer. The whites are much leaner than California wines and closer to crisp young northern Burgundies and the drier German styles.

Ferrante has distinguished itself as a regional winemaker, winning many national awards in large competitions for wines distinctive to the emerging regional character of Ohio.

www.ferrantewinery.com

THE RENAISSANCE OF OHIO'S WINE INDUSTRY

Today, Ohio has upward of 70 wineries. While a large number of them are small producers of sweet fruit wines, those making quality table wines have emerged into the national picture since the 1980s by adding European *vinifera* varieties to their portfolio of grapes, as have many other wineries in neighboring states.

The better Ohio wineries make wines from both old- and new-style grapes; old being native America grapes like Concord and Niagara, and French-American hybrids such as Cayuga, and new being classic European *vinifera* varieties, such as Chardonnay, Sauvignon Blanc, Pinot Noir and Cabernet Sauvignon.

4 | Debonné Vineyards
7743 Doty Rd., Madison, OH 44057; (440) 466-3485

About 3 miles (5 km) east of Route 528 (take the Madison exit off Interstate 90 and head south on 528 for about 2 miles/3 km) is one

▲ Debonné Vineyards is Ohio's largest estate winery.

of Ohio's most distinguished wineries. As well as the winery there is a chalet-style tasting room, gift shop, terrace and a garden with umbrella tables overlooking the vineyard. Tours of the large state-of-the-art facility include the fermentation tank area and barrel-aging room.

Debonné was started in 1971 by Tony and Rose Debevc, who have been joined in the day-to-day operation by their son, also called Tony. Debonné grows a wide variety of grapes in its 110 acres of vineyards. Debonné's list includes two Chardonnays, a reserve and regular bottling, as well as Pinot Gris, two Rieslings and a French hybrid white called Vidal Blanc, which is its best and most interesting wine. In reds, the Cabernet Franc has been successful and Debonné also makes very good Merlot and an unusual Pinot Noir and Syrah blend.

www.debonne.com

▲ Picking Cabernet Franc grapes for icewine at St. Joseph Vineyards

5 | Grand River Cellars Winery & Restaurant

5750 S. Madison Rd., Rte. 528, Madison, OH 44057; (440) 298-9838

Also south of the Madison exit, a few miles from Interstate 90, is this small impressive-looking winery that has been around since 1976. It has a full-service restaurant, making it a worthwhile stop for lunch or dinner while in the area.

Formerly Madison Wine Cellars, it was purchased in 2005 from its founders by a group including the Debevcs of Debonné Vineyards (see facing page) and other partners. Its premium wines are estate-grown Cabernet Franc, Pinot Grigio and Riesling—all bottled under the official Grand River Valley appellation (AVA). Proprietary wines include Grand Blush and Stonewood White Fox; other wines are made from a blend of locally grown grapes, and red and white wines purchased elsewhere.

www.grandrivercellars.com

6 | St. Joseph Vineyard

6060 Madison Rd., Thompson, OH 44086; (440) 298-3709

A few miles south of the exit for Madison off Interstate 90, the road changes from straight to rolling small hills and stands of trees, a state park and the Grand River. Just beyond is this unpretentious family-run winery, owned by Art and Doreen Pietrzyk, which has been getting national recognition and top medals in the country's more prestigious wine competitions. St. Joseph has also been making wine from European *vinifera* grapes since the mid-1980s and produces Sauvignon Blanc, Pinot Blanc, Chardonnay, Riesling, Vidal Blanc, icewine, Merlot, Shiraz, Pinot Noir and a Reserve Pinot Noir.

St. Joseph pays particular attention to agricultural practices in order to make complex and intense wines that reflect the regional character provided by the local climate and soil conditions. To do this, the winery has been careful about how it has orientated its vineyards toward the sun (important in this northerly region) and has planted them on a slight pitch in the land for natural irrigation. They also thin their crop throughout the growing season to get greater richness in the fruit. A deck outside the tasting room overlooks the vineyard.

findout more
• www.ohiowines.org
The website of the Ohio Wine Association, with maps, trails and links to wineries.

Southeast Pennsylvania

Pennsylvania has more than 100 wineries scattered throughout the state, but one of the most rewarding areas for the wine tourist to visit is the southeast Pennsylvania wine region. Not only are there several good wineries to visit here, but this is also the heart of Brandywine Valley, with its historic museums, art galleries, world-renowned gardens, antique shops and great restaurants. It's an easy hour's drive from Philadelphia or from the historic riverside town of Havre de Grace in northern Maryland.

As with other East Coast wine areas, the region is characterized by a moderate climate, and has a long growing season influenced by the Chesapeake and Delaware Bays. Most wineries here grow *vinifera* grapes such as Pinot Grigio, Chardonnay, Viognier, Pinot Noir and Cabernet Sauvignon; Italian varietals such as Sangiovese and Barbera thrive here as well.

◄ In early summer, the Paradocx vineyards are a sea of fresh green vines.

1 | Paradocx Vineyard

1833 Flint Hill Rd., Landenberg, PA 19350; (610) 255-5684

Paradocx Vineyard is the perfect starting place for this tour. First impressions tell us this winery is young, fresh and clever. The name Paradocx is a play on words—two doctors (a pair of docs) own the winery—wine must be good for you!

There is a new tasting room, which sits on over 100 acres of land, 30 of which are under vine. Paradocx was recently featured in *Wine Spectator* magazine for their clever packaging—they offer three wines in paint cans! These cans hold White Wash, a blend of Pinot Grigio and Chardonnay; Barn Red, a blend of Sangiovese and Cabernet; and Pail Pink, a blended rosé. Don't miss the crisp, fruity, award-winning Viognier. Leverage, a blend of Cabernet Sauvignon, Cabernet Franc and Petit Verdot, pairs very well with steak and the Sangiovese is medium-bodied and aged in American oak.

Paradocx is a family-friendly winery, hosting events throughout the year, such as summer concerts and holiday-oriented celebrations.

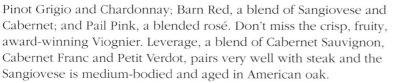

PDX

SANGIOVESE
CHESTER COUNTY PENNSYLVANIA
Alc. 13.5% by Vol.

www.paradocx.com

2 | Va La Winery

8820 Gap Newport Pike (Rte. 41), Avondale, PA 19311; (610) 268-2702

From Paradocx Vineyard, head southeast on Flint Hill Road, and left on Mercer Mill Road. Head up to Gap Newport Pike (Interstate 41 North). About 200 yards down the road, Va La Winery will be on the left—look for the white fence.

At Va La Winery, you can expect more than just stale crackers and a pitcher of water on the tasting bar. The years of self-sufficiency on this family-owned farm have given the owners a sense of pride when it comes to the homemade and local products that they feature, such as foccacia bread and local cheeses.

This is a small winery, producing around 700–900 cases of wine a year from vineyards planted in 1999. These intriguing blends are crafted in small batches and use unique combinations of grapes, mostly Italian red and white varieties. The philosophy here is that the wine reflects the land and the hard work and love that goes into it each year. Don't miss two popular blends, the red Va La Mahogony and the white Prima Donna. Va La hosts art shows, small concerts and special tastings throughout the year. You will often find a local recording artist playing the baby grand piano in the galleria, or hear a jazz trio in the vineyard in the backyard.

www.valavineyards.com

3 | Chaddsford Winery

632 Baltimore Pike, Chadds Ford, PA 19317; (610) 388-6221

Route 1 North/East will take you straight to the small country estate of Chaddsford, one of Pennsylvania's most highly acclaimed wineries. Founded by Eric and Lee Miller in 1982, this winery produces 25,000 cases annually. Enjoy the farm feel of this venue with its attractive seventeenth-century colonial barn, deck patio and picnic areas.

There is a wide variety of wines produced here—something for everyone, from high-end premium dry wines to fun seasonal wines, and nice regional wines in between. Be sure you try Due Rossi, an Italian blend of Sangiovese and Barbera, and Merican, a Bordeaux-style blend of Cabernet Sauvignon and Merlot.

Chaddsford's seasonal specialty wines include a spring wine that is young and green and a perfect patio wine for warmer days, and a fruity sangria for summer. Fall features a spiced apple wine, and winter is celebrated with a mulled wine called Holiday Spirit—a perfect holiday gift. If you are interested in a more technical tour, visit during the weekend, when a member of the winemaking team leads an in-depth tour. You can also try a reserve tasting hosted by a wine educator.

The winery hosts numerous events, such as the Brandywine Harvest Festival and Spiced Apple Days. You can also combine a visit to Chaddsford with a trip to the nearby famed Longwood Gardens and the Brandywine River Museum of American Art.

www.chaddsford.com

findout more

- **www.pennsylvaniawine.com**
  Information on the state's wine trails, wineries and special events.

- **www.thebrandywine.com**
  Ideas for visiting Brandywine Valley.

▲ Chaddsford offers plenty of festivals and events for the visitor, along with a relaxed atmosphere.

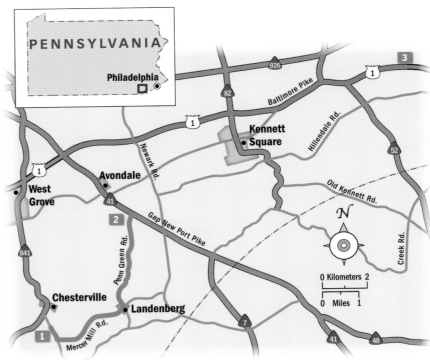

THE EASTERN REGION

PENNSYLVANIA

Frederick to Chesapeake

A drive through Maryland's wine country will fascinate both wine lover and history buff. This tour starts at Sugarloaf Mountain Vineyard, only 25 minutes from the Capital Beltway, making it the closest winery to Washington, D.C. It continues up through Baltimore, home of the East Coast's best fresh seafood and local charm. For sun worshippers and adventurers, take a spin out to Maryland's Eastern Shore, to one of the new premier wineries of the state: Bordeleau.

Maryland's scenery encompasses beaches, ski slopes and farmland. The diversity of conditions offers different kinds of wine and unique touring experiences. Fall is a rewarding time of year to visit. Not only are the vineyards being harvested, but Maryland's curtain of foliage begins to turn golden, amber and crimson. The wine-tour traveler has opportunities to visit wine festivals, historic tours, seafood festivals and other seasonal attractions.

◄ Elk Run is located in the peaceful Frederick County countryside.

1 | Sugarloaf Mountain Vineyard
18125 Comus Rd., Dickerson, MD 20842; (301) 605-0130

From Washington, D.C.'s, Capital Beltway, take Interstate 270 to exit 22, for Hyattstown/Barnesville. Take Route 109 to Comus Road and turn right. Sugarloaf Mountain Vineyard is 1.5 miles (2.5 km) down the road. You will spot the early 1900s large red barn, silo and windmill as you enter this 92-acre farm.

This welcoming family-owned-and-run operation will entice you with its award-winning Bordeaux-style wines. Comus (a blend of five Bordeaux varietals) and Cabernet Franc, both double gold-medal winners, lead the range of reds. If you're looking for something more refreshing while you sit on their outdoor patio, try the crisp, citrusy Pinot Grigio or rich, oaked Chardonnay.

This is a great place to start your Maryland tour, since there are many lovely B&Bs in the area, as well as local artisans, farmers and crafters. The winery is at the base of Sugarloaf Mountain, a conservation area that is open for hiking, biking, horseback riding and exploring.

www.smvwinery.com

2 | Black Ankle Vineyards
14463 Black Ankle Rd., Mt. Airy, MD 21771; (301) 829-3338

After leaving Sugarloaf Mountain Vineyard, stop for lunch in the historic city of Frederick. If you choose to go straight to Black Ankle, about 30 miles (50 km) away, go back to Route 109, then pick up Route 75 (Green Valley Road). At Libertytown, turn right onto Route 26 East (Liberty Road), and then turn left on Unionville Road. Follow this for over a mile and take a left on Black Ankle Road. As you follow this windy uphill road, you will see a sign for Black Ankle on the right.

Follow the road down the hill to the 100 percent wind-powered tasting room. This structure looks as if it has always been a part of the farm because everything from the straw-bale-insulated walls to the clay floors and handmade wooden tables and chairs is sourced from the land the winery stands on. Not only is the structure sustainable, but the farm uses biodynamic farming principles.

Be sure to stay a while on the patio or in the cozy tasting room to try the Leaf-Stone Syrah, the Crumbling Rock Bordeaux red blend or Bedlam, a wine made from the five white-grape varieties grown on the estate. All the wines are made in very limited quantities, but are beginning to build up a serious reputation.

www.blackankle.com

▲ Wildflowers thrive along with the biodynamically farmed vines at Black Ankle Vineyards.

3 | Elk Run Vineyards

15113 Liberty Rd., Mt. Airy, MD 21771; (410) 775-2513

Back on Liberty Road, you will find Elk Run Vineyards just 3 miles (5 km) down the road, on the right. Surrounded by beautiful Frederick County farmland, this rustic winery—recently named as one of the top 100 wineries on the East Coast—is flanked by vines on both sides of the road.

The winemakers' home, circa 1756, was once a tavern and sits on a property historically called the Resurvey of Cold Friday, which was a land grant from the King of England to Lord Baltimore in the early 1700s. Elk Run planted the first all-*vinifera* vineyard in Maryland and now grows some of the state's best Cabernet Franc and Gewürztraminer grapes.

Winemaker Fred Wilson uses old-world winemaking practices, and succeeds in making notable and award-winning wines vintage after vintage. His Cabernet Franc is becoming a signature wine, and there's also good Merlot and Cabernet Sauvignon, which is also used to make a sweet red, Sweet Katherine and a port labeled Lord Baltimore. Be sure to try the Gewürztraminer, which made a big splash at one of the inaugural balls in Washington, D.C. There are also delicious sparkling wines.

www.elkrun.com

Originally started in 1945 by Philip Wagner, Boordy Vineyards was purchased by the R. B. Deford family in 1980, and is now one of Maryland's largest wineries. Boordy produces award-winning Chardonnay, Cabernet Franc, Cabernet Sauvignon, and highlights some of Wagner's much-promoted hybrid varieties, including Vidal Blanc, Seyval Blanc and Chambourcin.

While keeping to traditional standards of wine-making, Boordy Vineyards has a fun and flirty side, too. They have a line of fruit wines, including a spiced wine, sangria and their most popular "Jazzberry" wine for the sweet wine lover in the group. Check out their website for seasonal events, like "Soup in the Cellar," concerts and farmers markets at the winery.

Fun Fact: Some of the scenes from the Julia Roberts and Richard Gere *Runaway Bride* (1999) movie were filmed at the winery!

www.boordy.com

5 | Fiore Winery

3026 Whiteford Rd., Pylesville, MD 21132; (410) 879-4007

Twenty miles (32 km) from Boordy Vineyards is a little piece of Italy, Fiore Winery. Leaving Boordy, turn left onto Long Green Pike. Turn left at Baldwin Mill Road (Route 165 North) for 15 miles (24 km). Take the third exit at the traffic circle onto Interstate 24. Turn right at Interstate 136 (Whiteford Road) and you will see Fiore on the right. Mike Fiore, owner and winemaker of Fiore Winery, came to the United

▲ Sugarloaf Mountain hosts a range of events for the wine tourist.

4 | Boordy Vineyards

12820 Long Green Pike, Hydes, MD 21082; (410) 592-5015

About an hour away from the wineries covered so far on this tour is Maryland's oldest winery, Boordy Vineyards. From Elk Run, head east on Liberty Road (Route 26 East) for 23 miles (37 km). Merge onto Interstate 695 north toward Towson. Take exit 29 (Cromwell Bridge Road) and bear sharp left over the bridge onto Glen Arm Road. Turn left onto Long Green Pike. After 2 miles (3 km), Boordy's entrance will be on the left.

Located in the Long Green Valley in Baltimore County, Boordy Vineyards is only 20 miles (32 km) from Baltimore's Inner Harbor. The farm, with its nineteenth-century buildings, is surrounded by rolling hills, preserved farms and winding roads. The tasting room is in the barn—be sure to take a peek at the 1830s stone wine cellar.

▲ Boordy Vineyards is Maryland's oldest winery.

States from Italy in 1962. It was here that he met his wife Rose, and they began their journey together. Mike was a product of generations of Italian winemaking, and before he left Italy he was the country's youngest winemaker and vineyard-owner.

Most of Fiore's wines are Italian in influence, but Maryland in origin. You can taste the passion and dedication that goes into every bottle. From big, bold reds to crisp and clean whites, the wines are well decorated in both international and national awards. Fiore is best known for its Proprietor's Reserve Chambourcin, but don't miss the Sangiovese, Cabernet Sauvignon, Chardonnay and Caronte, an intriguing red blend of Cabernet, Merlot and Sangiovese.

You should also try Fiore's distillery products—Limoncello and Grappa, two traditional Italian spirits. The Fiores peel crates and crates of lemons by hand to get the freshest lemon essence in their limoncello. The grappa is made from the skins of grapes that were crushed for wine.

www.fiorewinery.com

FIORE

MARYLAND

Chambourcin

DRY RED WINE

6 | Bordeleau Vineyards & Winery

3155 Noble Farm Rd., Eden, MD 21822; (410) 677-3334

If you have a few extra days, or are heading to Maryland's beaches before or after the tour, Bordeleau Vineyards & Winery is a must-see. It is located in Eden, south of Salisbury, on Maryland's Eastern Shore. Vines thrive here in the warm days and cool nights and the soil is sandy and well drained.

Bordeleau means "at the water's edge" in French and the beautiful home is depicted on the estate's wine labels. Owner and winemaker Tom Shelton grows 11 varieties of red and white grapes, including *vinifera* and hybrids; he is determined to make good wine rather than become a big player. Be sure to try the award-winning Cabernet Sauvignon, Cabernet Franc, Pinot Grigio and Chardonnay.

www.bordeleauwine.com

findout more

- **www.marylandwine.com**
  The official site of Maryland wine with information on wine trails.

- **www.chesapeakewinetrail.com**
  Covers wineries on the Eastern Shore.

▲ Fiore Winery specializes in all things Italian, both wines and spirits.

TOUR 74
Northern Virginia

A traveler heading west from the hustle and bustle of urban Washington, D.C., will soon be enjoying comforting vistas of cattle grazing on rolling green pastures and rows of neatly manicured grape vines. Virginia's wine history can be traced back to the "Acte 12" of 1619, when the House of Commons in London required landowners to plant 10 grapevines per acre.

Confederate and Union troops engaged in this area during the Civil War and there are planty of sites for the visitor. The Volstead Act prohibited wine production from 1920 until 1933. In 1971 the Virginia Farm Wineries Act promoted the return of wine production, and some of the first vineyards planted were in this area. Today these wineries are joined by new and innovative projects. Enjoy good wine, a good story and a good time here.

◀ Northern Virginia's rolling landscape, here in Fauquier County, provides good sites for quality grape-growing.

1 | Pearmund Cellars
6190 Georgetown Rd., Broad Run, VA 20137; (540) 347-3475

Head west from the Washington, D.C., area on Interstate 66 and take Exit 43 South on Route 29. You will arrive at Pearmund Cellars in about 45 minutes. The winery has a farmhouse feel with its columned porch and burgundy-colored roof. The property dates back to the 1740s, when tobacco was grown on the land. Grapes were first planted on the property in 1976. In 1991 Chris Pearmund, wine enthusiast and author, purchased the farm and initiated a raft of improvements.

The tasting room features a four-sided tasting bar that sits like an island in the middle of the tiled floor. The countertops are finished with rich wood. The popular winery won the People's Choice Award in 2007. Some wines worth trying are the German-style Riesling, with a sweet honeysuckle note; the buttery, creamy Old Vines Chardonnay; and the Lisa's Merlot, a smooth and supple garnet-colored wine with notes of cherry liqueur and cedar.

www.pearmundcellars.com

▲ Pearmund Cellars is on a historic property that used to grow tobacco.

2 | Mediterranean Cellars
8295 Falcon Glen Rd., Warrenton, VA 20186; (540) 428-1984

After leaving Pearmund, head south on Route 29 and then pick up U.S. 17 North. Turn left at Keith Road and you will soon arrive at Mediterranean Cellars.

The winery has a Grecian feel to it with its white columns, rock garden sculptures and rows of neatly trellised vines. Visitors can relax on the shaded patio and listen to the gurgling waterfall nearby. The wood-paneled barrel room is permeated with the heady aroma of oak and wine.

Jeweler Louis Papadopoulos made his first wine in his native Greece. He moved to northern Virginia in 1984 and opened Mediterranean Cellars in 2003. Taste the unique Rechina, a white wine patterned after a traditional Greek wine with resin notes. Don't miss the Cabernet Sauvignon, with cherry and cassis components.

www.mediterraneancellars.com

▲ Cattle farming sits side by side with viticulture in rural northern Virginia.

3 | Marterella Winery

8278 Falcon Glen Rd., Warrenton, VA 20186; (540) 347-1119

Just a short distance up Falcon Glen Road is Marterella Winery. The winery resembles an old southern house, and its wraparound front porch offers a fantastic view of the adjacent Blue Ridge Foothills. Owners Jerry and Kate Marterella invested in improvements between 2000 and 2003 but found themselves in dire straits when the local landowners' council tried to prevent them from selling wine from their tasting room. The Marterellas prevailed in 2009, when a jury ruled in their favor.

An authentic brick oven imported from Tuscany sits adjacent the tasting room, and wood-fired pizzas are baked in it on weekends.

Make sure to taste the crisp Pinot Grigio, the creamy Barrel Select Chardonnay and the Heritage dry Rosé, with refreshing cherry and strawberry flavors. Don't miss the Meritage, a Bordeaux-style red blend aged three years in French and American oak barrels.

www.marterellawines.com

4 | Gray Ghost Vineyards & Winery
14706 Lee Hwy., Amissville, VA 20106; (540) 937-4869

After leaving Marterella, take Highway 17 South and pick up Route 211 West to Amissville. This will take you to Gray Ghost Vineyards & Winery, named for a famous confederate colonel who operated in the area. The winery is a gray-and-white structure with gabled windows along the roofline. Al Kellert learned winemaking from his college chemistry professor. In 1986, he and his wife, Cheryl, purchased an apple orchard and began renovations and grape planting. The winery opened in 1994 and features an underground barrel room.

Some noteworthy wines are the Chardonnay, an aromatic, tropical Gewurztraminer and a Reserve Cabernet Sauvignon, made only in exceptional years exclusively from estate-grown grapes. The wine displays complex flavors of cherries and chocolate and well-integrated tannins. Make sure to taste the Adieu, an award-winning late-harvest sticky wine crafted from Vidal Blanc.

Nearby Washington, Virginia, offers accommodations at bed-and-breakfasts or the luxurious Inn at Little Washington.

www.grayghostvineyards.com

5 | Gadino Cellars
92 Schoolhouse Rd., Washington, VA 22747; (540) 987-9292

Gadino Cellars is about 2 miles (3 km) west of Washington, Virginia, off Route 211. The Italian-themed winery offers a sunny deck, a court for bocce ball (a variation of *boules*) and delicious cheeses and local sausages in their tasting room. The range includes a tangy Pinot Grigio and a barrel-fermented Viognier with heady notes of honeysuckle, peach and vanilla. Make sure to taste the Delfino Rosso, a twist on the standard Bordeaux blend, in which Petit Verdot is the primary grape; the wine is full-bodied with notes of spice and a tannic backbone.

www.gadinocellars.com

6 | Linden Vineyards
3708 Harrels Corner Rd., Linden, VA 22642; (540) 364-1997

Head north from Gadino and pick up Route 522 and then right on Route 635 to Linden. Linden winemaker Jim Law is regarded by many as the best winemaker in Virginia. Law purchased a hardscrabble farm in 1983 and began planting vines. He has a deep respect for the land, and Jim's philosophy is that wine is made in the vineyard, so he focuses on vineyard-management techniques to produce the best grapes possible. He also writes articles about winemaking for trade publications and is an avid chef.

Jim's goal is to produce white wines with a refreshing mineral component. The Avenius Sauvignon Blanc is a good example, made

Colonel John Singleton Mosby

THE GRAY GHOST
During the Civil War, Confederate Colonel John Singleton Mosby assembled a band of intelligent soldiers who were expert pistol shots, and employed guerilla tactics to harass the enemy. From northern Virginia they slipped behind enemy lines, cut telegraph wires and captured prisoners. Their method of warfare was to deny the enemy his supplies and munitions and to disrupt his communications. Mosby's most famous accomplishment was capturing Union general Edwin Stoughton by posing as a Union soldier and getting him drunk. General Robert E. Lee once exclaimed, "Hurrah for Mosby! I wish I had a hundred like him." Mosby's ability to operate silently behind enemy lines without being captured or suffering major losses earned him the nickname, the Gray Ghost.

in a crisp, fresh style. The nose is a medley of white grapefruit, lime zest, gooseberry and stone dust. For reds, he strives to blend individual components so the result is greater than the sum of the parts. His blending philosophy is reflected in the Hardscrabble Red, which displays notes of currants, rose petals and cherries delivered on a frame of dusty tannins. The Avenius Red, a blend of Petit Verdot and Cabernet Sauvignon grown at 1,300 feet (396 m) of elevation, on vines that are more than 10 years old, has aromas of black cherry, eucalyptus and cedar.

www.lindenvineyards.com

7 | Naked Mountain Vineyard & Winery

2747 Leeds Manor Rd., Markham, VA 22643; (540) 364-1609

Head north on Route 638 from Linden and take Interstate 66 East. Take Exit 18 and go north on Route 688 to Naked Mountain Vineyard. The winery is a brown wooden structure on a hillside surrounded by the majestic Blue Ridge Mountains. The winery features a deck with a stunning view and a stone hearth inside. Owners Bob and Phoebe Harper planted their first grapes alongside a river bed, but learned a hard lesson when they lost their first crop to an early frost. They moved to a higher elevation, where they first planted grapes at the current location in 1976. Over time, Naked Mountain developed a cult following for their delicious, buttery, barrel-fermented Chardonnay.

Relax in the warm, wood-paneled tasting room and savor the wines. The Chardonnay is Burgundian in style, with notes of orange,

spice and butter. Naked Mountain proves that Cabernet Franc is one of the best red wines for Virginia. The wine is complex and rich with notes of red fruits, black pepper and silky tannins.

www.nakedmtnwinery.com

8 | Barrel Oak Winery

3623 Grove La., Delaplane, VA 20144; (540) 364-6402

From Naked Mountain, go south on Route 688 and get back on Interstate 66 East. After about 3 miles (5 km) Virginia 55 North will take you to the aptly named Barrel Oak Winery. The winery sits on top of a green hill and looks a bit like a barn with its raised attic along the rooftop. The tasting room is warm and inviting, with rich wood paneling and a cathedral-like ceiling supported by exposed wooden beams. A stone patio outside offers stunning views of nearby Little Cobbler Mountain. Barrel staves attached to the bar provide a means to leash your pup at this dog-friendly winery. The beautiful hand-constructed building is environmentally friendly, using geothermal energy for heating, cooling and hot water.

Dog lovers Sharon and Brian Roeder opened the winery in 2008, and since that time have made many contributions to the community. Fundraisers for worthy causes are frequently held at the winery, and the Roeders donate 10 cents to charity for every bottle of wine sold.

Make sure to taste the Bowhaus White, a crisp blend of stainless-steel fermented Vidal and Sauvignon Blanc with notes of tropical fruits and peaches. The winery also makes an award-winning fruity Norton, a native Virginia red grape that is becoming appreciated by winemakers east of the Rockies.

www.barreloak.com

▲ The deck at Naked Mountain has stunning views of the nearby mountains.

▲ Vineyards in late fall at Naked Mountain up in the Blue Ridge Mountains

Monticello

The historic town of Charlottesville is in the heart of the Monticello viticultural area, and some of Virginia's best wineries are in the surrounding hills, where vineyards share the land with horse farms and lush green pastures.

Founding father Thomas Jefferson served wine at his nearby estate, Monticello, and students of history and connoisseurs will enjoy visiting the area. In colonial times England encouraged Virginia winemaking as an inexpensive alternative to European wines and Virginia eventually became the most prolific wine-producing colony. Winemaking suffered setbacks during the Civil War and the industry only began to recover in the 1970s when innovators grafted classic European grape varieties onto hearty native rootstocks. Today, great wines are made from the classic grapes Viognier and Cabernet Franc as well as the native American variety Norton.

◄ Thomas Jefferson's estate of Monticello is a must-see for visitors to Charlottesville.

1 | Keswick Vineyards
1575 Keswick Winery Dr., Keswick, VA 22947; (888) 244-3341

Take Route 250 east from Charlottesville toward Keswick Vineyards. The winery is covered with natural wood siding and features a plush front porch lounge. Owner Al Schornberg purchased the historic Edgewood estate in Albemarle County after narrowly surviving a plane crash. His near-death experience forced him to reevaluate his life, and he decided to focus on his passion: making wine. Confederate troops had camped at Keswick during the Civil War, and when the land was being prepared for vines, it was scanned with a metal detector and relics were unearthed and are on display in the wine-tasting room.

The talented South African Stephen Barnard crafts the wines. Barnard declined offers to work in prestigious California wineries because he sees potential in Virginia wine. Barnard's diligent winemaking paid off when Keswick 2007 Cabernet Sauvignon won the prestigious Governor's Cup in 2009. Other wines to try include Viognier and a dry red version of Touriga, the primary grape in Port.

www.keswickvineyards.com

▲ The view from the vineyards down toward Barboursville's winery

2 | Horton Vineyards

6399 Spotswood Trail, Gordonsville, VA 22942; (540) 832-7440

From Keswick, take the 231 north to Gordonsville and then east on Route 33. After a few miles you will see a stone turret rising from a building on the right. This is Horton Vineyards.

Dennis Horton was a defense contractor when he first tried his hand at growing grapes in Virginia in 1983. Lackluster results led him to visit Europe in search of grape varieties that would succeed in Virginia. Horton was one of the first to cultivate Viognier in Virginia. This thick-skinned white grape did so well that many other Virginia wineries have since followed suit. Today Horton cultivates a wide variety of grapes from all over the world.

Horton acquired the property in 1988, constructing the winery in 1992. After their first crush in 1993, the winery began winning medals, thanks to their innovative vineyard management and winemaking.

Today the winery produces a gamut of wines from a multitude of grape varieties spanning every style, from sweet fruit wines to dry single-barrel connoisseur wines. Don't miss the aromatic sparkling Viognier; the unique Rkatsiteli, a Russian grape with orange notes; and the spicy Rhône-style Stonecastle Red.

www.hvwine.com

3 | Barboursville Vineyards

17655 Winery Rd., Barboursville, VA 22923; (540) 832-3824

When leaving Horton, head east on Highway 33 to Barboursville. Travelers approaching the winery will see a domed tower rising from a white structure overlooking rows of neatly pruned vines.

Thomas Jefferson helped design the octagonal building that was home to Virginia governor James Barbour from 1811 until 1814. The building was destroyed by fire in 1884, leaving only a brick-and-mortar shell that can be observed on the property today.

Italian native Luca Paschina graduated from Italy's premier wine-making school and worked at wineries in Napa and New York. After consulting at Barboursville in 1990, he informed the Italian owners that if they were willing to invest in ideal vineyard-management systems, the finest wines on the East Coast could be produced there. They listened, and proved Luca right. In a recent blind wine tasting organized by the *Washington Post*, four wine professionals identified the Barboursville Octagon 2006 as Bordeaux. They praised its "cured meat, savory cassis, mint, mocha" flavors and its "dusty tannins."

The tasting room is a classy affair, offering wine paraphernalia and samples. Make sure to try the sparkling wine, the Reserve Cabernet Sauvignon and the Octagon. Palladio restaurant, named after Jefferson's favorite architect, offers international cuisine served with the estate's wines.

www.barboursvillewine.net

4 | Burnley Vineyards

4500 Winery La., Barboursville, VA 22923; (540) 832-2828

After leaving Barboursville Vineyards, head south on Highway 20 and you will arrive at the friendly Burnley Vineyards in a few minutes. The winery resembles a large split-level home and is adjacent to orderly rows of grape vines. The Reeder family planted their first grapes in 1977 and started producing their own wine in 1984. Currently they produce 5000 cases of wine annually from 31 acres of vineyard including Cabernet Sauvignon and Chardonnay.

A wooden-paneled guesthouse, known as Fernando's Hideaway, features a balcony overlooking the vineyards and offers a very relaxing stay.

The winery produces some sweet, whimsical wines such as Moon Mist, a sweet blend of white and orange Muscat grapes. On a more serious note, they offer an unfiltered Cabernet Sauvignon and Norton, a hardy American grape cultivated in Virginia long before before Prohibition and well suited to its humid climate.

After your visit head south on 20 and return to Charlottesville to relax before the next excursion.

www.burnleywines.com

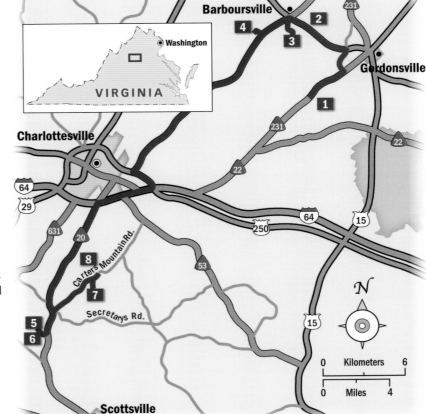

Randolph McElroy, Jr., a descendant of George Washington's attorney general, started the winery in 2000 and released the first wines in 2002. Randy hired winemaker Benoit Pineau, who learned winemaking in Bordeaux and honed his skills in Chile, Australia and California. Benoit makes the wines in the classic European style.

The winery coaxes a rich, complex red from the notoriously tannic Tannat grape. The deep wine has notes of plums and coffee. The estate-bottled Reserve Chardonnay displays creamy apple flavors and a buttery finish.

www.firstcolonywinery.com

▲ The hills around Charlottesville are home to some of Virginia's best vineyards.

5 | Virginia Wineworks and Michael Shaps Wines

1781 Harris Creek Way, Charlottesville, VA 22902; (434) 296-3438

Head south from Charlottesville on Route 20 for 12 miles (19 km) to Virginia Wineworks, where there are several lines of wines available at the tasting room. Michael Shaps wines are high-end and award-winning, produced from vineyards he supervises. The 2007 Chardonnay was thought to be white Burgundy by six wine professionals in a blind tasting organized by the *Washington Post*. The Michael Shaps Cabernet Franc also showed well in this tasting. One reason for its success is that it goes through an extended maceration for six weeks to extract tannins and give it aging potential. The Virginia Wineworks wines are made from Virginia grapes with value in mind. Try the Wineworks White, a blend of Viognier and Vidal Blanc, and the ready-to-drink Wineworks Red.

www.michaelshapswines.com

6 | First Colony Winery

1650 Harris Creek Rd., Charlottesville, VA 22902; (434) 979-7105

First Colony is a short distance from Virginia Wineworks. The winery is an inviting tan structure that resembles a mountain chalet. A warm, inviting wooden bar is backed by diamond-shaped wooden bins for wine storage. Tasty Amish cheeses, crackers and snacks accompany the wines and shaded patios feature vistas of rolling vineyards.

Portrait of Thomas Jefferson by Gilbert Stuart, 1805

THOMAS JEFFERSON, STATESMAN AND WINE LOVER

Founding father Thomas Jefferson, a true Renaissance man, constructed his ingenious home, Monticello, near Charlottesville. While Jefferson was ambassador to France, he toured famous French wine estates and kept a diary of his travels. Jefferson famously stated, "Good wine is a necessity of life for me."

Jefferson's cellar contained more than 1,000 bottles, including France's finest—Montrachet, Château Margaux and Yquem, which he served to his guests in Virginia. He planted some of the first European *vinifera* grapes in America, but those grapes never came to fruition, because horses trampled the vines. Jefferson's dream is kept alive today by Virginia wineries. Make sure to visit historic Monticello.

7 | Blenheim Vineyards

31 Blenheim Farm, Charlottesville, VA 22902; (434) 293-5366

After leaving First Colony, take Route 20 north to Blenheim Vineyards. Turn right at Carters Mountain Road. You will see a rich wood-and-glass structure with a steeply pitched roof peeking from the hillside. That is the winery.

The estate has a rich history that dates back to 1730, when John Carter purchased the property and named it after the site of a British battle victory in Bavaria in 1704. Thomas Jefferson and his bride once weathered a snowstorm there. Rock musician Dave Matthews acquired the property and completed the winery building in 2000.

The building is an energy miser: surrounding earth keeps the tasting room cool, while skylights are so effective that electric light is not needed on summer days. Visitors can look down through glass panels into the winemaking facility below.

Make sure to taste the creamy Blenheim Farm Chardonnay and luscious Cabernet Franc, both of which are composed entirely of grapes grown on the farm. The oak-aged Cabernet Franc has lush notes of cherries, tea and pepper.

www.blenheimvineyards.com

8 | Kluge Estate Winery and Vineyard

100 Grand Cru Dr., Charlottesville, VA 22902; (434) 977-3895

Kluge Estate Winery is just a short distance from Blenheim. The Farm Shop resembles a rough-hewn timber cabin situated among tall trees and cool green grass. The shop features gourmet coffee, cheeses, herbs grown on the estate and candles scented with Kluge wine. Topiaries and stone gardens add ambience, and there is a woodland trail nearby. The chef in the Farm Shop creates delicious culinary masterpieces.

Patricia Kluge acquired the property in 1999 and has spared no expense to produce world-class wines. An avid farmer, she visited wineries around the world and learned from the winemakers she met there.

The Kluge Estate Cru is a unique aperitif made by adding Virginia brandy to sweet Chardonnay juice and then aging in used bourbon barrels. This fortified wine displays aromas of toast, caramel and licorice, and a honeyed palate of white fruit. The winery is justifiably famous for their SP sparkling wine, produced by the classic method. It is crisp and fresh, with lively bubbles. Don't miss the Bordeaux-styled New World Red.

www.klugeestateonline.com

THE EASTERN REGION

VIRGINIA

▲ Kluge Estate makes an idyllic spot for a day out in the country.

Blue Ridge & Shenandoa

Western Virginia's Blue Ridge Mountains offer travelers a spectacular palette of majestic green mountains, rolling hills, quaint farmhouses and the occasional deer. The area has long been famous for delicious locally grown cabbage, corn and apples, but the mountains are now gaining a reputation for another type of produce—wine. Highland vineyards provide optimum conditions for ripening grapes to perfection.

There are several interesting wineries located near the friendly town of Roanoke that can be visited within a day's drive. Prepare to enjoy scenic vistas of rolling verdant hills, Christmas-tree farms and mountain landscapes as you travel to these wineries. October is a particularly beautiful time to visit, when brilliant autumn hues of orange, purple, red and green are on display.

◄ The Blue Ridge Parkway is a feature of this tour.

1 | Valhalla Vineyards
6500 Mt. Chestnut Rd., Roanoke, VA 24018; (540) 725-9463

A delightful day of traveling and wine tasting begins in Roanoke, Virginia. Heading south on Route 221, the traveler will arrive at Valhalla Vineyards in less than 30 minutes. After climbing a steep serpentine road between rows of well-pruned vines, the drive culminates at the mountaintop Cellar Door tasting room, a rustic stone-and-wood structure. Tall windows afford a spectacular hawk's-eye view of the patchwork quilt that is the valley below.

In 1994 Jim and Debra Vascik purchased a peach orchard, where they planted Syrah, Viognier, Cabernet Sauvignon, Merlot and other French grape varieties. The vineyard's 2,000-foot (610-m) elevation promotes a temperature inversion that helps protect young vines from spring frosts, while granite-laden soil contributes minerality to the wines. A cave was blasted into the side of a mountain for winemaking and barrel aging. The winery name is based on the Wagner opera theme.

Valhalla's reputation was established when their 1998 Syrah, a stunning wine with depth and power, won the prestigious Virginia Governor's Cup award.

Today Valhalla produces a variety of classically styled wines, including the barrel-fermented Rheingold Chardonnay, with its creamy texture, peach flavors and intriguing minerality. Their

signature wine, Gotterdammerung, is a bold blend of Cabernet Franc and Merlot. Don't miss the dense, portlike Late Harvest Alicante Bouschet.

www.valhallawines.com

2 | AmRhein Wine Cellars
9243 Patterson Dr., Bent Mountain, VA 24059; (540) 929-4632

After descending from Valhalla, continue south on Highway 221 to AmRhein Wine Cellars. The winery is surrounded by rising hillsides crisscrossed by rows of vines. Deer and wild turkey frequent the surrounding forest. The tasting room is adorned with colorful paintings by local artists. The wine labels are reproductions of these pieces. Patrons relax outside on the patio and enjoy live music, wines, and food from the kitchen.

The winery offers a broad selection of styles, from sweet whimsical wines to more serious Bordeaux-style offerings. The winery has earned acclaim for their Petit Verdot, a grape well suited for Virginia's mountain climate. The wine is dark and full-bodied, with a core of smooth red fruit flavors and hints of chocolate. AmRhein produces a rare, authentic icewine by allowing Vidal Blanc grapes to hang until freezing on the vine. The grapes are picked and crushed while frozen, yielding an intensely sweet nectar dessert wine with apricot notes.

Winery owner Russ Amrhein is of German descent and has visited wineries in Germany to learn more about their process. He produces a wine made from Traminette grapes, reminiscent of a German Riesling. The winery sponsors a fall Oktoberfest event, when the vibrant colors of oak, maple and hemlock are at their peak.

www.amrheinwine.com

---

3 | Villa Appalaccia
752 Rock Castle Gorge, Floyd, VA 24091; (540) 358-0357

After leaving AmRhein, continue south on Highway 221 for about 30 minutes to the town of Floyd. If you like smoked meats, locally raised free-range eggs and other produce, visit Sweet Providence Country Store before you get to Floyd. Galleries in Floyd display local art, and the Floyd Country Store features Bluegrass music. Local wines, cider and mead can be sampled at the tasting room in The Station.

Take Route 8 to the Blue Ridge Parkway and head south. Villa Appalaccia is about 30 minutes from Floyd. Just past Rocky Knob, a flowing red, white and green pennant will be visible on the left. It is attached to Villa Appalaccia winery, a sandy stucco structure resembling an Italian villa. On the winery porch, visitors can relax with a glass of wine and light foods from the kitchen while enjoying mountain vistas and refreshing breezes. The winery owners, Susanne Becker and Stephen Haskill, are aficionados of Italian wine and gastronomy. Their Italian-style wines include a medium-bodied red patterned after Chianti called Toscanello, and a crisp, lively, stainless-steel-fermented Pinot Grigio. A full-bodied red made from the Italian grape variety Aglianico displays deep color and a firm tannic backbone. The winery holds a semi-annual All Things Olive festival.

www.villaappalaccia.com

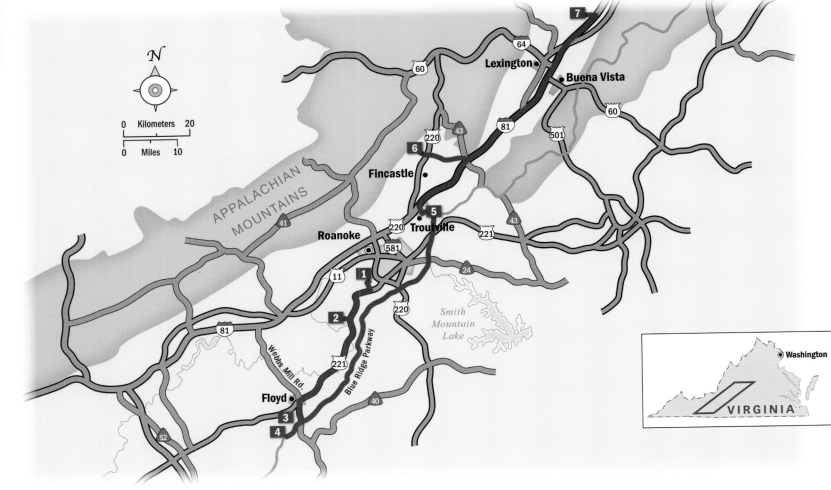

There is a fine dining restaurant with breathtaking views of the mountain landscape. After leaving Château Morrisette, you can enjoy the Blue Ridge Parkway scenery all the way back to Roanoke.

www.chateaumorrisette.com

▲ Château Morrisette's tasting room

4 | Château Morrisette

287 Winery Rd. SW, Floyd, VA 24091; (540) 593-2865

After leaving Villa Appalaccia, turn left on the Blue Ridge Parkway and you will arrive at Château Morrisette minutes later. Virginia wine pioneers William, Nancy and David Morrisette planted vines at this picturesque mountain location in 1978 and produced their first wine in 1982. Their hobby quickly grew out of hand and in 1999 a new winery and tasting room was built atop a ridge with breathtaking views. At more than 32,000 square feet (9,754 m²), this is one of the largest buildings constructed from salvaged timber in the country.

Today this hugely popular winery produces more than 60,000 cases of wine annually. The labels feature images of the winery's mascot, a friendly black Labrador. Our Dog Blue is a slightly sweet Riesling blend with apricot-citrus notes, while Black Dog is a smooth blended red of Cabernet, Chambourcin and Merlot. More serious wine lovers will appreciate the Cabernet Sauvignon for its cedar and cassis flavors on a frame of moderate tannins.

The Roanoke Star towers over the city.

ROANOKE, VIRGINIA

Roanoke was once headquarters for the Norfolk and Western Railway and is imbued with railroad lore. The extensive Roanoke shops produced some of the most majestic steam locomotives ever to roll over iron rails. Today the Virginia Museum of Transportation proudly displays magnificent iron horses. Visitors can climb into a caboose and listen to docents explain daily life on a train.

Luxurious lodging is available nearby at the Tudor-style Hotel Roanoke. The O. Winston Link Museum, located just below the historic hotel, displays surreal black-and-white photographs of steam locomotives taken shortly before their demise. A short walk will take visitors to the Roanoke Farmers Market, where local produce and works from local artisans are displayed on tables. A variety of restaurants offer a range of foods, from hot dogs to sushi. Peruse works of art at the stunning, futuristic Taubman Museum of Art.

The Roanoke Star—the world's largest freestanding, neon-lighted man-made star—towers over the city from its perch on Mill Mountain. Roanoke is known as the "Star City of the South."

5 | Fincastle Vineyard and Winery

203 Maple Ridge La., Fincastle, VA 24090; (540) 591-9000

From Roanoke, you can head north to more mountain wineries. Fincastle Vineyard and Winery is about a 40-minute drive from Roanoke, past Troutville off Route 11 North. There you will find a tasting room constructed of field stones adjacent to an old farmhouse that houses a charming bed-and-breakfast. The driveway passes through a meadow and rows of neatly manicured vines.

Owner David Sawyer likes to focus on quality, not quantity. He specializes in Cabernet Sauvignon and Cabernet Franc, a Bordeaux red grape well suited to Virginia's climate as it ripens early, before mold and rot can set in. The Cabernet Franc is ripe, juicy, deeply colored and delicious and it sells out in some vintages. Viognier also does well here, too, because its thick skin helps the grape resist vineyard fungi. Fincastle's version is barrel fermented, resulting in a rich, opulent white with honeysuckle aromatics and apricot notes.

Visit Fincastle while you are nearby—it's a nice place to walk about and observe the historic courthouse and Civil War monument.

www.fincastlewine.com

6 | Rockbridge Vineyard

35 Hill View La., Raphine, VA 24472; (888) 511-9463

After leaving Fincastle, head north on Route 11 toward historic Lexington. Pick up Interstate 81 north for a few miles and make a left turn at the Raphine exit. The drive will take less than an hour. Look for a red dairy barn, which is Rockbridge Vineyard.

Visitors will enjoy the rustic charm of this winery created from a dairy farm. Owner Shepherd Rouse is a native Virginian who learned how to make wine in California. He is one of few producers of Pinot Noir in the state and has won the Governor's Cup with his unctuous late-harvest dessert wine, V d'Or. The DeChiel Chardonnay and DeChiel Merlot are also well worth trying.

www.rockbridgevineyard.com

7 | Virginia Mountain Vineyards

4204 Old Fincastle Rd., Fincastle, VA 24090; (540) 473-2979

Virginia Mountain Vineyards is just north of Fincastle on top of Zion Hill. Owners David and Marie Gibbs planted vineyards in this beautiful mountain setting in 1998. Their fastidious vineyard management made their grapes sought after by other wineries and in 2000 they opened the winery, making their own wines— Chardonnay, Bordeaux-style reds and some lighthearted sweet wines. At harvest time a kilted bagpiper plays in the vineyard.

www.vmvines.com

regional events

Virginia Wine Expo □ February

Wine enthusiasts and avid connoisseurs congregate at this spectacular event to taste and purchase Virginia wines and sample regional food from the finest restaurants.   www.virginiawineexpo.com

Wine in the Woods □ May

Located at Symphony Woods in Columbia, MD, this festivals offers not just wine but also food, live entertainment, seminars, arts and crafts.
www.wineinthewoods.com

Great Tastes of Pennsylvania Wine & Food Festival □ June

Held at the Split Rock Resort in the Poconos, this two-day outdoor festival is a showcase for the state's finest wineries. Food vendors, educational seminars and music performances are designed to entertain.
www.splitrockresort.com/wine-festival.php

Visit Vintage Ohio □ August

This two-day summer event attracts 35,000 visitors each year and features delectable offerings from local wineries, restaurants, and artisans.
www.visitvintageohio.com

Maryland Wine Festival □ September

Wine tastings from local wineries, live music, gourmet foods, arts and crafts and wine education seminars attract thousands to this annual event.
www.marylandwine.com

Virginia Wine Festival □ September

Wine is served by the glass or bottle at the largest wine festival in Virginia. It features 60 Virginia wineries, gourmet food samples, seminars, concerts, arts and crafts and more   www.atwproductions.com

find out more

- **www.virginiawine.org**
Discover Virginia's wine country, wine trails, wineries and events.

- **www.virginia.org**
Lodgings, bed-and-breakfasts, wineries, spas and fun things to see and do in the state.

Acknowledgments and Credits

The publishers would like to thank the wineries and vineyards featured in this book, as well as the wine organizations and other professional bodies listed below, for their help with both information and images.

2 Shutterstock/Diane N. Ennis **5** (left) Nk'Mip; (center) Round Barn; (right) Doug Townsend **10** (above left) Shutterstock/Gosphotodesign; (above right) Cephas/Ian Shaw; (below left) Shutterstock/Konstantin Sutyagin; (below right) Cephas/Clay McLachlan **12** Cephas/Jerry Alexander **13** Shutterstock/Darren Baker **14** (left) Robert Mondavi; (right) CedarCreek **16-17** Shutterstock/Galina Barskaya **17** (left) Cephas/Mick Rock; (center) Quails' Gate; (right) Shutterstock/Chiyacat **18** (top left and right) Cherry Point; (center) Corbis; (below) Cherry Point **19** Blue Grouse **20** Vigneti Zanatta **21** (left) Butchart Gardens (right) Grgich Hills **22** (top left) Shutterstock/Santje; (top center) Domaine de Chaberton; (top right) Shutterstock/VIP Design USA; (center) Corbis/Sean White/Design Pics; (below) Domaine de Chaberton **23** Alamy/Gunter Marx **24** (top left) Shutterstock/Izaokas Sapiro; (top center, top right, below left and below right) Seven Stones; (center) BC Wine Institute **26** (top left) Shutterstock/Anson0618; (top right) Quails' Gate; (center) Corbis/Benjamin Rondel; (below) CedarCreek **27** (left) Summerhill Pyramid; (right) Quails' Gate **28** (top) Laughing Stock; (center) Alamy/First Light; (below) Poplar Grove **30** (top left) Burrowing Owl; (top center) Road 13; (top right) Jackson-Triggs Okanagan; (center) Hester Creek; (below) Jackson-Triggs Okanagan **31** Hester Creek **32** (above) Stoneboat; (below) Road 13 **33** (above) Burrowing Owl; (below) Nk'Mip **34** (top left) Shutterstock/Artern Mazunov; (top center) Shutterstock/Jerome Scholler; (top right) Shutterstock/MAIKO; (center) Lopez Island; (below) Bainbridge Island **35** Alamy/Chris Howes/Wild Places Photography **36** (top left) Shutterstock/Julija Sapic; (top right) Shutterstock/Lawrence Roberg; (center and below) Chateau Ste. Michelle **37** Columbia **38** (above, both) Brian Carter; (below) Novelty Hill **39** (left) DiStefano; (right) Herbfarm Restaurant **40** (top left) Tsillin; (top right) Vin du Lac; (center) Washington Wine Commission; (below) Alamy/Danita Delimont **41** Benson **42** (top left) Arbor Crest; (top right) Shutterstock/ VIP Design USA; (center) Alamy/Visions of Paradise.com; (below) Latah Creek; **43** (left) Arbor Crest; (right) Grgich Hills **44** (top left) Dunham; (top center) Shutterstock/Itay Uri; (top right) Tamarack; (center) Cephas/Mick Rock; (below left and right) L'Ecole Nº 41 **45** Cephas/Janis Miglavs **46** (below left) Cephas/Janis Miglavs; (above right) Dunham; (below right) Cephas/Mick Rock **47** (left) Chateau Ste. Michelle (right) Northstar **48** (top left) Kiona; (top right) Shutterstock/Tatiana Morozova; (center) Kiona; (below left) Chandler Reach; (below right) Fidelitas **49** Terra Blanca **50** (left above and below) Kiona; (right) Hedges **51** Col Solare **52** (top left) Claar; (top right) Thurston Wolfe; (center) Washington Wine Commission; (below) Claar **53** (left) Hyatt; (right) Cephas/Mick Rock **54** Desert Wind **55** (left) Kestrel (right) Cephas/Janis Miglavs **56** (top left) Shutterstock/Worytko Pawel; (top right) Sakala; (center) Alamy/FogStock; (below) Cascade Cliffs **57** (left) courtesy of Maryhill Museum of Art; (right) Maryhill **58** (top left) Dalles Area Chamber of Commerce; (top right, center and below) Phelps Creek **60** (top left) SakéOne; (top right and center) Montinore **61** (above left) Montinore (below) Hip CHICKS do WINE; (above right) Grgich Hills **62** (top left) Evergreen; (top right) Elk Cove; (center) WillaKenzie; (below) Adelsheim **63** (above and below) WillaKenzie **64** (above left) Elk Cove;

(above right) Cana's Feast; (below) Evergreen **65** (above left and right) Amity; (below) Evergreen **66** (top left) Duck Pond; (top right) Stoller; (center and below) Duck Pond **67** Erath **68** (left and above right) De Ponte; (below right) Sokol Blosser **69** (above) Sokol Blosser; (below) Stoller **70** (top left) Witness Tree; (top right) King; (center) Witness Tree **71** Witness Tree **72** (above) Willamette Valley Vineyards; (below) Silvan Ridge **73** (above and below) King **74** (top left and right) Abacela; (center) Alamy/Greg Vaughn; (below left) Brandborg; (below right) Spangler **75** (above) Abacela; (below) Brandborg **76** (top left and right) RoxyAnn; (center) Alamy/Imagebroker; (below) Cephas/Mick Rock **77** RoxyAnn **78** (top left and right) Parducci/Mendocino Wine Co.; (center and below) Saracina **79** Parducci/Mendocino Wine Co. **80** Cephas/Mick Rock **81** (above) Cephas/Kevin Judd; (below left) Pacific Star (below right) Fetzer **82** (top left) Handley; (top center) Roederer; (top right) Shutterstock/Chiyacat; (center) Cephas/R & K Muschenetz; (below) Cephas/Ian Shaw **83** (above) Scharffenberger; (below) Roederer **84** Cephas/Ian Shaw **85** Cephas/Jerry Alexander **86** (top left and center) Sbragia Family; (top right) Hanna; (center) Sbragia; (below) Dry Creek **87** Sbragia Family **88** (above and below) Stonestreet **89** Hanna **90** (all) Dutton Goldfield **91** (above) Cephas/Mick Rock; (below) Moshin **92** (both) Hop Kiln **93** (above left) J; (above right) Grgich Hills; (below) Rodney Strong **94** (top left) Sebastiani; (top center and right) Chateau St. Jean; (center) Cephas/Janet Miglavs; (below) Sebastiani **95** Ravenswood **96** (above) Imagery; (below) Kunde Family **97** (left) Kenwood; (right) Cephas/Clay McLachlan **98** Chateau St. Jean **99** (left) Matanzas Creek; (right) Alamy/Stephen Voss **100** (top left and center) Gloria Ferrer; (top right) Shutterstock/Dusan Zidar; (center) Cephas/Ted Stefanski; (below) Truchard **101** (above) Etude; (below left) Folio Winemakers' Studio; (below right) Saintsbury **102** Domaine Carneros **103** (left) Schug Carneros; (right) Gloria Ferrer **104** (top left and right) Clos du Val; (center) Cephas/Mick Rock; (below) HdV Wines **105** (left) Clos du Val; (right) Stag's Leap Wine Cellars **106** Darioush **107** Cephas/Bruce Fleming **108** (above) Cephas/R & K Muschenetz; (below) Duckhorn **109** (all) Chateau Montelena **110** (top left) Charles Krug; (top center) Cephas/Herbert Lehmann; (top right) Charles Krug; (center) Beringer; (below left) Charles Krug; (below right) Beringer **111** Charles Krug **112** Cephas/Bruce Fleming **113** (above left and below) Frog's Leap; (right) Cephas/Ted Stefanski **114** (left) Cephas/Mick Rock; (right, above and below) St. Supéry **115** (left) St. Supéry; (right) Domaine Chandon **116** (top left and right) Grgich Hills; (center) Cephas/Charlie Napasnapper; (below) Provenance **117** Cephas/Bruce Fleming **118** (above) Cephas/Bruce Fleming; (below) Larry Schmitz **119** (left) Robert Mondavi; (right) Cephas/Mick Rock **120** (top left and right) Von Strasser; (center) Cephas/Mick Rock; (below) Hess Collection/Goldsworthy **121** Spring Mountain **122** (left) Terra Valentine; (right) Pride Mountain **123** (above left) Von Strasser; (below left) Cephas/Jerry Alexander; (right) Schramsberg **124** (top left) Vino Noceto; (top right) Shutterstock/Karin Lau; (center) Karly **125** Vino Noceto **126** (top left) Shutterstock/Kateryna Larina; (top right) Alamy/Cephas/Ian Shaw; (center) Alamy/Cephas/Mick Rock; (below) Wente **127** Wente **128** (top left) Poetic Cellars; (top right) Shutterstock/Kiyanochka; (center) Cephas/Mick Rock; (below) Lorna Prieta **129** Grgich Hills **130** (top left and right) Wrath; (center) Cephas/Ian Shaw; (below left) Paraiso (below right) Pessagno **131** (left) Wrath; (right) Cephas/Ian Shaw

132 (top left and right) Claiborne & Churchill; (center) Edna Valley Vineyard; (below left) Kynsi; (below right) Chamisal **133** Claiborne & Churchill **134** (top left) Kenneth Volk; (top right) Riverbench; (center) Kenneth Volk **135** (above) Kenneth Volk; (below) Cephas/Mick Rock **136** (top left) Shutterstock/ncn18; (top right) Shutterstock/puchan; (center) Alamy/Chuck Place **137** Cephas/Mick Rock **138** (top left) Shutterstock/Sebastian Knight; (top right) Cephas/R & K Muschenetz; (center) Alamy/Chip Morton; (below) Alamy/Anthony Arendt **140** (top) Colorado Wines; (center) Terror Creek; (below left) Two Rivers; (below right) Canyon Wind **141** Colorado Wines **142** (top left) Shutterstock/Oleg Golovnev; (top right) Shutterstock/Sergiy Zavgorodny; (center) Alamy/Stock Connection Distribution; (below left) BookCliff; (below right) Colorado Wines **143** Boulder Creek **144-145** iStock /Luminigraphics **145** (left) iStock/M Eric Honeycutt; (center) Stone Hill; (right) Shutterstock/Gosphotdesign **146** (top left) Chateau Grand Traverse; (top center) Brys; (top right and center) Chateau Chantal; **147** Chateau Chantal **148** (top left) Bel Lago; (top center) Black Star; (top right and center) Left Foot Charley; (below) L. Mawby **149** Black Star Farms **150** (top left) Round Barn; (top center) Tabor Hill; (top right) Karma Vista; (center) Corbis/Walter Bibikow; (below) St. Julian **151** Karma Vista **152** (above) Tabor Hill; (below) Round Barn **153** (left) Round Barn; (right) Tabor Hill **154** (top) Wollersheim; (center) Alamy/Don Smetzer; (below) Wollersheim **155** (both) Weggy **156** (top left) Lynfred; (top right) Fox Valley; (center and below) Lynfred **157** Shutterstock/Liv Friis-Larsen **158** Alamy/Jason Lindsey **159** (left) Fox Valley; (right) Grgich Hills **160** (top left) Les Bourgeois; (top center) Shutterstock/Gyukli Gyula; (top right) Baltimore Bend; (center) Alamy/Corbis RF; (below) Les Bourgeois **161** Baltimore Bend **162** (top left) Stone Hill; (top center and right) Adam Puchta; (center) Visit Missouri/Hermann **161** Alamy/Don Smetzer **162** (above and below left) Stone Hill; (below right) Adam Puchta **165** (above) St. James; (below) Alamy/Photostock-Israel **166** (all) Montelle **167** Augusta **168** (top left) Twin Oaks; (top right) Shutterstock/Rachel Coe; (center) Chaumette; (bottom right) Crown Valley **169** Twin Oaks **170** (top left) Neal & Janice Newsom; (top right) Steve Werblow; (center) Steve Werblow; (below) McPherson **171** Shutterstock/Brandon Siedel **172** (left) Alamy/Andre Jenny; (right) Llano Estacado **173** Cap*Rock **174** (top left) Inwood; (top right) Dallas Food and Wine Festival; (center) Alamy/Corbis Premium RF; (below) Times Ten Cellars **175** Dallas Food and Wine Festival **176** (top left and right) Fuqua; (below left) Inwood **177** Grapevine **178** (top left) Becker/Michael Page; (top right) Flat Creek; (center) Cephas/R & K Muschenetz **179** Shutterstock/Gosphotodesign **180** (left above and below) Texas Hill; (right) Flat Creek **181** (left) Flat Creek; (right) Grgich Hills **182-183** Cephas/Mick Rock; **183** (left) Cephas/Mick Rock; (center) Shutterstock/Chiyacat; (right) Cephas/Mick Rock **184** (top, center and right) Doug Townsend; (center) Alamy/All Canada Photos; (below) Doug Townsend **185** L'Acadie **186** (left) Gaspereau; (right) Doug Townsend **187** (all) Jost **188** (top left) Vignoble de Sainte-Petronille; (top center) Shutterstock/Iofoto; (top right and center) Vignoble de Sainte-Petronille **189** Jost **192** (top left) The Grange of Prince Edward; (top right) Shutterstock/Konstantin Sutyagin; (center) Alamy/Klaus Lang; (below left) Norman Hardie; (below right) Margaret Mulligan **194** (above left) Huff; (above right) Long Dog; (below) Huff **195** (above) County Cider Company; **195** (below) Long Dog **196** (top left) Konzelmann; (top right) Strewn;

(center) Corbis/Jon Arnold/JAI; (below right and left) Konzelmann **197** Strewn **198** (top left) Shutterstock/John Keith; (top right) Shutterstock/Phil Date; (center) Jackson-Triggs Niagara; (below) Southbrook **199** (above left) Alamy/Brenda Kean; (below left) Jackson-Triggs Niagara; (below right) Grgich Hills **200** Chateau des Charmes **201** (both) Cephas/Kevin Argue **202** (top left) Cave Spring; (top right) Flat Rock; (center) Flat Rock; (below) Cave Spring **203** Flat Rock **204** (top left) Shutterstock/Gravicapa; (top right) Shutterstock/Maram; (center and below) Malivoire **206** (top left) Shutterstock/Junial Enterprises; (top right) Arrowhead Springs; (center) Arrowhead Springs; (below left) Marjim Manor; (below right) Arrowhead Springs **208** (top left) Shutterstock/Dmitriy Shironosov; (top center) Shutterstock/Konstantin Andy; (top right) Shutterstock/Julija Sapic; (center) Uncork New York! **209** Liberty **210** (top left) Uncork New York!; (top center) Dr. Frank's; (top right) Casa Larga; (center) Uncork New York!; (below left and right) Casa Larga **211** (above) New York Wine & Culinary Center/Dumwaiter Design; (below) Arbor Hill **212** (top left) Heron Hill; (top center and right) Dr. Frank's; (center) Uncork New York!; (below) Cephas/Mick Rock **213** (above left and below left) Dr. Frank's; (right) Hunt Country **214** (top left) Uncork New York!; (top right) Fox Run; (center) Uncork New York!; (below) Lamoreaux Landing **215** (above) Red Newt; (below) Wagner **216** Glenora **217** (above left) Hermann J. Wiemer; (below left and right) Fox Run **218** (all) Six Mile Creek **219** King Ferry **220** (above) Knapp; (below) Uncork New York! **221** (left) Knapp; (above right) Grgich Hills; (below right) Hosmer **222** (top left) Millbrook; (top right) Brotherhood; (center) Uncork New York!; (below left) Clinton; (below right) Uncork New York! **223** Stoutridge **224** (top left) Raphael; (top center) Castello di Borghese; (top right) Shutterstock; (center) Alamy/Reed Purvis; (below) Castello di Borghese **226** (above) Raphael; (below) Uncork New York! **227** (above) Channing Daughters (below) Wölffer **228** (top left) Shutterstock/Crolique; (top right) Shutterstock/Sherri R. Camp; (center) Alamy/Tom Uhlman; (below) Shutterstock/Olga Vasilkova **229** Alamy/Robert Harding Picture Library **230** (left) Cephas/Fred R. Palmer; (right) Debonné **231** (above left) Debonné; (below left) Grand River; (right) St. Joseph **232** (top left) Paradocx; (top right) Va La; (center and below) Paradocx **233** Chaddsford **234** (top left) Shutterstock/Velychko; (top right and center) Elk Run; (below) Sugarloaf Mountain **235** Black Ankle **236** (left) Sugarloaf Mountain; (above and below right) Boordy **237** (both) Fiore **238** (top left) Barrel Oak; (top right) Shutterstock/Brandon Bourdages; (center) Cephas/Mick Rock; (below) Pearmund **239** Alamy/Pat & Chuck Blackley **240** Anova Books Company **241** (both) Naked Mountain **242** (top left) Barboursville; (top center and top right) Kluge; (center) Alamy/Albert Knapp; (below left) Keswick; (below right) Alamy/Pat & Chuck Blackley **244** (left) Cephas/Mick Rock; (right) Corbis/Burstein Collection **245** (above left) Blenheim; (above right and below) Kluge **246** (top left) Villa Appalacia; (top right) Shutterstock/Dimitrijs Dimitrijevs; (center) Alamy/Stock Connection Distribution **247** Villa Appalacia **248** (above left and below) Château Morrisette; (above right) Alamy/Greg Philpott **249** Grgich Hills

Index